Studies in Celtic History XLV

THE GROWTH OF LAW IN MEDIEVAL WALES, *c*.1100–*c*.1500

STUDIES IN CELTIC HISTORY

ISSN 0261–9865

General editors
Dauvit Broun
Máire Ní Mhaonaigh
Huw Pryce

Studies in Celtic History aims to provide a forum for new research into all aspects of the history of Celtic-speaking peoples throughout the whole of the medieval period. The term 'history' is understood broadly: any study, regardless of discipline, which advances our knowledge and understanding of the history of Celtic-speaking peoples will be considered. Studies of primary sources, and of new methods of exploiting such sources, are encouraged.

Founded by Professor David Dumville, the series was relaunched under new editorship in 1997. Proposals or queries may be sent directly to the editors at the addresses given below; all submissions will receive prompt and informed consideration before being sent to expert readers.

Professor Dauvit Broun
Dauvit.broun@glasgow.ac.uk

Professor Máire Ní Mhaonaigh
mnm21@cam.ac.uk

Professor Huw Pryce
a.h.pryce@bangor.ac.uk

For titles already published in this series
see the end of this volume

THE GROWTH OF LAW IN MEDIEVAL WALES, *c*.1100–*c*.1500

SARA ELIN ROBERTS

THE BOYDELL PRESS

© Sara Elin Roberts 2022

All Rights Reserved. Except as permitted under current legislation no part of this work may be photocopied, stored in a retrieval system, published, performed in public, adapted, broadcast, transmitted, recorded or reproduced in any form or by any means, without the prior permission of the copyright owner

The right of Sara Elin Roberts to be identified as the author of this work has been asserted in accordance with sections 77 and 78 of the Copyright, Designs and Patents Act 1988

First published 2022
The Boydell Press, Woodbridge

Paperback edition published 2026

ISBN 978 1 78327 726 1 (harback)
ISBN 978 1 83765 359 1 (paperback)

The Boydell Press is an imprint of Boydell & Brewer Ltd
and of Boydell & Brewer Inc.
website: www.boydellandbrewer.com

Our Authorised Representative for product safety in the EU is Easy Access System Europe – Mustamäe tee 50, 10621 Tallinn, Estonia, gpsr.requests@easproject.com

A catalogue record of this publication is available
from the British Library

The publisher has no responsibility for the continued existence or accuracy of URLs for external or third-party internet websites referred to in this book, and does not guarantee that any content on such websites is, or will remain, accurate or appropriate

Tim
Iestyn
Goronwy

CONTENTS

Illustrations	ix
Abbreviations	xi
Law Manuscripts and Sigla	xv
Preface	xix

PART I: READING THE LAW, SHAPING THE LAW

1.	Introduction: Medieval Welsh Law and the Lawtexts	3
2.	'A Rather Laborious and Harassing Occupation': *Ancient Laws and Institutes of Wales* and the Historiography of the Welsh Laws	23
3.	'Rei a dyweit': Lawyers and the Law in Medieval Wales	49
	Appendix – 'Rei a dyweit'	87

PART II: A NEW APPROACH TO CYFRAITH HYWEL

4.	'All Additional and Later Matter': The 'Anomalous Laws' and the Lawtexts	103
5.	'Achwannec kyureith dylyedus y chynnal': the Blegywryd Redaction	133
6.	'O gyureith Hywel Da, a'e arueroed, a'e gynneuodeu': The Development of the Redaction Manuscripts	161
7.	'Much matter not elsewhere to be found': The Non-Redaction Lawbooks	187
	Conclusion	209

Acknowledgements	213
Glossary	215
Bibliography	219
Index	235
Index of Manuscripts	243

ILLUSTRATIONS

Map

Map of Medieval Wales and the March with relevant places marked	xxii

Figures

1.	Title Page of *Ancient Laws and Institutes of Wales*	35
2.	Oxford, Jesus College MS 57, p. 184	132

Tables

1.1.	The Iorwerth Redaction Manuscripts, organised by date	11
1.2.	The Blegywryd Redaction Manuscripts, organised by date	14
1.3.	The Cyfnerth Redaction Manuscripts, organised by date	16
1.4.	The Latin Manuscripts, organised by date	18
1.5.	Non-redaction Welsh law manuscripts, organised by date	19
2.1.	The Distribution of the Manuscripts in AL I	31–32
2.2.	The Anomalous Laws: AL II	37
2.3.	Editions of redaction texts of the Welsh laws	39
3.1.	The 'Debate Pattern' in Iorwerth Manuscripts	76–77
4.1.	Manuscripts containing *Llyfr Damweiniau*	106–107
4.2.	*Ancient Laws* and *Cynghawsedd*	110
4.3.	*Llyfr Cynghawsedd* as presented in *AL* VII	112
4.4.	The *cynghawsedd* in *AL* VIII	115

Illustrations

4.5. The *cynghawsedd* and organisation of *AL* IX	117
4.6. Plaints in *Ancient Laws*	122
4.7. Manuscripts containing *Holiadon*	125
5.1. *Arferion Cyfraith* and other connected sections	138
5.2. The Tripartite Divisions	140
5.3. *Arferion Cyfraith* in the Blegywryd manuscripts	146
5.4. *Ancient Laws*: Dimetian Code Book III	148
5.5. The Third Section of Bost	150–151
5.6. The Second Part of J	154–155
5.7. The LBostJ texts in other manuscripts	155–156
6.1. Quire 10 of O, fol. 74–76	176
6.2. The Three Columns of Law in Y	177–178
7.1. Manuscripts designated as 'anomalous'	190–191
7.2. Manuscript Mor and its contents	203–204

Full credit details are provided in the captions to the images in the text. The author and publisher are grateful to all the institutions and individuals for permission to reproduce the materials in which they hold copyright. Every effort has been made to trace the copyright holders; apologies are offered for any omission, and the publisher will be pleased to add any necessary acknowledgement in subsequent editions.

ABBREVIATIONS

Medieval Welsh law is a subject area that abounds in abbreviations, including the use of a lengthy list of manuscript sigla. The Appendix gives the full list of Welsh law manuscript sigla. This is a list of abbreviations commonly used in the field, but an attempt has been made to avoid the overuse of abbreviations and acronyms. Certain conventions are used for referring to some edited texts of the laws, and these are explained here.

AL   *Ancient Laws and Institutes of Wales*, ed. Aneurin Owen (London, 2 vols., 1841). References to the first volume take the format AL I if referring to the first volume in general, or to the three individual parts using the abbreviated form AL VC/GC/DC (for Venedotian/Gwentian/Dimetian Code). References to the second volume follow the format of book, chapter and section, with the use of capital Roman numerals, lowercase Roman numerals, and Arabic numerals respectively, e.g. AL VII.i.22. AL II starts at Book IV and continues to Book XIV.

ALD   G. Angharad Elias, *Yr Ail Lyfr Du o'r Waun. Golygiad Beirniadol ac Eglurhaol o Lsgr. Peniarth 164 (H)* (Texts and Studies in Medieval Welsh Law V, 2 vols., Cambridge, 2018).

DC   The Dimetian Code, in the first volume of *Ancient Laws and Institutes of Wales*, ed. Aneurin Owen (London, 1841).

DwC   Dafydd Jenkins, *Damweiniau Colan* (Aberystwyth, 1973).

GC   The Gwentian Code, in the first volume of *Ancient Laws and Institutes of Wales*, ed. Aneurin Owen (London, 1841).

GPC2   *Geiriadur Prifysgol Cymru: A Dictionary of the Welsh Language* (Second Edition, Cardiff, 2006), also *GPC Online*. University of Wales Centre for Advanced Welsh & Celtic Studies, 2014.

J(ed.)   *Cyfreithiau Hywel Dda yn ôl Llawysgrif Coleg yr Iesu LVII*, ed. Melville Richards (Cardiff, 1990). References are to page and line numbers.

Leges Wallicae   *Cyfreithjeu Hywel Dda ac Ereill seu Leges Wallicae Ecclesiasticae & Civiles Hoeli Boni et Aliorum Walliae Principum* ed. William Wotton and Moses Williams (London, 1730).

Abbreviations

LlBleg *Llyfr Blegywryd*, ed. Stephen J. Williams and J. Enoch Powell (Cardiff, 1942). References are to page and line numbers. *Bleg.* is a short form occasionally used to refer to the published edition.

LlCol *Llyfr Colan*, ed. Dafydd Jenkins (Cardiff, 1963).

LlIor *Llyfr Iorwerth: A Critical Text of the* Venedotian Code *of Medieval Welsh Law*, ed. Aled Rhys Wiliam (Cardiff, 1960). References to complete sections are prefaced by the section symbol §, and references to more specific sections are to section/sentence numbers e.g. 89/5. (There are no line numbers in this edition.)

LAL *Lawyers and Laymen: Studies in the History of Law Presented to Professor Dafydd Jenkins on his seventy-fifth birthday, Gŵyl Ddewi 1986*, ed. T. M. Charles-Edwards, Morfydd E. Owen and D. B. Walters (Cardiff, 1986).

LT *The Legal Triads of Medieval Wales*, ed. Sara Elin Roberts (Cardiff, 2007). References are to page numbers, and also to triad numbers e.g. Q121.

LTMW Dafydd Jenkins, *The Law of Hywel Dda: Law Texts from Medieval Wales* (Llandysul, 2000). References are to page and line numbers.

LTWL *The Latin Texts of the Welsh Laws*, ed. H. D. Emanuel (Cardiff, 1967). References are to page and line numbers.

Machlud *Machlud Cyfraith Hywel: Golygiad Beirniadol ac Eglurhaol o Lsgr. BL Add. 22356 (S)*, ed. Christine James (published online in 2013 in the series Texts and Studies in Medieval Welsh Law, <http://cyfraith-hywel.org.uk/cy/machlud-cyf-hyw.php>). References are to sentence numbers.

ODNB *Oxford Dictionary of National Biography* (Oxford University Press, 2004).

OED *The Oxford English Dictionary: OED Online* (Oxford University Press, 2021).

Pomffred *Llawysgrif Pomffred: An Edition and Study of Peniarth MS 259B*, ed. Sara Elin Roberts (Leiden and Boston, 2011). References are to sentence numbers.

RWMS Daniel Huws, *A Repertory of Welsh Manuscripts and Scribes c.800–c.1800* (Aberystwyth, 2022).

TCC *Tair Colofn Cyfraith. The Three Columns of Law in Medieval Wales: Homicide, Theft and Fire*, ed. T. M. Charles-Edwards and Paul Russell (Welsh Legal History Society Vol. V, Bangor, 2005).

VC The Venedotian Code, in the first volume of *Ancient Laws and Institutes of Wales*, ed. Aneurin Owen (London, 1841).

Abbreviations

WKC *The Welsh King and his Court*, ed. T. M. Charles-Edwards, Morfydd E. Owen and Paul Russell (Cardiff, 2000).

WLW *The Welsh Law of Women,* ed. Dafydd Jenkins and Morfydd E. Owen (Cardiff, 1980).

WML *Welsh Medieval Law, Being a Text of the Laws of Howel the Good*, ed. A. W. Wade-Evans (Oxford, 1909; repr. Darmstadt, 1979). References are to page and line number.

LAW MANUSCRIPTS AND SIGLA

A NLW Peniarth MS 29
Iorwerth redaction, $s.$xiii^{med}. Black Book of Chirk.

An NLW Peniarth MS 166
Linked to Blegywryd redaction, $s.$xvi^1.

As NLW Peniarth MS 175
No redaction text, $s.$xv^2. North-east Wales, linked to Mor, Z and H. Previously assigned the 'Anglo-Saxon' siglum of a capital A with a bar across the top.

B BL Cotton Titus MS D II
Iorwerth redaction, $s.$xiii^2.

Bost NLW MS 24029A
Blegywryd redaction, $s.$xiv^2, in Boston, Mass. until 2014.

C BL Cotton Caligula MS A III
Iorwerth redaction, $s.$xiii^{med}.

Col NLW Peniarth MS 30
Linked to Iorwerth tradition, $s.$xiii^{med}.

Crd Cardiff MS 2.7
Blegywryd redaction, $s.$xv^2. Largely a copy of L. Cardiff 2 in the *Report*.

D NLW Peniarth MS 32
Iorwerth redaction, $c.$1404.

E BL Additional MS 14,931
Iorwerth redaction, $s.$xiii^2.

Ep NLW Peniarth MS 258
Blegywryd redaction, $s.$xv^2. Copy of Q, one of the hands is Lewys Glyn Cothi. Previously assigned an 'Epsilon' symbol.

F NLW Peniarth MS 34
No redaction text, $s.$xv^2.

G NLW Peniarth MS 35
Iorwerth redaction, $s.$xiv^1. Same hand as U.

H NLW Peniarth MS 164
No redaction text, $s.$xiv^2. North-east Wales, linked to As, Mor and Z.

I NLW Peniarth MS 38
Blegywryd redaction, $s.$xiv/xv.

J Oxford, Jesus College MS 57
Blegywryd redaction, s.xiv/xv, hand of Hywel Fychan (one of the scribes of the Red Book of Hergest).

Law Manuscripts and Sigla

K **NLW Peniarth MS 40**
Iorwerth redaction, >1469. Hand of Lewys Glyn Cothi (fl. 1447–1489), linked to Cefnllys, Carmarthenshire.

L **BL Cotton Titus MS D IX**
Blegywryd redaction, $s.\text{xiv}^{\text{med}}$.

Llan **NLW Llanstephan MS 29**
Blegywryd redaction, $s.\text{xv/xvi}$.

Lew **NLW Peniarth MS 39**
Iorwerth redaction, $s.\text{xv}^{\text{med}}$, hand of Lewys Ysgolhaig, likely Carmarthenshire.

M **NLW Peniarth MS 33**
Blegywryd redaction, $s.\text{xv}^1$.

Mk **Bodorgan Manuscript**
Cyfnerth redaction, $s.\text{xiv}^1$. In private ownership.

Mor **NLW Peniarth MS 36C**
No redaction text, $s.\text{xv}^2$. Owned by William Morgan, north-east Wales, linked to As, Z and H. Previously assigned the 'Anglo-Saxon' siglum of an uncial M.

N **NLW Peniarth MS 36B**
Blegywryd redaction, $s.\text{xiv}^1$, hand of Gwilym Wasta.

O **NLW Peniarth MS 36A**
Blegywryd redaction, $s.\text{xiv}^1$, hand of Gwilym Wasta.

P **NLW Peniarth MS 259A**
Blegywryd redaction, $s.\text{xv}^2$. Copy of Q.

Q **NLW Wynnstay MS 36**
Blegywryd redaction, 1440s.

R **NLW Peniarth MS 31**
Blegywryd redaction, $s.\text{xiv}^1$.

S **BL Additional MS 22,356**
Blegywryd redaction, $s.\text{xv}^{\text{med}}$. Same hand as Tim.

T **BL Harleian MS 958**
Blegywryd redaction, $s.\text{xiv}^{\text{med}}$.

Tim **NLW Llanstephan MS 116**
Blegywryd redaction, $s.\text{xv}^{\text{med}}$. Same hand as S.

Tr **Cambridge, Trinity College MS O.7.1**
Blegywryd redaction, $s.\text{xiv}^1$, hand of Gwilym Wasta.

U **NLW Peniarth MS 37**
Cyfnerth redaction, $s.\text{xiv}^1$. Same hand as G.

V **BL Harleian MS 4353**
Cyfnerth redaction, $s.\text{xiv}^1$.

W **BL Cotton Cleopatra MS A XIV**
Cyfnerth redaction, $s.\text{xiv}^1$.

X   BL Cotton Cleopatra MS B V
Cyfnerth redaction, $s.\text{xiv}^{\text{med}}$.

Y   NLW MS 20143A
Cyfnerth Laws of Court, mainly Blegywryd Laws of Country, $s.\text{xiv}^2$.

Z   NLW Peniarth MS 259B
Cyfnerth redaction, $s.\text{xvi}^{\text{med}}$. Written on paper, said to be a copy of an earlier text which was at Pontefract. Hands of Richard Longford and his amanuensis. North-east Wales, linked to As, Mor and H.

Latin A   NLW Peniarth MS 28
An early Latin text of the laws originating in Gwynedd. $s.\text{xiii}^{\text{med}}$.

Latin B   BL Cotton Vespasian MS E XI
Latin text of the laws incorporating material from different exemplars. $s.\text{xiii}^{\text{med}}$.

Latin C   BL Harleian MS 1796
Incomplete manuscript with links to Anglesey. $s.\text{xiii}^{\text{med}}$.

Latin D   Oxford, Bodleian Rawlinson MS C 821
A version of this text, but not this manuscript, was translated into Welsh to form the Blegywryd redaction. $s.\text{xiii/xiv}$.

Latin E   Cambridge, Corpus Christi College MS 454, Oxford, Merton College 323
Two recensions. Linked to Latin B and sharing some material. $s.\text{xv}^1$, and c.1583.

PREFACE

'The literature produced by a profession is often the clearest guide to the state of its intellectual development'.[1] On this basis, then, the story presented by the literature of the medieval Welsh lawyer suggests a very high state of intellectual development. The medieval manuscripts preserving a text of Cyfraith Hywel, the law of medieval Wales, comprise the largest single corpus of manuscripts of any genre surviving in middle Welsh. The manuscripts themselves are varied, evidencing considerable editing and reorganising of the abundant material available to the lawyers and compilers. As such, a study of the legal texts and their development in medieval Wales may reveal a highly developed legal profession, and sheds light on the cultural life and political development of the country at that time.

This study is a full examination of the contents of the law manuscripts, the material that was drawn into them, how the manuscripts are structured, parallel texts in the law manuscripts and their occurrence, and the reasons for including the material in the way it was incorporated. It is primarily a textual study, although consideration is given to the context of this collation and editing by the jurists, the legal scholars in medieval Wales, and in addition to looking at the working methods of the compilers of the lawtexts, the reasons for their work are examined as well. As the main focus of the work is on the law manuscripts, the discussion in the first chapter on medieval Welsh law and its background, with a survey of the manuscripts, is the starting point. The background information presented in the introduction to the manuscripts in Chapter 1 is essential for understanding the following chapters, but the descriptions of the redactions and of the manuscripts within them is designed to be a ready-reckoner, which may be returned to during the discussion in the following chapters, although every attempt is made to keep the subject clear and further information on the manuscripts is added in context. A full list of the law manuscripts by sigla is also included at the start of the work, following the abbreviations, and may serve to avoid confusion as sigla will usually be used rather than full details of each manuscript.

Looking at what was in the manuscripts and where the material occurs, rather than the substance of the laws themselves, may seem a strange approach to the understanding of the law in medieval Wales, but this should not be the case. Patrick Wormald argued that 'the texts [of Old English law] have proved so baffling because they have been read with the expectation that a ninth- or tenth-century law-code would be like one of the twelfth or nineteenth. Codes must instead be approached as artefacts of their own time. That means so far as possible examining them through the eyes of their own time.'[2] Indeed, this approach may have something to offer the historians of other European traditions as well. It is striking that this has not been done in full before – or, at least, not since Aneurin Owen's full edition of the laws in *Ancient Laws and Institutes of Wales* in 1841. Owen's work makes it difficult to get

---

[1] Baker, *An Introduction*, 175.
[2] Wormald, *The Making of English Law*, xii.

a clear picture of what each manuscript contains and, in any case, more material and more manuscripts have come to light since the nineteenth century.

The aim of this monograph is to examine the texts of medieval Welsh law, in the context of legal development and the political circumstances surrounding their compilation. Working from the premise that the limitations in our understanding of the texts inhibit our awareness of the environment(s) in which they were created, the volume challenges the traditional division of the native legal writings into 'core' material and (clearly subsidiary) 'additions', and it offers a new model for understanding the lawtexts.

In order to reframe Welsh law and society in the period 1100–1500, this volume will take several approaches. Part I – *Reading the Law, Shaping the Law*, looks at the way the law has been viewed by historians and academics specialising in the field, as well as giving a medieval context to the creation of the Welsh lawbooks. Chapter 1 will present the subject matter and sources, looking at the manuscripts and their distribution. Following this introduction, Chapter 2 will focus on the historiography of the legal manuscripts, and consider how studies of the texts have led to editorial decisions being made that have shaped the way scholars have dealt with them. Particular attention will be given to Aneurin Owen and his ground-breaking edition, *Ancient Laws*. This work was divided into two volumes: volume one, comprising the Codes, and a second volume, comprising 'The Anomalous Laws'. This has led to a division in the way the texts have been viewed and to some texts being relegated to a secondary position, or called 'additional material', largely because of Owen's editorial decision. The concept of 'additional material' will be questioned.

The final chapter in this section, Chapter 3, turns to the people behind the law manuscripts, and indeed, the people behind the law itself. The work of the justice in medieval Wales will be studied, with a comparison of the different roles taken by the professional justices in north Wales and the landowners in south Wales who were called to sit in justice. Further, in south Wales a new group of legal professionals developed after the conquest, the *dosbarthwyr*. After examining the roles of the lawyers, attention will be given to how and why their roles should have and did affect the lawbooks, and why the nature of the extant lawbooks in medieval Wales is directly linked to the men who were making, and using, the law in medieval Wales.

Part II of the work, *A New Approach to Cyfraith Hywel*, will demonstrate a new way of viewing the material, following on from the discussion in Part I. The focus here will be on looking at the manuscripts in their own context, rather than within the confines of traditional historiographical constructs. Turning to the textual side of the study, subsequent chapters will examine various aspects of the makeup of the lawtexts, with a particular focus on material that has been deemed 'additional', 'later', or even 'anomalous'; and the division of the texts into 'core' sections versus 'tails' will be discussed and questioned in full. Chapter 4 will look at the texts which comprise the second volume of *Ancient Laws*, and will suggest that these texts should not be viewed as 'additional' at all. Instead, they should be elevated to the same status as the texts in the first volume, and be examined in their own context, with a focus on the purpose behind them, as well as the form taken by these texts.

Following on from the discussion of 'additional material', Chapter 5 introduces a new discussion of the Blegywryd redaction manuscripts. These lengthy manuscripts have often been divided into sections comprising a 'main text' and a 'tail' of so-called additional material. This chapter will suggest a different reading of the Blegywryd manuscripts. The demarcation in the material itself is not as straightforward as has been assumed, and therefore the start of the 'tail' material is unclear.

Preface

Indeed, the suggestion here will be that there is no such thing as a 'tail' in these manuscripts. Instead, the Blegywryd manuscripts – like the Iorwerth manuscripts – divide into three parts, comprised of the Laws of Court, the Laws of Country, and *Arferion Cyfraith* ('practices/customs of law'). The third part is far longer than has been supposed, but it serves a similar purpose to the Test Book in Iorwerth: it is practical material, for the use of lawyers in their working lives. The material in *Arferion Cyfraith* is examined and shown to have a heavy emphasis on procedural explanations and to include models for practice and material for the training of lawyers. There is no clear end-point to the *Arferion Cyfraith* section: rather, it was open-ended and could include various material, but with an emphasis on how the law was carried out. This is the southern equivalent of the Iorwerth Test Book.

Chapter 6 follows on from the discussion in the first part of the work, primarily in Chapter 3, and gives full consideration to the concept of the 'tail'. Once again, the manuscripts will be examined in their own right, and the material found included in the so-called 'tail' will be restored to prominence. How the material was incorporated, where else it occurs and the relationship between certain groups of these manuscripts will be given full consideration, but with an emphasis on giving all of the law equal billing.

Chapter 7 will take a manuscript-by-manuscript reading, and will examine the purpose of certain manuscripts that have been dismissed as falling outside a specific redaction or being 'anomalous' as they do not conform to the pattern of the basic redactions as set out by Owen and others. However, each of the manuscripts has certain characteristics that give them all their own value: many reveal the law that would have been used in certain areas of Wales (or, indeed, in the March where Welsh law continued to be practised and developed), or the use of certain learned people. The focus here will be on the nature of the material included in these manuscripts and why it was important: their lack of a text that can be assigned to a particular redaction is immaterial to the value of these manuscripts.

As well as examining specific manuscripts and the material contained within them, texts that have hitherto been neglected to a great extent, there is a focus here on the lawyers and the legal compilers, and their working situation: how they worked, and why they worked on the lawtexts in this way. Rethinking scholars' long-held beliefs about the structure and divisions of these medieval texts will shed light on those social and political processes that helped to shape, change and consolidate Welsh law and legal thinking in the later medieval period.

*Map of Medieval Wales and the March with relevant places marked.
Map drawn by Cath D'Alton.*

Part I

Reading the Law, Shaping the Law

1

INTRODUCTION:
MEDIEVAL WELSH LAW AND THE LAWTEXTS

Several academic disciplines benefit from the rich and extensive corpus of lawtexts of medieval Wales. Manuscripts of Welsh law occur among the earliest Welsh manuscripts, dating from the mid-thirteenth century.[1] The lengthy prose texts of Welsh law are important sources for the study of the Middle Welsh language. The manuscripts themselves are important evidence for the field of medieval Welsh codicology, and the scripts and their scribes illuminate the development of medieval Welsh palaeography. The law contained within these books is crucial for legal historians and legal scholars, and historians refer to the legal texts as a source on medieval society, politics and intellectual thought. The study of the medieval Welsh lawtexts is central to many aspects of studies on medieval Wales.

Despite its importance, the field of medieval Welsh law has however suffered somewhat from an image problem, and detailed study of the texts is confined to a small group of specialists. A highly accomplished scholar once joked to me that Seminar Cyfraith Hywel, the academic group focusing on the study of the Welsh lawtexts, was like a secret society that spoke in code, with the inner circle referring to 'Q' and 'J', which outsiders could not follow. Another academic with an expertise in the extremely complex twelfth- and thirteenth-century Gogynfeirdd praise poetry described the field of Welsh law as 'very difficult'. While it is pleasing to imagine that my own subject area is the rocket science of medieval Wales, the reality is that the topic itself is straightforward. This may not necessarily seem to be the case for a scholar whose expertise is in Middle Welsh narrative prose or poetry, as they confront a different situation: unlike Welsh law, those areas of study do not tend to have to deal with numerous manuscripts with many significant differences in the texts,[2] but this is a matter of acquiring familiarity with a certain working procedure. Getting to the actual material is trickier, requiring a study of the manuscripts and texts and their relationships to each other. The aim of this chapter is to provide such an overview, offering a brief history and context for the Welsh laws in general, and then discussing the different manuscripts and texts, thus setting the scene for the textual studies that follow.

---

[1] See for example, Huws, *Medieval Welsh Manuscripts*, 58: in the list of manuscripts by date, nine are listed under 'Saec. XIII med.', and six of those are law manuscripts, three in Welsh and three in Latin.

[2] This is certainly true before the fourteenth century, but the work of the *cywyddwyr*, Dafydd ap Gwilym and his contemporaries, is a different matter. With thanks to Barry Lewis for discussing this with me.

The Growth of Law in Medieval Wales, c.1100–c.1500

The Law of Medieval Wales

Unlike its great neighbour England, Wales in the middle ages was a country consisting of various territories, each with its own rulers, rather than being united, however nominally, under one king (although there are one or two exceptions when the country was under the rule of one king or prince).³ This makes discussing medieval Wales as a separate entity problematic. In the early period there were several kingdoms or territories, but conquest and consolidation led to some of the regions expanding and vying for control. The best-known of the kingdoms was Gwynedd, in the north, covering Snowdonia, the Llŷn peninsula and Anglesey at various times, with its eastern and southern boundaries constantly changing.⁴ Despite early Norman incursions into Gwynedd, the dynasty established by Gruffudd ap Cynan (*c*.1055–1137) came to rule the most powerful of the Welsh territories, up to the conquest of Wales by Edward I of England in 1282. That war was thus led largely against the Prince of Wales, Llywelyn ap Gruffudd (*c*.1223–1282).⁵ Powys, in the east, was another major territory and was ruled by the descendants of Bleddyn ap Cynfyn (d. 1075), although its proximity to England coloured its political ambitions.⁶ The southern kingdoms, including Deheubarth which was ruled by Hywel ap Cadell (d. 949/950) in the tenth century, Morgannwg, Brycheiniog and other lands, remained independent from both Gwynedd and also from England, although Morgannwg and Brycheiniog were conquered by the Normans before 1100. These and other regions in south Wales were thus within the March, the area colonised by the Normans and formed by the borderlands between England and Wales, but which also spread across the south of Wales and up to the river Teifi, and west as far as Pembrokeshire.⁷ The March was, legally, a separate entity made up of lordships, some of whose rulers had considerable powers. A definition of medieval Wales, then, depends on the particular region under consideration, and there was considerable variety in the language, fortunes, rule, politics and foreign policy in all its various kingdoms.

Despite the apparent disjointed nature of the Welsh territories in this period, there were, however, some unifying factors, which means that it is possible to talk about Wales as a whole in this period. One of these aspects was the law. This distinguished the Welsh as a separate people, distinct from others, and offered a sense of national identity: 'The definition of law and of those subject to it served to draw the lines of national and racial division more sharply and precisely ... Welshmen could now be increasingly distinguished from Englishmen by the law

---

³ Studies of this period and these rulers include the excellent introduction by Maund, *The Welsh Kings*.
⁴ David Stephenson rightly points out that the traditional historiography is often Gwynedd-centric, but offers a superb and broad new reading of Welsh history moving the focus to other territories in his excellent monograph: Stephenson, *Medieval Wales*.
⁵ Maund, *The Welsh Kings*, 78–85, on Gruffudd ap Cynan; 129–147 on Llywelyn ap Gruffudd. On Llywelyn ap Gruffudd and the conquest of Wales, see Smith, *Llywelyn ap Gruffudd*, English version published in 2014. Other studies include Carr, *Llywelyn ap Gruffudd*; Morris, *The Welsh Wars of Edward I*.
⁶ On medieval Powys, see the excellent studies by David Stephenson: *Medieval Powys*, and *Medieval Wales*. On Bleddyn ap Cynfyn see also Maund, *The Welsh Kings*, 71–77.
⁷ For studies on the March, see for example Davies, *Lordship and Society*; Rees, *South Wales and the March*; Lieberman, *The March of Wales*; Lieberman, *The Medieval March of Wales*; Edwards, 'The Normans and the Welsh March'; Maund, *The Welsh Kings*, 46–50. See also Stephenson, *Medieval Wales*, 9–12 and Chapter 3 in the same work, 63–83.

to which they were subject.'[8] It was assumed, in the lawtexts, that the legal rules contained within applied to all of the inhabitants of Wales, whichever region they were from and whichever ruler governed them – indeed, on the latter point, while some rulers are named in the laws as contributors, the way the texts are written avoids mention of specific rulers and current politics. Law is the main institution that identifies the medieval Welsh as a single people – more so than their language or their geographical region and its boundaries.

Cyfraith Hywel, the law of medieval Wales, was the only legal system said to apply to the whole of Wales, although what exactly was meant by 'Wales' is less certain.[9] It was different from the Common Law in England, and also from Canon Law, the law of the church, although some references within it acknowledge the different rules of the church.[10] This was very much a home-grown legal tradition, and has been described in the past as a *volksrecht* system, a law of the people.[11] The legal texts make it abundantly clear that this was lawyer-created law.[12] Despite the grandiose naming of King Hywel ap Cadell in the opening words of most texts of the law – and indeed the use of his name as a shorthand for the legal system – this was not a top-down system, and the law in its entirety was not promulgated or created by any royal person. However, princes and rulers could, and did, adapt or contribute to the law: there are references to both Bleddyn ap Cynfyn (d. 1075) and Rhys ap Gruffudd (The Lord Rhys, c.1132–1197) doing so.[13] The law was known in Welsh as Cyfraith Hywel (the Law of Hywel), the attribution being to Hywel ap Cadell (Hywel Dda, d. 949/950), a tenth-century ruler of the south Wales kingdom of Dyfed, who managed to extend his dominion through conquest and alliance to include a large part of Wales (the lawbooks claim that he held all of Wales). What he contributed to the law is uncertain, however.[14] The prologues to the law manuscripts are the only evidence (although not conclusive)[15] for Hywel engaging in any legal activity, although, for the period, he had a relatively stable reign with few challenges; this stability may have meant that culture, both legal and otherwise, could flourish during that time.[16] Unfortunately there is no evidence of any cultural renaissance under his rule either, but there is very little evidence for tenth-century Wales in

---

[8] Davies, 'Law and National Identity', 53.

[9] Magna Carta c.56 refers to 'the Law of Wales' as contrasted with the law of England and the law of the March. A section of the Iorwerth text however seems to imply that Cyfraith Hywel had a jurisdiction extending beyond Offa's Dyke, which would encompass large parts of the March: *LlIor*, 89/5.

[10] On this, see the superb full study: Pryce, *Native Law and the Church*.

[11] This is suggested by Dafydd Jenkins, in contrast to the *kaiserrecht* (royal or imperial law) civil- and common-law systems: Jenkins, 'The Significance of the Law of Hywel', 63; it should be remembered that the Welsh law has early origins.

[12] Charles-Edwards, *Wales and the Britons*, 269–270.

[13] Bleddyn ap Cynfyn is quoted in the Iorwerth texts as changing the numbers of acres in each toft, and compensation rules for stolen property; according to some of the Blegywryd texts, Rhys ap Gruffudd set down sworn appraisal (in the law of theft) for all animals. *LTMW*, 98, 164.

[14] Maund, *The Welsh Kings*, 46–48. Binchy argued that the restructuring of dynastic succession in Welsh law 'may be safely ascribed to Hywel Dda'. Binchy, *Celtic and Anglo-Saxon Kingship*, 30.

[15] The general shortage of evidence for tenth-century Wales means that it cannot be argued either way. 'On present evidence we cannot prove that Hywel made an important contribution to Welsh law; but neither can we disprove it, and the most plausible explanation for his unanimous inclusion in the prologues remains that his reputation as a lawgiver had a historical basis', Pryce, 'The Prologues', 166; see also Edwards, 'Hywel Dda and the Welsh Law-books', 155.

[16] Charles-Edwards, *Wales and the Britons*, 270.

general, and so this kind of activity may have taken place but is unattested; evidence from England shows that Hywel had regular links and contact with Athelstan of Mercia (c.894–939, ruled from 924, and became 'King of the English' from 927 to his death), who was known as a lawmaker.[17]

Hywel ap Cadell was also known, apparently from an early period, and in his death notices in some chronicles, by the intriguing epithet 'Good', which may suggest that he was a particularly religious ruler: he did go on pilgrimage to Rome in 928 or 929.[18] There is a general paucity of evidence for early medieval Welsh rulers, and thus very little meaning can be attributed to the lack of evidence for any cultural activity by Hywel ap Cadell. His reputation as a lawgiver may be rooted in historical fact that is no longer substantiated by historical evidence.[19]

The legal system of medieval Wales may have started to develop as early as the post-Roman period, but the earliest manuscripts containing a text of the laws date from the mid-thirteenth century, as do all the earliest surviving books written in Welsh.[20] The earliest extant link between Hywel's name and the lawtexts occurs in the lawtexts themselves, in the Prologues, an introductory section giving the story of the creation of the laws, and the first part of any Welsh lawbook.[21] The Prologues may well have been composed to give the Welsh laws imagined royal and ecclesiastical origins, as a defence against the harsh criticism of the Welsh laws by English clerics, a criticism made in part as a means of justifying war.[22] However, while the Prologues are not contemporary with Hywel Dda, there are no earlier manuscripts of Welsh law *lacking* the attribution to the king, and therefore they do suggest an earlier origin to the tradition, perhaps dating to the twelfth century or even before. It is notable that, as Pryce points out, the Prologues in all of the law manuscripts are unanimous in naming Hywel as the lawgiver.[23] The Prologues may have a different historical and political origin and may not prove or disprove the link to Hywel ap Cadell, but Pryce states: 'If, as J. Goronwy Edwards convincingly argued, the prologues to the Welsh lawbooks have little to offer the historian of tenth-century Wales, they nevertheless deserve to be studied as historical sources for the period of their redaction.'[24] This is true to a great extent of different parts of the lawbooks, but tracing the origins and a start date for medieval Welsh law will remain hugely problematic.

---

[17] *LTMW*, xi–xvi; Maund, *The Welsh Kings*, 48. Charles-Edwards discusses two schools of thought on Hywel Dda and the laws: either to accept the attribution, or to see 'the attribution as belonging to a wider European pattern by which lawbooks of the twelfth and thirteenth centuries were attributed to authoritative figures of the past', Charles-Edwards, *Wales and the Britons*, 268.

[18] The earliest datable occurrence of the epithet 'da' is in the Book of Llandaf: Gwenogvryn Evans, *The Book of Llan Dâv*, 241, 248. See also Jones, *Brut y Tywysogyon*, 8, 'howel da vab cadell vrenhin pen a molyant yr holl vrytanyeit'; *Annales Cambriae: The C text*, 21, 'Howel rex britonum congnomento bonus moritur'. His pilgrimage to Rome is listed in all versions of *Annales Cambriae*, see <http://croniclau.bangor.ac.uk/chronicles.php.en>, accessed 28/11/2021. The epithet 'Da' is not found with references to Hywel in contemporary sources, and J. E. Lloyd stated that it 'obtained an early currency from the prefaces to the editions of the Laws': Lloyd, *A History of Wales*, 333 n.48.

[19] Pryce, 'The Prologues', 166. See also Charles-Edwards, *Wales and the Britons*, 268.

[20] Huws, *Medieval Welsh Manuscripts*, 13.

[21] For an example see *LTMW*, 1.

[22] *LTMW*, xiii. See also p. 1 where there is an example of a prologue; Pryce, *Native Law and the Church*, 71–72.

[23] Pryce, 'The Prologues', 166.

[24] *Ibid.*, 181.

Introduction: Medieval Welsh Law and the Lawtexts

One of the problems with dating Cyfraith Hywel as a whole is that the lawbooks are unlikely to have had one continuous period of creation, and so the extant manuscripts contain different layers of texts from different periods. Examples of early passages include the section known as Saith Esgopty Dyfed ('The Seven Bishop-Houses of Dyfed'), discussed in detail by Thomas Charles-Edwards, who dates the original of the text to the second half of the ninth century or the beginning of the tenth.[25] The texts show borrowing from an Irish collection of canons, knowledge of which may have reached Wales in the tenth or twelfth century,[26] and they also show that the Welsh lawtexts were open to influence from other traditions. In these early examples, the lawtexts borrowed from, and were influenced by, sections of Irish law, and there has been considerable discussion by historians on the Welsh lawtexts as the outcome of early and native legal development.[27] The Welsh lawtexts could have an origin shared with Irish law and legal texts, perhaps originating in the tenth-century world of Hywel Dda, but they can also be viewed as a reflection of European-wide trends in lawmaking dating to the twelfth and thirteenth century, as the Welsh contribution to the 'general resurgence in law taking place in Western Europe as a whole'.[28] The lawtexts do not therefore give an accurate picture of Welsh society at one and the same period in the Middle Ages, although various parts of the laws may be roughly datable.[29]

The texts of the earliest manuscripts point to an earlier exemplar. This pushes back the date of the creation of at least part of the laws to an earlier date, a century or more before the thirteenth century.[30] However, while the law itself may be early, the texts of the law as contained in manuscripts are not dated to the tenth century, to the time of Hywel ap Cadell, and there are little to no traces of early orthography, word forms or grammatical constructions in the extant texts; however, this does not necessarily mean that sections or manuscripts of Welsh law were not written in Old Welsh.[31] The nature of some of the content of the lawtexts however may point to a pre-Norman origin, and it is doubtless true that there were some legal texts being written in Wales in a period earlier than the thirteenth century.[32] Added to this, there are two surviving legal texts in Old Welsh, and these support the theory that at least some legal texts were being recorded in the vernacular in at least one part of Wales.[33]

The piece known as the Surexit Memorandum, on the margins of the manuscript of the Lichfield Gospels, records the resolution of a legal dispute, written into the Gospel book in the first half of the ninth century, perhaps soon after the case was resolved.[34] The Book of Llandaf, a Gospel book containing a twelfth-century

---

[25] Charles-Edwards, 'The Seven Bishop-Houses', 268–269.

[26] Pryce, 'Early Irish Canons', 122. See also Owen, 'The *Excerpta*', 171–195.

[27] See the summary in Stacey, *Law and the Imagination*, 11–12.

[28] See the discussion on this point and the link to Hywel Dda, and the implication of the interpretations, in Charles-Edwards, *Wales and the Britons*, 267–272; Stacey, *Law and the Imagination*, 12.

[29] Jenkins, *Cyfraith Hywel*, 3, 9.

[30] Charles-Edwards, *The Welsh Laws*, 70–72.

[31] Huws, *Medieval Welsh Manuscripts*, 37. Old Welsh is the language from around the eighth century to the twelfth century, and it was followed by Middle Welsh, up to the fourteenth century. Koch, *Celtic Culture: A Historical Encyclopedia*, 1757. On the transmission of texts in manuscripts see Charles-Edwards, 'The Textual Tradition of Medieval Welsh', 23–39.

[32] Charles-Edwards, *The Welsh Laws*, 73–74.

[33] *Ibid.*, 74–75.

[34] On the Surexit, see Jenkins and Owen, 'The Welsh Marginalia', Parts I and II; more recently, Eska and Wolf, 'The *Surexit* Memorandum Revisited', which discusses the dating on p. 20.

collection of documents relating to the history of that church, also includes the famous text of *Breint Teilo*, a document detailing the liberties of St Teilo, supposedly the first bishop of Llandaf and the founder of that church, and also of the church at Llandeilo Fawr in Carmarthenshire. The *Breint Teilo* text in the Book of Llandaf was previously thought to have been written in Old Welsh from the start, but it has been thoroughly reassessed recently by Paul Russell, who suggests that the Welsh text may not be the earliest form, and that the Latin text that accompanies it in the Book of Llandaf may be the original.[35] Whether or not the Welsh version of *Breint Teilo* was the original, the wording within the piece is similar to that of Welsh law, and this may suggest an earlier origin for the Welsh lawtexts, even if that is as a translation of a Latin text.[36]

Cyfraith Hywel is likely to be early, and is certainly earlier than the first manuscripts that attest to it. There is some evidence that Cyfraith Hywel was in operation, in part at least, and in certain regions, in the thirteenth century, and it is likely to have been in operation in the twelfth century too, if not earlier. The earliest manuscripts originate from Gwynedd, which was enjoying a period of stability and dominance under Llywelyn ab Iorwerth, c.1200–1240, from which much cultural activity resulted.[37] There is considerable evidence for the development of the legal texts under his rule in Gwynedd, and the work of reorganising and reformulating the laws was undertaken in that period.[38] There was, however, a definite north/south divide in Wales and this is apparent in the lawtexts as well. While the Law of Hywel as a legal tradition (and the 'law of Wales' referred to in Magna Carta) was seen to apply to the whole of Wales, there were certainly regional variations and, as will be seen, different texts were developed in different regions. Unsurprisingly perhaps, it is highly likely that there was a different method of practising the law in different regions, and this is reflected in the lawtexts and their description of the role of the professionally trained jurist in north Wales, whereas in south Wales the landowner would be called upon to play a legal role.[39] The extent to which this regional variety is reflected in the lawtexts themselves varies, but the development of the lawtexts, the growth of the law, may have taken a different form in different regions.

The law may have experienced a golden era in Gwynedd between 1216 and 1240, and may have continued from that point, but the political situation changed in Gwynedd under the rule of Llywelyn ab Iorwerth's grandson, Llywelyn ap Gruffudd. During the reign of Henry III, Llywelyn was able to develop Gwynedd, but in the latter part of his reign he suffered largely because England also had one of its mightiest kings, Edward I, at the same time. Wales was conquered following the death of Llywelyn ap Gruffudd in 1282 and the execution of his younger brother Dafydd ap Gruffudd in 1283, and the territories held by Llywelyn ap Gruffudd as Prince of Wales passed to the English crown. The consolidation of the conquest included making provisions for the law in Wales, and this was done in the Statute of Wales,

---

[35] Russell, *Priuilegium Sancti Teliaui*, 41–68.

[36] *Ibid.*, 63.

[37] On Llywelyn ab Iorwerth's reign see Maund, *The Welsh Kings*, 115–126; see also the chapter in Lloyd, *A History of Wales*, 612–693; Davies, *The Age of Conquest*, 236–251.

[38] This aspect will be explored more fully in this work, in particular in Chapter 3, which will explore the development of the Iorwerth texts, but also in Chapter 4, which considers particular genres, some of them closely linked to the Iorwerth development, including *cynghawsedd* (model pleading) and *damweiniau* (eventualities).

[39] See Chapter 3, 59–61, where this is discussed in more detail.

1284, the legal document that set out the constitutional situation for the government of the new Principality of North Wales. However, as Llinos Beverley Smith notes, the Statute of Wales was more of 'an outline scheme for the government of the king's lands in Wales' than an official declaration of post-conquest legal practice.[40] According to the provisions of the Statute, Welsh law was permitted to continue in all areas other than criminal law, and so it was not an attempt to transplant English law into the conquered territories as is sometimes supposed.[41] In addition, the Statute of Wales only applied to the lands conquered by Edward I in 1282, and not to the whole of Wales, and so parts of south Wales, as well as the March of Wales, remained independent in a legal sense. As such, Welsh law continued beyond the conquest of Wales in some regions and, even in the conquered lands, English law did not supplant it. In addition, manuscripts of Welsh law were still being created and copied, and there were some innovations in the lawtexts that post-date the conquest of 1282. There is no question that, in some areas, at least some parts of the lawtexts were still applicable and useful, and were also necessary.

The March of Wales was one of these areas where the law may still have been applicable in part. Running along the borderlands between England and Wales and into large parts of south Wales, it was comprised of lordships, and the Marcher lords had a greater degree of independence from the English crown.[42] As such, the Lords Marcher were able to formulate their own laws, and often did so by drawing on both legal traditions – as well as on customs and other sources – which were familiar to them. As a result, law and legal practice in the March may reflect a combination of both Welsh and English law.[43] In these areas, Welsh law continued to be copied, and indeed created and written, but in a changed form.[44]

The later development of Welsh law, the manuscripts created after the conquest and the law being created after that time, is largely traced to south Wales and to the March of Wales. While there is evidence that law was being created, rewritten and revised in Gwynedd, it was largely happening during the golden age, the thirteenth century, and before the conquest of Wales; but for the development of Welsh law and the making of the later lawtexts, as far as the surviving manuscripts are concerned the focus must move from Gwynedd,[45] and, as will be evident, much reworking and development was taking place.

The Lawtexts of Medieval Wales

Any study of the Welsh lawtexts should begin with the manuscripts. There are over 40 complete medieval manuscripts of Welsh law, which is a relatively high number of manuscripts for any genre, highlighting the importance of the law and the need for written copies of it. Most of these manuscripts present a text of the laws that is unique in some senses, although each text may have similarities in order and content to

---

[40] Smith, 'The Statute of Wales', 134.
[41] Brand, 'An English Legal Historian', 37, and *passim*.
[42] Davies, *Lordship and Society*, vii, 3–4. See also Lieberman, *The March of Wales*, 81–84; and Lieberman, *The Medieval March of Wales*, 218–219.
[43] See Davies' seminal study 'The Law of the March'.
[44] See for example Roberts, 'Legal Practice'.
[45] One notable exception is the now-lost Llanforda manuscript, dating from the start of the fourteenth century and intended for use in Meirionnydd; Jenkins, 'Llawysgrif Goll Llanforda', 93, 99.

other extant law manuscripts, and there is much repetition of material across the texts, including in those manuscripts that are said to contain later or 'additional' material.

Most of the Welsh law manuscripts can be categorised into groups, known as redactions, although a small number of the manuscripts do not fit into any of the recognised redactions. Each redaction-text of Welsh law is comprised of a number of tractates (sub-sections, essays even) on various topics, and the tractates are usually fairly fixed in content, although the order may vary. However, as well as the commonly occurring tractates, many law manuscripts also include other sections of law that do not occur in as many manuscripts. This factor, together with Aneurin Owen's edition of the laws, *Ancient Laws*, which will be discussed in detail in the next chapter, has led to the division of the legal material into two parts: the 'main text' material, seen to be the 'standard' tractates that would make up the lawtexts; and then anything that does not fit into the 'standard' number of tractates. This latter material has been variously described as 'anomalous', later, 'additional', and as forming a 'tail' to a manuscript. The main focus of this study will be on this so-called additional material, and the way it relates to the other legal material within the law manuscripts. In addition, the division is problematic when one considers the manuscripts of Welsh law which contain very few or even none of the 'standard' or expected tractates from a redaction, but are comprised purely of legal material. The division is therefore highly contentious, but still a well-known attempt to categorise the Welsh law manuscripts, and one that is frequently seen in scholarly discussions of the laws.

Before looking at the material they contain, the manuscripts themselves and their place in the traditional organisation of the Welsh law material need to be examined in detail. The categorisation of manuscripts into redactions, with each manuscript sharing similar features, is accepted, and so this introduction will examine the manuscripts of Welsh law by redaction. Further detail on the dating and contents of the manuscripts can be found in studies with a focus on that aspect, such as the work of Daniel Huws, who has published widely on the topic.[46]

The Manuscripts of Welsh Law

It has long been known that the Welsh law texts could be divided into groups, and this was a feature of the earliest editions of Cyfraith Hywel. The antiquary and manuscript collector William Maurice (1620–1680), in his manuscript compilation of the law manuscripts preserved in Wynnstay 37 and 38, may have been the first both to attempt a full study of a number of law manuscripts, and also to divide the manuscripts into groups, which he called *Alpha*, *Ior* and *Beta*.[47] In the first printed edition of the laws, William Wotton and Moses Williams did not organise the material in the

---

[46] On the dating of the manuscripts, see *RWMS*; also Huws, *Medieval Welsh Manuscripts*. Dr Huws has contributed widely on the manuscripts to various works published by Seminar Cyfraith Hywel, for example, *WLW*, *LAL*, *WKC*, *TCC*. Each of these volumes has a full essay by Daniel Huws on the manuscripts used in the edition. The Welsh law website <http://www.cyfraith-hywel.org.uk> has a short description of each of the law manuscripts, and also has databases listing the contents of those manuscripts. My thanks go to Dr Huws in this present work, for his assistance and his generosity. The dates and descriptions of the manuscripts given here owe much to Daniel Huws, and I am grateful to him for discussing these matters with me, both in person and in correspondence.

[47] Jenkins, 'Deddfgrawn William Maurice', 36.

same way, and did not draw on Maurice's work either, which rendered their book less organised in some ways, although it had its own organisational structure.[48]

Aneurin Owen certainly made use of Maurice's manuscripts, even if he did not make that fact known in *Ancient Laws*; there is a receipt acknowledging from Owen the return of Maurice's manuscripts along with some others from the Wynnstay library.[49] His work follows a similar order to Maurice's manuscripts, but Owen renamed the redactions (or 'Codes' as he called them) according to geographical links, which he perceived, and following his concept of the original books created at the instigation of King Hywel ap Cadell.[50] The material that did not fit into his categorisation of the Codes was deemed 'anomalous', but he conceded that this was a very important part of the lawtexts. His Codes were called Venedotian, pertaining to Gwynedd; Dimetian, pertaining to Dyfed; and the Gwentian Code, belonging to Gwent, as he felt the texts had been created in those areas. His linking of the Venedotian Code to Gwynedd is still accurate; the Dimetian Code was created in south Wales, in Deheubarth (which was largely coterminous with the ancient kingdom of Dyfed); but the Gwentian Code is a misnomer: it was actually associated with Deheubarth in south Wales, and the lands under the rule of Lord Rhys in the twelfth century.[51] As a result, in his edition of the texts of that redaction, the Reverend A. W. Wade-Evans proposed that the Codes should be renamed, doing away with the geographical designations, and suggested naming the groups of texts after the jurists given pre-eminence in the Prologues to each group.[52] The Venedotian Code became the Iorwerth redaction; the Dimetian Code was renamed Blegywryd; and the Gwentian Code, the focus of Wade-Evans's edition, became known as the Cyfnerth redaction. These names are the standard categorisation of the Welsh law manuscripts to this day. Aneurin Owen's work was not completely superseded, however; the sigla that he assigned to the manuscripts are still used.[53]

(a) Iorwerth

Table 1.1: *The Iorwerth Redaction Manuscripts, organised by date*

Siglum	Manuscript Call Number	Date
A	NLW Peniarth MS 29	$s.\text{xiii}^{med}$
C	BL Cotton Caligula MS A III	$s.\text{xiii}^{med}$
E	BL Additional MS 14,931	$s.\text{xiii}^2$
B	BL Cotton Titus MS D II	$s.\text{xiii}^2$
G	NLW Peniarth MS 35	$s.\text{xiv}^1$
D	NLW Peniarth MS 32	$c.1404$
K	NLW Peniarth MS 40	>1469
Lew	NLW Peniarth MS 39	$s.\text{xv}^{med}$

---

[48] *Leges Wallicae*; see also the highly entertaining account of the creation of *Leges Wallicae* in Stoker, 'William Wotton's Exile and Redemption'.
[49] Jenkins, 'Deddfgrawn William Maurice', 36.
[50] AL, Introduction, xviii–xxi.
[51] Charles-Edwards, *The Welsh Laws*, 18–19.
[52] *WML*, vii–xii.
[53] AL, Introduction, xxv–xxxii.

The manuscripts in the Iorwerth redaction are the oldest of the Welsh law manuscripts, and several of the manuscripts are among the earliest in the Welsh language.[54] The Iorwerth redaction is based in Gwynedd, and Aneurin Owen was correct in deeming it the Venedotian Code; the redaction has since been named after Iorwerth ap Madog (fl. ?1240-?1268), a jurist who is named in the prologue and who can be traced in genealogies.[55] The Iorwerth manuscripts are organised and systematic texts, with markers throughout – short sections stating 'Here begins …', 'Here ends …' – making the divisions within the text clear and obvious. The Iorwerth texts also have a tripartite division: they are split into the Laws of Court, detailing the royal court; the Laws of Country, covering laws on matters such as land, contract, buying and selling, and the relationships between people; and the Justices' Test Book, which is said to contain material that a lawyer needed to know. The Test Book comprises the Three Columns of Law (homicide, theft and fire); the Value of Wild and Tame (listing all of the characteristics of animals of which a man may make use); and sections on agriculture, such as *Cyfar* ('co-tillage') and Corn Damage (on animal damage to crops in the fields). The latter two sections were called the 'appendix' to the Test Book by Dafydd Jenkins because, in his view, unlike the Three Columns and Wild and Tame, they are not named in the introduction to the Test Book as part of the book, but are probably to be included under *ac a perthyn arnadunt* ('what pertains to them').[56] However, there are differences in the texts in different manuscripts, and the evidence for the existence of the 'appendix' is not strong.[57]

Parts of the Iorwerth texts may have been organised, compiled, or even created – in the case of the Test Book or parts of it – by Iorwerth ap Madog himself.[58] His exact role and his link to the redaction now named after him may not be entirely certain, but it is striking that he was contemporary with the earliest manuscripts in this redaction, A and C, and that parts of the Iorwerth Test Book have been described in modern scholarship as 'current law'.[59] All of this points to the fact that the Iorwerth redaction in its extant form in the thirteenth-century manuscripts reflects the legal activity taking place in Gwynedd under the rule of Llywelyn ab Iorwerth (c.1200–1240). Some parts of the texts, such as the Laws of Court, were older and carried into the new compilation; but several sections in the Test Book may have been created or at least put together in the thirteenth century. As such, parts of the Iorwerth redaction can be dated, tentatively, although dating the laws as a whole remains problematic.

---

[54] See for example the table of medieval Welsh vernacular manuscripts in Huws, *Medieval Welsh Manuscripts*, 58–64, where Iorwerth A and C are listed among the nine manuscripts from the mid-thirteenth century, and B and E date from the late thirteenth century.

[55] Iorwerth ap Madog was discussed by Dafydd Jenkins in 'Iorwerth ap Madog', trans. and rev. in Jenkins, 'A Family of Medieval Welsh Lawyers'; also in Jenkins, 'Iorwerth ap Madog a Hywel Dda', and Jenkins, 'Yr Ynad Coch'.

[56] *LlIor*, 104/2; Jenkins, *Hunting and Husbandry*, 2. See also Chapter 3, 67–68.

[57] Manuscript B has an explicit stating *Ac yuelly e teruynha e Llyuer Prauf* ('And so ends the *Llyfr Prawf*'), which occurs before the value of houses and equipment, and *Cyfar* and Corn Damage: *LlIor*, 138/14. Other manuscripts, however, have an explicit, which suggests that the 'appendix' is in fact part of the *Llyfr Prawf*: manuscript C ends after the Corn Damage section with the Latin explicit *Explicit libellus probationis legum curialium Walliae. Amen.* ('Here ends the Test Book of the Laws of Wales. Amen.'); see AL VC III.xxv.46. Manuscript K has an explicit at the end of the value of equipment, which states that the *Llyfr Prawf* ends at this point: AL VC III.xxii.251. It is not at all clear where the *Llyfr Prawf* ends.

[58] Charles-Edwards, *The Welsh Laws*, 23–24; 29–30.

[59] Jenkins, *Agricultural Co-Operation*, 2.

Introduction: Medieval Welsh Law and the Lawtexts

A, 'The Black Book of Chirk', was considered by Aneurin Owen and J. Gwenogvryn Evans to be the earliest of the Welsh law manuscripts, and Aneurin Owen used it as the basis of his Venedotian Code. The orthography of the manuscript is unusual and has caused problems, but Paul Russell's excellent and detailed study of the orthography revealed that while there are some Old Welsh orthographical elements, it is not a representative of Old Welsh; however, the exemplar used by the scribes may have had late survivals of Old Welsh orthography.[60] The other early Iorwerth manuscript is C, a manuscript that is incomplete. This manuscript may have been created at Clynnog Fawr (on the north coast of the Llŷn peninsula, and the principal church of St Beuno),[61] not long after Iorwerth ap Madog's work on the Iorwerth redaction, and it may have been written by 'perhaps not a young man, old-fashioned in his ways'.[62]

B was the base text for the standard printed edition of the Iorwerth redaction, Aled Rhys Wiliam's *LlIor*. B has particular interest because it offers a different version of Iorwerth, and appears to remove references to Iorwerth ap Madog deliberately.[63] D and E are both full copies of the Iorwerth redaction and both contain a copy of *Llyfr Damweiniau* (Eventualities, sentences stating 'if X happens, then Y is to follow').[64] B also has a copy of *Llyfr Cynghawsedd* (model pleadings).

G as it exists today is not a complete text of Iorwerth, and the manuscript's quires are disordered. It contains *damweiniau* and *cynghawsedd*, and also other material that is not found elsewhere. One of the manuscripts' scribes was also the scribe of U of the Cyfnerth redaction. Despite it being an early Iorwerth manuscript it has been much neglected.[65] K is a later Iorwerth text, preceded by a calendar, and followed by a collection of triads shared with manuscript Q of the Blegywryd redaction; a full collection of *damweiniau* also shared with Q; and a plaint that is also found, in a different version, in the Boston manuscript of the Blegywryd redaction.[66] The manuscript can be linked to Cefnllys in Radnorshire, and is in the hand of the poet and scribe Lewys Glyn Cothi. The latest medieval Iorwerth manuscript, Lew, like G does not follow the Iorwerth order and has other material, including *damweiniau* and *cynghawsedd*. It is in the hand of the scribe Lewys Ysgolhaig.[67]

Only manuscript B of the Iorwerth redaction has been edited in full, although there is a facsimile of manuscript A.[68] Transcripts of all of these manuscripts apart from K and Lew are available online.[69] *WLW* based its edition of the Law of Women on G; *LAL* took the text of Suretyship from C; and in *TCC*, the Three Columns

---

[60] Russell, 'Scribal (In)Competence', 140–145, 165, 170.

[61] Clynnog Fawr was also a traditional Welsh *clas* (religious community). See Pryce, *Native Law and the Church*, 186–188.

[62] Huws, 'Cotton Caligula A iii', 121. This is the fullest study of the text and history of manuscript C.

[63] With thanks to Professor Thomas Charles-Edwards, who discussed this in his unpublished paper on the Iorwerth redaction.

[64] Stacey, 'Legal Writing in Medieval Wales', 59.

[65] Wiliam, 'Llyfr Cynghawsedd', 73–85, presents an edition of the *Llyfr Cynghawsedd* text from G, but rearranged into a more logical order. He also edited sections of G in Wiliam, *Llyfr Cynog*.

[66] See the study of K in Owen, 'A Fifteenth-Century Lawbook'. The Boston manuscript is known as 'Bost', and is discussed below.

[67] Huws, *Medieval Welsh Manuscripts*, 61.

[68] *LlIor*; Evans, *Facsimile of the Chirk Codex*.

[69] *Rhyddiaith Gymraeg 1300–1425* <http://www.rhyddiaithganoloesol.caerdydd.ac.uk/>; and also 13th Century Welsh Prose Manuscripts, <https://pure.aber.ac.uk/portal/en/datasets/13thcentury-

of Law was taken from E, with a full parallel text of the same section from B. In addition, a full translation largely based on the edition in *LlIor* was made by Dafydd Jenkins and published as *LTMW*.

(b) Blegywryd

Table 1.2: The Blegywryd Redaction Manuscripts, organised by date

Siglum	Manuscript Call Number	Date
N	NLW Peniarth MS 36B	$s.xiv^1$ *Gwilym Wasta*
O	NLW Peniarth MS 36A	$s.xiv^1$ *Gwilym Wasta*
Tr	Cambridge, Trinity College MS O.7.1	$s.xiv^1$ *Gwilym Wasta*
R	NLW Peniarth MS 31	$s.xiv^1$
T	BL Harleian MS 958	$s.xiv^{med}$
L	BL Cotton Titus MS D IX	$s.xiv^{med}$
Y	NLW MS 20143A	$s.xiv^2$
Bost	NLW MS 24029A	$s.xiv^2$
I	NLW Peniarth MS 38	$s.xiv/xv$
J	Oxford, Jesus College MS 57	$s.xiv/xv$ *Hand of Hywel Fychan*
M	NLW Peniarth MS 33	$s.xv^1$
Q	NLW Wynnstay MS 36	1440s
P	NLW Peniarth MS 259A	$s.xv^2$ *Copy of Q*
Ep	NLW Peniarth MS 258	$s.xv^2$ *Copy of Q*
S	BL Additional MS 22,356	$s.xv^{med}$ *Same hand as Tim*
Tim	NLW Llanstephan MS 116	$s.xv^{med}$ *Same hand as S*
Llan	NLW Llanstephan MS 29	$s.xv/xvi$
Crd	Cardiff, Central Library MS 2.7	$s.xv^2$ *Copy of L*

The Blegywryd redaction with its 17 manuscripts is the redaction or group with the most surviving manuscripts. Despite the high number of manuscripts, the text is often close across the manuscripts, at least for certain tractates, and there is considerable similarity in order between the texts, although further sub-grouping can be discerned. The redaction is linked to south Wales and, indeed, none of the extant manuscripts have a northern provenance. Dating the Blegywryd redaction is problematic, since there is variation in the dates of the manuscripts – from the early fourteenth century to the late fifteenth century – and there is a considerable amount of material found in some manuscripts that is not found in the shorter texts: this may be accounted for by different origins and dating.

The Blegywryd redaction was in large part a translation of a version of Latin D, but the text that was translated appears to have been a sister text of the extant Latin D (Oxford, Bodleian Rawlinson C 821), and none of the extant Blegywryd manuscripts

---

middle-welsh-prose-manuscripts(3abf4ef1-e364-4cce-859d-92bf4035b303).html>, accessed 29/11/21.

appear to be the original translation.⁷⁰ However, since the extant manuscript of Latin D is dated to the late thirteenth century or the early fourteenth century, this shows that parts of the Blegywryd redaction go back to *c*.1300, at least in Latin versions, closer than the earliest manuscripts of Blegywryd to the putative date of the formation of the Iorwerth redaction.

Three of the earliest Blegywryd manuscripts, N, O, and Tr, are in the hand of a scribe called Gwilym Wasta ('Gwilym the Good Servant'), who was also an English burgess in Dinefwr, Carmarthenshire: Gwilym Wasta can be located in the early fourteenth century from record sources.⁷¹ These texts are notable in that they do not have a copy of the Laws of Court, and this may have been omitted because it was no longer of use – there is a colophon by the scribe that states as much. However, the manuscripts are laconic in general, and that has led Paul Russell to suggest that this may have less to do with a deliberate omission and more to do with working from a laconic exemplar.⁷²

R also dates from the first half of the fourteenth century, and T is a little later, from the mid-fourteenth century. Each of these manuscripts have their end wanting, but contain the basic text as it was presented in the printed edition, *LlBleg*. From the late fourteenth century, the Boston manuscript, Bost, has lacunae but has further material at the end of the manuscript. The same material is also found in L, another mid-fourteenth-century manuscript. M is early fifteenth century, as is Cardiff 2.7, which is a copy of L by the same scribe as F.⁷³

Several of the later Blegywryd manuscripts have more material in them than the earlier texts. J is a late fourteenth-/early fifteenth-century manuscript, and it has the same fuller Blegywryd text that is found in Bost and in L, and also continues with texts derived from the Iorwerth redaction.⁷⁴ It is in the hand of Hywel Fychan fab Hywel Goch of Buellt (Builth), one of the scribes of the Red Book of Hergest, the most important compilation of Welsh prose – but not including law – and poetry and one of the most important medieval Welsh manuscripts.

Y is a composite manuscript: the Laws of Court are from Cyfnerth, but the remainder of the manuscript is Blegywryd, with material from other redactions, including Cyfnerth, interspersed; it is an important Blegywryd text, and early, as it dates from the second half of the fourteenth century.

I is also late fourteenth-/early fifteenth-century, and it is the only one of the later manuscripts that only contains the text found in *LlBleg* and nothing else, but it is wanting its end. The text in I is related to the first part of S, a large manuscript from the fifteenth century, and S also has an extended text, some of which may have been taken from a book known as *Rhol Dafydd Llwyd* (Dafydd Llwyd's Roll). Some of the same material occurs in S's sister manuscript, in the same hand, Tim. Unfortunately, Tim is missing around two quires at the beginning, further text at the end, and has lacunae.

Q is a beautiful mid-fifteenth-century manuscript with a heavily edited Blegywryd text, and is augmented by several texts including *damweiniau*, triads, plaints and proverbs. Two early copies were made of this manuscript, both within 50 years of its creation (and thus dating from the second half of the fifteenth century). The

---

⁷⁰ Emanuel, 'Llyfr Blegywryd', and with a newer version in Emanuel, 'The Book of Blegywryd'.
⁷¹ Owen and Jenkins, 'Gwilym Was Da', 429.
⁷² Russell, '*Canyt oes aruer*'. Daniel Huws, in a paper at Seminar Cyfraith Hywel in 2016, disagreed with this view. See the discussion in Chapter 5, below.
⁷³ *RWMS*.
⁷⁴ See the full discussion in Chapter 5, 149–155.

copies are P and Ep. Llan is the latest Blegywryd manuscript, late fifteenth-/early sixteenth-century. It has several lacunae.

Several of the Blegywryd manuscripts have been edited and published. The earliest edition of a Blegywryd text was that of Stephen J. Williams and J. Enoch Powell, which based the text on manuscripts O and Tr, with the Laws of Court and the very last sentences taken from L (as Tr ends mid-sentence) and, as such, it is a composite edition.[75] The text of that edition was also translated by Melville Richards and published separately.[76] Manuscript J was edited in its entirety, but it is itself a text composed of a Blegywryd first part, and more varied material, mostly Iorwerth, in the second part.[77] Another highly important, and later, Blegywryd manuscript was examined and edited by Christine James for her doctoral thesis; the focus of her edition is manuscript S.[78] A facsimile transcript of Tim, the sister manuscript of S, was published by Timothy Lewis.[79] All of the earlier Blegywryd manuscripts are available as transcripts online, but the manuscripts that are not included are the later S, Tim, Q, P, Ep and Llan.[80] The tractate studies published by Seminar Cyfraith Hywel have not included a Blegywryd text, but the triad tractate from Q was published in a study of the legal triads.[81]

(c) Cyfnerth

Table 1.3: The Cyfnerth Redaction Manuscripts, organised by date

Siglum	Manuscript Call Number	Date
Mk	Bodorgan Manuscript	$s.xiv^1$
U	NLW Peniarth MS 37	$s.xiv^1$
W	BL Cotton Cleopatra MS A XIV	$s.xiv^1$ Same hand as V
V	BL Harleian MS 4353	$s.xiv^1$ Same hand as W
X	BL Cotton Cleopatra MS B V	$s.xiv^{med}$
Y	NLW MS 20143A	$s.xiv^2$
Z	NLW Peniarth MS 259B	$s.xvi^1$

The Cyfnerth redaction is often said to be the earliest version of the Welsh laws, although the manuscripts are of a date with the early Blegywryd manuscripts, and some of them have close similarity to the Blegywryd redaction. While textual relationships can be discerned for the Iorwerth and Blegywryd manuscripts, the Cyfnerth manuscripts are problematic and are individual texts; it is very difficult indeed to determine a 'core' Cyfnerth text (although several tractates do occur across the manuscripts and they are similar in form and content) and Dafydd Jenkins's conspectus of the Cyfnerth manuscripts demonstrated the complexity of the redaction.[82] The texts

---

[75] *LlBleg*, 131 – apart from the first page, the text on the final page of the edition is taken from L, and it comprises 10 lines.

[76] *J(ed.)*.

[77] *J(ed.)*.

[78] This was published online in 2013 as *Machlud*. It is forthcoming as a printed book.

[79] Lewis, *Llanstephan MS. 116*.

[80] *Rhyddiaith Gymraeg 1300–1425* <http://www.rhyddiaithganoloesol.caerdydd.ac.uk/>.

[81] *LT*.

[82] Jenkins, *Conspectus*.

themselves are the shortest texts of Welsh law, perhaps because of the early nature of the texts, but they do share features with the other redactions of Welsh law and, at times, the early development of the laws can be seen in the Cyfnerth texts. The redaction has a tractate comprising of a collection of triads, a feature that is developed in the Latin and in the Blegywryd redactions.[83] The Cyfnerth texts may show similarity to some of the Latin texts, as well as having sections that form the basis for some parts of the developed Iorwerth texts (for example, a section in Cyfnerth appears to be the inspiration for the complex and highly developed *Cyfar* ('co-tillage') section in the Iorwerth Test Book).[84] The Cyfnerth texts are largely southern, although two of the manuscripts, X and Z, show northern affinities.[85]

Cyfnerth U is the shortest text and was the basis of Owen's Gwentian Code.[86] X may represent a basic Cyfnerth redaction text. The text in X is similar to that in Z, is the latest of the Welsh law manuscripts, written on paper. Z is dated to the sixteenth century and can be firmly located in north-east Wales, and while the manuscript is late in date, it is undoubtedly a copy of earlier exemplars, with the original Cyfnerth text probably dating from the mid-fourteenth century like that in X.[87]

V and W were written by the same scribe and are very close, and have much material that is also found in the Blegywryd redaction; both are in the same hand as that of Llyfr Taliesin, and W appears to be the earlier of the two.[88] Wade-Evans suggested calling these manuscripts 'the composite book of Cyvnerth and Blegywryd', but it is uncertain whether V and W were borrowing material directly from a Blegywryd text, or whether there was an element of shared development between the manuscripts.[89] W also appears to reflect early Iorwerth influence in south Wales.[90] To V and W can be added Mk, a manuscript that remains in private ownership, and, that, as a result, was omitted from both AL and Wade-Evans's *WML*.

Y can be considered with the Cyfnerth manuscripts, although only the Laws of Court from that manuscript are Cyfnerth. The Laws of Court in Y show close similarity to those in X.[91] As the manuscript was lost from public view shortly after the publication of *Ancient Laws* and up to 1969, the text is yet to be the subject of a full study, but the Blegywryd part of the manuscript has Cyfnerth and other material interspersed with the Blegywryd text.[92]

There are two edited texts of the Cyfnerth redaction, and both also include a translation. Wade-Evans's early edition was based on the laconic manuscript V, with the gaps filled from its sister manuscript W; and the edition of the Pontefract manuscript, Z, is a single-manuscript edition.[93] *WLW* used Mk as the base text for the

---

[83] *LT*, Introduction.
[84] See Chapter 3, below, 68–72.
[85] *Pomffred*, 7–8.
[86] AL GC.
[87] *Pomffred*, 23.
[88] Huws, 'B.L. Cotton Cleopatra A.xiv', 133. See also Haycock, 'Llyfr Taliesin', 359–360. Haycock argues that the manuscripts may have originated from south-east Wales, by a clerically-trained scribe, perhaps working in an ecclesiastical or monastic centre, and she tentatively suggests Glamorgan as a location for this centre; Haycock, 'Llyfr Taliesin', 364–367.
[89] *WML*.
[90] Charles-Edwards, 'The Texts', 117.
[91] *WKC*, 431.
[92] *WKC*, 420–424.
[93] *Pomffred*.

Cyfnerth Law of Women; *LAL* used W; the edition of the Laws of Court in *WKC* was based on Y; and the Three Columns of Law were taken from X in *TCC*. Other than Z, which has been published as a modern edition, there are online transcripts of all extant Cyfnerth manuscripts.[94]

(d) Latin

Table 1.4: The Latin Manuscripts, organised by date

Siglum	Manuscript Call Number	Date
Latin A	NLW Peniarth MS 28	$s.\text{xiii}^{\text{med}}$
Latin B	BL Cotton Vespasian MS E.xi	$s.\text{xiii}^{\text{med}}$
Latin C	BL Harleian MS 1796	$s.\text{xiii}^{\text{med}}$
Latin D	Oxford, Bodleian Rawlinson MS C 821	$s.\text{xiii/xiv}$
Latin E	Cambridge, Corpus Christi College MS 454	$s.\text{xv}^{1}$

The Latin manuscripts only form a group because they share the same language and are in Latin rather than in Welsh, although Emanuel considered them as a group; but Russell argues that the Latin texts are 'all part of the same tradition' (with the Welsh texts) and rather than only viewing them in the context of the other Latin texts, their place in the law manuscript tradition in general needs to be considered: 'the language in which they were written is secondary to the significance of the content'.[95] The Latin texts appear to be older than the Welsh redactions.

Latin A is a beautiful manuscript, with its famous illustrations of officers of the court and animals.[96] The text is the shortest of the complete Latin manuscripts, and has similarities to the southern Cyfnerth texts. Latin B is a complex manuscript but highly important, and has material from several other strata. The text of Latin B probably originated in south Wales but moved north.[97] Latin C is an Anglesey text, but it is not complete; Russell notes that 'if any correspondence with vernacular texts can be identified, it is usually with Ior' but starting from a Latin text within the same tradition as Latin A and Latin B.[98] Latin E may be derived in part from a version of Latin B, but with further material added, and it is a heavily revised version of the laws. Some texts in the manuscript have a north-east Wales connection. In addition, there are three manuscript witnesses to it.[99] A version of Latin D, but not the extant manuscript, was combined with other texts, translated into Welsh and became the Blegywryd redaction, and Latin D, especially its passages in Welsh, may be called the earliest witness to the Blegywryd redaction.[100]

---

[94] *Rhyddiaith Gymraeg 1300–1425* <http://www.rhyddiaithganoloesol.caerdydd.ac.uk/>.
[95] *Welsh Law in Medieval Anglesey*, xviii–xix.
[96] The manuscript has been digitised and can be viewed online at the National Library of Wales' Digital Mirror, <https://www.llgc.org.uk/discover/digital-gallery/manuscripts/the-middle-ages/laws-of-hywel-dda/>, accessed 26/11/21.
[97] *Welsh Law in Medieval Anglesey*, xvii.
[98] *Ibid.*, xxxv.
[99] See Russell, *Vita Griffini Filii Conani*, 17–25.
[100] Emanuel, 'Llyfr Blegywryd', 23–28; and Emanuel, 'The Book of Blegywryd', 161–170.

Introduction: Medieval Welsh Law and the Lawtexts

All of the manuscripts were edited by Hywel Emanuel in his *LTWL*, although the text is problematic as he based his editions on the assumption that all of the Latin texts were derived from Latin A, which he took to be the oldest version. This view has since been superseded.[101] Latin C has benefited recently from a new edition by Paul Russell, including a translation.[102] Latin A has a translation published separately, but on the whole the Latin manuscripts have been neglected in favour of the Welsh redactions.[103] The tractate studies produced by Seminar Cyfraith Hywel have included a Latin text: Latin A for *WLW*; Latin E for *LAL*; *WKC* used Latin B; and the basis for the Three Columns in *TCC* was Latin D.

(e) Other manuscripts

Table 1.5: *Non-redaction Welsh Law Manuscripts, organised by date*

Siglum	Manuscript Call Number	Date
Col	LW Peniarth MS 30	$s.\text{xiii}^{\text{med}}$
H	NLW Peniarth MS 164	$s.\text{xiv}^2$
F	NLW Peniarth MS 34	$s.\text{xv}^2$
As	NLW Peniarth MS 175	$s.\text{xv}^2$
Mor	NLW Peniarth MS 36C	$s.\text{xv}^2$
An	NLW Peniarth MS 166	$s.\text{xvi}^1$

The remaining manuscripts are all manuscripts in Welsh that do not appear to contain a full text that fits into one of the three redactions listed above, although they may be linked to one of the redactions or contain material from one or more of them.

The earliest manuscript is Col, named 'Colan' by the seventeenth-century scholar William Maurice. It is of a date with some of the earlier Iorwerth manuscripts, and has been described as a 'revised form' of Iorwerth.[104] There is no doubt that the text in Col is linked to the Iorwerth redaction, but the manuscript does not fit easily into that redaction despite containing some of the same material in a different presentation. The manuscript is not complete. The early date of the manuscript is also very interesting and is a reflection of the revising and editing of the lawtexts in Gwynedd during the time of Llywelyn ab Iorwerth. The first part of Col was edited and published by Dafydd Jenkins in 1963; the collection of *damweiniau* which forms the second part of Col was edited and published separately by him at a later date.[105]

H has also benefitted from a recent edition. It is a complex manuscript that stands alone in the legal tradition to a great extent.[106] It is a manuscript containing an enormous collection of triads as well as other legal material such as some *cynghawsedd* (model pleadings), and it is linked to north-east Wales; it shares some material with Cyfnerth Z, and also with the two manuscripts containing a collection

---

[101] Russell, *Welsh Law in Medieval Anglesey*, xvii; Huws, 'Leges Howelda at Canterbury', and Huws, 'Leges Howelda at Canterbury: A Further Note'.
[102] Russell, *Welsh Law in Medieval Anglesey*.
[103] Fletcher, *Latin Redaction A*.
[104] Charles-Edwards, *The Welsh Laws*, 21.
[105] *LlCol*; *DwC*.
[106] *ALD*.

of *cynghawsedd* from north-east Wales, As and Mor.[107] Both of these manuscripts, As and Mor, are also of north-east Wales and are clearly linked to each other, and they are largely comprised of a separate collection of *cynghawsedd* (which itself further divides into two parts) although other material does occur in the manuscripts. The same collections of *cynghawsedd* are also found in Cyfnerth Z.[108]

F is also linked to the Iorwerth redaction but is a manuscript that has not been studied in great detail and no edition of it currently exists.[109] The manuscript is set up in a similar way to the manuscripts from the redactions, with a prologue that is linked to the Iorwerth redaction, but it does not contain a full text of the laws – there are no Laws of Court, but there are sections of the Three Columns and Suretyship. However, the manuscript contains *damweiniau* and *cynghawsedd*, and Aled Rhys Wiliam describes it as the Iorwerth manuscript with the fullest collection of 'additional' material.[110]

NLW Peniarth MS 166, given the siglum An by Seminar Cyfraith Hywel, was not used by Aneurin Owen and it is a sixteenth-century text of the laws, containing some material that is not found elsewhere, although parts of the manuscript show an affinity with other extant lawtexts, such as Blegywryd S.[111] Some sections of the manuscript correspond to the Blegywryd redaction.[112] This is an important manuscript, in the south Wales tradition, which will be examined more fully in Chapter 7, as will each of the non-redaction manuscripts discussed in this section.

Conclusion

In many ways, each manuscript of Welsh law deserves a full study and an edition, but this is unlikely to happen any time soon. Instead, the next most valuable undertaking is to list what is contained in each manuscript in order to give the scholar of medieval Welsh law – and indeed, scholars of medieval Wales in general – an overview of what there is. This was done as part of the Cyfraith Hywel website, where the databases opened out the contents of the Welsh law manuscripts and made possible this study of the significance of the material.[113]

It was also the approach taken, for the Cyfnerth manuscripts, by Dafydd Jenkins in his *Conspectus*.[114] As it is, at the present time, the editions of Welsh law can be highly misleading, in terms of the material presented and also of the way the material has been presented. The edition in *LlBleg*, for example, appears as a standard representation of the Blegywryd redaction, but in fact it is representative of two early manuscripts (O and Tr), with much of the triad collection and the Laws of Court supplied from a third manuscript, L, since both O and Tr have their end wanting

---

[107] Roberts, 'Law Texts and their Sources'.

[108] *Pomffred*, 39–41.

[109] Some work on the manuscript was carried out by Aled Rhys Wiliam, published as Wiliam, 'Y Deddfgronau Cymraeg'.

[110] Wiliam, 'Y Deddfgronau Cymraeg', 97.

[111] Elias, 'Cam o'r Tywyllwch', 107. The manuscript was also included by Thomas Charles-Edwards in his list of Welsh law manuscripts, but it has received little attention by scholars in the field until recently: Charles-Edwards, *The Welsh Laws*, 102.

[112] *Ibid.*, 109.

[113] <http://www.cyfraith-hywel.org.uk>.

[114] Jenkins, *Conspectus*. The Cyfraith Hywel website also follows the same method of listing contents: <www.cyfraith-hywel.org.uk>.

and lack the Laws of Court.[115] This approach, however, disguises the true nature of Blegywryd L, and indeed of O and Tr, which have a note explaining the missing Laws of Court.[116] In addition, it omits important material at the end of that manuscript, following the triad collection. This material is critical to the understanding of the development of the Blegywryd text, and the final part of the Blegywryd redaction may reveal a great deal about the development of the whole redaction, if not of the later development of Welsh law in general.

In the same way, *LlIor* represents the Iorwerth redaction, and it is a good edition, but the manuscript chosen, B, has significant differences from the other manuscripts in the same redaction. It also does not present the entirety of manuscript B – the collection of *cynghawsedd* at the end of that manuscript is not included in the edition in *LlIor*. Unlike B, all of the Iorwerth manuscripts apart from those that are incomplete at the end have a collection of *damweiniau* as the final part of the manuscript rather than *cynghawsedd*. This selection has meant that both *cynghawsedd* and the very important *damweiniau* collections have been treated separately and, indeed, are seen as being 'separate' to the Iorwerth text. Both of the aforementioned works also share the same form of title: *Llyfr Blegywryd, Llyfr Iorwerth*. The very wording of the title gives the edited texts an authority that did not exist in the context of the manuscripts that were edited. They also imply that the edited manuscripts contain all of the Book of Blegywryd or Iorwerth, but this is not a realistic portrayal of either the manuscripts or of the way the law was presented in the medieval Welsh manuscripts.

As the legal material available to scholars of medieval Wales is coloured in this way, and does not give the complete picture, medieval Welsh law has developed a reputation for being a 'difficult' subject, fraught with problems of interpretation. This monograph aims to deal with manuscripts and also with redactions, but by breaking down the divisions between the different types of material, and making the entire corpus of Welsh law a subject for study. This will have wide-ranging consequences for the understanding of the manuscripts, the written culture, the legal and scholarly work in medieval Wales, as well as the history and political situation in Wales in the middle ages. The law is central to our understanding of medieval Wales, and this study will return the legal texts to the status they deserve, and will examine the growth of the law of medieval Wales as a gateway to understanding politics, governance and society in Wales in the middle ages.

---

[115] *LlBleg*, xxxix–xli, explains this situation, but it is also incorporated into a brief discussion on Enoch Powell's concept of 'floating sections', which was later expanded and published as a journal article: Powell, 'Floating Sections in the Law of Hywel', 29–34. The text of Tr ends mid-sentence, but it is uncertain how much was lost.

[116] See Owen and Jenkins, 'Gwilym Was Da', 429.

2

'A RATHER LABORIOUS AND HARASSING OCCUPATION': *ANCIENT LAWS AND INSTITUTES OF WALES* AND THE HISTORIOGRAPHY OF THE WELSH LAWS

The laws of medieval Wales are a rich and valuable historical source. With more than 40 manuscripts containing lengthy texts, there is plenty of material upon which the historian can draw – as can lawyers, legal historians and those interested in linguistics or literature. R. R. Davies declared that 'whatever their shortcomings and pitfalls ... the historian neglects the legal texts at his peril'.[1] Davies's summary of the problems of dealing with the legal texts for historians stemmed from the problems in dating the texts, which 'contain, pell-mell, tractates and individual dicta drawn from widely differing periods and contexts. Such chronological uncertainty is the despair of the historian.'[2]

Davies goes on to emphasise the purpose of the lawtexts. Giving the surprising and amusing example of a husband's right to reclaim his ex-wife if he could catch her before she had finished climbing into bed with her next husband, he states that the section

> has about it that air of unreality which hardly fosters confidence in the validity of the law-texts as a guide to the central issues of social custom. Such indeed they were not meant to be: they were, it must be repeated, lawyers' manuals, not guidebooks for social observers. ... [The historian] for his own part can liberate the textual expert from some of the constricting fundamentalism of textual studies of the laws, by showing how and how far *Cyfraith Hywel* was operated and modified in late medieval Wales.[3]

Davies's critical point about the purpose of the lawtexts is central to my study. The same 'constricting fundamentalism' may account for how surprisingly few published editions or studies of law manuscripts there are, especially when set against the large number of extant manuscripts.

The textual work on the Welsh lawtexts, and in particular the work of early editors, has coloured the subject area in a very specific way. The aim of the studies was usually to understand the way the legal texts worked as texts, and to present the material in a usable way, but the editors were, on the whole, working with certain presuppositions – demonstrating Davies's 'constricting fundamentalism' – which led to certain parts of the texts being treated differently. Large sections of legal texts were separated and accorded a different status by editors having preconceived ideas about the genesis of the texts, and formulating a framework for some aspects. While

---

[1] Davies, 'The Status of Women', 94.
[2] *Ibid.*, 93.
[3] *Ibid.*, 94. See also Stacey, *Law and the Imagination*, 9–11.

there certainly are differences in the texts – chronological, stylistic or, indeed, their different purposes – the early editors gave some sections priority over others, even if this was unintentional. This present study intends to remove these presuppositions and see the subject area in a different way.

By looking at some of the assumptions made by the editors of the Welsh lawtexts, whether clearly stated or implied, much can be revealed about the nature of the editions themselves. That is not to say that the published editions have no value; to the contrary, the edited texts are the crucial way of studying the contents of the manuscripts. But, often, the material that is *not* edited and that has not been examined tells us a great deal more about the nature of the Welsh lawtexts than the material that has been examined in earlier generations.

This chapter, then, will look at the editions of the Welsh lawtexts, starting with early editions, and focusing particularly on Aneurin Owen's *Ancient Laws and Institutes of Wales* (1841). It will consider how Owen (and others) approached the work, and how Owen in particular dealt with the multiplicity of texts and versions of the laws in the manuscripts that he viewed. Some textual decisions have led to the laws being viewed in a particular way even today, but I aim to show that this is misleading and that the manuscripts should be viewed as complete texts, moving away from the colouring by earlier editors.

Classifying Manuscripts and Texts

The first stage in looking at the law manuscripts has always traditionally been distributing the manuscripts into groups and organising the large bulk of material. Most of the lawtexts, but particularly so in the earlier manuscripts, are presented as codes of law, as single books whose nature implies that each contains all of the law of Wales. They follow a fairly formal structure, starting with the prologue discussing Hywel Dda and the origins of the Welsh laws.[4] Rather than being disorganised texts, the law manuscripts are subdivided into recognisable sections, often, but not always, thematically organised. Charles-Edwards states that the texts 'are arranged as a sequence of tracts – or tractates as they have come to be known by students of Welsh law. Sometimes these tractates bear titles. In this way they resemble the tracts of the early eighth-century Irish lawbook, the Senchas Már.'[5]

Some of the Welsh law tractates are more formal than others, however, and there is much variety in the nature and form of the tractates found in the law manuscripts. Among the more recognisable tractates that occur in many of the manuscripts, there is the Laws of Court, usually the lengthy opening book in a law manuscript, detailing the royal court and the officials of the king, and giving the laws a royal link.[6] The Laws of Country are made up of several shorter tractates, including *inter alia* the Law of Women, Land Law, Suretyship (Contract), the Three Columns of Law (homicide, theft and fire) and sections of law on animals and agriculture. A collection of triads,

---

[4] See Chapter 1.
[5] Charles-Edwards, *The Welsh Laws*, 23.
[6] In one Iorwerth manuscript, B, this tractate is called *Lleuer Llys* ('the Book of the Court'): *Lllor*, 43/13; this use of *llyfr* may simply be as 'one of the main divisions of a larger work': *GPC*2, s.v. llyfr[1] (a).

sentences listing legal rules or situations in threes, also form a tractate included in most of the law manuscripts.[7]

There is considerable repetition of material across the 40 or so law manuscripts and, while each manuscript is a unique text of the law, the majority can be assigned to a group or redaction, with manuscripts of that group showing similarities in order and content. As was discussed in the previous chapter, there are three recognised Welsh redactions, and the manuscripts in a redaction usually contain the same material or the same collections of tractates, and these often follow a similar order.[8] In general, it is the form of the text in a manuscript that assigns it to one of the Welsh redactions. The concept of grouping the Welsh manuscripts into redactions is a useful way of distributing the texts. It is useful as it recognises that, while each manuscript is a unique text, it is still likely to be linked to other manuscripts, and this makes the high number of Welsh law manuscripts more manageable. It makes it possible to focus on specific aspects of the text, and it may also show the development of legal ideas reflecting changing society. This study therefore does not reject the concept of the three Welsh redactions.

A broader question is whether the concept of a redaction or book following a certain pattern had any meaning for the medieval lawyers. There was a clear sense of particular books of law having pre-eminence, and books named after famous lawyers were prized.[9] Iorwerth ap Madog had the concept that his book – or the Test Book, a section of the Iorwerth texts – was drawing on other books of law.[10] There was also an awareness of the distinctiveness of some books – as shown by references to *llyuyr Hywel* ('the Book of Hywel') and *lleuyr e Ty Guyn* ('the Book of the White House')[11] – but while certain texts are discussed as particular entities, on the whole the lawbooks were not necessarily compiled with a sense of being a certain type of lawbook, with the material selected because it belonged to a redaction or group. Rather, the aim was to have a selection of books to consult, and so it does not appear that the concept of the redaction was a consideration for the medieval Welsh lawyer, although certain books may have had some significance.[12]

One of the problems that arises with the neat classifications of law manuscripts into the three Welsh redactions is that there are several manuscripts that do not fit the pattern, as was noted in the previous chapter. These are still manuscripts of Welsh law, but they may not include recognisable tractates such as the Laws of Court, and they may not be set out in the same way as other law manuscripts, lacking the formal organisation of opening with the prologue and proceeding through tractates on different subjects. They may appear to be more miscellaneous in nature, or chaotic in structure. But even then they may well have texts found in other manuscripts, and may have short passages that do fit into one of the Welsh redactions. Much of the focus of the following chapters will be on these manuscripts and the texts within them, and what they tell us about the nature of Welsh legal texts. The way these manuscripts and texts have been viewed, and are viewed today, originates in the earliest studies of the Welsh laws, and they have been affected by the difficulties faced by early editors in dealing with these manuscripts. The difficulty stems from having a

---

[7] *LT*.

[8] This is not as true of the Latin manuscripts, as they are grouped together because they are in Latin.

[9] See Chapter 3, 50–54.

[10] See Chapter 3, 67.

[11] AL VII.i.9, and see n. 67 below; *LlCol*, §528.

[12] See Chapter 4, 103.

multiplicity of manuscripts with similarities, and yet huge differences between the texts, as well as in presuppositions about the origins of Welsh law.

Early Editions of the Welsh Laws[13]

The Welsh laws have been studied since the seventeenth century, and some editorial decisions made as early as that still have an impact. The first edition, in manuscript form, was William Maurice's 'Corpus Hoelianum', also known as his *Deddfgrawn* ('law anthology'), created 1660–1663 and preserved in manuscripts Wynnstay 37 and 38.[14] Maurice was an antiquary and manuscript collector, the owner of several important Welsh manuscripts including one fine law manuscript, and he also spent time studying and copying those manuscripts. His legal compilation is the first attempt to categorise and distribute the contents of the Welsh law manuscripts, and it includes diligent editing work giving variant readings from at least ten manuscripts.[15] Aneurin Owen drew upon his work in his own *Ancient Laws*, but William Maurice's *Deddfgrawn* was not used for the first printed edition of the Welsh laws.

William Wotton and Moses Williams worked together on *Leges Wallicae*, which appeared in print in 1730, three years after Wotton's death.[16] Moses Williams (1685–1742) was a cleric and scholar, with considerable expertise in Welsh manuscripts; he had access to several important libraries.[17] The work had been started by William Wotton (1666–1727). Wotton, a child prodigy and a highly talented linguist, had been destined for a high career in the church, but he had several weaknesses: he was described as 'a most excellent preacher, but a drunken whoring soul',[18] and both his drinking and his whoring led to considerable debts.[19] As a result, in 1714 he and his wife and daughter fled his living in Milton Keynes and escaped to Carmarthen, where he lived in disguise as 'Dr Edwards'. Wotton's former sponsor, William Wake, Bishop of Lincoln but Archbishop of Canterbury from 1716, suggested that Wotton could work on the laws, as a way to occupy him and help him move on from his financial difficulties and his drinking problems. In the long run, it may have been envisaged that he could move back into favour and perhaps regain his career in the church. Wake presumably expected a study of one manuscript, but the task did not work out as planned. Wotton had to learn Welsh to work on the laws – which he did in just over a year – and he translated the Welsh texts into Latin in the multi-text edition. However, the attempt to organise the various texts of the Welsh law manuscripts caused Wotton untold distress. During the time spent working on *Leges Wallicae*, his health deteriorated, his wife died, and he lost his daughter's dowry in the South Sea Bubble. Wotton had many difficulties with the work, including gaining access to the

---

[13] The following four sections, 'Early Editions of the Welsh Laws', 'Aneurin Owen and the *Ancient Laws*', 'Editing the Law Manuscripts – *Ancient Laws*' and 'The Anomalous Laws', are a slightly revised form of my chapter Roberts, 'A Rather Laborious'. I am grateful to Brill for permission to republish a version that work here.

[14] Jenkins, 'Deddfgrawn William Maurice', 33.

[15] Huws, 'Maurice, William (1619/20–1680)', *ODNB*.

[16] *Leges Wallicae*.

[17] Bowen, 'Moses Williams (1685–1742)', *Dictionary of Welsh Biography*.

[18] Jackson, *The Diary of Abraham de la Pryme*, 29.

[19] An excellent account of the highly entertaining tale of Wotton's work on the Welsh laws and the creation of *Leges Wallicae* can be found in Stoker, 'William Wotton's Exile and Redemption'.

manuscripts – he could not travel far, and certainly not to England, because of his creditors – but his collaborator Moses Williams had no such blots on his character, and he helped Wotton by bringing him manuscripts, as well as making considerable contributions to the text itself. Wotton died before the work was published, but Wotton's son-in-law assisted Williams in getting *Leges Wallicae* to press. Dafydd Jenkins has suggested that looking at William Maurice's manuscript would have suggested a better classification of the lawtexts to Wotton and Williams, but Moses Williams did not visit Llanforda (where the manuscripts were kept at that time) until 1728, by which time the *Leges Wallicae* must have already gone to press.[20]

Aneurin Owen and the *Ancient Laws*

The first modern edition of the Welsh laws, *Ancient Laws*, was published in two volumes in 1841.[21] Fortunately for him, the editor appears to have escaped the personal problems faced by some previous editors. Aneurin Owen (1792–1851) was the only son of the well-known antiquarian and London Welsh literary figure William Owen Pughe.[22] Although Aneurin Owen attended school for a short while, he was mainly educated by his father.[23] Glenda Carr, in her biography of Owen's father, argues that Aneurin Owen is unlikely to have been the true author of *Ancient Laws*: apart from allegedly not being able to speak Welsh fluently until his marriage at the age of 27, there is evidence from Pughe's diaries that he was helping Aneurin learn his craft as a scholar, and was even responsible for copying manuscripts, translating texts and organising the work for Aneurin.[24] Indeed, Carr states '*Rhaid gofyn yn ddifrifol faint o ôl llaw William Owen Pughe sydd ar waith ei fab*' ('It must be asked in all seriousness how much of William Owen Pughe's hand is visible in the work of his son'). They visited libraries together, and Pughe was in London more often than Aneurin was, since Aneurin farmed at the family farm of Nantglyn in Denbighshire, and it was Pughe who met regularly with Henry Petrie, the overseer of the bigger project in which the work on the Welsh laws was included.[25] Whether or not he was the true author of the work, Aneurin Owen is the man who is credited with it, and there was no mention of his father (who had died by that time) in his acknowledgements – whether that omission is significant is debatable.[26]

The idea of a study of the Welsh laws originated not with Aneurin Owen but with an earlier scholar, John Humphreys Parry, a London Welshman like Pughe who was involved in the literary work which was being undertaken in the city at the time. Parry became the secretary of the Cymmrodorion society, and established the literary magazine *The Cambro-Briton*.[27] He had a troubled life, with financial difficulties,

---

[20] Jenkins, 'Deddfgrawn William Maurice', 36. Jenkins states that *Leges Wallicae* was already published by 1728 but it did not appear in print until 1730 and had that date on the published book.

[21] AL.

[22] For the life of William Owen Pughe, see the excellent biography by Carr: *William Owen Pughe*. She also discusses Aneurin Owen.

[23] Lloyd, 'Owen, Aneurin (1792–1851)', ODNB.

[24] Carr, *William Owen Pughe*, 247–248.

[25] *Ibid.*, 248.

[26] *Ibid.*, 250.

[27] *Ibid.*, 203. The Honourable Society of the Cymmrodorion is the only one of the London Welsh learned societies that is still going today.

and died young following a brawl near the Prince of Wales tavern in Pentonville.[28] Before his death, he had started working on the Welsh chronicle *Brut y Tywysogion* and also on Welsh law, with the intention of publishing an edition of both. His papers were inherited by Pughe and, as a result, he came to know Henry Petrie, a Fellow of the Society of Antiquaries, and the keeper of records in the Tower of London.[29] Petrie had been tasked with producing a 'corpus historicum' of all materials on English history. John Humphreys Parry's plan of publishing an edition of early history works, the *Monumenta Historica Britannica*, including Welsh texts, was incorporated into this wider plan.[30] The 'epic collection of source material' was publicly funded and published by the Record Commission, and Aneurin Owen became involved in this work from the late 1820s when he took over Parry's role, probably organised for him through his father's connections.[31] Owen's Welsh work was divided into two: an edition of the laws, and an edition of the 'Chronicle of the Princes'.[32] Despite the problems in gaining a usable reading of the texts and the size of the task, the work on the laws appeared in 1841, as *Ancient Laws*, and was highly praised – at the time, Owen was particularly commended for dividing the Welsh material into the three redactions in his 'improved edition of Wotton's *Leges Cambriae*'.[33] However, Owen's work on the chronicles towards the same aim was not published, although the version of *Brut y Tywysogion* edited by ab Ithel in 1860 was shown – in print – to be the work of Owen, uncredited, 'with a trifling verbal alteration in certain sentences'.[34] The anonymous reviewer[35] had a high opinion of Owen's work:

> No Welsh archaeologist since the days of Edward Lhwyd has appeared superior to Aneurin Owen. He was employed by the Record Commissioners for the Welsh part of their labours, and he *exhausted* the subject. We look into his *reliquia*, we test his accuracy, we go over his ground: it is all done, it is all correct; we have all that we want, as far as the state of archaeological research extended at the date of Aneurin Owen's decease. His *magnum opus* is undoubtedly the *Laws of Howel Dda*: the two Chronicles, which he edited, are but *opuscula*: still they are of very great value, and they reflect the highest credit on his memory ... Nobody has undertaken such a task since; and very few have been qualified for it.[36]

Despite producing a highly praised masterpiece that is still in use today (although with some caveats), Aneurin Owen struggled with his edition of the laws.[37] Tasked with the work of creating an edition of the Welsh law manuscripts, Owen discovered

---

[28] *Ibid.*, 211.
[29] *Ibid.*, 212.
[30] Pollard, 'Petrie, (Frederick) Henry', ODNB. The *Monumenta Historica Britannica* and Owen's role in it, particularly his work on the chronicles, is discussed in Guy, 'Historical Scholars', 74–78.
[31] Guy, 'Historical Scholars', 74; Carr, *William Owen Pughe*, 212.
[32] On Owen's work on the *Brut*, see Jones, *Brut y Tywysogyon*, xxix–xxxi.
[33] Review of *Brut y Tywysogion*, 94.
[34] *Ibid.*, 95.
[35] The anonymous reviewer was Harry Longueville Jones: Guy, 'Historical Scholars', 76–77, and n.30.
[36] Review of *Brut y Tywysogion*, 94.
[37] Guy states that although Owen created variorum editions – true of AL as well as his work on the Chronicles – 'his textual work was generally sound': Guy, 'Historical Scholars', 74.

that his original plan of adapting or working from the earliest printed edition of the laws, *Leges Wallicae*, was not feasible and so it was 'reluctantly abandoned'.[38] The reason for changing the scheme and starting afresh was explained in his Introduction to be due to the nature of the material in the manuscripts:

> It was apparent that the sense of the text was admirably rendered, and the notes and glossary worthy of the accomplished coadjutors in these labours: but the plan upon which Dr. Wotton proceeded with the Leges Wallicæ was the adoption of one form of laws as the foundation of his text, interspersed with which were various readings, which differed widely from the text, and sometimes were contradictory of it. The cause of this anomaly was unexplained, and upon its being investigated it appeared that there were three distinct forms of laws existing, the parts of which had been dislocated by the Editor, and so arranged as to suit the order of the manuscript which he had adopted as his text, from the conviction of its being the most ancient and uniform of the whole.
>
> Upon further research these three independent codes were found to belong respectively to Venedotia or North Wales, Dimetia or South Wales, and one adapted to Gwent or South-east Wales. The dialect of each class of copies corroborated this supposition, which was established by allusions in them which dissipated all doubt.
>
> It was therefore evident that justice could not be done to the subject without allotting to each respectively its proper station, by which the discrepancies above alluded to are satisfactorily explained, the contrary usages of each district rightly attributed, and the consistency of each class of Codes preserved. Consequently a re-modelling of the materials became necessary.[39]

Owen was happy with the new division and the way this presented the material in a more orderly fashion, saying so in one of his letters to Henry Petrie:

> The division of the laws into 3 codes has simplified the coup d'œil, & rendered the investigation to the reader more satisfactory. In Wotton we are surprized at the very great & unaccountable variance in the Mss. but the distribution of each to its respective province, the courts of N & S Wales being differently constituted & the practise dissimilar, explains the anomaly.[40]

The task that faced Aneurin Owen was huge. He had to examine all of the extant manuscripts of medieval Welsh law, and work out a scheme for presenting those texts. Since the texts are almost all unique, editorial decisions had to be made about determining a base text, and how to deal with the other manuscripts – it would not have been practical to present each manuscript individually since they are all lengthy. Owen worked out that the manuscripts could be put into groups showing similarities in content and order, and he decided on three groups for the Welsh manuscripts that he had seen. This was a concept first employed by William Maurice in his manuscript edition of the laws, but it was not used by Wotton and Williams, which is why Aneurin Owen felt that he could not replicate that work. While it is not stated in the book,

---

[38] AL, Introduction, viii.
[39] *Ibid.*
[40] PRO 36/44, 5. The correspondence from Aneurin Owen to Henry Petrie is preserved in PRO 36/44, and is a collection of letters on various topics including Welsh chronicles, and occasional references to the laws. The letters were passed via stage coach and were received by Petrie at the Tower of London, where he was Keeper of Records.

Aneurin Owen did use William Maurice's edition and drew upon it, particularly in his first volume. William Maurice's manuscripts were at the Wynnstay library by that time, and Owen visited the library at Wynnstay Hall; there is a slip from 1851 acknowledging Owen's return of several law manuscripts, including Maurice's edition in Wynnstay 37 and 38.[41] The lax filing system in that library meant that all the manuscripts Owen had borrowed, including the valuable law manuscript Q, Wynnstay 36, and Maurice's two manuscripts containing the edition, were still together in a box in the muniment room seven years later, and so escaped the devastating fire that overtook the library in 1858.

Editing the Law Manuscripts – *Ancient Laws*

For his magnum opus, Owen set about viewing all of the Welsh law manuscripts available to him. He viewed 29 Welsh manuscripts, three Latin manuscripts, texts of the Statute of Rhuddlan (the post-conquest legal settlement for Edward I's territories in the Principality), and a section taken from *The Myvyrian Archaiology of Wales*, which included work by the antiquary and eccentric scholar Iolo Morganwg, containing what are now known to be forgeries.[42] Most of the Welsh law manuscripts were given an identifying siglum by Owen, for easy reference, using letters of the alphabet and – since he had more manuscripts than letters of the alphabet – (allegedly) 'Saxon' characters.[43] These sigla are still used today in referring to the law manuscripts. Three of the Latin manuscripts were presented as 'a few Latin transcripts' and, while Owen was familiar with all five versions of the laws in Latin, he did not give the Latin manuscripts as much attention as the Welsh manuscripts, offering transcripts with very little discussion.[44]

Once he had gathered together his manuscripts, Owen categorised them, following a similar method to that employed by William Maurice. In his Introduction, Owen demonstrated that he perceived geographical links to the law manuscripts, and he had a concept of original books created at the instigation of Hywel ap Cadell.[45] Owen appears to have taken the story describing Hywel as a lawmaker in the Prologues at face value: 'To him are we indebted for the collections of laws which pass

---

[41] Jenkins, 'Deddfgrawn William Maurice', 36.

[42] AL, Introduction, xxv–xxxiv. The manuscript containing the forgeries, presented in AL XIII, was not listed with the other manuscripts used since Owen only used the text in *The Myvyrian Archaiology of Wales* and, despite stressing that the triads contained there 'are of the greatest importance', Owen was suspicious of them – 'their antiquity is very dubious' – and attributed them to the sixteenth century: AL, Introduction, xx. Iolo Morganwg was a Welsh scholar and poet, a collector of manuscripts, and a successful and convincing forger. He was eccentric and a heavy laudanum user. An excellent introduction to Iolo Morganwg and his work is Jenkins, *A Rattleskull Genius*.

[43] AL, Introduction, xxv–xxxii. The 'Saxon' characters have now been replaced with sigla that can be more easily reproduced electronically.

[44] AL, title pages. Owen was aware of all six manuscripts but presented an untranslated text of Latin A, B and C, numbered 1–3 under the heading 'Leges Wallicae' at the end of his second volume. In his introduction he refers to manuscripts in the Bodleian Library, Merton College Oxford and Trinity College Cambridge; these are Latin D and the two Recensions of Latin E respectively, Owen, AL, Introduction, xxxiii–xxiv.

[45] AL, Introduction, xviii–xxi. On Hywel Dda and his relationship with the making of the lawbooks, see Chapter 1, 5–6.

under the name of the Laws of Hywel dda.'[46] Because of this, Owen believed that the three books said (in the Prologues) to be deposited in the three Welsh royal courts at Aberffraw, Dinefwr and Mathrafal were genuine, and that they were uniform texts, but that 'shortly after a variance must have occurred' that caused the differences between the manuscripts.[47] As a result of this 'variance', he stated that 'a necessity arose for Codes to comprise the respective ordinances and usages prevalent in each district'.[48] 'Code' is no longer used in discussing the Welsh lawtexts, but to Owen the manuscripts of Welsh law contained a 'Code' of law, that is, a formalised and final collection of written laws specific to a particular region. He therefore distributed the Welsh manuscripts he had used into three Codes, each named after a geographical region of Wales. These Codes form Owen's first volume. The categorisation made by Owen is still largely followed, although some manuscripts were misplaced by him, and the names of the groups have been changed.[49] For a comparison of the manuscripts listed in Table 2.1, see the five tables and discussion in Chapter 1, as well as in the full list of manuscripts at the start of this book.

Table 2.1: The Distribution of the Manuscripts in AL I

Siglum	Shelfmark	Re-classification
'The Venedotian Code' (Iorwerth Redaction)		
A	NLW Peniarth MS 29	
B	BL Cotton Titus MS D II	
C	BL Cotton Caligula MS A III	
D	NLW Peniarth MS 32	
E	BL Additional MS 14,931	
F	NLW Peniarth MS 34	*Non-redaction*
G	NLW Peniarth MS 35	
H	NLW Peniarth MS 164	*Non-redaction*
'The Dimetian Code' (Blegywryd Redaction)		
I	NLW Peniarth MS 38	
J	Oxford, Jesus College MS 57	*Iorwerth second half*
K	NLW MS Peniarth MS 40	*Iorwerth*
L	BL Cotton Titus MS D IX	
M	NLW Peniarth MS 33	

---

[46] AL, Introduction, x. See Chapter 1 for a discussion of Hywel Dda and the lawbooks.

[47] AL, Introduction, xviii. To be fair to Owen, large sections of the laws are very close to other manuscripts of the same group, and several of the simpler manuscripts are uniform in order and/or content. See also the discussion on the concept of the Model Lawbook, below, 39–45.

[48] AL, Introduction, xviii. On the second page of his Introduction, Owen first uses 'codes' without a capital C, but by the end of the same paragraph he capitalised the word and continued to do so throughout the remainder of the Introduction; see AL, Introduction, viii.

[49] Wade-Evans suggested renaming the groups according to individuals given pre-eminence in the texts as it 'seems therefore advisable for the time being to abandon "territorial" designations'. He also felt that the laws originated in Powys; *WML*, viii–xii.

(Table 2.1 continued)

Siglum	Shelfmark	Re-classification
N	NLW Peniarth MS 36B	
O	NLW Peniarth MS 36A	
P	NLW Peniarth MS 259A	*Copy of Q*
Q	NLW Wynnstay MS 36	
R	NLW Peniarth MS 31	
S	BL Additional MS 22356	
T	BL Harleian MS 958	
'The Gwentian Code' (Cyfnerth Redaction)		
U	NLW Peniarth MS 37	
V	BL Harleian MS 4353	
W	BL Cotton Cleopatra MS A XIV	
X	BL Cotton Cleopatra MS B V	
Y	NLW MS 20143A	*Cyfnerth Laws of Court, remainder Blegywryd*
Z	NLW Peniarth MS 259B	

Owen's Venedotian Code, now the Iorwerth redaction, was discussed first because he saw A, 'The Black Book of Chirk', as the oldest version of the laws in Welsh.[50] Manuscripts F and H are no longer included in this redaction, but manuscript K has been moved into this group; and Peniarth 39, Lew, was discovered after Owen's time and belongs in this group. Owen's largest group was his Dimetian Code and, since Owen's time, five manuscripts have been added to this group – Tr, and Bost, which had gone to Boston, Massachusetts, by the time Owen was working, but which was used for the earlier *Leges Wallicae*;[51] both were unknown to Owen. Ep was not assigned to a redaction by Owen but is a full copy of manuscript Q and belongs in this group;[52] and Tim and Llan were presumably not known to Owen. This is now known as the Blegywryd redaction. Owen's Gwentian Code has been renamed the Cyfnerth redaction, to which today is added Mk, the Meyrick or Bodorgan manuscript, which was then – as now – in private ownership and of which Owen was not aware. Y has been reconsidered and is a composite text: the Laws of Court are from the Cyfnerth redaction, but the remainder of the manuscript is largely Blegywryd material.[53]

Once Owen had viewed the manuscripts and presumably transcribed them in their entirety, his aim was to present the text in a usable form, presenting a variorum edition.[54]

---

[50] See the discussion in Chapter 1, 11–13.
[51] Owen, 'Llawysgrif Gyfreithiol Goll', 338–343.
[52] Roberts, 'Creu Trefn o Anhrefn', 402.
[53] See Huws, 'National Library of Wales MS 20143A', 420.
[54] Guy, 'Historical Scholars', 76.

> The operose task of collating the various matters contained in these Manuscripts and distributing them in their respective classes having been gone through, the enquirer may now ascertain the reading of every existing Manuscript of each description, with the exception of some fragments of no importance, and may also estimate the form and character of each version, and scrutinize the validity of the conclusions that induced the classifications here adopted.[55]

Owen's working method can still be viewed as a standard and sensible approach today. Although he does not reveal the details of his method in his Introduction, his working process appears to have been to choose a base manuscript. In the case of his Venedotian and Dimetian codes, he selected the manuscript that was in his view the oldest version of the text, but for his Gwentian code he used the manuscript 'not from any superiority, but as being the simplest; most of the others being anomalous, and containing much matter extracted from the Dimetian form'.[56] The text for each of his Codes would be taken from his base manuscript and presented as it appeared in the manuscript, with 'no transpositions of matter, nor ... any incongruity of arrangement'.[57] In that sense, this is a very useful method since Owen was not combining texts, and his statement that the order of the base manuscripts were followed is mostly true[58] throughout his work – it is also true of the texts in his second volume, The Anomalous Laws. Once he had selected the base manuscript for his text, a loosely edited transcript was presented, along with an English translation on the facing page. For the Welsh text, variant readings were given from the other manuscripts of the same code where possible, although Owen would occasionally admit that things did not always work to plan. For example, when it came to the complex Gwentian Code, he struggled with some of the manuscripts and, by the time he had reached Book II of the Gwentian Code, after the Laws of Court, he took drastic measures, and decided to stop giving variant readings from Z: 'Z. is carelessly transcribed and has many chasms, [it] will only be noticed when important variations or new matter occur'.[59] Occasionally, a different version of the text would be presented at the bottom of the page, when the version was too different for Owen to incorporate it into his main text or present it using his usual method of giving variant readings.[60] Corrections or additions to his main text were presented in square brackets in the text, with a numbered footnote giving the base manuscript for the variation.

The apparatus itself often appears to be intractable, but a variation of Owen's method is still used today for critical texts, although in a simplified form, and omitting the confusing 'ticks':

> The notes are commonly referred to by a small numeral: thus, (^{1}); and in special cases by a small *Italic* letter: thus, (^{a}). Explanatory foot-notes are distinguished by a Roman letter: thus, (^{a}). There is also used another mark, called a tick: thus, ('). In the body of the text this mark shows the end of the passage, for which a various reading is to be found; and in the notes a corresponding tick has been placed immediately after the

---

[55] AL, Introduction, xxxv.
[56] *Ibid.*, xxxi.
[57] *Ibid.*, xxxv.
[58] Two sections have been moved in his Venedotian Code (Iorwerth): *Y Naw Tafodiog* ('The Nine Tongued-Ones') was moved so that it came after the law of women.
[59] AL GC II.i n.11; see also *Pomffred*, 20. Owen did not note any important variations or additions from Z after that statement.
[60] See, for example, AL VC III.i.10–VC III.ii.13.

numeral or *Italic letter*. In cases where two or more Manuscripts vary as to the length of the passage about which they differ, the point in the text at which each terminates is marked by one or more ticks, according to the number of conflicting Manuscripts : thus, (′) (″) (‴) (⁗) and so on.[61]

Despite sounding horrifically complex, the process does in fact work well, even if it is a little confusing to a new reader. It enables a good sense of the manuscripts to be obtained, although the order of the contents of the manuscripts used for variant readings is less clear, mainly because page or folio numbers are not used in the edition. But, generally speaking, the Codes in *Ancient Laws* still function as a usable text: even if they only fully represent the selected base texts, at least they provide a guide to where else the material is available. Wade-Evans, however, clearly found it difficult to navigate:

> The Books of Gwynedd, Blegywryd, and Cyvnerth, however, are produced in such a way that the various MSS. of each particular class are interblended, so that it is with the greatest difficulty that any particular one may be distinguished. Indeed, in the case of the majority of the MSS., it is impossible to do so. Moreover, by arranging the texts so that they fall into books, chapters, and sections, and by consequently attempting to bring them into harmony, the confusion becomes hopeless. The table of contents also and the indices are most jejune, misleading every beginner who takes up the book. There are besides other serious defects.[62]

Wade-Evans was very mindful of the students of early medieval Wales and warned them 'to be wary, for he treads enchanted ground ... Many are they who have boldly entered here only to succumb to the charm of this realm of phantasy and illusion'; his safeguard for these dangerous risks was to 'keep closely to the laws of Howel' as presented in his edition.[63]

The Anomalous Laws

Fairly early on in his work, Owen discovered that the Welsh law manuscripts did not organise themselves effectively and tidily into the scheme that he had in mind. This was so problematic that it caused some delay: 'The labour incurred in the collation, and in the care required in the printing and correction of such complicated matter, were the causes of a longer delay in the publication than could have been anticipated, and which the Editor greatly regrets.'[64] Owen's worry and the troublesome nature of his work are apparent in that statement: in a letter to Henry Petrie, he describes the work as 'a rather laborious and harassing occupation'.[65] Owen still had the material that he could not fit into his neat organised structure, and that appeared to be extraneous to his neat Codes. His procrustean answer to make the material fit together neatly was to divide the work, placing the Codes in his first volume, and the 'Anomalous Laws' in his second. This structure reshaped the Welsh laws into a new but artificial

---

[61] AL, Introduction, xxiv.
[62] *WML*, liii–liv.
[63] *WML*, liv–lv.
[64] AL, Introduction, xxxv.
[65] PRO 36/44.

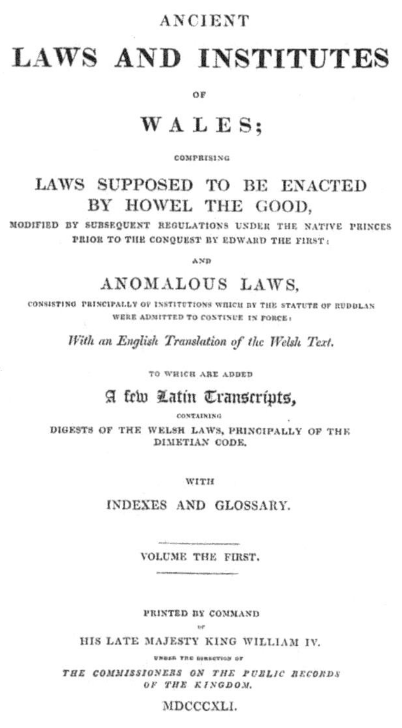

> ANCIENT
> # LAWS AND INSTITUTES
> OF
> ## WALES;
> COMPRISING
> ### LAWS SUPPOSED TO BE ENACTED BY HOWEL THE GOOD,
> MODIFIED BY SUBSEQUENT REGULATIONS UNDER THE NATIVE PRINCES PRIOR TO THE CONQUEST BY EDWARD THE FIRST;
> AND
> ### ANOMALOUS LAWS,
> CONSISTING PRINCIPALLY OF INSTITUTIONS WHICH BY THE STATUTE OF RUDDLAN WERE ADMITTED TO CONTINUE IN FORCE:
>
> *With an English Translation of the Welsh Text.*
>
> TO WHICH ARE ADDED
> ### A few Latin Transcripts,
> CONTAINING
> DIGESTS OF THE WELSH LAWS, PRINCIPALLY OF THE DIMETIAN CODE,
>
> WITH
> INDEXES AND GLOSSARY.
>
> VOLUME THE FIRST.
>
> PRINTED BY COMMAND
> OF
> HIS LATE MAJESTY KING WILLIAM IV.
> UNDER THE DIRECTION OF
> *THE COMMISSIONERS ON THE PUBLIC RECORDS OF THE KINGDOM.*
> MDCCCXLI.

Figure 1: Title page of Ancient Laws and Institutes of Wales, *ed. Aneurin Owen (London, 1841).*

form, not found in the manuscripts, although this is naturally a problem with any edited work. Owen was aware of this issue and raised it in his introduction: 'The ANOMALOUS or WELSH LAWS constitute an important portion of the Work. Under this head are given such anomalous chapters as are respectively found in those Manuscripts which afforded the texts for the regular Codes, and also all additional and later matter, wherever found. Herein are comprehended legal dicta and decisions, pleadings, and elucidatory matter.'[66]

The word 'anomalous' is an adjective from the noun 'anomaly' meaning that it is something that 'deviates from what is standard, normal, or expected'.[67] This is why Aneurin Owen used the term to refer to some of the legal material with which he was dealing; but in order to use the term, he also had to have a sense of what was standard. Owen's use of 'anomalous' appears to have been very specific, and he had a very definite sense of what constituted 'anomalous' material. He also seemed to have very clear ideas of how the manuscripts were formed, and extremely strict opinions on which material belonged in which class or Code. To Owen, the 'standard' material

---

[66] AL, Introduction, xx.
[67] 'anomaly, n.', *OED*.

were his three Codes, which themselves derived from a single original book created by Hywel Dda in the assembly at Whitland.[68] His 'anomalous' material, then, deviated from this standard, but it was simply a standard that Owen had devised, based on his concept of the origins of the Welsh laws.[69] Given that many of the manuscripts were similar, including the same contents and following a similar order – the very features that meant that he could classify them into his three Codes – anything in addition to this material, anything that was not found in the majority of the manuscripts, were the texts he included under the heading 'anomalous'. Indeed, the full wording of the title page of *Ancient Laws and Institutes of Wales* makes this clear:

> ANCIENT LAWS AND INSTITUTES OF WALES; comprising LAWS SUPPOSED TO BE ENACTED BY HOWEL THE GOOD, modified by subsequent regulations under the native princes prior to the conquest by Edward the First; and ANOMALOUS LAWS, consisting principally of institutions which by the Statute of Ruddlan were admitted to continue in force: with an English Translation of the Welsh Text. To which are added A few Latin Transcripts, containing DIGESTS OF THE WELSH LAWS, PRINCIPALLY OF THE DIMETIAN CODE.

In addition to his concept of the 'anomalous' material deviating from the material in his Codes, Owen also seemed to organise the material chronologically. The original Welsh laws were the work of Hywel Dda, and thus dated to the tenth century; Owen did not think that these 'original' laws had survived apart from the versions in his Codes, which were the regional derivatives of the same official law, and dated to the time of the post-Hywelian princes of Wales. The 'anomalous' laws he saw as post-conquest, and were the parts of the Welsh laws that were allowed to continue according to the Statute of Rhuddlan (Statute of Wales, 1284). He included the Statute of Rhuddlan in his second volume, along with three Latin texts, but Owen had little to say on the Latin versions of the Welsh laws.

To Aneurin Owen, the 'anomalous' texts had a specific meaning, and it was 'an important portion of the Work'.[70] Despite this, his portioning of the material has led to more emphasis being given to the first volume, Owen's 'Codes', and far less to the second volume. In looking at the laws, it is time to move away from Owen's inaccurate division, and view the manuscripts as a whole. Like Owen, I do not see the 'anomalous' material as being necessarily unimportant or peripheral, but rather than seeing it as something that does not fit into a usual pattern – with that pattern artificially fixed by Owen in the first place – I would prefer to see the material in its own right, and considered in the context of the manuscript(s) in which the text occurs. The 'anomalous' texts should not be separated from any other legal texts that are found in the manuscripts of Welsh law.

Some clues to how Owen arrived at the division can be found in the law manuscripts themselves. Charles-Edwards points out that manuscript U marks the division between the previous law texts in the manuscript and the following *damweiniau* (a collection of sentences that give special circumstances, often called 'eventualities')

---

[68] See AL, Introduction, xviii.

[69] It should be noted however in the *cynghawsedd* in AL VII.i.9, there is a description of a legal case for land and a reference to the seating plan: *ac yna e mae yaun eysted en kyureythyaul, mal y dyweyt llyuyr Hywel* ('and then it is right to sit in the legal manner, as is stated in the book of Hywel'); this seating plan is found in the Iorwerth redaction: *LlIor*, §73. This gives Owen an early source for his approach.

[70] AL, Introduction, xx.

by saying that it is turning to looking at *damweiniau*.⁷¹ Aneurin Owen refers to 'anomalous' material that occurred in his manuscripts, often appended to the main Code but sometimes found among the 'Code' material. In his description of manuscript U, Owen uses 'anomalous' to refer to anything that 'interrupted' his basic Gwentian text, and that could be material taken from another Code (the Dimetian, in this case).⁷² Owen was of course also guided by practical considerations, and his organisation also helped to keep the size of the work and its cost under control.

In addition, there are some manuscripts that defy categorisation into the recognisable groups. Owen was aware of some of these manuscripts, since he listed them after the manuscripts in the Codes, under the (puzzling) heading 'The Welsh or Anomalous Laws'.⁷³ These manuscripts, four of them in all, were assigned 'characters from the Saxon alphabet', since Owen had exhausted letters of the Roman alphabet. In reality, these were not strictly Old English letters: Ð may be a capital thorn, but ϵ looks more like a Greek Epsilon or a Cyrillic form; Owen's siglum for As, Ꞻ, is similar to capital A forms in the Lindisfarne Gospels, and Mor was given an uncial ᛘ.⁷⁴ Owen's assigned sigla have also had the unfortunate effect of contributing to their classification as 'other' or even 'weird', and has even made referring to them problematic on modern computers. This group has been expanded since other manuscripts have come to light after Owen's time, and some manuscripts have been moved into this group from the main Codes. Much of the material from these manuscripts can be found in Aneurin Owen's Second Volume, 'The Anomalous Laws'.

Table 2.2: The Anomalous Laws: AL II

'The Anomalous or Welsh Manuscripts' (Non-redaction texts)		
Ep	NLW Peniarth MS 258	*Copy of Q, actually Blegywryd*
As	NLW Peniarth MS 175	*Cynghawsedd (model pleadings) collections*
Mor	NLW Peniarth MS 36C	*Cynghawsedd (model pleadings) collections*
Dd	BL Additional MS 31,055	*Plaints as only legal material*⁷⁵
Manuscripts now seen as non-redaction		
F	NLW Peniarth MS 34	*Non-redaction, previously Venedotian*
H	NLW Peniarth MS 164	*Non-redaction, previously Venedotian*⁷⁶
An	NLW Peniarth MS 166	*Non-redaction, not used by Owen*⁷⁷

---

[71] Charles-Edwards, *The Welsh Laws*, 26.
[72] AL, Introduction, xxxi.
[73] *Ibid.*, xxxii. His use of 'Welsh' here is not explained, but may refer to a more general or unknown geographical origin, as opposed to the 'regional' texts found in his Codes. This list is followed by his 'Leges Wallicae', giving the Latin texts he used.
[74] With thanks to Barry Lewis for pointing out to me that what I had been calling a 'curvy capital M' for several decades working on Cyfraith Hywel is actually an uncial M.
[75] Ð (now Dd) was described as 'excerpts from the White Book of Hergest'. On this manuscript, see Roberts, 'Plaints', 229–230, and also Chapters 4 and 6, below.
[76] F and H have definite northern links but do not contain enough text to allow them to fit into Owen's Venedotian Code. See Chapter 7, below.
[77] Peniarth MS 166, given the siglum An by Seminar Cyfraith Hywel in 2016, was not used by Aneurin Owen. See Elias, 'Cam o'r Tywyllwch', 107. See also Chapter 7 below.

That the partitioning of the material in AL II is a divide imposed by Owen, and is a flawed way of looking at the law manuscripts, is shown by the fact that there is little or no evidence that the creators or redactors of the lawbooks saw such a division within their material. One point to support this is that many of the law manuscripts contain a 'Code' as well as material in Owen's 'anomalous' second volume. This suggests that this is all law, all part of the same book, rather than being material that needed to be divided in any way.

A closer look at the material in Owen's second volume also supports the argument that there was no real division in the texts, either in importance, or even in how they were included in the manuscript. Owen's particular *modus operandi* seems to have been to look at any given manuscript and determine which material fitted into one of his Codes. For example, let us take manuscript Q, Wynnstay 36. Many of the texts in that manuscript are similar to the corresponding texts in manuscript L, his base text for the Dimetian Code. He therefore gave variant readings from Q on his text of the Dimetian Code. Occasionally, he might come across a sentence in Q that was not in L; this could be added as a variant reading if it was in a Dimetian Code section. However, when Owen came across a section of text that was not in L, and did not match anything in his Dimetian Code, he assumed that it was a later addition and so placed it in the relevant chapter of his Anomalous Laws volume.[78] The system worked for him – but it emphasises the fact that the texts included in AL II were taken from some of the same manuscripts used in his first volume, since they also contain a 'Code' of law. In some cases it was interspersed with the 'Code' material, which does not suggest that it was added at a later date, or as an afterthought.

There was more of an element of selection in Owen's second volume than in the first, since the material was thinned down to some extent, to avoid repetition. For example, Book XIV of the Anomalous Laws is comprised of triads, found in manuscript H. These triads are not part of the triad collections in any of his three Codes.[79] But, if he came across a triad in H that was similar to something that he had in his Dimetian Code, say, he omitted that triad from his Book XIV. This reduced the size of the volume, naturally, but it does make it difficult when examining a Welsh law manuscript to find which of the material is in *Ancient Laws*, and which is not. But, more importantly, perhaps, it shows that the material is not divisible as Owen divided it. The material in AL II may not be different, or necessarily 'new' law. It may even present older material in a different form, or develop ideas found in other parts of the texts. Added to the fact that the material may all come from the same manuscript, it is hard to see a clear division on any grounds.

If the material was genuinely miscellaneous or 'additional' or was less important or had a different status to the material in Owen's 'Codes', then one would expect this to be reflected in the way it was presented. But Owen's second volume, and the material in it, is thematic and well-organised. It is divided into Books IV–XIV. The first six books are arranged by different genres: Books IV–VI present *damweiniau* ('eventualities'), collections of sentences stating 'if X happens, then

---

[78] Looking at the Iorwerth manuscripts, the situation is a little different: the material that is common to those manuscripts before they diverge – with manuscripts A and E ending with *damweiniau*, and B ending with *cynghawsedd* – is the material that makes up Owen's 'Code'.

[79] *ALD*, lxvi–lxix.

Y is to follow'.[80] Books VII–IX are collections of *cynghawsedd* ('model pleadings').[81] Book XII is also thematic, looking at plaints, the initial statement in a legal process.[82] The remaining books are organised by individual manuscripts: Book X is material taken from Q; XI is from S; and XIV is from H. Book IX combines both ideas – it is genre based but it is also taken from manuscripts As and Mor. In addition, the thematic collections in Books IV–IX are also organised by manuscript, working systematically through manuscripts containing different collections of material on the same genre. Book XIII was also manuscript-based, but the manuscript was a later forgery by Iolo Morganwg and is not counted among the law manuscripts today.[83]

Owen created his second volume because of his concept of the basic texts, the original books, of Welsh law, with elements that he felt were old and general to all the Codes – some of them he even traced back to some early 'White House book'. As such, the material in his second volume did not fit in with this scheme. Some of the material had a different purpose or context, perhaps; and much of the material was different and indeed probably later than the material in his first volume. But the division of the texts is problematic, and it does not necessarily reflect the way the medieval lawyers viewed the material. It is based on a later interpretation of the law manuscripts and their genesis.

The Model Lawbook and the 'Additional Material'

Owen's division of the material had a significant impact on later studies of the Welsh law manuscripts. Traditionally, editions of the laws after Owen's time have presented single manuscripts from particular redactions. Each of the redactions has been represented, and these texts are often viewed as basic statements of the different redactions, and are quoted as such.

Table 2.3: Editions of Redaction Texts of the Welsh Laws[84]

Redaction	Edition	Date
Cyfnerth	*Welsh Medieval Law*, A. W. Wade-Evans	1909
Cyfnerth	*Llawysgrif Pomffred*, S. E. Roberts	2011
Blegywryd	*Llyfr Blegywryd*, S. J. Williams & J. E. Powell	1942
Blegywryd	*Coleg yr Iesu LVII*, M. Richards (Revised edition)	1990
Iorwerth	*Llyfr Iorwerth*, A. Rh. Wiliam	1960

---

[80] Charles-Edwards, *The Welsh Laws*, 49.
[81] Charles-Edwards, '*Cynghawsedd*'; Stacey, 'Learning to Plead'; and Charles-Edwards, *The Welsh Laws*, 53–67.
[82] Roberts, 'Plaints'; and Roberts, 'More Plaints'.
[83] See n.42, above; the text was taken from the *Myvyrian Archaiology*.
[84] The Latin manuscripts of Welsh law were published as a single volume – an act that perhaps has led to them being viewed as a single entity or group: *LTWL*. Paul Russell's edition of a single text from one manuscript has advanced the field considerably, and is a major contribution to the study of the Latin texts: *Welsh Law in Medieval Anglesey*.

The Iorwerth redaction is the only one that has not had a new edition in the last 30 years or so. The early editions are still used as authoritative texts, and it is interesting that in most of these editions Aneurin Owen's division of the Code versus the Anomalous material held its ground. The law manuscripts themselves do not, on the whole, divide the material as neatly as has been done in *Ancient Laws*. This will be explored in more depth in the following chapters, but here it should be stressed that while there are colophons in the manuscripts that note a change of subject, there is nothing to mark a change in status between the material. In addition, several scholars have a concept of an 'original lawbook', or a 'model lawbook', and what this would contain. Defining such a lawbook naturally means that there is material in the extant law manuscripts that does not fit into the scheme, and this has led to the material being seen as 'additional'.[85]

The earliest modern edition of the laws, and the first since Aneurin Owen's publication, was *Welsh Medieval Law* by Rev. Arthur Wade-Evans. A clergyman with views considered to be unorthodox in some ways,[86] he wrote several works on Welsh history. His contribution to Welsh law, the first edition since *Ancient Laws*, was 'intended primarily for the student of the political history of Wales', and his introduction, with a detailed overview of pre-Norman Welsh history, focused on the unity of Wales.[87] It is a valuable edition, with an emphasis on presenting a usable text of the laws, and since his emphasis was on the early history of Wales rather than on the laws themselves, Wade-Evans cannot be said to have engaged with the arguments regarding the early composition of the laws to a great extent. He acknowledged assistance from J. Gwenogvryn Evans (whose *Report* Wade-Evans was able to use before it had all been published) and Sir John Rhŷs, and while Wade-Evans was critical of aspects of *Ancient Laws* he also admitted that his own translation was based on Owen's.[88] His critique of Owen's three 'Codes' was a major step forward and his renaming of the redactions is still followed today.[89] As far as the origins of Cyfraith Hywel are concerned, it is clear that Wade-Evans felt that all the extant manuscripts were based on one original, 'which, in our present state of information, we may suppose to have been a "Book of the White House"', referring to Col, but he says little more on the subject and his wording seems to imply some serious doubts.[90] His focus was on early Welsh history, with an emphasis on the unity of Wales, before 'the Normans had ... interfered with Welsh affairs', and Hywel ap Cadell's contribution to this unity was to 'bring the whole of the Welsh people under one law'.[91] Wade-Evans's work on comparing the different texts and manuscripts was a major step forward for the field, but he had less of a focus on the nature of the laws and was using them for his own historical arguments, and summarised the situation well: 'The law is the law of Howel, but it is the law of Howel as modified and amplified both by the varying customs of different parts of Wales and also by the changes which are taking place

---

[85] Owen used the heading 'Additional Law' as chapter headings for Books X and XI. It referred to material which he could not categorise into genres from Q and S.
[86] James and Roberts, 'Wade-Evans, Arthur Wade (Arthur Wade Evans), (1875–1964)', *Dictionary of Welsh Biography*.
[87] *WML*, iii.
[88] *WML*, iii.
[89] *WML*, viii–x.
[90] *WML*, vii.
[91] *WML*, xix, l.

throughout three and a half critical centuries.'⁹² He produced an early useful text, and did so largely without imposing textual divisions or views on the manuscripts he used.

Llyfr Blegywryd, the first edition focusing on the Blegywryd redaction, was a joint enterprise between two authors, Stephen J. Williams and J. Enoch Powell. Far better known as a politician, Powell was a Fellow in Classics at Trinity College Cambridge, and came across the Welsh law manuscript⁹³ at the Wren Library of the college. He taught himself enough Middle Welsh to start translating the text, and his journal article on the manuscript led to a collaboration with Williams, a well-known scholar of middle Welsh texts, and the first published edition of a Blegywryd text.⁹⁴ The concept of 'additional material' is one that affects the Blegywryd redaction most heavily, as several of the manuscripts within that group have material that does not follow the scheme presented by the editors of *LlBleg*.⁹⁵ That scheme was naturally bound with Enoch Powell's idea of what was and was not law.

The introduction delineates clearly Williams's and Powell's contributions to the introduction.⁹⁶ Enoch Powell was responsible for the sections on the text, but incorporated his earlier ideas on the Welsh laws, including his 'floating sections' theory, which was praised by Aled Rhys Wiliam.⁹⁷ Published as a journal article, this was his attempt to explain the differences between the law manuscripts, the 'wide divergences in the matter of section-order'.⁹⁸ He assigned the different order of the sections in the Blegywryd manuscripts to 'floating sections', added later when relevant. Because the sections were often lengthy, he surmised that they would have been added as slips of parchment, incorporated later, citing Bracton as a parallel.⁹⁹ Powell considered various sections, but triads were clearly a particular problem: he rejected triads and claimed that they were not law but '*crynodebau o gyfreithiau neu arferion cyfraith*' ('summaries of laws or legal customs/practices'), and that they were added at a later point to the text.¹⁰⁰ To him, triads were not law.¹⁰¹ His argument was that law consisted of rules, backed by a royal power, and therefore they have binding force; but this is not the case with triads, which are for teaching purposes, and are customs.¹⁰² He also had a concept of an original book of law, with binding force, to

---

⁹² *WML*, xx.

⁹³ This is now known as Tr, and is Cambridge, Trinity College MS O.7.1; it was not known to Aneurin Owen or used in the earlier work, *Leges Wallicae*.

⁹⁴ Heffer, *Like the Roman*, 29. Powell, 'The Trinity College Manuscript', 120–124. According to Stephen J. Williams's obituary by D. Ben Rees, 'Williams contacted Powell, then a Fellow of Trinity College, Cambridge, after reading his article in a bulletin of Welsh studies on "The Floating Sections of the Laws of Hywel Dda". Powell contributed a chapter to the final volume and a long friendship between the two scholars followed.' *The Independent*, 7 August 1992.

⁹⁵ This matter is discussed in full in Part II of this work.

⁹⁶ *LlBleg*.

⁹⁷ *LlBleg*, xxxix. Also, Powell, 'Floating Sections'.

⁹⁸ Powell, 'Floating Sections', 27.

⁹⁹ *Ibid.*, 28.

¹⁰⁰ *LlBleg*, xlii–xliii.

¹⁰¹ '*Nid cyfreithiau yw trioedd, ond crynodebau o gyfreithiau neu arferion cyfraith, wedi eu llunio ar ddull nodweddiadol modd y cofid hwy'n hawdd.*' ('Triads are not laws, but summaries of laws or legal custom, made in a distinctive form so that they would be easily remembered'), *LlBleg*, xlii–xliii.

¹⁰² Powell, 'Floating Sections', 29.

which triads were a later addition. Powell's 'floating sections' theory and his idea of what was law are no longer followed, largely because they were based on a concept of law that was alien to the Welsh tradition.[103]

It is clear from the introduction to *LlBleg* that Powell was attempting to recreate the exemplar of 'Llyfr Blegywryd' – a concept which Wiliam shared in relation to the Iorwerth redaction, although Wiliam was not attempting to recreate the 'Book of Iorwerth'.[104] Powell also makes it clear that the extant manuscripts do not represent the lost Book of Blegywryd, and also that Owen's work needed to be superseded by a 'correct and clear' edition of an early text from very few manuscripts.[105] His edition aimed to recreate the exemplar of OTr (the two manuscripts on which he based *LlBleg*, with lacunae filled from manuscript L[106]) but stated that even that exemplar was not the original 'Llyfr Blegywryd'.[107]

LlBleg is often seen as presenting the 'basis' of the Blegywryd redaction, but the editor Enoch Powell had his own ideas about material that did not belong in the original lawbook.[108] In addition, the editors omitted material that is found near the end of manuscript L, thus reducing the texts included in the Blegywryd redaction, although Owen had included that material in his Dimetian Code rather than in his Anomalous Laws.[109] The decision to omit the material presented in AL DC III was probably on the basis that the main edition in *LlBleg* focused on manuscripts O and Tr, but both of those manuscripts are defective and have their end wanting. L, which contains the material found in AL DC III, was only used for filling lacunae. It is notable however that neither O nor Tr have the Laws of Court, possibly omitted deliberately, but in *LlBleg* the Laws of Court were filled in from L.[110] The edition therefore does not even give a true picture of its base manuscripts.

The Iorwerth redaction is neater and better organised than the Blegywryd redaction, but it has not escaped the same division of the material. The editor of the only edition to date of the Iorwerth redaction, Aled Rhys Wiliam, focused on manuscript B, but ended his edition before the collection of model pleadings at the end of the manuscript – this is material that was in Owen's Anomalous Laws, in Book VII – and so divided his manuscript in the same way that the Iorwerth text had been divided in *Ancient Laws*.[111] The origin of the decision to separate the legal material in two may be rooted in the bipartite division of *Ancient Laws*, but the view that some material is 'additional' is a persistent one and it is found in most of the modern editions in varying degrees.

In his edition in *LlIor*, Aled Rhys Wiliam made the decision to omit the *cynghawsedd* (model pleadings) found in his manuscript, B: 'B has been reproduced in full, save the last twelve folios (which contain the Cynghawsedd).'[112] The explanation was that he had a concept of the 'original Book of Iorwerth', and his intention in

---

[103] *LT*, 11–13.
[104] *LlBleg*, xlv.
[105] *LlBleg*, xlv.
[106] *LlBleg*, xxxix.
[107] *LlBleg*, xlv.
[108] *LlBleg*, xxxix–xlvi. For a discussion of Powell's 'Floating Sections' theory see *LT*, 11–15.
[109] AL DC III.
[110] On this see Russell, '*Canyt oes aruer*'.
[111] *LlIor*.
[112] *LlIor*, xxxvii.

his edition was to look at the Iorwerth manuscripts and trace their relationships back to this 'original Book of Iorwerth'.[113] Unfortunately, we do not get a clear outline of what this book would have been – although Wiliam states that none of the extant manuscripts represent it – but some hints are given regarding what was *not* in this book.[114] It appears that Aled Rhys Wiliam was following a similar idea to that of Owen's, and his 'original Book of Iorwerth' may have been the first version of the law for Gwynedd,[115] and closer to Aneurin Owen's second stage, where the 'variance' appeared and regional 'Codes' came into being.

Wiliam does not use the words 'additional material' but rather states that there are 'certain evidences of accretions to the original text', with more of these in the later manuscripts and, as such, he says that Enoch Powell's 'Floating Sections' are 'aptly named'.[116] It is perhaps under the influence of Powell that Wiliam accepts that triads are 'accretions', but to this adds the 'Book of Pleadings (Cynghawsedd), part of the Book of Cynog, the Privileges of Arfon, and the two bodies of Case-law (Damweiniau), all of which were derived from sources other than the Book of Iorwerth'.[117] To Wiliam, none of the material in Owen's second volume would be part of his original Book of Iorwerth, and all of those genres are examples of 'additional material'.[118]

The problem with this of course is that the material would not have been divided at all were it not for Owen's editorial decision, and Wiliam makes no comment on the fact that the manuscript does not emphasise a different status to the material. In Wiliam's edition, following B, the text of Corn Damage ends, and has a closing sentence – *Ac yuelly e teruynyr am lugyr yt* ('And so ends concerning Corn Damage') – but otherwise continues with the next text, without a title or anything to denote a change of material. Wiliam, however, states that the *damweiniau* (classed by him as 'additional material') are different:

> The Damweiniau differ from the Book of Iorwerth in that they are not a coherent, well-ordered exposition of a subject but a mass of short unrelated passages, with every appearance of being a collection of legal notes and precepts based on current legal practice. No MS. mentions them in its Preamble. We may conclude that they were a gradually solidifying mass of rules which in the thirteenth century had not acquired the status and systematic lay-out of the Books of the great lawyers.[119]

This is not a convincing argument, since it is doubtful that any other part of the lawbooks had a particularly special status – Land Law, for example, or the Three Columns of Law – and it is unclear what the 'Books of the great lawyers' were. Wiliam may be referring to his 'Book of Iorwerth', but again that is a modern construct to some extent, not reflected in the medieval lawtexts.

A collection of *damweiniau* is found in most Iorwerth manuscripts, but they are usually treated separately. Dafydd Jenkins's edited the collection of *damweiniau* from the early manuscript Col, but his edition of the first part of the manuscript

---

[113] *LlIor*, xxi, xxiii.

[114] *LlIor*, xxi.

[115] He notes that Iorwerth ap Madog's floruit was c.1220–1240, and that the original would therefore date to the first half of the thirteenth century. *LlIor*, xxxvi, n.8.

[116] *LlIor*, xxi; xxiii.

[117] *LlIor*, xxiv.

[118] See also note 69 above, with the reference in *Llyfr Cynghawsedd* to 'Llyfr Hywel'.

[119] *LlIor*, xxxii–xxxiii.

was published earlier, omitting the large collection of *damweiniau* in the same manuscript.[120] The *cynghawsedd* texts, like the *damweiniau* linked to the Iorwerth manuscripts, have suffered particularly, as there is no modern edition of them, only the texts in *Ancient Laws*.[121]

Not every scholar has been lured into the false dichotomy of Owen's division between proper law and anomalous material. Dafydd Jenkins, in his edition of Col, published before *LlIor*, is more careful in his discussion of the text, and indeed in general Jenkins did not engage with the division of the material. However, *LlCol* only presented the first part of Col, and he later published the second part, *damweiniau*, separately – although he made it clear that he had intended to give *damweiniau* a fuller treatment.[122] He notes in his introduction to *LlCol*: 'And although some [law] books confine themselves to "damweiniau" type subjects, the main [law] books offer something which was intended to be a complete statement of the law, and that statement can be taken from the other material, as has been done in this edition and in other editions.'[123] Having said that, Jenkins did not afford more importance to the material in the first part of Peniarth 30, presented as *LlCol*, over the material from the latter part in his *DwCol*, and did not use any language to suggest a division. Rather, he stated that there is no obvious or clear division in the manuscript between 'Llyfr Colan' and 'Llyfr y Damweiniau', and neither is there a division between the two equivalent parts in the Black Book of Chirk (Iorwerth A).[124]

Thomas Charles-Edwards examined the lawtexts as a whole in his introductory volume to the Welsh laws.[125] Like Jenkins, he does not use the word 'additional' and makes it very clear that there is no difference between the various type of material in the lawtexts; indeed his interest in *damweiniau* and *cynghawsedd* focuses on those sections found in the 'Anomalous Laws' in the *Ancient Laws*.[126] He makes it clear that the distinction between the 'Versions' ('Codes') and the Anomalous Laws, including the Latin texts, was made by Owen and has its negative aspects, with the latter 'relegated ... to a supporting role'.[127]

More recent scholarship on the lawtexts has tended to step away from the attempts to recreate archetypes or trace the texts back to the original assembly of Hywel Dda at Whitland. There remain different views on the link (or lack thereof) between Hywel ap Cadell and the extant law manuscripts, but there is some consensus that there existed 'some sort of Model Lawbook [which] underlies our extant texts that probably pre-dates the composition of Cyfn in the late twelfth century'.[128] The concept of a Model Lawbook refers to an early archetype, one that existed before the three

---

[120] *LlCol*; *DwC*.

[121] *Cynghawsedd* will be discussed more fully in Chapter 4.

[122] *DwC*, vii.

[123] *LlCol*, xxiii–xxiv. 'Ac er bod rhai llyfrau'n eu cyfyngu eu hunain i bynciau "damweiniol", mae'r prif lyfrau'n cynnig peth a fwriedir yn ddatganiad cyflawn o'r gyfraith, a gellir tynnu'r datganiad hwnnw oddi wrth y defnydd arall, fel y gwnaed yn yr argraffiad hwn ac argraffiadau eraill.'

[124] *LlCol*, xxiv n.10. Slightly more problematic is the argument that *LlCol* is seen as a revised version of Iorwerth, but the text of the *Damweiniau* is more uniform across the different versions of it – the *damweiniau* in the same manuscript as the Colan text is not a different version of that collection.

[125] Charles-Edwards, *The Welsh Laws*.

[126] *Ibid.*, 17. He states that the Anomalous Laws are 'unfortunately' entitled.

[127] *Ibid.*, 25–26.

[128] Stacey, *Law and the Imagination*, 14.

main redactions and indeed may have been a common textual archetype for them. There is no doubt that some sections of the lawbooks are earlier than others, many with pre-Norman origins; in addition, all of the extant manuscripts of Welsh law are likely to be a copy of at least one earlier exemplar. Charles-Edwards argues that these early texts may have been in the Model Lawbook. There were independent written traditions of law in both Gwynedd and Deheubarth by the end of the twelfth century, and there are enough similarities in the way these texts are organised to show that both traditions 'are likely to go back to a single earlier "model-lawbook"'.[129]

Paul Russell, in his study of the Three Columns of Law tractate (on homicide, theft and arson) considers the sections of the tractate that are likely to be earlier, and suggests a possible order for the material in the Model Lawbook.[130] Charles-Edwards takes a broader view and considers the material found across most of the lawbooks – focusing on the texts found in Owen's first volume, as much of the material in the second volume is indisputably later in date – and discusses the probable date or antiquity of the sections; the parts that can be called early or pre-Norman are likely to have been in the Model Lawbook.[131] As Stacey points out, this tells us little of the dating of the Model Lawbook (indeed, some scholars such as Pryce suggest an early twelfth-century date), and it does not tell us more about the form of the Model Lawbook.[132] Neither does it prove – or disprove – the Hywelian link.[133] While the Model Lawbook would be earlier than the three redactions and was an archetype for them, it is less clear whether it was the same as the text from Hywel's time; it is more likely that it derived from at least one other archetype.[134] But the concept of the Model Lawbook is crucial when, as Charles-Edwards states, the texts may need to be used as evidence for pre-Norman Wales. It also answers the problem set out by R. R. Davies, and discussed at the start of this chapter, and the 'chronological uncertainty' he described as 'the despair of the historian'.[135] As a historian, Charles-Edwards points out that these texts are not as chronologically uncertain as they first appear, and are useful even as historical sources.

The pitfalls that arise in attempting to recreate a Model Lawbook on the basis of the extant manuscripts, as can be seen in many of the main editions of the redaction texts, is that this can colour the way the material in any particular manuscript is treated. While contemporary scholars can discuss the Model Lawbook and its contents without dismissing or reducing the importance of the legal material that was not in it, several of the published editions in the early to mid-twentieth century emphasised the early, or original, material at the cost of the other texts.

---

[129] Charles-Edwards, *Wales and the Britons*, 269.

[130] Russell, 'The Arrangement and Development', 84–85. This theory looks at the shape of the Iorwerth text before the material that now forms the Test Book was taken out of the Laws of Country, and also the disruption to the collection of 'Nines', with *Y Naw Tafodiog* ('the Nine Tongued-Ones') left behind.

[131] Charles-Edwards, *Wales and the Britons*, 271–272. The focus on the texts in AL I is reasonable as it has been shown, by Charles-Edwards and others, that texts such as the *damweiniau* and *cynghawsedd* are later in date in any case.

[132] Stacey, *Law and the Imagination*, 15–16.

[133] *Ibid.*, 16. 'For even if Hywel had presided over the compiling of a written lawbook, there is no guarantee that it and the Model Lawbook were one and the same.'

[134] On the possible archetypes, see the discussion on Iorwerth, and particularly the stemmata, in Charles-Edwards, 'The Textual Tradition of Llyfr Iorwerth', 21–45.

[135] Davies, 'The Status of Women', 93.

The editorial decisions made in *LlBleg* and in *LlIor* appear to have represented a turning point in how the material is viewed and, despite the earlier edition by Owen, *LlIor* and *LlBleg* made the demarcation between the 'main' texts and the 'additional' material very clear, in a way that had not been done before. Powell's attempt to recreate 'Llyfr Blegywryd' and his concept of the nature of law led him to reject (wrongly) some of the material as 'not law', and thus divided the legal texts. There was no entertaining of the possibility that this perfect 'Llyfr Blegywryd' may not have existed at any stage. Aled Rhys Wiliam followed, with less of an emphasis on recreating the original exemplar, but with more of an emphasis on the 'accretions' and weeding out the material to present some perfect text. But in all of this, the preoccupations of the editors, particularly Enoch Powell, added unsubstantiated interpretations to the field. The 'additional material' was afforded a secondary position, in contrast to the elevation of their editions, given the authoritative titles *Llyfr Blegywryd* and *Llyfr Iorwerth*, and thus the appearance of a fixed statement of law.[136]

The fullest discussion of a complex manuscript, containing a considerable amount of material outside of the expected tractates, is found in Christine James's excellent doctoral thesis from 1984.[137] The work focuses on manuscript S, and its sister text (in the same hand) Tim, with the emphasis on both books being manuscripts for the use of practitioners of law, for administering the law in the courts.[138] James notes that the main criticism to be levelled at *Ancient Laws* is the division of the material into 'Codes' versus 'Anomalous Laws', a decision she attributes correctly to Owen's concept of a 'core' version of the law, possibly even traceable to Hywel Dda and the meeting in Whitland.[139] She notes that several manuscripts, and particularly the later texts, contain material from one of the redactions, but may also have material from other redactions too, plus other material that would be found in AL II.[140] Manuscript S is an example of that kind of composite text, and James sees a clear division between the 'main text' and the 'tail' of the manuscript, with an adapted colophon to show where the 'tail' starts.[141] While acknowledging the division, James gives all the material in the manuscript the same importance and treatment, and does not really divide her manuscript on the grounds of origin or superiority. If anything, James focuses more closely on the material in the latter part of manuscript S, but this was the first full study of any such manuscript, and the first important edition to move away from emphasising the redaction or 'Code' part of the lawtexts on the grounds that it provided a view of some early core statement of the law. In her discussion of the second part of S, James refers to different types of 'additional material' found in the 'tail' of S: the material taken from the 'Codes', and other 'additional material', which can be divided into '*deunydd ychwanegol traddodiadol a deunydd ychwanegol diweddarach*' ('traditional additional material and later additional material').[142] In doing so she follows earlier editors in making all the 'additional material' additional

---

[136] Charles-Edwards states that the titles using 'Llyfr' for the statement of laws are unlikely to be correct, with the exception of 'Llyfr Iorwerth'. Charles-Edwards, *The Welsh Laws*, 19.

[137] James, 'Golygiad o BL Add. 22,356'; a revised version of the work was published online as *Machlud*.

[138] *Machlud*, viii.

[139] *Machlud*, x–xi.

[140] *Machlud*, xii.

[141] *Machlud*, xii, xxi. This colophon is discussed more fully in Chapter 5, and S is discussed in Chapter 6.

[142] *Machlud*, xii, xiii.

to the 'Code' in the manuscript, even if it has been taken from the 'Codes' of other redactions. Her examination of all the material in S was a major step forward for the field, and it cannot be denied that the first part of S does indeed conform to material found in other Blegywryd manuscripts.

In her study of S, James suggests calling the later, 'composite' manuscripts like S *Deddfgronau* (legal compilations or anthologies, the plural form of *deddfgrawn*), following a suggestion made by Aled Rhys Wiliam in an article on '*Y Deddfgronau Cymraeg*' ('The Welsh *Deddfgronau*').[143] He referred to William Maurice's legal compilation in two manuscripts, Wynnstay 37 and 38, called '*Deddfgrawn* William Maurice'; Wiliam noted that '*ei enw yntau ar ei waith yn gwneud y tro yn iawn wrth gyfeirio at gasgliadau eraill o gyfraith ychwanegol*' ('his [Maurice's] own name on his work will do well in referring to other collections of additional law').[144] Wiliam's *Deddfgronau* focused on manuscripts with little or no material from Owen's Codes.[145] James's emphasis on the practical aspect of the manuscripts that incorporate a variety of texts from various exemplars certainly contextualises the manuscripts in a way that had not been done before, but also took an important step away from the traditional division of 'Code' versus 'Other'. By looking at S in its entirety, and emphasising the context of the material as well as that of the creation of the manuscript, James created a new direction for studies on Welsh laws, and forced a much-needed breach between the views of Aneurin Owen and study of the laws in the late twentieth and twenty-first century.

Conclusion

Despite the early date of the publication, *Ancient Laws* remains a valuable work for studying the Welsh law manuscripts, and credit is due to Aneurin Owen who made great strides in dealing with the large bulk of legal material by categorising it and giving it some kind of order. Several of his editorial decisions still stand, in a modified form, and his work set the foundations for modern editions of the Welsh laws. The work is now dated, and has been partially superseded by more recent editions, but it is still a valuable contribution to the field.

The main issue with *Ancient Laws* is the division that the work imposed on the texts in the law manuscripts, and the continued references to 'additional material', or the 'tails' of manuscripts. In his study, while avoiding use of terminology such as 'additional', and not adhering to the concept of manuscripts with 'tails', Thomas Charles-Edwards made a very important point about the variety found in the law manuscripts. He attributes the differences between the texts to the 'eclecticism of lawyers' who were compiling their texts from a 'variety of sources'.[146] This has led to some of the manuscripts having a 'chaotic structure', and he also notes, importantly, that while one tractate of the lawbooks may show a particular relationship between lawbooks, the same relationship may not be there for other tractates.[147]

---

[143] *Machlud*, xii; Wiliam, 'Y Deddfgronau Cymraeg'.

[144] Wiliam, 'Y Deddfgronau Cymraeg', 97.

[145] *Ibid.*, 97.

[146] Charles-Edwards, *The Welsh Laws*, 45.

[147] *Ibid.*, 45–46. His example discusses Latin B: 'One reason for the chaotic structure of Latin B is its readiness to use material from a variety of sources.'

This is an important point. The problems that stem from Owen's construct are that there was a fixed idea of a pattern that the laws ought to follow, and to which the Codes were seen as belonging, but the Anomalous laws did not.[148] If the idea of a 'model lawbook' is correct, then there was at least a fairly fixed idea of such a pattern. The problem perhaps is with overemphasising this pattern at the cost of material that does not conform, and dismissing other patterns, or the development of the texts. Rather than distributing the texts into 'Core sections' and 'Anomalous Laws', or separating manuscripts into 'main text' and a 'tail' comprised of 'additional material', the new approach should be more open-minded, and each section of law should be assessed on its own merits, in its own context. The concept of the three Welsh redactions does work, and texts do group together, but they should not be afforded any pre-eminence, and the study of the lawtexts needs to move away from seeking the 'core' text of Cyfraith Hywel, or a 'basic statement' of law. The manuscripts and studies of certain texts show that this may not exist, and it is not an accurate way to view the laws.

Instead, the different sections of the lawbooks should be examined on their own terms. A section of law may only occur in two or three manuscripts, and may not be found in all manuscripts of one redaction; this does not mean that it is secondary or not part of some 'real lawbook'. Instead, it should be considered for what it is: a text of law available in a particular area, or a section written for a specific purpose. Instead of looking at manuscripts as those containing a 'main text' and a 'tail', the division should be lost; these are manuscripts that contain material from a number of sources, and often the first part may be a statement, a collection of tractates, which is found in a similar form in several other manuscripts too, linked to a redaction. Other parts of it are not found in as many texts, and this may be to do with local availability, or the interests of the compilers, rather than with the status of the material. Finally, rather than looking at material as being 'additional' to other parts of a lawbook, each lawbook should be viewed on its own terms, and all of the contents should be seen as making up a specific lawbook for a specific purpose – much as was done by Christine James in her study of S.

Taking this approach will give a new picture of Cyfraith Hywel, and will reveal the growth of the law in medieval Wales. It will elevate all parts of the law to the same status, and open the field to give a full picture of the laws, their practice, and the men who made them, which will have huge benefits for all those wanting to examine medieval Wales through the context of the lawtexts.

---

[148] *Ibid.*, 26–27.

3

'REI A DYWEIT':
LAWYERS AND THE LAW IN MEDIEVAL WALES

The literature produced by a profession is often the clearest guide to the state of its intellectual development. It is, of course, possible for courts and administrative systems to function without books; but it is impossible for a body of law to develop very far without the interposition of writing.[1]

Professor Sir John Baker, in his *Introduction to English Legal History*, devoted a chapter to 'Legal Literature', examining surviving examples from England such as the important treatises called *Glanville* and *Bracton*, formularies, reports of cases, and studies of law in the early modern period. If the field of Cyfraith Hywel is subjected to the test that Baker proposed, it comes out of this very well, rich as it is in written sources. This is not the place to discuss the differences between the English Common Law that Baker considered and the law of medieval Wales, but the 'character and limitations'[2] of the manuscripts of Cyfraith Hywel have been the subject of intense study for at least 200 years, starting with the earliest published editions of the lawtexts.

There has been much discussion of the nature of the genesis of Cyfraith Hywel in scholarly publications, and whether Hywel Dda himself wrote or created any part of the legal texts as they stand today.[3] But, as Baker states, such evidence as there is will have to come from the extant written sources. We may be able to acknowledge now-lost exemplars, or trace the origins of the texts to an earlier period, but for solid evidence, the focus must be placed on the manuscripts that we have today. This chapter will therefore look at those texts and what they tell us about the growth of law in medieval Wales – the hints we are given about the people behind their creation, where they drew their material from, the way the texts were constructed, and why they take the form they have today. Only by taking that view will it be possible to move away from the constraints and constructs imposed on the subject area by the editors of the early publications of texts.

In the past, it was traditional to describe Cyfraith Hywel as a *volksrecht* system, a 'law of the people': Dafydd Jenkins states that 'the law they [the lawbooks] contain is Volksrecht, not *Kaiserrecht*', contrasting one with the other.[4] In reality, the legal

---

[1] Baker, *An Introduction*, 175.

[2] *Ibid.*, 175: 'Even if law may exist, and indeed develop, in an unwritten form, our vision of the past is necessarily circumscribed by the written word; our knowledge must be derived from those written sources which the accidents of time have preserved, and therefore we need to be aware of their character and limitations.'

[3] See discussion in Chapter 1.

[4] Jenkins, 'Significance', 56. Jenkins may have been using '*volksrecht*' as a contrast to '*kaiserrecht*' rather than thinking about lawyers' or judges' law, and there are elements of both in medieval

system of medieval Wales was lawyer-made law, created by the lawyers and for the lawyers. Far from being a collection of customs that developed among local communities, this was a scholarly legal system, drawing on wider European traditions of lawmaking, and with a written form predating the extant manuscripts. While the law applied to all of society (be that throughout Wales or on a more regional basis, and notwithstanding variation over time), the men who needed the law were the lawyers. R. R. Davies indeed stressed this point: the purpose of the lawbooks should be kept in mind – they were not intended to be a historical source or to tell us about society in medieval Wales, in a particular region, at any specific point in time. They were 'lawyers' manuals, not guidebooks for social observers'.[5] Davies suggested looking at how the law worked in late medieval Wales as a way of escaping the 'problems' of the textual studies, but taking a different approach to the texts may also be to work in parallel with Davies's suggestion, without dismissing the texts themselves altogether: using those very texts to determine how the law worked.

In order to get a sense of the nature of the texts and the men who created them, several aspects will be considered here. This study will begin by looking at the lawyers – including looking at particular 'famed' lawyers named in the manuscripts themselves – who they were, and what we can learn about their role. In this section we will look at the work undertaken by these lawyers on the manuscripts as they exist today, showing that the law was being discussed and developed by lawyers over time, rather than being treated as an immutable, fossilised relic handed down from previous generations. This will be followed by questioning why these men, the compilers of the lawbooks, were doing this work – in particular, how did the law operate in their view, and what was the purpose of the books. Finally, the lawtexts themselves will be examined in detail for evidence of their intended use, and how the compilers were moulding their material for the purposes of the lawbooks.

Lawyers and Lawbooks

The obvious place to start considering the role of the lawyer in medieval Wales would be to look in the written historical records for evidence of men who operated as lawyers or justices, *ynad* (pl. *yneid*) in Welsh, and work from that basis. However, outside the law manuscripts we lack early alternative sources: Stacey notes that it is only in the second half of the thirteenth century that there is 'non-lawbook evidence' for the professional Welsh judges.[6] There is however some additional historical evidence for actual lawyers who worked in Gwynedd during the Age of the Princes since, as members of the academic elite classes, evidence for the lawyers' existence – along with the poets, who were often related to the lawyers – sometimes appears in genealogies. The best-known example of this is the poet Gruffudd ab yr Ynad Coch, who composed a famous elegy to Prince Llywelyn ap Gruffudd (r. 1246–1282); his father has the nickname 'The Red Justice/Judge'.[7] The genealogies name other

---

Welsh law. While this was not conceived as law promulgated by kings, there are examples of kings adapting the law, and Hywel ap Cadell is named as the person behind the legal system as a whole.

[5] Davies, 'The Status of Women and the Practice of Marriage', 94.
[6] Stacey, 'Hywel in the World', 182.
[7] See Jenkins, 'A Family of Welsh Lawyers', 125; Roberts, 'Addysg Broffesiynol', 6–7. Stacey questions some of Jenkins's conclusions in Stacey, 'Hywel in the World', 184. See also Charles-Edwards,

lawyers in the same family – Iorwerth ap Madog and Cyfnerth ap Morgenau – as well as poets, including Einion ap Gwalchmai, whose father was also a poet, and Guy notes that 'members of this family had a reputation for deep involvement with written literary activity'.[8] Guy makes the persuasive argument that the genealogical text itself was created in a 'secular literary environment maintained by a family like that of Iorwerth ap Madog, akin to a 'law-school', and the genealogy is dated to the early thirteenth century.[9]

The lawbooks name several pre-eminent lawyers, as has been noted many times, and the names of some of these lawyers have been adopted as the modern names for the redactions. The Blegywryd redaction was named after Blegywryd Athro, who not only appears in the prologues to that redaction but is also mentioned in some Cyfnerth redaction manuscripts, in Latin D, and in later manuscripts such as S and Z. He is described as a scholar rather than as a lawyer, and the epithet *Athro* often implies a church link, but he is credited in Cyfnerth manuscripts V and Mk with composing lawbooks: *A'r llyfr hwn Blegywryd ysgolhaig a'i hysgrifennodd, canys ef oedd orau ar gof a chyfreithiau* ('And this book was written by Blegywryd the scholar, since he was the best on memory and laws'). *Ysgolhaig* is certainly ecclesiastical. Hywel Emanuel noted that this attribution is dubious on various levels, but that it also differs from that of Iorwerth ap Madog since Iorwerth was credited within the lawbook itself, but Blegywryd is named only in the Prologue.[10] This means that he is credited in a general way but, unlike Iorwerth ap Madog, Blegywryd is not shown 'to have made specific contributions on points of law': his contribution is more abstract.[11] Emanuel also notes that Blegywryd is only named in manuscripts of one particular redaction and does not feature in any of the other redactions, unlike Iorwerth ap Madog (and others).[12] It is difficult to connect the reference to Blegywryd in the laws to a known historical figure, but there are clerics called Blegywryd in the Book of Llandaf, and one of these may be the same person.[13] Nothing concrete can be surmised about legal activity from the hand of Blegywryd, and there is no other supporting evidence about his role, but the attribution of legal activity by him is clear enough.

There is a stronger case for other named lawyers. In some lawbooks there is a reference to another cleric responsible for a part of the laws: in manuscript Q there is a section called *Llyfr Cynyr ap Cadwgan* ('The Book of Cynyr ap Cadwgan'). Cynyr ap Cadwgan appears in the records as the Abbot of Llandinam, and there is evidence of his legal work in ecclesiastical sources: he acted as a clerical jurist in a case in Arwystli.[14] The attribution in manuscript Q is followed by text that is said to be from his book, but while the start of the book is marked, the end is not, so the length of

---

'The Textual Tradition of Llyfr Iorwerth', 25.

[8] Guy, *Medieval Welsh Genealogy*, 221. There is evidence that the role of poet and lawyer could be combined; the poet Gwalchmai, himself from a well-known family of poets who became landholders in Anglesey, seems to have been an 'advocate' to Prince Owain Gwynedd (1137–1170) and was certainly influential in the royal court. Stephenson, *Governance of Gwynedd*, 14. Stephenson also states that Gwalchmai's son Einion may also have combined the role of poet and lawyer, and was a witness to some charters: *ibid.*, 210.

[9] Guy, *Medieval Welsh Genealogy*, 222.

[10] Emanuel, 'Blegywryd and the Welsh Laws', 257.

[11] *Ibid.*, 257.

[12] *Ibid.*, 256–257.

[13] Davies, *The Llandaff Charters*, 122, 150.

[14] Pryce, *Native Law and the Church*, 34–35. See also Elias, *Llyfr Cynyr ap Cadwgan*.

this 'book' is unknown. The short section that follows the attribution is a general piece on learning, although it may have been based on an existing triad found in one law manuscript.[15] The existence of the book and the attribution to Cynyr seems to suggest that the lawtexts were open to including works written by expert lawyers, but the case of Cynyr ap Cadwgan, the clerical jurist, also suggests that the definition of lawyer or legal scholar could be a flexible one.

The Cyfnerth redaction is named after Cyfnerth ap Morgenau; both he and his father, Morgenau, appear to have been lawyers.[16] They may be the earliest of the lawyers known to be associated with the creation or the redrafting of the lawtexts: they are referred to in some Cyfnerth prologues, but perhaps more interesting is that the Test Book prologue in Iorwerth states that Iorwerth ap Madog drew on 'the book of Cyfnerth ap Morgenau' (among other named books) for his own work.[17] The work of Cyfnerth (and/or that of his father) may have been well-known in Gwynedd, and there is also a reference to an extant book of law made by them, rather than to more general, unspecific, legal activity. There is evidence outside of the lawbooks for the existence of Cyfnerth and Morgenau: Morgenau was from a family of lawyers, and Morgenau and his family held land in Dinas Dinlle.[18] It appears that father and son were invited to Anglesey – Jenkins suggests to fill judicial posts – and they also held land there, in Llanddyfnan.[19] The Cyfnerth redaction was shown by Huw Pryce to be linked to Maelienydd, but that Cyfnerth and Morgenau were based in Gwynedd or Anglesey suggests how their books may have been available for Iorwerth ap Madog, and the book of theirs used by Iorwerth ap Madog does not necessarily need to mean a text of the extant Cyfnerth redaction.[20]

An alternative version of the main prologue of the laws, found in only two manuscripts, lists several people involved with the creation of the laws, and who are said to have assisted Hywel Dda at Whitland: of all the wisest men from all parts of Wales, the 12 wisest were selected to make the law.

> A llyma henwe y gwyr hyny oll, nid amgen Morgenev Ynad, Kyfnerth i vab, Gweir vab Rvvawn, Gronwy vab Moriddic, Kedwyδ Ynad, Iddic Ynad, Gwrbri Hen o Is Kennyn, Gwrnerth Lwyd i vab, Meddwan ail Kerist, Gwyn Vayr (perchenawc ar Lan Tafhwin, bioedd y ty y gwnaythbwyd y gyfraith ynddo), Bledrws vab Bleiddvd. Brewgawryd [sic] Archddiagon Llan Daf oedd yr ysgolhaic, a doctor ynghyfraith yr amerawdr ac ynghyfraith eglwys.

> And here are the names of all those men, namely Morgenau Ynad, Cyfnerth his son, Gwair son of Rhufon, Goronwy son of Moriddig, Cedwydd Ynad, Iddig Ynad, Gwrbri Hen from Is-Cennen, Gwrnerth Lwyd his son, Meddwan ail Cerist, Gwyn Faer (the owner of Llantafwyn, the house in which the law was made belonged to him), Bledrws son of Bleiddydd. Blegywryd Archdeacon of Llandaf was the cleric, and a doctor in the law of the emperor and in the law of the church.[21]

---

[15] For the section see Roberts and James, *Archwilio Cymru'r Oesoedd Canol*.

[16] Guy, *Medieval Welsh Genealogy*, 221.

[17] See *LTMW*, 141.

[18] See Jenkins, 'A Family of Welsh Lawyers', 124–127. Father and son may have been related to Iorwerth ap Madog; Guy, *Medieval Welsh Genealogy*, 221.

[19] Jenkins, 'A Family of Welsh Lawyers', 128–129.

[20] Pryce, 'The Prologues', 165; see also Owen, 'The Laws of Court from Cyfnerth', 429.

[21] *Pomffred*, 196–199.

This is likely to be a later composition – it does not occur in any early manuscripts – and most of the names cannot be linked to existing people found in the records; but then again that much is true of many names in early medieval Wales.[22] Iddig Ynad may be one of the family of Iorwerth ap Madog.[23] Gwrnerth Lwyd is named in a Latin verse at the end of the manuscript of Latin D, and a note also states that he was the court judge of Hywel Dda himself.[24] Goronwy ap Moriddig, however, is perhaps the most neglected of the named authors of Welsh law. Despite being in the shadow of his more famous colleagues Iorwerth ap Madog and Cyfnerth ap Morgenau, Goronwy has the further cachet of being named within a lawbook as the person responsible for a legal rule. This is not unusual in itself, for others are named in this way, but such naming is usually confined to princes or rulers rather than to legal scholars. In addition, rather than being named in the Iorwerth text – allegedly drawn at least in part from his book – it is the Blegywryd text that refers to him:

> Gronw ab Moridic a dywedei na dyly gwr, yr bot gan wreic gwr arall a'r wreic yn da genti, talu dim idaw tra ganmolo hi y gweithret; ac or byd honheit y gweithret, y wreic a dyly talu y sarhaet y'r gwr, neu y gwr a'e gwrthotto yn ryd.[25]

> Goronwy ap Moridic stated that a man, despite copulating with another man's wife with the wife's consent, should not pay anything to him [the husband] as long as she praises the deed; and if the deed is publicly known, the wife is to pay his *sarhaed* to the husband, or the husband may freely reject her.

The section occurs near the end of the women tractate, and is found in all Blegywryd manuscripts containing the section, and also more tellingly in Latin D, which is the earliest text containing the reference, the extant manuscript dating from the late thirteenth century. References to the redactors by name in this way are relatively rare in the manuscripts, although when the texts state *nynheu a deweyt* ('we say'), the earliest readers would doubtless have known who was meant by *nynheu*. The comment naming Goronwy ap Moriddig does not state that he was more important than the other possible redactors, but reference to a legal comment by him may refer to the existence of some work – in a book, or stated orally (even in a law lesson) and noted down – which can be linked to him, and which was known to an early compiler of a Blegywryd text, be that in Latin or in Welsh. In addition, work originating from Goronwy was also available to Iorwerth ap Madog in the creation of his Test Book, according to the preface[26] – although it is interesting that the legal amendment linked to Goronwy ap Moriddig is actually on the law of women and the payment of *sarhaed*, and not on any of the subjects included in the Iorwerth Test Book. It may be the case that there was a book of law of some kind linked to Goronwy ap Moriddig, perhaps even named after him. The fact that it was named in the Test Book acknowledgements does point to its existence, even if its contents cannot be traced in the Test Book itself.

There is other evidence for Goronwy ap Moriddig's existence. Pryce notes that he may be the same person as the Goronwy ap Moriddig who was a witness in an

---

[22] See Owen, 'Royal Propaganda', 226–229.
[23] Jenkins, 'A Family of Welsh Lawyers', 126.
[24] Owen, 'Royal Propaganda', 227–228.
[25] *LlBleg*, 67.
[26] See *LTMW*, 141, and the text quoted below, 67.

inquest in 1274 to the rights of St Asaph, and he was most probably a layman.[27] The inquest refers to events that happened c.1230, and while Morfydd Owen states that the dates in that text are too late for the man to be the lawbook author,[28] Pryce notes that 'Goronwy ... could well have composed a lawbook in the second quarter of the thirteenth century that was then incorporated into the Iorwerth Redaction's Test Book by c.1250'.[29] Because Goronwy ap Moriddig seems to have existed, and because there is later evidence for men such as Cynyr ap Cadwgan who were involved in written legal work, there is no reason to doubt that the other lawyers named in the lawbooks also existed, and that the preface to the Test Book naming (some of) the sources used by Iorwerth ap Madog had its basis in fact.

Iorwerth ap Madog was studied in some detail by Dafydd Jenkins, whose work on the genealogies and records locating the legal families of north Wales was a major contribution to the field.[30] Iorwerth ap Madog ap Rhahawd (fl. ?1240–?1268) would have lived in north Wales, in Gwynedd, and is named as being responsible for the Iorwerth Test Book. He may have been from a family of poets and lawyers.[31]

The exact nature of Iowerth ap Madog's work is not clear, but despite this Jenkins noted that even if the attribution was later than Iorwerth's own time, he 'was regarded in his day as a high authority on the law'.[32] Iorwerth ap Madog was living and working at roughly the same time that the earliest Iorwerth manuscripts were made, and he lived and worked in Gwynedd, in Arfon Uwch Gwyrfai.[33] In addition, there is a reference in the Test Book prologue to the texts available to Iorwerth. He was not working alone nor was he starting from scratch – he had other texts by well-known lawyers to draw upon. This is an important point to note in relation to the nature of Welsh law. While some of the Welsh lawtexts may appear to be conservative and static, describing an idealised situation from a long-gone time, there is plenty of evidence within the lawtexts themselves that suggests that learned men were free to adapt, rewrite, edit or even create legal texts for their own or other purposes, and furthermore, there is evidence of men doing just that. The evidence is not confined to professional jurists in Gwynedd such as Iorwerth, Cyfnerth and Goronwy ap Moriddig, but is attested for clerical jurists such as Blegywryd and Cynyr ap Cadwgan. And there is even evidence that the Welsh princes were involved in changing the law – Bleddyn ap Cynfyn and Rhys ap Gruffudd are well-known examples named in the law[34] – which shows that the Welsh lawtexts were dynamic and adaptable, and changed regularly according to need.

---

[27] Pryce, *Native Law and the Church*, 93, acknowledging *LTWL*, 61.

[28] Owen, 'Shame and Reparation', 53.

[29] Pryce, *Native Law and the Church*, 93–94. Emanuel was very sceptical of 'the pretended list of those laymen' who assisted Hywel Dda in creating his books of law, but Pryce accurately points out that these men were credited with being used for the Iorwerth Test Book, not for Hywel Dda's purported book. *LTWL*, 61.

[30] See Jenkins, 'A Family of Welsh Lawyers', *passim*. See also Stacey, 'Hywel in the World', 184–185, who questions Jenkins's handling of the genealogy, but the actual existence of Iorwerth ap Madog is not in question. See also Guy, *Medieval Welsh Genealogy*, 221–222.

[31] Jenkins, 'A Family of Welsh Lawyers', 129; Guy, *Medieval Welsh Genealogy*, 221.

[32] Jenkins, 'A Family of Welsh Lawyers', 132.

[33] Charles-Edwards, 'The Textual Tradition of Llyfr Iorwerth', 42–43, and 25–29.

[34] Rhys ap Gruffudd is named in the Blegywryd redaction as supporting sworn appraisal for animals who were stolen; Bleddyn ap Cynfyn is named in the Iorwerth redaction linked to his decision on sworn appraisal too, as well as on fixing land measurements. *LTMW*, 164, 165, 98.

The Role of the Justice in Medieval Wales

Having looked for evidence of the existence of named lawyers in medieval Wales, the next step is to look at what evidence there is for the work that lawyers or judges did – and indeed, whether there is a distinction to be drawn between lawyer and judge. According to the lawtexts, the lawyer was a very important person in Welsh society, placed only slightly lower than the king himself; although this perhaps is to be expected when it is considered that the lawyers were creating the laws themselves – they would be unlikely to do anything other than maintain their own social standing.[35] Like the poets (who were often closely linked to the lawyers), their high status was largely down to the fact that they had particular skills, focused on words and learning. That the poets were politically important in medieval Wales may be surprising to modern eyes, but the lawyers' other role as advisors to the rulers is not particularly unusual even today, since law and power do tend to go hand-in-hand.

The lawtexts have sections dedicated to the justice, not only within the Laws of Court (since the justice was one of the officers of the royal court) but also in other sections in some texts that look at the justice and his work. Further information on the way the justices worked can be found throughout the texts, particularly in sections such as *cynghawsedd* (model pleading), and the lengthy legal case for land found in the Land Law tractate of the Iorwerth redaction. In order to have a picture of the work of the justice in medieval Wales and the way these men operated, which could affect the lawtexts directly, a survey of the role of the justice according to the Welsh lawtexts is first necessary.

One of the first things that needs to be discussed is a matter of terminology. There are two words used in the law to refer to the lawyer or justice: *ynad* and *brawdwr*. *Ynad*, plural *yneid*, has an older form, *ygneid*, and it may derive from the Indo-European root **gnō*, 'to know'.[36] *Ynad* is still the word for a magistrate in modern Welsh, but the suggested translations in *GPC* also include 'justice, judge, one who is learned in law' as well as 'wise man'. *Brawdwr* (plural *brawdwyr*) is *brawd* + *gŵr*, and *brawd* here means judgement, so the *brawdwr* is one who judges, or a judge or justice.[37] Robin Stacey argues that there is an absence of an established judicial terminology in medieval Wales, compared to that in Ireland; *ynad* may have had a broader meaning of 'wise man'.[38] In his study of the Court Justice, J. Beverley Smith notes that *iudex curie* is used consistently in Latin, but there is more variation in the Welsh – in Iorwerth texts *ynad* is more common, and in Blegywryd *brawdwr llys*, although both terms are used in all of the texts.[39] Beverley Smith summarises that *ynad*, *brawdwr* and *iudex* are all best described as judge, which is entirely accurate when looking at the officer of the court, and a large part of the work of an *ynad* or a *brawdwr* was to sit in judgement.[40] Here, however, the word 'justice' will be used, as the wider context will be under consideration. It also leaves the terminology more open to other interpretations.

---

[35] *WKC*, 445; *LlBleg*, 58.12–14.
[36] *GPC2*, s.v. ynad, yngnad. See also the Glossary in *WLW*, 220–221.
[37] *GPC2*, s.v. brawd², brawdwr.
[38] Stacey, 'Hywel in the World', 193–194.
[39] Beverley Smith, '*Ynad Llys, Brawdwr Llys, Iudex Curie*', 94.
[40] *Ibid.*, 94.

Another factor that needs to be kept in mind is that there appears to have been a north/south divide in Wales in the work of the justice to some extent, and this may in part explain the varying frequency of the terms in the different redactions.[41] The main difference is that in north Wales the justices appear to have been trained specialists. Some evidence to support this is found in the Iorwerth Test Book, where the training of justices is set out in the preface; the Test Book itself is sometimes called *Llyfr Prawf Ynaid*.[42] In addition, the list of question-and-answer sentences, clearly for the use of legal training or in legal schools, often have the title *Profi Ynadon*. In Deheubarth, and in the Blegywryd texts, it is stated that landowners could be called upon to sit in justice, although the trained justice does appear to have been known as well:[43]

> Tri ry6 vra6d6yr yssyd ygkymru her6yd kyfreith Hy6el: bra6d6r llys penydya6l her6yd s6yd, gyt a brenhin Dinef6r ac Aberffra6 yn 6astat; ac vn bra6t6r kym6t neu cantref her6yd s6yd, ym pop llys o dadleueu G6yned a Pho6ys; a bra6d6r o vreint y tir ym pop llys kym6t neu cantref o Deheubarth, nyt amgen, pop perchena6c tir.
>
> There are three kinds of judges in Wales according to the law of Hywel: the judge of the daily court by virtue of office, continually with the king of Dinefwr and Aberffraw; and one judge of commote or cantref by virtue of office, in every court of pleading in Gwynedd and Powys; and a judge by privilege of land in every court of a commote or cantref in Deheubarth, namely, every owner of land.[44]

The justice occurs at various points – and in different guises – in the lawtexts. The main section, which has a particular focus on the justice and his role, is found in the Laws of Court, where he is listed in all redactions as one of the principal officers of the court. The focus of the section is to list his rights and entitlements, and so little is said about the exact duties of the justice at this point – that was probably not the focus of the passage in the Laws of Court, and this is true of the other officers too, although their entitlements and so on are usually linked to their function. There is one comment on the justice's duties, that 'his is the task of indicating the privilege and duty and offices of the court',[45] but Beverley Smith notes that this shows more of 'a concern with the needs of the household rather than the functions of the king's court as a court of law with a duty of justice to others than those who constituted the household'.[46] The royal court was not a court of law and, while the rulers had their own importance according to the laws, they were not the ultimate dispensers of judgement. Indeed, in the description of the legal case for land set out in the Iorwerth texts, the king is presiding but it is the justices who declare the judgement.[47] Beverley Smith also notes that the Court Justice was also not the ultimate legal judge: he did not appear to have primacy over all other justices in Wales according to the law,

---

[41] Glossary, *WLW*, 220.
[42] *LTMW*, 274.
[43] Stacey, 'Hywel in the World', 180–181.
[44] *LT*, 198–199.
[45] See *WKC*, 451; from Cyfnerth. The wording of the section differs slightly in the different redactions, but the substance is similar in all of the redactions with none of them giving more or different details on the work of the court justice.
[46] Beverley Smith, '*Ynad Llys, Brawdwr Llys, Iudex Curie*', 99.
[47] *LlIor*, 77/35–37. The king releases the hostages, and provides political force, but the justice is responsible for the judgement, and summarising the arguments as witness and for the future memory of what has been judged.

and he was 'not readily envisaged as the head of a judiciary'.[48] He may, however, have had an important role in testing the other justices or those wanting to join the profession (although this role is not detailed in the lawtexts), and Beverley Smith suggests that once he had examined the other justices he had little or nothing to do with them.[49] Indeed, the only hint at the role of the court justice in this section is the reference to making wrong judgements:

> O'r gŵrthŵynebha neb yr ygnat llys am a uarnho rodet deu ŵystyl yn llaŵ y brenhin; ac o'r methlir yr ygnat llys, diuarnedic uid y geir, a thalet werth y tauaŵt y'r brenhin ac odyna na uarnet byth. O'r methlir y llall talet y sarhaet y'r ygnat llys ac y'r brenhin werth y tauaŵt.

> If anyone oppose the court justice concerning what he judges let him put two pledges in the king's hand; and if the court justice be foiled, his word will be without legal judgement and let him pay the value of his tongue to the king and then let him never more give judgement. If the other be foiled let him pay his *sarhaed* to the court justice and the value of his tongue to the king.[50]

The Court Justice section in the Laws of Court has a similar content across the redactions, although the Blegywryd redaction has more of an emphasis on procedure. While the picture is not at all clear, it seems that the court justice gave judgements that could then be questioned – this aspect will be discussed shortly; it appears that he would conclude a case by stating which party won, and he also worked alone.[51] In addition, the court justice's section in Blegywryd is followed by a section which is called *Brawdwr a Brawd* ('Judges and Judgement'), made up of triads and extensions or explanations on the three items in the triad,[52] detailing the role of the (court) justice. Much of the short section focuses on querying judgements.[53] The duties are outlined in the triad that opens the section:

> Tri pheth a perthyn y vraŵdŵr: vn yŵ dillŵg kyfarcheu ŵrth reit y brenhin, eil yŵ datcanu a dosparth kynheneu y myŵn llys, trydyd yŵ yr hyn a dospartho trŵy varn, y gatarnhav trŵy ŵystyl a braŵtlyfyr, ot ymŵystlir ac ef, neu, os gouyn idaŵ y brenhin heb ymŵystlaŵ.

> Three things pertain to a justice: one is to issue pronouncements at the king's need, the second is to set forth and settle disputes in court, the third is that whatever he may determine by judgement, he should confirm by a pledge and a lawbook, if pledges are exchanged with him, or, if the king asks him without pledging.[54]

This Blegywryd section expands on the duties of the justice: he clearly had a role in the king's court, making official pronouncements, and he had the role of a judge,

---

[48] Beverley Smith, '*Ynad Llys, Brawdwr Llys, Iudex Curie*', 104.

[49] *Ibid.*, 103–104. However, there are instances in the lawtexts where several judges work together, for example *LlIor*, 78/1, and 76/3.

[50] *WKC*, 450–451; from Cyfnerth. This is a problematic passage, since it is uncertain who would decide whether the appeal is correct or not.

[51] See *LlBleg*, 15.25–16.9.

[52] *LT*, 7–9.

[53] *LlBleg*, 17.19–18.21.

[54] *LT*, 94–95.

though the option was available to a litigant of questioning his judgements. The justice also appears to be a court official who explains the legal process, and also settled cases within court. His role, according to this section, is firmly linked to the court of law and not to arbitration, although he may well have played a part in extra-curial legal processes. Both Rees Davies and Beverley Smith acknowledge that the justice no doubt had a role in arbitration, which was central to dispute regulation,[55] and the role of the justice and arbitration as an alternative or parallel route is supported in evidence outside the lawbooks, such as a description of a legal procedure from Brycheiniog.[56] In addition, the justice is highly likely to have acted as a legal advisor or expert, and people may have approached the justice for advice and guidance, but again evidence from the lawbooks on all aspects of the justice's work is scarce. Since the focus of the lawbooks is on the formal action, the evidence there is confined to the justice's role as the judge in actual legal cases.

While the lawtexts give some hints as to procedure, what the justice actually did when he acted in his role is less clear, although some suggestions are found in the *cynghawsedd* sections, particularly in the Iorwerth case for land. In that case, there are two justices present and one is assumed to be more senior than the other, although the senior one is not necessarily the court justice.[57] The senior justice leads the session and is in control of the procedure – it is assumed that he would know each step in the process, and explains it to the claimants. He listens to the claims made, and decides which is the better argument or case, and the justices make the decision in the case; in the legal case for land the role of the justice is akin to that of a modern-day judge.[58] He also had a similar role in suretyship cases. Suretyship, a personal action, was designed to be carried out between the parties, but the Iorwerth text outlines a situation – in the first few sentences of the tractate – where the debtor wants to deny that a man is a surety for him, and the first step is to approach the justice, who questions both sides (the surety and the debtor), hears their oaths, and then goes out to judge the matter.[59] The *Llyfr Cynghawsedd* texts have a different focus and mainly give the statements and expectations of procedure in court, but the regular references to judgement being made, and the occasional references to the justice(s) being present, assume a similar role for the justice, as the decision-maker in legal cases. There are also sections that discuss the role of the justice in cases, and rules on impartiality.[60] The *cynghawsedd* from north-east Wales also sees the judge as running the legal case and being in charge of the procedure as well as the decision.[61] Much of the evidence from the lawbooks themselves sees the justice's role as running the legal sessions, hearing the proof and 'in the light of the proof, to make his adjudication and impose the appropriate penalty (*camlwrw*) in accordance with Welsh law. He was thereby the interpreter and arbiter of the processes laid down by law.'[62]

---

[55] Davies, 'The Administration of Law', 259; Beverley Smith, 'Judgement under the Law of Wales', 64. See also Llinos Beverley Smith, 'Disputes and Settlements', 835–860.
[56] Roberts, 'Legal Practice in Fifteenth-Century Brycheiniog', 307–323.
[57] *LTMW*, 85. In land cases the court justice takes two-thirds of the fee if there are two justices, but if there are more than two his share of the fee is equal to two of the others. *LlIor*, 78/1.
[58] *LTMW*, 87–89. See also Beverley Smith, 'Judgement under the Law of Wales', 65.
[59] *LAL*, 140–143. See also Beverley Smith, 'Judgement under the Law of Wales', 67–68.
[60] AL, VII.i.30–40.
[61] *Pomffred*, 224–225.
[62] Davies, 'The Administration of Law', 267.

Brawdwyr O Fraint Tir – The Landowner Justices

Brawdwr herwyd breint y dir, tra gynhalyo tir, breint brawdwr a gynneil ef drwy y tir. Sarhaet brawdwr swydawc, herwyd breint y swyd y telir idaw. Sarhaet hagen brawdwr heb swyd, namyn trwy vreint y dir, herwyd breint y tir y telir idaw.[63]

A justice by privilege of land, while he holds land, he holds the status of a justice through his land. The *sarhaed* of an office-holding justice, that is paid to him according to the status of his office. The *sarhaed* of a justice without an office, however, namely one according to privilege of land, it is paid to him according to the status of his land.

In his highly important article on 'Judgement Under the Law of Wales', J. Beverley Smith looks at the different types of justices in the laws, and considers their role both within the Welsh legal process but also in the wider context of the changing political and legal landscape of Wales.[64] He considers the contrast between the professional judges described by the Iorwerth lawbooks and the judges by privilege of land in south Wales and elsewhere, and also looks at wider evidence beyond the lawtexts and from post-conquest Wales; his emphasis in his study is on the 'collective judgements' and the apparent shift to this type of process – a shift witnessed in other countries and other legal traditions too.[65] However, his study also notes that the Welsh legal system as outlined in the Welsh lawtexts emphasised the professional judge but also allowed for other methods, and that the concept of collective responsibility for judgements in Deheubarth may have developed because of the political circumstances after the conquest.[66] This summary assumes that judgement by a professional justice was the original method throughout Wales, and from an early date, but he argued that the role of landowners as judges, such as was said to exist in the south, was a development of the thirteenth century, after the conquest of 1282.[67] Beverley Smith's conclusions show again that there was an inherent flexibility in the laws. It is not surprising that legal practice and the role of the justice changed with time, and this is particularly the case in the period after the thirteenth-century Edwardian conquest of Wales. The lawtexts themselves allowed for such changes to happen.

There are several passages in the lawbooks that reference the landowner judges in south Wales. The triad listing the three different justices, the third being the landowner justice, occurs in the Blegywryd manuscripts, but the same reference is not found in the Cyfnerth or Iorwerth manuscripts. There are two versions in Latin D, but only the first has the same reference to the landowner justice; the second version refers to a justice who gives *iudicium curie in qua non sit iudex* swytawc, *sed iudices per dignitatem curie* ('the judgement of a court in which the judge is not *swyddog* [holding office], but is a justice for the dignity of the court').[68] There are not many references to the *brawdwr o fraint swydd*, the landowner justice, and often the word *brawdwr* is used in the Iorwerth texts as *brawdwr llys* (the 'court justice'). As Stacey notes, when it comes to the justices, 'the professional identity and vocabulary [was]

---

[63] *J(ed.)*, 11.15–19.
[64] Beverley Smith, 'Judgement under the Law of Wales', 63–103.
[65] Ibid., 82–86, 95, 101.
[66] Ibid., 101.
[67] See also Stacey's summary, Stacey, 'Hywel in the World', 181.
[68] *LTWL*, 382 and also 342.

still in flux' at the time of writing the lawbooks.[69] This may account for statements where both *ynad* and *brawdwr* are used interchangeably.[70]

It may also be the case that in the post-conquest period, there were fewer highly trained justices around – while the Blegywryd lawbooks make provision for the landowner justices, the same lawbooks also outline a procedure on training someone who is *agkyurwys ac amharawt yghyureith* ('unskilled and unready in law') to be a *brawdwr llys* ('court justice'). The process involves learning book law (with reference to certain parts of the lawtexts) and observing legal cases and law in practice for a whole year, before undergoing a ceremony and swearing an oath and the exchange of tokens to signify taking up office.[71] Further evidence for the relaxing of the formal training for justices can be witnessed in discussions in the Blegywryd texts on the duties of the justice, in a section entitled *Swydd a Braint Brawdwr* ('The Office and Status of a Judge') in modern editions. This is always separate to the Laws of Court, and so Blegywryd texts missing the Laws of Court still have details on the justice.[72] *Swydd a Braint Brawdwr* is, like the Court Justice section in Blegywryd, largely made up of triads: this may be a case of using triads to confer authority.[73] It outlines the different types of justices in Wales and, in addition, offers some comments on the role of the justice, with the focus on the work of the landowner justices. They were to make judgements, and the focus is on the fixed times for reaching a judgement (with different timescales for different types of justices). The section hints at the difficulties of taking on the role and making the decisions – the landowner justices may have been given the office, but had not received the same training as the court justice. They also seem to be working without the full court personnel available to them, perhaps because they are not in the setting of the royal court.

> Os brawdwyr o vreint tir a archant yspeit am vrawt, ae o betruster, ae o eisseu rei o wyr y llys, y rei kyndrychawl a gaffant oet heb dwng…[74]

> If justices by virtue of land request a period for [reaching] judgement, either because of uncertainty, or because of a lack of some of the men of the court, the ones present may have a delay without swearing…

There is a focus in the section on disputing judgements, and it is followed by a lengthy section on wrong judgements, and then a discussion on the verdict of the country. This part of the lawbook has the air of a handbook for non-professional jurists, as it is full of practical points – what needs to be heard in court, who has the right to act as a justice and who does not, and the role of clerics in the justice system. As is noted by Beverley Smith, this shows it was written for non-professional justices in south

---

[69] Stacey, 'Hywel in the World', 194.

[70] For example, *Pomffred*, 204–205, where '*ynad*' is used, as well as '*ynad llys*' for the senior justice, and also '*brawdwr*' is used of the office when the justice is no longer allowed to be an '*ynad*'. The section is taken from the *cynghawsedd* (pleadings) section of the manuscript, which is likely to date to the thirteenth century or, in the case of this text, after the conquest of Wales by Edward I in 1282.

[71] *LlBleg*, 16.16–17.18.

[72] Beverley Smith, '*Ynad Llys, Brawdwr Llys, Iudex Curie*', 109.

[73] Stacey, *The Road to Judgment*, 188.

[74] *J(ed.)*, 45.21–23.

Wales, who sat as a team as compared to the professional judges of north Wales who generally worked alone.

Setting aside the usual problem of a lack of evidence outside of the lawbooks – although it should be noted that while there is some evidence for the work of *ynaid* and *brawdwyr* and *sapientes*, there is none whatsoever for the landowner justice – there is a distinct lack of detail and explanation of the role in the lawtexts themselves. Beverley Smith states that the concept of having every landholder sitting in judgement was 'uneasily accommodated in the existing legal redactions of the thirteenth century', but he claims that the situation ultimately superseded professional judgement.[75] Perhaps the key to understanding the situation in Deheubarth is to look at the later situation, and look at men who held offices relating to justice, for whom there is evidence in the post-conquest period: the *dosbarthwyr*.

Dosbarthwyr

As discussed, there is little to no evidence, outside of the lawbooks, for 'justices by privilege of land', allegedly responsible for legal decisions in Deheubarth.[76] However, there is evidence for men called *dosbarthwyr*, who were men with some expertise in Cyfraith Hywel.[77] *Dosbarthwyr* are mentioned in post-conquest records, but there is also one reference in the lawtexts: in the lengthy triad on procedure, *Tair gorsedd dygynull* ('Three specially convened courts') found in later lawtexts in a section focusing on procedure.[78]

> Eil datleu dygynull yѡ damѡeinaѡ y haѡlѡr neu amdiffynnѡr ameu dosparth a ѡnel aѡdurdaѡtѡyr a vѡynt alѡedigion o bleit y brenhin, megis y dyѡedir yn y cam dosparth... Os hѡynteu a ѡatta nat ynt achѡyssaѡl o rei a dѡetter arnadunt, yna y dylyir, o bleit y brenhin, kymell doethion o'i kygelloryaetheu o pop parth y adnabot beth a dyѡedynt y dosparthѡyr ae gѡir ae geu, a hynny o rei a odefir o pob parth. Os yn achѡyssaѡl y hardiѡedir, neu vot yn ampriodaѡl y dosparth yn y gyfreith, bit difodedic heb amgen gosp; cany ossodet yn y gyfreith ymѡystlaѡ yn erbyn dosparthѡyr. Canyt oes vreint braѡtѡr y ryѡ dosparth hѡnnѡ, onyt gan y odef, heb ѡneuthur ameu, val y dyѡetpѡyt o'r blaen. Ac yna y dyly y brenhin gossot braѡtѡr penyadur y ѡneuthur tervyn tragyѡyd am y gynnen trѡy varn.

> A second [kind of] specially convened pleadings occurs when it happens that a claimant or a defendant doubts the verdict made by authorities who may be called on behalf of the king, as it said in relation to a false verdict... If they deny that they are responsible for those things which are attributed to them, then, on behalf of the king, wise men should be required [to come] from their *cynghellor*-ships on every side to make a recognition as to whether what they may say is true or false, and those [wise men] are to consist of persons accepted on each side. If they are found to be responsible, or that

---

[75] Beverley Smith, 'Judgement under the Law of Wales', 75, 93.
[76] *Ibid.*, 74.
[77] James, 'Dafydd (Llwyd)', 157–158.
[78] *LT*, 210–215 notes that the triad occurs in Q, S and Tim, but much of it also occurs in Lew. That the section containing this reference to *dosbarthwyr* occurs in those manuscripts is significant, since those manuscripts, S and Tim in particular, had a specific purpose as legal practitioners' handbooks (see Part II where these manuscripts are discussed, and Chapter 6 in particular). The section is not found in the majority of the Blegywryd manuscripts and there are no references to the *dosbarthwyr* in the Iorwerth manuscripts or those dating to before the conquest or shortly afterwards.

the verdict is improper in law, let it be extinguished without any further penalty; for mutual pledging against *dosparthwyr* was not established in the law. For such a verdict as that does not enjoy the status of a judge, unless it has been accepted, without doubt being expressed, as has been said previously. And then the king should set a chief judge to make a final termination of the dispute through judgement.[79]

The *dosbarthwyr* would be called upon to correct judgements made by 'authorities' working for the king. They were a higher level of legal official, paid by the crown.[80] There are records of the existence of such men.[81] James shows that the men who acted as *dosbarthwyr* were noblemen with an important role in the cultural and literary life of their day. They could be patrons and even poets themselves, and they also had books made for them.[82] A section of manuscripts Tim and S is said to be from *Rhol Dafydd Llwyd*, ('Dafydd Llwyd's Roll'), and Dafydd Llwyd ap Gwilym appears to have worked as a *dosbarthwr* in south Wales in the late fourteenth century.[83] The Blegywryd texts outline the procedure to follow for a doubted judgement made by justices by privilege of land, and this involved turning to a lawbook. In the only extant recorded case involving *dosbarthwyr*, sections of Cyfraith Hywel were quoted.[84] James suggests that manuscripts S and Tim, with their focus on procedure and administration of law, and including a section purported to be from a Roll belonging to an existing *dosbarthwr*, were books intended to be used by *dosbarthwyr* in court. In addition, the larger-than-average physical size of these manuscripts suggests that they were higher in status than other lawbooks, perhaps as the reference books used by justices.[85]

The emphasis on recourse to written lawtexts may explain the nature of some of the extant lawbooks, and may even testify to their use in legal cases in south Wales.[86] The format of the books, as well as their content and the emphasis within the sections that were copied and recopied, is testament to their intended purpose and the legal context of their creation. It also suggests that the Iorwerth lawbooks had a different purpose, which may go some of the way to explain the structure and focus of the Iorwerth manuscripts: these were more formal texts, and were the work of the professional justices in Gwynedd before the conquest. However, it may be the case that the description of the situation and work of the professional justices outlined in Iorwerth, and the contrasting legal setup in post-conquest south Wales, was not an abrupt change, and was not a move away from the 'classical' Iorwerth setup. Beverley Smith argues convincingly for a change in the way judgements were made in medieval Wales, but also notes that the system of professional justices outlined in the

---

[79] *LT*, 214–215. '*Dosparth*' is translated here as a 'verdict', and '*dosbarthwr*' seems to mean 'one who makes a decision [in law]'. The word is found in several places in the Blegywryd texts in relation to the role of the justice, and the section on procedure, which includes this triad, also has a long triad on *camddosbarth*, 'wrong decision/verdict'.

[80] James, 'Dafydd (Llwyd)', 157.

[81] *Machlud*, xvii; Beverley Smith, '*Ynad Llys, Brawdwr Llys, Iudex Curie*', 110. James assumes that the crown-appointed justices whose decision came under question were the 'landowner justices', but this is not made explicit in the text. However, this section may be a clearer reference to the '*brawdwyr o fraint tir*', and they do not have to have been amateur landowners.

[82] *Machlud*, xxii–xxiii; James, 'Dafydd (Llwyd)', *passim*.

[83] *Machlud*, xxi; James, 'Dafydd (Llwyd)', 158.

[84] *Machlud*, xvii, xx.

[85] *Machlud*, xxii.

[86] There is evidence of turning to written law in a case from Cydweli in 1510: Beverley Smith, 'Judgement Under the Law of Wales', 77–78.

Iorwerth texts also allowed for other methods of making judgements.[87] And, taking this further, there was considerable flexibility and an openness to change written into the same lawbooks. The Blegywryd lawbooks may reflect the different situation in Deheubarth, giving rise to a need for a variety of different legal texts and books. Meanwhile, the Iorwerth lawbooks, which reflect the more traditional situation in pre-conquest Gwynedd, have their own inbuilt flexibility.

The Lawbooks and the Law

Having looked at the role of the lawyers, it is time to turn to the purpose of the books they used. The lawbooks were designed as authoritative books of law. This is obvious from the opening sentence of the prologues linking them to King Hywel ap Cadell:

> Howel Da o rat Duw, mab Kadell, brenhin Kymry oll ...[88]

> Hywel Dda son of Cadell, by the grace of God, king of all Wales ...

It has been shown that the prologues to the Welsh lawbooks may have been fiction, but the purpose of the prologues was to give the books and the law itself a necessary authority: the law was both royal and Christian and was not a casual compilation.[89] This is further emphasised by the first tractate in most of the lawbooks. The Laws of Court were always placed at the start of the lawbooks, following the prologue; the Laws of Court may have been an outdated fossil, but they were retained to emphasise the royal background of the law itself.[90] The Laws of Court were omitted in some of the Blegywryd lawbooks, but by that stage the nature of the law and the work of the lawyers had most likely changed in medieval Wales and the need to 'protect' Cyfraith Hywel by emphasising its royal background may have receded.[91] However, there are several signs that there was room for manoeuvre and flexibility even while the compilers of the lawtexts may have wanted them to appear authoritative and fixed: in the Iorwerth and Blegywryd redactions there are texts that have the same tractates in the same order, suggesting a recognisable form of the law. It appears that the Iorwerth redaction was rewritten, and that there was scholarly work being carried out on the text in thirteenth-century Gwynedd. We have a statement in several of the earliest manuscripts that Iorwerth ap Madog, a justice, had reworked part of the text. The section that received Iorwerth's attention was the Test Book, the part of the Iorwerth manuscripts that the justices were required to learn by heart. The authority of the

---

[87] Beverley Smith, 'Judgement under the Law of Wales', 101.
[88] *J(ed.)*, 1.
[89] Pryce, 'The Prologues', 176.
[90] Jenkins, 'Prolegomena to the Laws of the Court', 16–17.
[91] It is interesting to note, however, that those lawbooks that are lacking the Laws of Court as a deliberate act (rather than due to a loss of leaves) do include a prologue. The Gwilym Wasta manuscripts, N, O and Tr, all start with a Blegywryd prologue, and then have sections on the justice from the Laws of Court but also have a statement that the Laws of Court have been omitted. S may be linked to these manuscripts as S is also lacking the Laws of Court but it also has a prologue, as is a related text, I, which has the same opening as S. This may point to the omission of the Laws of Court as a deliberate act rather than because of a general loss. Russell, 'Canyt oes aruer', 183, 186. Iorwerth manuscript K opens with the Iorwerth Test Book, following a calendar, but the Test Book preface is used instead of a Iorwerth Laws of Court prologue.

law – in both Iorwerth texts and other redactions – was found in the presentation of 'traditional' tractates, including the Laws of Court, and this made these books of law look familiar, but the main use of the books was found in the latter part which had a focus on practical application and the administration of law.[92] The Test Book would fit in with this scheme, as would the *Llyfr Damweiniau*.

It seems that the Iorwerth lawbooks were also extremely flexible from the outset, as is shown with the existence of Col, often called a 'revised version' of the Iorwerth redaction. Col, Peniarth 30, is a manuscript that stands alone in the Welsh lawbook tradition.[93] Dating from the thirteenth century, this early text is clearly linked to the Iorwerth redaction but takes a different form, and includes much material that is not found in the other Iorwerth manuscripts; its second half is a copy of an extensive version of *Llyfr Damweiniau*.[94] The fact that Col was created and preserved does not take us away from the idea of the authoritative lawbook taking a fixed form. Iorwerth ap Madog's reorganisation was copied more than once – Col and B both derive from a text of the same type as C and E – but while that version of Iorwerth has a preeminent position, there was flexibility in how it was presented. Manuscript B belongs to the same Iorwerth tradition as C, D and Col (and is similar in date) but has a different version of the *galanas* tractate, exchanges the *damweiniau* for *cynghawsedd*, and seems deliberately to remove references to Iorwerth ap Madog. This suggests that there was more than one way of writing law in thirteenth-century Gwynedd, but nevertheless it starts with the Iorwerth text. And because that flexibility already existed, it allowed for the rewriting, the adapting and the development of law, both in its written form but also in practice.

Dafydd Jenkins suggested that the reason Col was created was because the lawbooks refer to choosing the best judgement in a legal case; it is uncertain how it was decided whether a judgement was the best one, but the reasoning behind a decision may have had some sway, and in his view Col had 'strong' justifications and discussions, so the lawbook may have had considerable respect.[95] The Blegywryd law manuscripts regularly emphasise the importance of consulting books in order to practise the law and to conclude legal cases and reach the best and most accurate outcome. In the extended section on the justice in the Blegywryd Laws of Court (a section considered to be important enough to include even if the Laws of Court themselves were being omitted), there is a discussion on how to deal with a landowner justice who was accused of making a wrong verdict.

> Ac ual hynn y dosperthir: yn gyntaf y dyly y brenhin yn hedychawl gwarandaw yn y llys amrysson y neb a wrthwynepo y'r brawdwr; ac odyna atteb y brawdwr ol yn ol. Odyna y neb a dywetto yn erbyn y brawdwr a dyly dangos o lyfyr kyfreith brawt teilyngach no'r honn a dangosses y brawdwr, os dichawn; ac uelly y goruyd ef y brawdwr; onys dichawn, y brawdwr bieu goruot, kany dichawn neb anheilyngu brawt yn erbyn gwystyl y brawdwr, ony eill ynteu dangos brawt a uo teilyngach yn ysgriuennedic. Os yr amrysson o'r deu erbyn yn erbyn a vyd ynghyfreith ysgriuennedic, y dosparth a dodir ar y kanonwyr a rueront o wironed; a'r hwnn a weler yn nessaf y'r wironed, teilyngaf yw y chynnal yn y gyfreith.[96]

---

[92] I would argue that this is also the case with the Blegywryd manuscripts. See Chapter 5.
[93] *LlCol*, xv.
[94] *LlCol*, xv. Col is discussed in more detail in Chapter 7.
[95] *LlCol*, xxxiii.
[96] *J(ed.)*, 46.30–47.3.

And this is how it is decided: first the king is to hear peacefully in his court the argument of the person who opposes the justice; and then the justice shall answer in turn. Then the person who speaks against the justice is to produce from a law book a more correct judgement than the one which the justice produced, if he can; and so he overcomes the justice; if he cannot, the advantage belongs to the justice, because no one can discredit a judgement against the pledge of the justice, unless he can produce a more worthy decision in written law. If the dispute of the two is against each other in written law, the decision is to be referred to canonists experienced in truth; and the one which is seen to be closest to the truth, that is the most worthy to be maintained in the law.

Or dyweit neb ar y brawdwr varnu cam varn arnaw, rodent eu deu wystyl yll deu yn llaw y brenhin, ac os y brawdwr a orvydir, a chyfreith yscriuennedic yn dangos y oruot, talet y'r brenhin y swyda gwerth y dauawt; ac odyna na varnet vyth. Ny dylyir credu barn na'e chymryt rwng deu wystyl am vrawt, onyt vn a dangosser yng kyfreith ysgriuenedic.[97]

If anybody states that the justice has judged a wrong judgement to him, let them both place their two pledges in the hand of the king, and if the justice is defeated, and written law shows that that he is defeated, let him pay the king his office and the value of his tongue; and from then on let him never judge again. A judgement is not to be believed nor taken between two who have pledged on a judgement, unless one is shown in written law.

The written judgements appear to have been very authoritative and it was akin to a trump card for the claimant – it could make or break a justice. But the implication perhaps is that the justice would have done his homework in advance and consulted several books – although this is in a section discussing the landowner justices in south Wales. However, the hint that the claimant may also be able to find a (better, winning) judgement in a written text is intriguing; this assumes some expertise from the claimant too, although perhaps the expertise would be gained via a trained legal representative.[98] The whole process, however, suggests that a number of lawbooks would be available in court, and that they were essential for procedure. Unfortunately, there are no indications as to the kind of books that could be cited or used in this way – we can assume that there may also have been various kinds, including the *brawdlyfr* mentioned in the *cynghawsedd*, presumably books of judgements or even case notes.[99]

The justice was expected to consult the books, and ensure that he pronounced the best possible outcome to a legal case – the penalty for a wrong judgement was that he would be prevented from acting as justice again and have to pay the value of his tongue, a massive sum, to the king. But this may be another example of the laws setting out scenarios that were unlikely to happen in practice, as a salutary lesson

---

[97] *J(ed.)*, 11.8–14.

[98] There are references to legal representatives or 'helpers' in the lawtexts: the *cyngaws* and the *canllaw*. Jenkins states that the difference between the two is not clear, 'nor is it known whether either would be professional as being paid or as having been trained. Both helped litigants with the technicalities of presenting their cases', *LTMW*, 322–323. In Blegywryd the *cyngaws* is described as having the responsibility of bringing legal cases to a conclusion: *LlBleg*, 121.2–4. The expert help in these passages may be provided by the *cyngaws*, and a successful appeal of this sort would surely launch the career of a *cyngaws*.

[99] This is discussed in more detail in Chapter 4.

on how to conduct certain cases. Perhaps the point here is in fact symbolic – that the justice would be highly unlikely to be found wanting. Despite the section being included in the Blegywryd redaction discussions of the justice by privilege of land, perhaps the subtext to this section is that such justices, even if not professional, nevertheless still had the necessary legal background and expertise, so that to challenge them would require specialist legal knowledge and access to books that the ordinary lay claimant would be highly unlikely to have. The threat to a justice that he would never be able to judge again in the case of being found to have made a wrong judgement was very serious (and expensive), but perhaps that threat was largely rhetorical because the justice was expected to know what he was doing – training or no training – and he was unlikely to be found wanting.

The suggestion that there were numerous books of written law available to be used, and that they were even actually used in practice, is supported by a sentence in the section on the value of dogs:

> Gwerth damdwng a vyd ar bop peth ny bo gwerth kyfreith arnaw yn yscriuenedic.[100]
>
> A sworn appraisal value is to be applied to everything which does not have a written legal value.

The suggestion that there are lists of legal values for most items is interesting, and ties in with the lists found as part of the Value of Wild and Tame in the lawbooks, particularly the lengthy list of values for various items in Iorwerth that may have been copied with this purpose in mind. The difficulty however is in working out whether the idea of a written list of the value of items came first, or whether the sentence was added to the lawbook in the knowledge that there were plenty of lists available to consult and that the exceptions were to be dealt with by sworn appraisal to remove the need of adding to the list every time a new situation came up.

That the law emphasises the use of books in this way is supported by the comments in the lawtexts that suggest that there were several versions of the law circulating in books, even in early thirteenth-century Gwynedd. These may have been the books that were available for use in legal cases. The compiler of Col drew on several texts, some of them in Latin, and the introduction to the Iorwerth Test Book states that Iorwerth ap Madog created his work from several sources.[101] The reference to at least six books, three of them by named authors, closely links the practice of law and the creation of the lawbooks. The men who possessed these books were most likely legal practitioners, like Iorwerth ap Madog himself, and there is nothing to suggest that they did not create their books themselves; they are likely to have put together books containing material which they deemed to be useful. Iorwerth ap Madog stands out only in that versions of his book have possibly survived, at least in part. There are of course references to other books in the lawtexts. *Llyfr Cynog* is problematic: Cynog is better known as a saint and this may be an attribution to a saint to elevate the book for religious reasons, or out of respect for the saint himself.[102] Cynyr ap Cadwgan was a practitioner and he has a book named after him.[103] Latin B and manuscript G

---

[100] *J(ed.)*, 56.29–31; *LlBleg*, 54.9–11.

[101] Manuscript D, NLW Peniarth MS 32, pp. 112–113; translated in *LTMW*, 141.

[102] It is possible for lawyers to become saints, and St Thomas More is one example. On Llyfr Cynog see Elias, '*Llyfr Cynog of Cyfraith Hywel*', 27–47.

[103] *Ibid.*

appear to refer to a *Llyfr Iestyn*, a deathbed book of judgements (*iudicia* or *urodyeu*, from 'brawd', 'verdicts', in G) by an old man called Iustinus who was claimed to be contemporary with Hywel Dda.[104] Manuscript Tim mentions *Rhol Dafydd Llwyd*, and Dafydd Llwyd existed and worked as a *dosbarthwr*. Perhaps these books were collections of the best judgements as outlined in the procedure in the lawtexts, the best outcome to legal cases that the people who owned and most likely created them had dealt with personally.

The Scholarly Work of Iorwerth ap Madog

Iorwerth ap Madog has been credited with creating the redaction that is now named after him. Of the names given to redactions of Welsh law, Charles-Edwards believes that the Iorwerth designation is the only one that is likely to be correct.[105] The attribution to Iorwerth is found at the start of the Test Book in some manuscripts.

> A'r llevyr hvn a gynvllvs Yorwerth vap Madavc o lyvyr Kyvnerth vap Morgenev ac o lyvyr Gweyr vap Rvuavn ac o lyvyr Goronwy vap Morydyc, a hen lyfr y Ty Gwyn, ac ygyt a henny o'r llyvrev gorev a kavas hevyt eg Gwyned a Phowys a Dehevparth. A'r llyvyr hvn a elwyr e Llyvyr Prav sef ew henny teyr kolovyn kyvreyth a gwerth gwyllt a dof ac a berthyn ar hynny.[106]

> And Iorwerth ap Madog compiled this book from the book of Cyfnerth ap Morgenau and from the book of Gwair ap Rhufon and from the book of Goronwy ap Moriddig, and from the old book of the White House, and in addition to that from the best books that he found also in Gwynedd and in Powys and in Deheubarth. And this book is called the *Llyfr Prawf*, that is the three columns of law and the value of wild and tame and those things which pertain to that.

The exact nature of Iorwerth ap Madog's work cannot be ascertained from this prologue. While the entire text of a Iorwerth lawbook is now attributed to him, the reference in the attribution from the manuscripts is vague: he was responsible for 'this book', but 'this book' may be the Test Book only rather than the entire Iorwerth redaction. The Test Book seems to have been known as a book in its own right, and towards the end of the section there is a reference to the Test Book specifically as 'this book'. However, if Iorwerth ap Madog was responsible for the removal of material from the Laws of Country to make the Test Book, that act changed the shape of the lawbook, which would mean that Iorwerth ap Madog was responsible for the transformation and thus the entire lawbook in its new form.[107] That Iorwerth ap Madog was seen as a legal scholar and recognised as such is found in a further reference to his opinion in the *Damweiniau*: there, in a discussion on stock, the views of two different sets of lawyers are set out on the subject, but the definitive view seems to be Iorwerth ap Madog's.[108]

---

[104] *Pomffred*, 33.

[105] Charles-Edwards, *The Welsh Laws*, 19.

[106] Taken from manuscript C, Cotton Caligula A III, f. 180b. The same passage is also found in other Iorwerth manuscripts but without the reference to the Book of the White House: see *TCC*, 262–263.

[107] Charles-Edwards, 'The Textual Tradition of Llyfr Iorwerth', 28–29.

[108] AL IV.iii.2.

Dafydd Jenkins stated that Iorwerth ap Madog was only responsible for the addition of what Jenkins called the 'appendix' to the Test Book, rather than the whole book, and that the Test Book itself had already been put together before Iorwerth's time.[109] That view has been superseded by more recent discussions on the subject, and Charles-Edwards notes that even if only the Test Book was the work of Iorwerth ap Madog, he was also responsible for the shape of the text: by 'removing portions of what had been the Laws of Country and using them to form Llyfr Prawf' his actions also affected the new form of the Laws of Country as well as the Test Book.[110] The texts are not in agreement on what was, and what was not, included in the Test Book: manuscript B has an explicit stating that the Test Book ends after the value of trees, and before the values of houses and equipment, and *Cyfar* ('co-tillage') and Corn Damage, but this is not found in the other Iorwerth manuscripts. The 'appendix' therefore is only really clear in B, and there is no reason for preferring that reading.[111] Iorwerth C has a Latin explicit after the Corn Damage section and at the end of the manuscript, which states that everything previous was in the Test Book: *Explicit libellus probationis legum curialium Walliae. Amen.* ('Here ends the Test Book of the Laws of Wales. Amen.')[112] In any case, the list of values of houses and equipment, *Cyfar* and Corn Damage are stated fairly clearly to have been composed by Iorwerth ap Madog, or at the very least written down by him. Accepting Dafydd Jenkins's dating of Iorwerth ap Madog to the middle of the thirteenth century means that the date of committing these sections to writing (in the text) must be the same – they occur in the earliest Iorwerth manuscripts, and the sections may even have been composed at the same time.[113] As one of the very few datable sections of Welsh law, they deserve further consideration.

Cyfar and Corn Damage

In the texts, a list of equipment usually occurs first, and is followed by *Cyfar*, and then Corn Damage, which is where *Lllor* ends.[114] The values of houses and equipment also occur in Cyfnerth, with the latter as a list and a given value. There is an expanded form of the list in manuscript Z but it is a later manuscript and it may have been influenced by other texts; however, the version in Z seems closer to that in Iorwerth than it does to the other Cyfnerth texts.[115] It appears that the Iorwerth list of

---

[109] *LTMW*, 274; Jenkins, 'A Family of Welsh Lawyers', 132; *LlCol*, xxv n.18. Jenkins's suspicion may be due to a closing sentence after a section on the value of trees in the Iorwerth manuscripts; see e.g. Manuscript C, BL Cotton Caligula MS A III, f. 190v: *Llyma re weles Yorwerth vap Madawc vap Rahavt vot en grynno y escryvenny, nyt amgen a gwerth e tey ar deodrevyn, a chyvar, a llvgyr yt. Kyntaf ew onadónt ...* ['Here Iorwerth ap Madog ap Rhawd saw that it would be useful to write namely the value of houses and equipment, and *Cyfar*, and Corn Damage. The first of them is ...'].

[110] Charles-Edwards, 'The Textual Tradition of Llyfr Iorwerth', 28–29.

[111] *Lllor*, 138/14. Manuscript K has an explicit stating that the Value of Wild and Tame ends before the value of limbs and other material: AL VC III.xxii.251.

[112] AL VC III.xxv.46.

[113] Charles-Edwards, 'The Textual Tradition of Llyfr Iorwerth', 28–29.

[114] The manuscript (B) continues with *Llyfr Cynghawsedd* where *Llyfr Damweiniau* would be found in most other early Iorwerth texts.

[115] *Pomffred*, 124–137, and see note on 302.

values is an expanded version of a similar list in Cyfnerth, but it is interesting to note that there are some references in the Cyfnerth list to the opinions of other lawyers. It is difficult to determine whether this is an original composition or the work that was carried out on the section since it is a bare list.

Dafydd Jenkins discussed *Cyfar* in some detail and presented an edited version of the text from Colan.[116] He describes *Cyfar* as 'perhaps the most interesting piece of material to be found anywhere in the corpus of Welsh law',[117] for various reasons: textually, as an example of legal drafting, and historically as it 'suggests the increasing importance of efficient arable farming in thirteenth-century Wales, which in turn suggests increasing population and increasing pressure on land'.[118] He discusses the detail of the contract, which assumes co-operative ploughing of 12 acres with a wooden plough and iron coulter and share, and a team of eight oxen led by a ploughman and controlled by a driver. The section is not found in Blegywryd or in Cyfnerth, but there is a sentence in the Cyfnerth texts that refers to *cyfar*.[119] *Cyfar* in Iorwerth takes what was probably a well-known concept, and writes it out – this is probably because it was needed, and it most likely reflects the changing social situation as Jenkins suggested. But despite the potentially new format, there remains a link to the well-known lawtexts which knew of the term and the action described.[120]

Corn Damage is a slightly different case but it has some similarity to *Cyfar* in Iorwerth – it is in the Test Book, it is seemingly attributed to Iorwerth ap Madog, and it links to the Cyfnerth texts in a similar way. Corn Damage fits in with the preoccupation with compensation in the Welsh laws, but it also had its own importance as agriculture and animals were a highly important part of everyday life in medieval Wales. The section, a 'named' section of Welsh law with its start and end marked,[121] discusses how to compensate for damage or loss caused by animals to growing crops, and emphasises the animal owner's responsibility for his animals as well as the responsibilities of the crop farmer. Such a section is common in medieval law and is found widely in tracts from England, Ireland and the Continent. It also occurs in all versions of Welsh law, although the text shows development in its Iorwerth form. The text is complete in all Cyfnerth manuscripts, and is found with other sections on animals in that redaction (after bees in U, W, X and Z, and after cats and dogs in V and Mk), although it is a stand-alone section in Cyfnerth. The text is fairly uniform in the Cyfnerth manuscripts, but Z and U have some additional sentences on the end, with U putting more of an emphasis on pigs. The material on pigs in U echoes the Blegywryd section *Moch mewn coed ac ŷd* ('Pigs in woods and corn'), which is not part of the Corn Damage section in Blegywryd but was probably included since pigs caused more damage than other animals because of their rooting. In Blegywryd, the tractate is missing in manuscripts R, P and N, which are laconic, and its beginning is missing in O for the same reason. It occurs in full in the other Blegywryd manuscripts and the readings are very similar across the versions. The Blegywryd version

---

[116] Jenkins, *Agricultural Co-Operation*.

[117] *Ibid.*, 1.

[118] *Ibid.*, 2.

[119] The sentence also occurs in Latin A and Latin B but not in Blegywryd. *LlCol*, 68.

[120] There are references to *comar*, the Irish equivalent of *cyfar*, in the Irish legal texts; while there is no tract on *comar*, the references show that it had a set of rules which were similar to the Welsh ones.

[121] See *LlIor*, 154/1, 'am llugyr yt'; 160/9, 'Ac yuelly e teruynyr am lugyr yt'; the heading of the section in manuscript U is 'kyfreith yt a gwarchay', see AL, heading to GC II.xxviii.

is also very similar to the Cyfnerth version of the same tractate, and the values for the animals are the same. The version in Latin D is also the same as that in Blegywryd, and it is written entirely in Welsh in Latin D. This suggests strongly that this was an early written text that was included as it was into the extant Latin D manuscript, and it was not translated. It may explain the similarity between the Blegywryd version and the Cyfnerth version, since there is very little change in the text across the two redactions or in Latin D. It is difficult to suggest why it was not translated in Latin D, however, but it may be that it was in Welsh in the first place, and that no adapting of the material took place.

The basic concept of Corn Damage as set out in the tractate in Cyfnerth/Blegywryd is that it states what the compensation should be when an animal has been found on someone's crop. The tractate is ordered by animal and the compensation varies as different animals behave differently. While the tractate is called 'Impounding and Corn Damage' in U, there is very little discussion of impounding on the whole in this version of the text. However, the version in Iorwerth is different and has a much heavier focus on impounding. The Iorwerth Corn Damage tractate is considerably longer than that in Cyfnerth/Blegywryd, and it is orderly and well-written. The focus in Iorwerth is less on the payment or penalty for having one's animal caught on someone else's crop, but rather on how to go about catching and holding the animals, giving different rules for different times of the year according to the agricultural cycle. The payment for releasing animals from the pound is given. In Iorwerth the Corn Damage tractate is a text on impounding, and a self-help action – the owner of the crop does not have to seek out the owner of the animal, but rather he holds the animal so that its owner can claim it and thus admit liability. To have the animal returned its owner must pay, or else lose the animal; either way, this ensures compensation for the crop farmer.

There is also a Corn Damage section in Col, and Dafydd Jenkins states that there is little difference between the versions in Col and Iorwerth, but that Col is clearer and better organised, although the text in Col breaks off, which Jenkins attributes to missing leaves in an exemplar of Col, as there is no natural break in the text at this point.[122] Col also has an interesting reference to an older tradition, where the situation in 'Cyfraith Hywel' is described (interesting in that the text in Col does not identify with 'Cyfraith Hywel') but then we are told how Bleddyn ap Cynfyn changed the rules on pigs.[123] There is an awareness here of an older tradition for the same piece of law, that there was a different practice, but it was changed. It also emphasises the age (and venerability) of the piece of law. Both the Iorwerth and Col versions of the text may be derived from a text similar to the one in the Cyfnerth manuscripts, and there is evidence for this happening in other sections too.[124]

The evidence from the Latin texts is less useful. There are only four lines of the tractate in Latin C, which is a fragmentary text, and the section in Latin A, B and E is very short (it is broken down into several even shorter sections in Latin E) and follows the same idea as in the Cyfnerth/Blegywryd version. Latin E also includes

---

[122] *LlCol*, 76.

[123] *LlCol*, §184.

[124] At the end of the Corn Damage section in Z, there are additional rules that are not in Corn Damage in the other Cyfnerth manuscripts, although some of them are in X as well. These additional rules in Z are echoed in other sections (not Corn Damage) in Iorwerth. Among these sections in Z is material that is found in the *torri troed anifail* ('breaking an animal's foot') section in Iorwerth, so there may be a Cyfnerth basis for this section in Iorwerth. Jenkins, *Cyfraith Hywel*, 10.

the proverb *tal glan gwedy halauc lw* (*telitor wedi haloc lw* in Cyfnerth/Blegywryd; 'clean payment/it is paid for a fouled oath') in Welsh, but this is not found in the Iorwerth version.[125] However, one of the Latin E sections of the text also includes the proverb-style saying that is given in Iorwerth: *Et hic est locus ubi animal domitum capit silvestre, a llyna e guyllt a deyle y dof* ('and that is the wild one which the tame one catches').[126]

The text itself is a subject that seems to have been under discussion early on, since the Cyfnerth version has a rare example – for that tractate – of different views by jurists, and it gives an old and new version of the compensation for some animals.[127] It would make sense that the Cyfnerth version of the text was the original version, and the standard version in general use, copied into the lawtexts – including in Welsh into Latin D. It was a fairly static piece of law. However, it was rewritten in a different form in Iorwerth, perhaps derived from the Cyfnerth version, or with the knowledge that there was a known section called *Llwgr Yd* in the lawtexts. It is possible that the section was rewritten to reflect actual practice, and that the Cyfnerth/Blegywryd version was old and outdated; the Iorwerth version is innovative. But the interesting issue with Corn Damage in Iorwerth is that there is some overlap with English practice. Jenkins noted that Corn Damage was similar to 'Cattle Trespass' in Common Law, but in fact the Iorwerth Corn Damage is perhaps closer to an action called 'Distress Damage Feasant'.[128] This was a self-help action in England, and is described as being 'dictated as well by good sense as by human nature'.[129] In Distress Damage Feasant a person could impound trespassing animals as security for compensation, and the system seems to have worked in a very similar fashion to the Iorwerth Corn Damage section.

Jenkins suggested that the developed version of Corn Damage in Iorwerth and the *Cyfar* section, where the Iorwerth tract details the obligations that stemmed from the contract that the participants made with each other, reflected real, current legal usage, and this is likely to be the case.[130] Both sections are similar in that they appear to take an earlier bit of law, found in Cyfnerth texts, and they are either rewritten to reflect actual practice, or are written out in full with details on the procedure in the case of *Cyfar*. This may be the work of Iorwerth ap Madog, but if not Iorwerth himself, these sections of the Test Book show that justices in Gwynedd in the mid-thirteenth century were reworking older sections of law and incorporating them into their books. This served a dual purpose. It made the lawbook more useful and perhaps even more up-to-date, but it also kept the link to the authority of the traditional Cyfraith Hywel lawbooks, maintaining terms or even concepts that were seen to be part of the traditional law of Wales. Stacey emphasises this duality, the mixing of the 'current and archaic', in her work on suretyship (contract) in the Welsh laws. The old had the purpose of overlaying tradition and giving authority, including to sections newly created to reflect contemporary practice: 'To sanction their work, the lawyers needed to retain and perhaps even to embellish what was old.'[131]

---

[125] *LTWL*, 489; *Pomffred*, 104–105, #511. There is a different version in Blegywryd: *J(ed.)*, 77.30.

[126] *LTWL*, 507; *Lllor*, 156/6; *LTMW*, 205.

[127] *Pomffred*, #496.

[128] *LTMW*, 305. On Distress Damage Feasant, see Williams, *Liability for Animals*.

[129] Williams, *Liability for Animals*, 7.

[130] Jenkins, *Cyfraith Hywel*, 90.

[131] Stacey, *The Road to Judgment*, 181; Chapter 7, 179–198 on 'Past and Present in the Law of Hywel' focuses on this very aspect. A further example, that of the right of a woman to stand as

Finally, the Corn Damage section and its parallels with the English Distress Damage Feasant action may be very revealing. Dafydd Jenkins states that these sections are '*cyfraith fyw*' ('living law'),[132] but what Corn Damage shows is that Welsh law was not being practiced or studied in a vacuum, but in a situation that had regular contact with England. In the case of *Cyfar* and Corn Damage, 'their addition is a sign that population was increasing, so that pressure on land was also increasing when the tractates were written', but it also tells us a great deal about the circumstances of law and legal contact in thirteenth-century Gwynedd.[133]

Custom and Law

Important though the lawbooks were as a source of law determining the outcome of a dispute, there is evidence showing that the law set out in the lawbooks was not treated as being the only possible source of law. The texts contain reference to the acceptance of unwritten law and to custom.

Some hints on how to find the best possible outcome for a legal case – apart from having several lawbooks to hand – are found in the Blegywryd texts, in a section that is found nearer the end of the manuscripts, usually preceding *Arferion Cyfraith*.

> Cyfraith Anysgrifenedig
>
> Beth bynnac nyt yscriuenner mywn kyfreith ac a aller trwy dylyet y gyffelybu y'r hynn a yscriuennwyt yn ossodedic, kynhaladwy vyd yn lle kyfreith yn y dadleueu, kany ellir yscriuennu pop peth o'r a vo reit y dywedut neu y varnu. Kyfreith heuyt a dyweit, 'o'r kyffelybyon, kyffelyb varn a dylyir'.[134]

> Unwritten Law
>
> Whatever is not written in law and can through right be compared to that which is stated in writing, it is to be maintained in the place of law in pleadings, because it is not possible to write everything which it is necessary to state or to judge. Law also says, 'from similar [cases], there is to be a similar judgement'.[135]

The discussion on unwritten law appears to add a further level of flexibility – and also suggests that there were no scribes recording all the judgements in medieval Wales. While the procedure for questioning judgements emphasises the importance of finding a better, or the best, written judgement, the section on the inclusion of unwritten law points out that it would be impossible to write down absolutely everything, and therefore if something is more or less the same as a piece of law written in a lawbook, then it may be included. It allowed the justices some discretion and interpretation of

---

surety, is discussed by Stacey in 'The Archaic Core of Llyfr Iorwerth', 23–27. 'Ior's compiler, anxious that his lawbook reflect what he knew to be contemporary practice, chose nevertheless to reinterpret rather than to abandon the old material with which he was working.'

[132] Jenkins, *Cyfraith Hywel*, 12.

[133] Jenkins, *Hunting and Husbandry*, 2.

[134] *J(ed.)*, 85.37–86.5. The title is not found in the manuscripts.

[135] Robin Stacey points out that the quoted statement in this passage corresponds to a similar statement in Bracton, and Julian's Digest Book, and a similar statement is found in the *Collectio Canonum Hibernensis*; the Welsh lawyers were part of a wider European tradition. With thanks to Robin Stacey for discussing this matter with me.

decisions. This places an emphasis on consistency and fairness in the law, and also predictability, so that people know the consequences of particular actions – and they have the additional benefit of being able to settle out of court. This section of Welsh law looks like an earlier step in establishing precedent (or something like it) in the first place, and while the Welsh lawbooks cannot be called 'precedent books' and have no similarity to such things, they may be the result of discussions on subjects such as the best outcome in legal cases within the courts.

In addition, the section on unwritten law is preceded by another very important section on procedures to follow in judgements, and this takes the form of a series of triads.

Cynefodau

Teir kynnefawt yssyd: kynnefawt a erlit kyfreith – kynhaladwy yw; a chynnefawt a raculaena kyfreith – or byd awdurdawt brenhinyaeth idi, kynhaladwy yw; kynnefawt a lyckro kyfreith, ny dylyir y chynnal.

Tri pheth a gadarnhaa kynnefawt: aduwynder, a gallu, ac awdurdawt.

Tri pheth a wanha kynnefawt: gorthrymder, ac angheugant uonhed, a dryc angreith. A hi a wrthledir rac dryc angreith.[136]

Customs

There are three customs: a custom which follows law, it is to be upheld; and a custom which precedes law, if it have royal authority, it is to be upheld; and a custom which corrupts law, it is not to be upheld.

Three things which strengthen custom: fairness, and competence, and authority.

Three things which weaken a custom: oppression, and doubtful origin, and bad example. And it [i.e. *cynefod*] is confounded by bad example.

The lawtexts state quite clearly that the justices used lawbooks in order to determine whether a decision was correct or not. The symbolic threat of the justice losing his position and having to pay the value of his tongue to the king if he was found to be wrong suggests that the justice was expected to do much of the work of checking the books himself to ensure that he had made the correct decision. But the section preceding the treatment of incorporating unwritten law discusses customs, and this is a clue to how the law got into the lawbooks in the first place. Dafydd Jenkins discussed this in an article in 1990, and stated there that nowhere in the laws is 'custom' defined.[137] However, he notes that in relation to medieval Wales and the Welsh lawtexts, 'the general principle in our period is quite clearly that the authority of a legal rule comes neither from custom nor from the sovereign but from its being written in a lawbook'.[138] This is presumably why the triads on custom are included in the Blegywryd texts, and why they are in their position, preceding a section on unwritten law, and then *Arferion Cyfraith*. This is an attempt at summarising how the justice was to decide whether what he was using, or wanted to use, was appropriate or even good, and whether it should be included in his lawbook to be used in court as

---

[136] *J(ed.)*, 85.29–36. The title is not found in the manuscripts.
[137] Jenkins, 'Custom in Welsh Medieval Law', 426.
[138] *Ibid.*

one of the options from which the correct judgement would be chosen. The lawbooks had to come from somewhere, and while custom was one of the possible sources, this does not mean that this was a true *volksrecht* system: scholarly individuals created their books, and if those books were then deemed authoritative by others they would be cited accordingly, regardless of the origin of the rules.

The first of the three triads on custom gives guidelines as to whether a justice could accept what was said to be custom or not, and the suggestions are very basic indeed – customs were to be followed if they were in accordance with the law or if they had royal authority, but otherwise customs that stated matters that were contrary to law were not to be followed.[139] This assumes some knowledge of the law and suggests that there was somewhere the justice could verify what the law said. The other pair of triads state the things that make a custom a good one to follow, and the opposite situation, and again they are fairly basic ideas; if a custom is fair, competent (or from a good source) and has authority, the nature of which is left unstated, then the custom is 'strong' and presumably can be followed. However, if the custom is introduced through oppression or is forced on the justice or the people, or is of doubtful origin – again the exact nature of doubtful origin is not explained – and is basically a bad custom, then it is not to be followed; and if it is a bad custom it is to be disregarded completely. A further triad found in the triad collection in all Blegywryd manuscripts states the importance of customs to the law.

Tri pheth a tyrr ar gyfreith: amot, a defaʋt gyfyaʋn, ac agheu.

Three things that cut across law: contract, and a just custom, and death.[140]

Amod was the general word used in the lawtexts for a contract, but it could also refer to a special form of contract.[141] Death is an amusing third item.[142] But according to this triad an appropriate custom can override law – the custom should be followed. The section on customs in general is rather unclear on determining exactly what made a custom 'just' and whether it even could override law.

The importance of custom to the work of the Welsh justice is outlined in the Court Justice's section in the Blegywryd Laws of Court – it occurs in all Blegywryd manuscripts except O, T, Llan, Bost and Tim, and it is also in Latin D. The section states the procedure if a king wishes to place *nebun anghyfrwys ac amparawt* ('someone unskilled/untrained and unready/inexperienced') as a court justice.[143] The person is to shadow the existing justices and spend time in the court watching and learning, and he must know the Three Columns of Law, and the Value of Wild and Tame, but must also spend time 'learning laws and practices and customs and the

---

[139] Jenkins discusses the exact meaning of the triad in detail in his study: *Ibid.*, 428–429.

[140] *LT*, 136–137; the translation 'cut across' for 'tyrr ar' follows *Ibid.*, 428.

[141] *LTMW*, 252.

[142] In *LT*, the reading *angeu*, 'death', was followed, since it occurs in the majority of the manuscripts, but some of the manuscripts have the reading *angen*, 'necessity'. Naturally there is a minim issue here too, but in Latin D, where the triad occurs in Welsh, Emanuel chose the reading '*agheu*', but a note states that the copy of his D1 has '*angeu* altered marginally to *angen*'. *LTWL*, 373. Cf. 'Aghen a dyrr dedyf', found in the collection of proverbs in manuscript Q, and transcribed thus in the full transcript of the manuscript.

[143] *J(ed.)*, 11.

ordinances of the King which pertain to authority'.[144] The order of the sentence varies in the texts. The majority of the manuscripts have the items listed in the same order in which they occur in J:

> dyscu kyfreitheu a gossodedigaethau y brenhin ac arueroed a deuoteu a berthynont wrth awdurdawt ...[145]

In manuscripts L and Tr the order is the one found in *LlBleg*, which was taken from L at that point, and which was translated by Jenkins in the translation given above.

> dyscu kyureitheu ac arueroed a deuodeu a gossodedigaetheu y brenhin a berthynont vrth aỏdurdaỏt ac yn bennaf ...

S has a different version not shared by any others, and seems to have removed the reference to the king, which would accord with S being later and written in post-conquest south Wales, or alternatively this could be a case of eyeskip.

> dyscu kyfreith a gossotdedigaetheu a berthynnynt ỏrth audyrdaỏt ...

The version in Latin D is also different – apart from being in Latin – and focuses on royal authority. This version may be the earliest since Latin D predates the Blegywryd redaction, but Latin D has '*que usu ... habentur*' as its version of *defodau* and *arferoedd*, both words for custom, but keeps it vague with *aliorum*, 'other people'.

> et addiscere leges et constituciones regis, nec non, si poterit, aliorum que usu et auctoritate habentur ...[146]

> and to learn the laws and regulations of the king, as well as, if he can, of others, which are held by practice and authority ...

Despite the Blegywryd texts' insistence on custom being an important aspect of what the court justice needed to know, and the vague suggestions of how to incorporate custom into law (and when not to do so), there are very few references to custom in the Blegywryd texts. Naturally, most of the law may have originated from custom at one stage, but finding sections that could be attributed to custom, or sections that could be said to be newly-added, is very difficult if not impossible in the Blegywryd texts. That may be because the lawbooks were necessary to support judgements in court; as a result, all of the sections of the Blegywryd lawtexts were presented as definitive, and had authority that left no room for doubt. Manuscripts S and Tim may have been created as a book for a *dosbarthwr*, and were intended for use in court to prove judgements and find the best possible outcome and, as a result, there is little to refer to the making of the law or any hints at alternatives or doubts in those manuscripts. Their purpose was to give the final answer, and this is largely true of the Blegywryd redaction as a whole.

---

[144] *LTMW, 142.*
[145] *J(ed.)*, 11. A similar version is found in M, Q and its copies Ep and P, R, I, N and Y on f. 57r.
[146] *LTWL*, 325.

The 'Debate Pattern'

The lawbooks show that the contents of the law were not fixed. There are topics upon which the law was at some stage debated, with different views as to the correct answer being given, showing the work of lawyers (named and unnamed) in developing the law over time. While there is one reference to an alternative view in the Blegywryd texts,[147] and a handful in the Cyfnerth texts, mainly in sections discussing animals and sworn appraisal of objects,[148] the Iorwerth texts have several examples of various options in the legal rules. Throughout the Iorwerth texts there are sentences that state that there was some discussion on the exact letter of the law, and opposing views are presented.[149] This may show more of the background of the making of the law, and where the justices were getting their material as well as the debates surrounding procedure or process in the law.

> Rey a dyweyt na dygwyd gwystyl o law vach hyt em pen vn dyd a blwydyn; e kyvreyth a dyweyt e dygwyd gwystyl o law try dyn en y oet. Esef ew e try dyn henny ...

> Some say that a gage is not forfeit from the hand of a surety for a period of a day and a year; the law says that a gage is forfeit from the hand of three persons at its appointed time. Those three persons are ...[150]

> Pwy bynnac a gwystlo gwystyl adevedyc a thebygw ohonaw ef vrth nat oes vach arnaw bot en anylys e gwystyl hwnnw, e kyvreyth a dyweyt dygwydaw e gwystyl hvnnv a'y vot en dylys.

> Whoever should give an acknowledged gage and suppose that because there is no surety for it that gage is not immune from claim, the law says that that gage is forfeit and that it is immune from claim.[151]

All of the early manuscripts of the Iorwerth redaction, A, B, C, D and E, have many examples of this pattern. It suggests ongoing discussion of the laws or at the very least that there were attempts to resolve or close debate on a given subject.

Table 3.1: The 'Debate Pattern' in Iorwerth Manuscripts

Section or Tractate	No. of Examples	Notes
Laws of Court		
List of Officers	2	Queen's groom, Watchman
Laws of Country		
Law of Women	4	Sections contain *damweiniau* form

---

[147] In *LlBleg*, 37.26, there is a reference to a statement on the number of witnesses in 'the law of Rome', and the statement looks to be a contrast with Welsh law; but the note by the editors shows that the statement has been somewhat mistranslated into Welsh and in the Latin texts it is simply showing their knowledge of 'the law of Rome' with no comparison. *LlBleg*, 183.

[148] See *Pomffred*, ##925, 954, 496 and 156.

[149] See the texts following this chapter.

[150] *LAL*, 154–155; see also *LlIor*, 66/1–2.

[151] *LAL*, 146–147; see also *LlIor*, 62/9.

Suretyship	11	Sections contain *damweiniau* form
Land Law	11	Sections contain *damweiniau* form
Family Law	2	
Test Book		
The Three Columns of Law	8	
The Value of Wild and Tame	2	Less descriptive prose
Value of Equipment	2	Less descriptive prose
Cyfar	5	Organised tractate
Corn Damage	1	Re-edited tractate
Llyfr Damweiniau		
Damweiniau I and II	7	

In the Laws of Court, there are only two examples of the pattern, and both are sentences in a section discussing a particular officer – the Queen's Chief Groom in the first case, and the Watchman in the second.[152] Neither of these officers is particularly high ranking: the queen's officers are in a separate section, and the Watchman is one of the additional officers 'by custom'. The discussion on the Queen's Chief Groom states that some claim that his protection goes as far as the King's Chief Groom, but 'others' give a different view, and the text does not settle for one or the other. In the case of the Watchman, there is a brief sentence that states that some say that he is entitled to the eyes of the animals killed in the court, but again the text does not confirm or reject this notion. That there are only two examples of these sentences in the lengthy Laws of Court section, and no real decision is made in either case, is probably significant since the Laws of Court was an old section, fixed, and most likely outdated by the time of the creation of the earliest extant Iorwerth manuscripts. There was unlikely to be much discussion on the contents of the Laws of the Court by the mid-thirteenth century, and so the text may not have been heavily amended.[153] But since it is already known that Iorwerth ap Madog and/or other lawyers were still working on the lawtexts in thirteenth-century Gwynedd means that it is less surprising that there are many more references to various opinions and options in other parts of the Iorwerth texts. It is also not surprising that the nature of the references vary depending on the section in which they occur, as the tractates were not all from the same date.

The highest number of examples of this pattern appear in the Suretyship section in the Iorwerth texts, which has 11 of them.[154] There are also 11 in Land Law, though that is a longer section.[155] These tractates have textual similarities. They appear to have been developed for the Iorwerth redaction: Suretyship, for example, has a high number of *damweiniau*-style sentences, stating 'if it happens that …'; and Land Law

---

[152] See the texts in the Appendix to this chapter, nos. 1 and 2.

[153] See, however, the changes made to the queen's officers, possibly under the influence of Queen Joan, the wife of Llywelyn ab Iorwerth. See Pryce, 'The Household Priest', 93; and Stacey, 'King, Queen and Edling', 55. Robin Stacey argues that the Laws of Court do have contemporary relevance and were being frequently amended, but as a vehicle for political commentary rather than for legal reasons: Stacey, *Law and the Imagination*, 56–88.

[154] 7–17 in the Appendix.

[155] 18–28 in the Appendix.

has a section of *cynghawsedd* discussing the procedure in an action for land. Neither of these passages are found in the Cyfnerth or Blegywryd texts, and these tractates are sections where Iorwerth deviates more from the other redactions.[156] In the case of Suretyship, all examples of the discussion pattern occurs in sections that follow the *o derfydd* format, similar to *Llyfr Damweiniau*, and this gives it the air of a debate in a law school rather than a formal written text. The same is true of the occurrences of the pattern in Land Law – in general, the sentence containing the pattern will start with *o derfydd*. This may suggest that the sections of Land Law and Suretyship containing debate and differing opinions – 'some say' and 'we say' – or those with the clear statement 'the law says', are sections of the Iorwerth text that were being discussed by lawyers, in legal schools even, and that the Iorwerth text as is extant in the earliest manuscripts is a work-in-progress and an attempt to bring together differing views and determine or state the best version of the law.

There are four examples of the pattern in the Law of Women, but this is a tractate that is fairly similar across the redactions.[157] Only one of them suggests that there is a debate – 'some lawyers' versus 'us' – and the remainder simply refer to what the law states, or the stance taken by this text, on a particular matter to give it more force. However, as with the examples in Land Law and Suretyship, in the Law of Women the pattern occurs in sections that are worded as *damweiniau*, opening with *o derfydd*. Linked to the Law of Women is the section on Family Law, discussing children and inheritance, but this tractate is of a different nature. There are many self-conscious references to this being a written text – *E deu uab rydywedassam ny uchot* ('the two sons we named above') – and referring back to something to avoid rewriting things that have already been explained in full. There are only two examples of debate here, and both state that some may be uncertain about the situation but then follows with *e keureyth a dyweyt* ('the law states'), making it very clear.[158] This section clearly has a written tradition and it is also organised and orderly – and Iorwerth's form may be a more final one. Sections of the text do occur in Cyfnerth and Blegywryd but not as an orderly section.

Further support to the suggestion that the Family Law tractate was rewritten for the Iorwerth redaction can be found in the use that is made of a triad in the text. The triad, *Tri dygyngoll cenedl* ('The three dire losses of a kindred'), occurs at different points in the different redactions, and in the Blegywryd redaction the triad is found in the Three Columns of Law section as it refers to homicide.[159] In Iorwerth, however, there is an introductory section and the triad is not presented with the usual 'triad heading' but it is broken down to some extent – this may be because whoever was writing the section on Family Law had a triad in a text that he was using, and he rewrote it within his essay.[160] However, judging by the material included at this point the compiler of the text was not using anything resembling an extant Cyfnerth or Blegywryd text containing the triad, as the version of the triad in Iorwerth is different.[161] This use of the triad may be further evidence that this section on Family Law

---

[156] Several of the Iorwerth tractates have a systematic text followed by miscellanea on the same subject, and the second part of the tractates often take the form of *damweiniau* or other genres. Daube, 'Codes and Coda', 75, 81, 97–98.

[157] 3–6 in the Appendix.

[158] 29–30 in the Appendix.

[159] Roberts, '*Tri Dygyngoll Cenedl*', 167.

[160] *Ibid.*, 169–170.

[161] *Ibid.*, 170, 173.

was formally written, and done so in a way that removed much of the debate on the subject – unlike the Suretyship and Land Law sections in Iorwerth.

The same is broadly true of the contents of the Test Book in Iorwerth. While the debate pattern does occur in the Test Book, it does so less frequently than in the Land Law and Suretyship sections, and again the Three Columns tractate has more references to written law, which suggests at least an attempt at a more formal text.[162] The Value of Wild and Tame has far fewer examples, only two, as does the list of values of equipment, but both of these texts are more like handbooks than other sections of the laws, and their prose is less descriptive.[163] The Test Book was the text that justices needed to know in order to practise, and as such it may be that the discussion on the best procedure or the best outcome had already concluded by the time of the earliest manuscripts of Iorwerth. The list of equipment, Corn Damage, and the neatly constructed *Cyfar* (Co-tillage) contract make up the remainder of the Test Book. Corn Damage has only one example of the debate pattern but, by contrast, *Cyfar*, a well-written and organised tractate, has several examples.[164] The Test Book may have been the work of Iorwerth ap Madog, where sections from the Laws of Country were moved to make a new book, but the nature of *Cyfar* and Corn Damage is rather different. *Cyfar* does not occur in Cyfnerth or Blegywryd, apart from a passing sentence in Cyfnerth naming the procedure, and may have been written up as a contract in thirteenth-century Gwynedd, perhaps even by Iorwerth ap Madog himself; it may have been the subject of discussion in certain circles, and the creator of the section may have written in full the procedure that was being – or was to be – followed in a *Cyfar* situation but with reference to other opinions. All of the examples in *Cyfar* state 'the law says' rather than presenting different views; manuscripts E and A usually have 'we say' rather than 'the law says', again suggesting discussion in juristic circles. This may be an attempt at having clarity in the rules in this newly-created section, and it confers authority. The Corn Damage section is different – Corn Damage occurs in Cyfnerth, Blegywryd and the Latin texts, but it is rewritten in a different format for Iorwerth's version in the Test Book. There may have been less discussion on this section, and perhaps what was said in an earlier text was the starting point for the new version, so there was less of a need to discuss with others, since existing written texts were being consulted.

These regular references to variant law or legal debate in the Iorwerth texts may tell us a great deal about the circumstances of creating the texts themselves. Iorwerth ap Madog may not have been the only justice working on a legal text, or reworking written texts that he had at his disposal – certainly there is evidence to show that the redactor of Col was also doing this at roughly the same time – but it also shows that the law was not a fixed text, that there was room for discussion, and that some at least of the discussion could be incorporated into the lawtexts. Some parts of the Iorwerth texts may have been written out in a formal way, such as *Cyfar*; but it may be the case that other parts were less formal and more a work in progress – this certainly seems to be the case for Suretyship and Land Law, and perhaps also in *Llyfr Damweiniau*, which has seven examples of the pattern.[165] And it is in these sections that we see most evidence of using different sources to create the law, but not all of them written sources, and perhaps this shows how custom could be incorporated into the law in

---

[162] 31–33 in the Appendix.

[163] 39–40 and 41–42, respectively, in the Appendix.

[164] 48, and 43–47 in the Appendix.

[165] 49–55 in the Appendix.

the Iorwerth texts. This compares with the later Blegywryd procedures on customs and incorporating unwritten law.

The Blegywryd texts have a more formal appearance and do not 'show their workings' in the same way, perhaps because they were intended as a definitive text on which to base judgements in court. However, while there is little or no emphasis in the Iorwerth texts for using the written texts in actual legal cases (as opposed to training lawyers), and the Iorwerth texts may be the work of lawyers, there is some interesting evidence in one of the manuscripts for an attempt at greater formality in the text itself. Manuscript B is the subject of the only modern edition of a Iorwerth text and, as such, *LlIor* (along with the highly valuable translation made by Dafydd Jenkins) is the text that is relied upon by scholars working on the field.[166] Manuscript B is one of the earliest law manuscripts, and is only slightly later than manuscript A, the Black Book of Chirk. Thomas Charles-Edwards, in his re-examination of the Iorwerth text, noted that manuscript B seemed to show 'a consistent hostility, or at least studied lack of interest, in the name of Iorwerth ap Madog', since the Test Book preface naming Iorwerth, as well as the entire *Llyfr Damweiniau*, were omitted altogether or replaced by *cynghawsedd*. B's Test Book preface is a shorter version with no reference to Iorwerth ap Madog.[167]

> Llyma e gueles e doethyon bot en grynno escryuennu guerth e tey a'r doodreuyn, ac am kyuar a llugyr yt, ygyt a'r Llyuer Prauf.[168]

> Here the wise men saw that it would be useful to write the value of the houses and the equipment, and about *Cyfar* and Corn Damage, together with the Test Book.

Llyfr Damweiniau is another section of law where occasionally the debate pattern appears,[169] but perhaps the most significant of these is the reference to Iorwerth ap Madog himself.

> Rey a dyweyt panyu dyn amdyuenhedyc, [hynny] yu kyuarch kyfyll. Ereyll a dyweyt panyu derwen a ladher yn agkyuarch ar trew tat pryodaur, a dylyu dody mantell arnau o'y gudyau rac y welet, a bot yn waratwyd y'r trew tadauc y welet. Jorwerth uab Madauc eyssyoes a dyweyt panyu hun yu kyuarch kyfyll yn yaun: sew yu hynny, pan ...[170]

> Some say that when a man has been cut off from everything, that is *cyfarch cyffyll*. Others say that it is when an oak is felled without permission on the patrimony of a proprietor, a mantle ought to be put on it to hide it from sight, and that it is an insult to the patrimonial to see it. Iorwerth ap Madog however states that it is this that is rightly a *cyfarch cyffyll*: that is, when ...

---

[166] *LlIor*; *LTMW*.

[167] Charles-Edwards, 'The Textual Tradition', 42.

[168] *LlIor*, §139. The note gives the reading in other manuscripts in place of 'doethyon': Yorverth vap madavc vap rahavt C; yoruerth am madauc E; yoruerth vab madauc A. In fact, the wording of the preface is almost dismissive of the Test Book itself – it is the last item listed. The text does not see the Test Book as containing *Cyfar*, Corn Damage, or the value of houses and equipment, so presumably only the Three Columns of Law and the Value of Wild and Tame.

[169] There are more examples of the construction in Damweiniau I than in Damweiniau II (see Chapter 4), and it is not as common in either as it is in the Iorwerth texts.

[170] Manuscript E, BL Additional MS 14931, 100–101. The word *amdyuenhedyc* is very problematic.

According to this section, Iorwerth ap Madog was active in legal discussion in the region and he is linked to *Llyfr Damweiniau*, as a legal authority. It is this reference that may have led the compiler of Iorwerth B to omit the *damweiniau* entirely, and remove all traces of Iorwerth ap Madog from his manuscript.[171] The *Llyfr Cynghawsedd*, which the compiler appended to his Iorwerth text, instead has no debate or discussion and is a straightforward model of how to plead.

In addition, there is another interesting development in manuscript B, in its treatment of the debate pattern sections. Rather than have the usual 'some say ... we say' construction found in the other Iorwerth texts, B has something more authoritative: 'some say ... the law says'. All self-referencing 'we say' examples appear as 'the law' instead in B. This may be a further attempt to give B more authority, and also to place the text at a remove from the law schools or the discussions of jurists. Rather than being something that was under discussion, debate in B is over, and the actual form of the law is fixed. That B did not include a collection of *damweiniau* at the end of the manuscript is also interesting: *damweiniau* are full of legal discussions and have less force, but the compiler of B seems to have been less keen on the open-ended discussion and instead included *cynghawsedd*, which are model pleadings but which take a very prescriptive approach to the legal cases and does not include the familiar debate pattern (although there is debate in direct speech in *cynghawsedd*). This suggests two things: first, that B wanted to avoid the link to Iorwerth ap Madog and the discussions among justices, perhaps to present a version of the law with no argument or discussion; and also that it seems that the Test Book did not actually end with Corn Damage and something else was expected to follow. For the other Iorwerth texts the ending was a version of *Llyfr Damweiniau*, but B substituted this with the more formal and perhaps more authoritative *Llyfr Cynghawsedd* instead.

Powys and the Law

One final aspect of the subject of creating the law needs to be discussed, and that is the relationship between the lawtexts and the different customs that could exist in different places. The Iorwerth texts have a clear Gwynedd origin, and the Blegywryd texts are generally later and belong to south Wales. There is evidence for a clear written tradition in Gwynedd and Deheubarth, and all discussions on law and legal texts refer to these two major regions with their own lawbook traditions and manuscripts. David Stephenson, talking generally about medieval Welsh history, notes that 'discussion tends to be centred on the rulers of Gwynedd, and their rise to be princes of a wider Welsh polity, though the similarly ambitious and successful Lord Rhys of Deheubarth is also accorded much attention ... it would be wrong to assume that they represent anything like a comprehensive portrayal of the multifaceted political dynamics of Wales'.[172] The third major region in Wales in the central middle ages was Powys, and it is not omitted from the lawbooks. Indeed, in a section found in some fifteenth-century manuscripts, the *sarhaed* (payment for a deliberate injury) is listed for four countries. The fourth is England, but in this list Powys follows Gwynedd, and is listed before Deheubarth.[173] This is unlikely to be a text that originated in south

---

[171] Charles-Edwards, 'The *Galanas* Tractate in Iorwerth', 102.
[172] Stephenson, *Medieval Wales c.1050–1332*, 1.
[173] See *Pomffred*, 158–159: *Pwybynac a syrhao neb o werin o bedair gwlad, nid amgen Gwynedd, Powys, Deheubarth, a Lloygyr* ... / Whoever causes *sarhaed* to anyone of the natives of four

Wales. This representation of medieval Wales in the lawbooks is likely to originate from around the mid-twelfth century, when Powys was at its height and could be counted as 'one of the major realms of twelfth-century Wales'.[174] While there had been an extensive ancient kingdom of Powys, during the tenth and eleventh centuries much of it had been subordinate to Gwynedd and some parts were under English rule; it took shape as a result of territorial acquisitions under Maredudd ap Bleddyn, whose son Madog ap Maredudd (ruled 1132–1160) was responsible for Powys's 'Age of Eminence'.[175] The political circumstances in Powys, therefore, were rather different to those of its neighbour in Gwynedd, and a natural consequence of that is that there is likely to be a different legal culture in Powys.

Charles-Edwards states:

> There is no evidence that any surviving lawbook derives from Powys. While the division of Wales into three major units probably reflects an earlier stage when the political claims of Powys were more generously treated by the lawyers, the generally unfavourable thrust of the existing lawbooks is unmistakeable ... One of the defects of Welsh law as evidence is, therefore, the lack of a lawbook from Powys.[176]

The Cyfnerth text as has been noted had links to Maelienydd, but there is no corresponding lawbook tradition from Powys to rival that in thirteenth-century Gwynedd, or the later lawbooks of Deheubarth. Cyfraith Hywel was of course intended to apply to every Welshman, but the political history of Wales may have made this impossible. It is certain that there was a legal tradition in Powys and it would have been originally a very Welsh legal system, part of the Cyfraith Hywel tradition; the difference is that it may not have been a written system in the way that the Iorwerth redaction can be seen as evidence of the legal system for Gwynedd.

There are some sections of the extant lawbooks, however, that have a clear link to Powys. The aforementioned *Llyfr Cynyr ap Cadwgan*, a short text on legal theory, is linked to a man for whom there is other evidence, and Cynyr ap Cadwgan (and his sons) worked as legal experts in Arwystli, which was part of Powys at various points in its history.[177] David Stephenson has also discussed the Powysian links of *Llyfr Cynog* in some detail, and although he describes it quite accurately as 'something of an enigma', he shows that it holds Bleddyn ap Cynfyn, the eleventh-century ruler, king of Gwynedd but ancestor of the Powys dynasty, in high regard.[178] Bleddyn ap Cynfyn was certainly active in law – apart from the references in *Llyfr Cynog*, there is a reference in the Iorwerth texts to his activity as a lawmaker.[179] Stephenson

---

countries, namely Gwynedd, Powys, Deheubarth, and England ....

[174] Stephenson, *Medieval Powys*, 38.

[175] *Ibid.*, 1–8, 23, 38, *passim*. Chapter 2 is titled 'The Age of Eminence: Madog ap Maredudd'.

[176] Charles-Edwards, *The Welsh Laws*, 44. A further problem is the position of Rhwng Gwy a Hafren in relation to Powys, and defining Powys in the middle ages: see Charles-Edwards, 'Dynastic Succession in Early Medieval Wales', 80–83.

[177] AL IV.i.28–29 follows a discussion on the death of clerics, and states that in cases of disputes among clerics, *eneyt or clas a dele barnu udunt* ('justices from the *clas* [pre-Norman monastic community in Wales] are to judge for them', but disputes between lay lords and ecclesiastical are to be decided by *egneyt er argluyt* ('the justices of the lord').

[178] Stephenson, *Medieval Powys*, 210–211.

[179] See *LTMW*, 98, where the text states that Bleddyn ap Cynfyn changed the number of acres for the division of land; and 165 where he is stated to have fixed the rules on sworn appraisal instead of 'payment and second payment'.

concludes that 'in part of Wales at least the law of Bleddyn did not replace the law of Hywel but operated alongside that law and enjoyed something approaching parity of esteem. It is hard to avoid the suspicion that the law of Bleddyn was or became primarily a Powysian law.'[180] However, it is possible to go further – the law of Bleddyn, be it in *Llyfr Cynog* or elsewhere, not only worked in parallel to Welsh law but it was sometimes incorporated into it, as is shown with the reference to Bleddyn's adaptation of the law of sworn appraisal.[181]

That the laws could incorporate customs, assuming that they were appropriate for inclusion, is stated in the Blegywryd texts, and one of the things to consider when looking at the use of custom in the laws was whether the custom 'preceded' law, or had royal authority, and if that was the case then the custom was to be 'upheld'. Bleddyn ap Cynfyn had a clear royal authority. Having said that, Rhys ap Gruffudd was said to have involved himself in lawmaking too:

> Pop peth ar ny bo arnaw gwerth kyfreith, damdwng a geffir amdanaw herwyd kyfreith Howel. Rys uab Gruffud, arbennic Deheubarth, trwy duundeb a'e wlat a ossodes gwerth damdwng ar bop llwdyn, nyt amgen no thyngu o'r perchen y talei y lwdyn y gwerth a wnelei arnaw ac y kaffei yna yrdaw.[182]

> For everything which has no legal value, sworn appraisal is allowed according to the law of Hywel. Rhys ap Gruffudd, the suzerain of Deheubarth, by agreement with his country laid down sworn appraisal for every beast, to wit, that the owner should swear that the beast was worth the value he put on it, and that he would get that for it.[183]

The comment on a custom 'preceding' law is complex and rather difficult to explain, but it may fit with the idea that unwritten law could be included as part of Welsh law, or as part of the matter available to a justice in south Wales (if not elsewhere); and it may be that the custom 'precedes' law before it is written, so the contrast is with written law. However, that Powys had laws is not in doubt, and references are found in Iorwerth to other customs in Powys.[184]

Reference is made there to an alternative procedure in Powys for accepting or denying a son from a kindred, in the Iorwerth Family Law section:[185]

> Herwyd guyr Powys, ony byd na that na penkenedel, deg wyr a deu ugeynt a'e kymer ac a'e guatta.[186]

> According to the men of Powys, if there is neither father nor chief of kindred, fifty men accept him and deny him.[187]

---

[180] Stephenson, *Medieval Powys*, 213.
[181] *LTMW*, 165.
[182] *J(ed.)*, 82.13–18.
[183] *LTMW*, 164.
[184] Outside of the lawbooks, there is a very important poem on *Breintiau Gwŷr Powys* ('The Liberties of the Men of Powys') by Cynddelw Brydydd Mawr. The poem is a legal appeal by the nobility in Powys against their rulers, and it was included in *Ancient Laws* as a piece of law. See Charles-Edwards and Jones, '*Breintiau Gwŷr Powys*', 191–223.
[185] On the Family Law section, see above, 78.
[186] *LlIor*, §103/4.
[187] *LTMW*, p. 137.

A more well-known reference to legal practice in Powys is found in Latin B, the *Naw Affaith* ('Nine Abetments') 'according to the men of Powys'.

> Hic incipit de tribus columnis iuris secundum Powissienses.
>
> Tres sunt columpne iuris *herwid guyr Powys: nau affeith galanas, nau affeith tan, nau affeith lledrat.*
>
> *Nau affeith galanas: Dirdra, guereictra, sarhaet, tewessiau cerh, gorduy, brat, kennadwri y rung bratwyr ay elin, gurthareith, lad y gelein.*[188]
>
> Here begin the Three Columns of Law according to the men of Powys.
>
> There are three columns of law according to the men of Powys: nine abetments of *galanas*, nine abetments of fire, nine abetments of theft.
>
> Nine abetments of *galanas*: dispute over land, dispute over a woman, insult, leading an assault, violence, treachery, taking messages between traitors and their enemy, defamation/opposition to law, killing/striking of the body.

This occurs before the *Naw Affaith* according to the men of Gwynedd, which is interesting and it may mean that the Gwynedd text was not the most important, or that the Powys text was not alternative in any way; these may be parallel laws. Russell states that Latin B is important as a text since it 'preserved arrangements and gatherings of material which have been re-edited or ironed out in other versions preserved elsewhere'.[189] However, in this case Latin B is not preserving a text that was written in Latin; the Powysian *Naw Affaith* has a Latin title but the text itself was in Welsh. This may suggest that the exemplar used by Latin B (assuming that there was one) was written in Welsh. A more difficult question to answer is whether there were laws being written in Powys: the written list referencing the way things were done in Powys may have been written from an outside perspective and, given the different political circumstances, it is unlikely that there was an extensive tradition of written law in Powys, at least not separate from the same process in Gwynedd. Powys may not be part of the great textual tradition, but it may have had its own tradition instead. Also, the Powysian *Naw Affaith* text has what appears to be an earlier use of *affaith*, and this suggests that perhaps in Powys there was an awareness of what should be included in the laws – and the *Naw Affaith* may be an 'expected' part of the Three Columns tractate – but either because there was no Iorwerth text available to copy, or because the writer of the section wanted it, the *Naw Affaith* text may have been created in Powys for Powys, not under the influence of Iorwerth.[190]

Conclusion

The discussion has centred on the men who may have been creating the lawbooks of medieval Wales, and the way they worked. The descriptions of the office of the justice found in the lawbooks suggest that there are reasons why the lawbooks often

---

[188] *LTWL*, 250–251.
[189] Russell, '*Y Naw Affaith*', 151.
[190] *Ibid.*, 152.

appear in a particular form – and looking at these reasons, the contexts for the creation of the lawbooks themselves, may free us from some of the problems imposed on the subject by the early editors of Welsh law. The second part of this work will turn to look in more detail at those constructs, and suggest a new approach to the Welsh lawbooks, but the starting point must surely be the texts themselves.

There was considerable flexibility written in to the lawtexts themselves, and the form of the lawtexts, despite being written down, was not necessarily fixed. This suggests that, in examining the lawtexts, we should be equally flexible. The lawtexts and the compilers behind them may have wanted the law to appear authoritative, even definitive, but the society to which it applied was ever-changing and, as a result, so was the law itself. There is plenty of evidence within the Iorwerth texts that the law was still a subject for discussion, and this is reflected in the very wording of some sections of the law. The 'debate pattern' also shows that there were several sources of law from which the lawbook redactors could and did choose. The law was open to incorporating custom and procedures that were being practised – there was indeed 'a sense among Welsh men of law that custom was a discrete component of their jurisprudential landscape'.[191] While the Blegywryd texts do not include the statements showing that discussion was taking place (the 'debate pattern') there is in those texts an explanation of how to incorporate customs into law and the importance of the written texts, but without making the written text exclusive. As Cavell states, 'In Wales the law books being produced in our period accommodate a carefully managed law–custom (very roughly, text–practice) relationship that operated smoothly within the native legal tradition.'[192]

The later Blegywryd lawbooks may have been used in court by *dosbarthwyr* as the very same written texts that they were said to need to prove their judgements or find the best outcome for a case and, as such, they may be rare survivals, but the tip of the iceberg in terms of the existence of mixed legal compilations. The Iorwerth texts on the other hand reveal the creation of the written texts from earlier works, and show the discussions held presumably between justices or perhaps in law schools (in whatever form these may have taken).

Several lawyers are named as the creators of books, or sections of lawbooks. Only some of these works survive, and even then determining the work of the named lawyer in a precise way is difficult. This may be because that would go against the grain of the work that the lawyers were doing. They were not creating law anew, but were drawing on a long written tradition, adapting customs that they knew to be in use, and adapting sections of law which they had at their disposal. There is some evidence of the rewriting of earlier sections of law to reflect contemporary practice, and taking a brief reference found in earlier lawtexts and creating a neat but full version of a specific section of law. The lawyers creating their lawbooks were open-minded, and were not afraid to include legal concepts or new ideas borrowed from England. Since they were open to all sources for making their books, the forms that their books took varied too. The main aim perhaps was to keep the law workable and current, and this meant changing and adding to the formal lawbooks.

In the context of English law, Professor Sir John Baker states 'As books became the repositories of legal learning, so lawyers became hungry for books.'[193] Similarly, the Welsh justices were not only hungry for books, but they were hungry for law in

---

[191] Cavell, 'Long Shadow', 1406.
[192] *Ibid.*, 1411.
[193] Baker, *An Introduction*, 175.

all its forms, and their attitude towards all things legal could be very wide-ranging and unlimited. All of this, the way all options were kept open, goes much of the way to explain the survival of the Welsh law well beyond the conquest of Wales, but may also explain the complexity of the surviving texts. The law of medieval Wales may 'suffer from what must be one of the most complicated textual traditions known to any field of study',[194] but that may be due in large part to the flexibility and open-mindedness of the men behind the texts.

---

[194] Stacey, *The Road to Judgment*, 17.

APPENDIX: 'REI A DYWEIT'

Presented here are the references to different legal opinions in the Welsh lawbooks. The Welsh texts are from the Iorwerth redaction, and are presented in the order in which they occur in the manuscript, noting the tractate in which they are found. Edited texts are from *LlIor* and references are to section and sentence number. The translations are from *LTMW*, references to page numbers. Notes and texts from other manuscripts are my translation unless otherwise stated.

Texts from *Llyfr Damweiniau* are taken from the stated manuscript and edited. Translations are my own. Cross-references to the texts in AL are given, following the standard form of uppercase Roman numerals for the book, lowercase Roman numerals for the chapter, and Arabic numerals for the sentence number.

See also Table 3.1, above.

Iorwerth

1. Laws of Court. LlIor, §24/4–5, LTMW, p. 29

E navd yv, herwyd rey, hyt ar penguastravt e brenhyn. Ereyll a dywet panyv hyt e parhao talym e march kentaf e'r urenhynes, dvyn e den a wnel e kam.

His protection, according to some, is as far as the King's Chief Groom; others say that it is to take the person who commits the offence for as long as the Queen's fastest horse continues to run.

2. Laws of Court. LlIor, §36/3, LTMW, p. 36

Rey a dyweyt e dele llegeyt er anyueyllyeyt a ladher en e llys, ac a dele e dyllat y am y cappan a'e hossaneu.

Some say that he is entitled to the eyes of the animals that are slaughtered in the court; and he is entitled to his clothing, in capes and hose.

3. Law of Women. LlIor, §50/3, LTMW, p. 51

Rey o'r egneyt ny at guat en erbyn henne; e keureyth eyssyoes a dyweyt e deleyr gadu e guat[1] mal e dewedassam ny uchot.
[1] e keureyth eyssyoes...gadu e guat] niny eissyoes a adόn wad ual y dywedassam ny uchot E, A

Some of the justices do not allow denial against that: the law however says that it is right to allow denial[1] as we have said above.
[1] the law however...allow denial] we however allow a denial as we stated above E, A

4. Law of Women. LlIor, §54/3, LTMW, p. 59

O deruyd e uorven dyweduet ar ur duen treys y arney a'r gur en guadu, a dyweduet o'r uoruen ony duc ef treys e arney hy e bot en uoruen, e kyureyth a dyweyt bot en yaun prouy ae moruen ae nyt moruen, canes e bot en uoruen yu e hardelu.

If it happens that a maiden says that a man has raped her and the man denies it, and the maiden says that if he has not raped her she is a maiden: the law says that it is proper to test whether she is a maiden or not a maiden, for her plea is that she is a maiden.

5. Law of Women. LlIor, §54/7, LTMW, p. 59

O deruyd rody gureyc y vr adan e haguedy, [ac enwy y da,][1] a chaffael kubel o'r da hyt yn oet un keynnyauc ac na chaffer honno, [nyny a dywedun y geill y gur yscar a hy ac na cafo dym o'r eydy: a][2] honno a elwyr un keynnyauc a aduc cant.
[1] *From E*
[2] *From E*

If it happens that a woman under her *agweddi* is given to a man, [and her goods are named,][1] and all the goods are received up to the last penny but that penny is not received, [we say that the man can separate from her and that he will get none of what is hers; and][2] that is called one penny which draws a hundred.
[1] *From E*
[2] *From E*

6. Law of Women. LlIor, §55/3, LTMW, p. 60

Keureyth a deweyt na dele gureyc cowyll guedy blodeuho onys dyheura e kefnessyuyeut e am e mam a'e that a'e brodyr a'e chuyoryd, ac o henne ene uont seyth nyn.

Law says that a woman is not entitled to *cowyll* after she begins to menstruate, unless her closest relatives vindicate her, that is to say her mother and father and brothers and sisters to the number of seven.

7. Suretyship. LlIor, §61/6–7, LTMW, p. 67

O deruyd e den kemryt llawer o ueychyeu ar beth, a mennu eu guadu o'r kynnogyn kymeynt ac a dywedassam ny uchot y wadu mach a dau e wadu pob un onadunt huenteu. Rey a uen ac un seyth wyr guadu, ket et uoent petwar meych ar ugeynt; e kyureuth eyssyoes a dyweyt hyt nat yaun ac nat aduuen.

If it happens that a person takes many sureties for a thing and the principal debtor wants to deny them, as many as we said above for denying a surety are needed for denying each of them. Some of the justices want to deny them with one set of seven men though they should be twenty-four sureties; the law however says that that is not proper and not competent.

Appendix: 'Rei a dyweit'

8. Suretyship. Lllor, §61/8, LTMW, p. 68

O deruyd e den tebygu bot en ryd mach o'e uechny o talu peth o'r dylyet ac hep talu kubyl, e keureyth a deweyt[1] na byd ryd ef a deleu ohonau bot en uach ar e keynnyauc dywethaf mal ar e gentaf.

[1] e keureyth a deweyt] nyny a dywedun E, A

If it happens that a person supposes that a surety is free from his suretyship by paying part of the debt, without paying the whole, the law says[1] that he will not be free, and that it is right for him to be a surety for the last penny as for the first.

[1] the law says] we say E, A

9. Suretyship. Lllor, §62/9, LTMW, p. 69

Pvybennac a vystlo guestel a tebygu ohanau urth nat oes uach arnau bot e guestel adeuedic en anylys, e keureyth a dyweyt[1] e dyguyd e guestel hunnu a'e uot en dylys.

[1] e keureyth a dyweyt] nyny a dywedun E, A

Whoever gages a gage, and supposes that as there is no surety for it, the gage is invalid: the law says that that gage will fall forfeit and that it is valid.

[1] the law says] we say E, A

10. Suretyship. Lllor, §62/14, LTMW, p. 70

O deruyd e den rody mach ar delyet e arall a guedy rody e mach menet e naud rac e delyet, e keureyth a deweyt[1] na dele ef naud rac henne, ac e dele e mach rody e uystyl e'r haulur neu enteu a watto e uechny.

[1] e keureyth a deweyt] nyny a dywedun E, A

If it happens that a person gives a surety for a debt to another, and after giving the surety goes into protection against the debt, the law says[1] that he is not entitled to protection against that, and that the surety is entitled to give his gage to the claimant, or else that he should deny his suretyship.

[1] the law says] we say E, A

11. Suretyship. Lllor, §64/6–7, LTMW, p. 71

Rey a deweyt ony men e mab hunnu seuyll en e uechny e mae uuch pen bed e tat e dele ef e guat ar keureyth; e keureyth a deweyt[1] eyssyoes na deleyr, canys e doethyon a dyweyt nat erlyt keureyth e byt un den, na nef yd el nac uffern, namen ene el y ar e daear. Sef achaus yu ...

[1] e keureyth a deweyt] nyny a dywedun E, A

Some say that if the son does not want to stand to the suretyship, it is right that he should make denial by law over his father's grave. The law says[1] nevertheless that it is not right: for the wise say that worldly law does not pursue any person (whether it is to heaven that he goes or to hell) save until he leaves the earth. This is the reason for it ...

[1] the law says] we say E, A

12. Suretyship. LlIor, §65/4, LTMW, p. 73

O deruyd e'r arwaessaf deweduet na dele talu namen kemeynt ac a gauas er e peth, pa ryu beth bennac uo, e keureyth a deweyt[1] deleu ohonau talu guerth keureyth e peth, pa ryu beth bennac uo.
[1] e keureyth a deweyt] e kyvreyth eyssyoes a deweyt C, niny a dywedun E, A

If it happens that the warrantor says that it is right for him to pay only as much as he received for the thing, whatsoever kind of thing it may be, the law says[1] that it is right for him to pay the legal value of the thing, whatsoever kind of thing it may be.
[1] the law says] the law already says C, we say E, A

13. Suretyship. LlIor, §65/9–10, LTMW, p. 73

E kyureyth a dyweyt hagen bot en uach e mach a rodho gureyc, canys puebennac a allo anylessu da, keureyth a deweyt[1] bot en ryd ydau e dylessu; a chanys gureyc a eyll anylessu da, e kyureyth a deweyt bot en reyt mach e genthy hytheu a bot en uach e mach a rodho. A chanys gur a watta hy, guyr a dele hytheu egyt a hy e wadu mach. (O deruyd e wreyc rody bruduv ar peth a'e wadu ohoney en keureythyaul, e keureyth a dyweyt[2] e mae guraged a'e guatta egyt a hy.)
[1] keureyth a deweyt] nynheu a dywedun E, A
[2] e keureyth a dyweyt] nyny a dywedun E, A

The law says however that the surety which a woman gives is a surety, for whosoever can invalidate property, law says[1] that it is free to him to validate it; and since a woman can invalidate property, the law says that a surety is needed from her and that the surety which she gives is a surety. And since it is a man that she is denying, she is entitled to men in support of her to deny a surety. If it happens that a woman gives a *briduw* for a thing and legally denies it, the law says[2] that it is women that deny it with her.
[1] law says] we say E, A
[2] the law says] we say E, A

14. Suretyship. LlIor, §66/1–2, LTMW, p. 75

Rey a deweyt na dyguyd guestel o lau uach hyt em pen un dyd a blueden; e keureyth a dyweyt[1] e dygued guestyl o law try dyn en e oet. Sef yu e rey henne...
[1] e keureyth a dyweyt] nyny a dywedun E, A

Some say that a gage does not fall forfeit from the hand of a surety until after a year and a day. The law says[1] that a gage falls forfeit at its due date from the hand of three persons; those three persons are...
[1] the law says] we say E, A

15. Suretyship. LlIor, §67/4, LTMW, pp. 77–78

O damweynnya e deu den bot keureyth erygthunt a'r neyll en galu am uach ar keureyth a'r llall en deweduet na dele rody mach ar keyreyth namen deleu ohonau ef oet urth e porth, a deweduet o'r haulur, 'Dyoer', hep ef, 'mach a deleaf uy: dele mach ne dele dym' – 'Dyoer', hep e llall, 'nyt mach ny uo mach ar dym; ac e my ny deley ty dym, canes adeuedyc gennyt tuhun nas deley' – e keureyth a dyweyt[1] na dele ef uach ar keureyth, can ardeluus e llall o oet urth porth, a phey rodey e mach keureyth dyannot a uedey, canyt oes oet en haul uach a kennogen.

[1] e keureyth a dyweyt] nyny a dywedun E, A

If it befalls two persons that there is litigation between them and one of them calls for surety for law, and the other says that he is not bound to give a surety for law but is entitled to a delay for aid, and the claimant says 'God knows,' says he, 'I am entitled to a surety: he is entitled to a surety who is entitled to nothing'; 'God knows,' says the other, 'he is no surety who is a surety for nothing, and from me you are not entitled to anything, for it is admitted by you yourself that you are not entitled': the law says[1] that he is not entitled to a surety for law, since the other pleaded a delay for aid, and if he gave the surety there would be immediate law, since there is no delay in a claim of surety and principal debtor.

[1] the law says] we say E, A

16. Suretyship. Lllor, §68/8, LTMW, p. 78

Ket dywetter e bot hy en uruduu, e keureyth a deweyt[1] nat bruduu ene keuarfo e llau a'e gylyd, ac nat mach ac nat goruodauc ene keuarfo e teyr llau ygyt.

[1] e keureyth a deweyt] nyny a dywedun E, A

Though it be said that it is a *briduw*, the law says[1] that there is no *briduw* until the hands meet each other, and that there is no surety and no *gorfodog* until the three hands meet together.

[1] the law says] we say E, A

17. Suretyship. Lllor, §69/8, LTMW, p. 79

O deruyd e den emadau ac arall eg guyd testyon am peth a mennu eylweyth e wadu ohonau, e keureyth a deweyt[1] na dele ef e wadu ene palloent e testyon.

[1] e keureyth a deweyt] nyny a dywedun E, A

If it happens that a person enters into a promise with another for a thing in the presence of witnesses, and he again wants to deny it, the law says[1] that he is not entitled to deny it until the witnesses fail.

[1] the law says] we say E, A

18. Land Law. Lllor, §75/3, LTMW, p. 86

O deruyd bot rey a ryuedho dody keytweyt a guybydyeyt o'r un pleyt, e keureyth a deweyt[1] y gellyr eny warandawher attep er amdyffynnur.

[1] e keureyth a deweyt] nyny a dywedun E, A

If it happens that there are some who are surprised that maintainers and knowers are offered by the same party, the law says[1] that it can be done until the defendant's answer is heard.

[1] the law says] we say E, A

19. Land Law. Lllor, §75/6, LTMW, p. 87

E keureyth a deweyt,[1] ket darfey y'r amdyffynnur atteb en gynt no'y holy ef o'r haulur, bot yn anolo yr attep eny warandawo ef er haul, ac yna rody attep.

[1] E keureyth a deweyt] nyny a dywedun E, A

The law says[1] that though the defendant may have answered before the claimant makes his claim against him, the answer is void until he hears the claim, and that then he should give answer.
[1] the law says] we say E, A

20. Land Law. Lllor, §80/1, LTMW, p. 94

Rey a dyweyt e mae gureyctra esyd petweryd llyssyant; e keureyth eyssyoes a dyweyt e mae o kenedel gelynyaeth yd henyu, a'e uot en tredyd.

Some say that woman-feud is a fourth ground of objection; the law however says that it is of the essence of enmity of kindred and is one of the three.

21. Land Law. Lllor, §81/5, LTMW, p. 96

O deruyd dyguydau dyd coll neu gaffael en amser cayat kyureyth am tyr a daear neu en amser dedon, rey a deweyt deleu e adnewydu en amser ryd eylweyth; e keureuth eyssyoes a dyweyt nat oes dym a annotto dyd coll a chaffael namen un peth: sef yu henne, na del cof e'r egnat e uraut amdanau; ac ot amheuyr, kreyrhaer ef, ac yna e rodyr oet e'r egnat e emgoffau ac e emdydan a guyr a uo hyn eu puyll noc ef.

If it happens that the day of loss or gain falls in the close season for law concerning land and earth, or in a blank time, some say that it is right to renew it again at the open season. The law however says that there is nothing which postpones a day of loss and gain save one thing: that is, that the justice does not remember the judgement for it; and if he is doubted, let him be put to the relics, and then a delay is given to the justice to remind himself and to discuss with others whose discretion is older than his.

22. Land Law. Lllor, §82/5, LTMW, p. 99

Ereyll a dyweyt e mae guyalen gyhyt a'r gur huyaf en e tref a'e lau uuch y pen, ac yn un ryu gerdet ar honno ac ar e llall.

Others say a rod as long as the tallest man in the townland with his hand stretched above his head, handled in the same way as the other.

23. Land Law. Lllor, §85/7, LTMW, p. 104

A honno a elwyr dyaspat uuch Annuuen, a chet dotter e dyaspat o henne allan, byth ny werendewyr. Ac ereyll a dyweyt na dele e nauuet dyn dody e dyaspat honno namen e uynet o pryodaur en ampryodaur.

And that is called *Diasbad uwch Annwfn*, and though that shriek be given thereafter, it will never be heard. And others say that the ninth person is not entitled to give that shriek, but that he has passed from proprietor to non-proprietor.

24. Land Law. Lllor, §86/3–5, LTMW, p. 107

Rey a deweyt na dele meybyon un wreyc tref tat o uamues namen un wreyc: sef yu honno, gureyc a rodho y that a'e brodyr e alltut. Ereyll a dyweyt ket rodho y

Appendix: 'Rei a dyweit'

chenedel hyhy e alltut ac nas rodho henne o deneon, na dele e meybyon hy tref tat. E keureyth eyssyoes a dyweyt bot teyr guraged a dele eu meybyon tref tat o uamues ...

Some say that the sons of no woman are entitled to patrimony by mother-right save those of one woman, that is, a woman whom her father and brothers give to an alien. Others say that though her kindred give her to an alien, if those persons do not give her, her sons are not entitled to mother-right. The law however says that there are three women whose sons are entitled to patrimony by mother-right ...

25. Land Law. LlIor, §86/7, LTMW, p. 108

Rey a deweyt am ueybyon e ryu wraged henne, ket buynt treftadogyon, nat ynt pryodoryon. E keureyth a dyweyt na chychuyn pryodaur rac ampryodaur ac e kechuyn pryodaur rac meybyon e ryu wraged henne, ae y ar peth ae y ar kubyl: ac urth henne e gat e kyureyth e rey henne en pryodoryon. A'r keureyth eyssyoes a dyweyt o byd suyd neu ureynt o'r tyr hunnu na cheyff ef dym ohanau ef hyt e tredegur, canys guell yu breynt pryodaur a gynwarchatwo tyr nogyt un newyd dyuot.

Some say of the sons of such women that though they are patrimonials they are not proprietors. The law says that a proprietor does not move before a non-proprietor and that a proprietor moves before the sons of such women (whether from part or from the whole); and therefore the law allows that these are proprietors. The law nevertheless says that if there is office or status from the land, he does not get that until the third man, for the status of a proprietor previously occupying land is better than that of one newly arrived.

26. Land Law. LlIor, §87/5, LTMW, p. 110

Keureyth eglues a dyweyt[1] na dele un mab tref tat namen e mab hynaf e'r tat o'r wreyc pryaut. Keureyth Hewel a'e barn e'r mab yeuhaf megys e'r hynaf, ac a uarn na dotter pechaut e tat na'e agkeureyth en erbyn e mab am tref e tat.
[1] Keureyth eglues a dyweyt] y gyureyth a dyly eylweyth E

Church law says[1] that no son is entitled to patrimony save the father's eldest son by the wedded wife. The law of Hywel adjudges it to the youngest son as to the eldest, and judges that the father's sin and his illegality should not be set against the son for his patrimony.
[1] Church law says] the law ought to a second time E

27. Land Law. LlIor, §87/8, LTMW, pp. 110–111

Rey a dyweyt o lledyr den am tyr deleu hunnu o'e etyued enteu en waettyr udunt guedy henne. E keureyth a dyweyt nat guaettyr urun namen a talher en keureythyaul guedy na bo dym ar helu e llourud a talho, nac o keynnyauc palader nac o dym arall, ac a uarn na deleyr llad un den namen e llourud ny wnel e kubyl; a'r tyr hunnu a deleyr e rannu erygthunt mal e deleyt rannu er alanas.

Some say that if a person is killed for land, his heirs are entitled to the land as blood-land after that. The law says that none is blood-land save what is legally paid over after the homicide has nothing to his name which he can pay, either from shaft penny or from anything else; and it judges that there is no right to kill any person save the homicide who does not pay in full. And it is right to share that land among them as it is right to share the *galanas*.

28. Land Law. LlIor, §89/1–6, LTMW, pp. 114, 116

E keureyth a deweyt e dele meybyon uchelwyr cadu argluydyaeth ... Ereyll a dyweyt na deleant uynet hyt ar e tredeguynt.

The law says that the sons of *uchelwyr* are entitled to maintain lordship ... Others say that they are not bound to go until the third wind.

29. Family Law. LlIor, §97/1, LTMW, p. 129

Rey esyd ar pedrus am ueychyogy gureyc, o llegryr, pa beth a deleyr amdanau: ae uynepwarth ae galanas. E keureyth a dyweyt panyu galanas a deleyr amdanau; sef achaus yu ...

Some are doubtful about the pregnancy of a woman, as to what the right for it is, if it is destroyed, whether *wynebwerth* or *galanas*. The law says that it is *galanas* to which there is a right in respect of it. This is the reason ...

30. Family Law. LlIor, §97/3, LTMW, p. 130

Rey a deweyt nat yaunach talu galanas gur amdanau ef nogyt un gureyc, cane wys beth yu ef, ae gur ae gureyc; e keureyth a deweyt bot en yaunhaf barnu en ol e peth pennaf, a bot galanas gur arnau a henne ene uedydhyer.

Some say that it is not more proper to pay the *galanas* of a man for it than that of a woman, since it is not known what it is, whether man or woman. The law says that it is most proper to judge according to the higher thing, and that there is a man's *galanas* for it, and that until it is baptised.

31. Three Columns of Law. LlIor, §104/10, LTMW, p. 143

Rey a deweyt panyu e'r kenedel e dau er aryant a dywedassam ny uchot; e keureyth a dyweyt panyu e'r argluyd yd ant, ac o guedyr, hyt na deleyr namen guat.

Some say that the money which we have specified above comes to the kindred. The law says that it goes to the Lord, and that if there is denial, there is no right save to denial.

32. Three Columns of Law. LlIor, §105/3–4, LTMW, p. 144

Sef yu messur galanas o keureyth, e sarhaet teyr gueyth herwyd y ureynt e den a ladher. Ereyll a deweyt panyu e den a uo teyr buu a thry ugeynt aryant e sarhaet, panyu teyr buu a thry ugeyn muu yu e werth, ac euelly herwyd mal e derchauo breynt pob den.

The legal measure of galanas is three times the sarhaed of the person killed, according to his status. Others say that for the person whose sarhaed is three kine and three score pence, the worth is three kine and three score kine; and similarly as every person's status rises.

Appendix: 'Rei a dyweit'

33. Three Columns of Law. Lllor, §111/15, LTMW, p. 156

O guedyr er affeythyoed rydywedassam ny uchot, kymeynt eu guat a guat llouryudyeyt. [Ereyll a deweyt am e reyth honno panyw pymwyr hep alltvdyon hep wyr not a'y gwatta; a henny ew kyvreyth Hewel en yavn.]¹
¹ *From C*

If the abetments we have named above are denied, their denial is as great as the denial of principal offenders. [Others say regarding that compurgation that it is five men without aliens without designated men deny it; and that is the true law of Hywel.] ¹
¹ *From C*

34. Three Columns of Law. Lllor, §111/28

[Ereyll a dyweyt y uot en eneyt uadeu ony cheyf y werth.]¹
¹ *From E*

[Others say that his life is forfeit unless he receives his value.] ¹
¹ *From E*

35. Three Columns of Law. Lllor, §113/6–8, LTMW, pp. 159–160

Ny byd eneyt uadeu ef yr caffael y dogen uanac, namen y uot en lleyder guerth. Ony eyll caffael e werth, y dyhol ual lleyder. Ereyll o'r keureythyeu a uyn gadu guat ydau er gyrr e raglau ual er gyrr perchennauc arall, a henne uuyhaf y coyllya guyr Guyned ydau.

His life will not be forfeit though sufficient information has been received, but he will be a sale thief; and if he cannot find his price, he is banished like a thief. Other forms of law wish to allow him denial against the lord's charge as against another owner's charge, and that is what the men of Gwynedd most believe in.

36. Three Columns of Law. Lllor, §115/2, LTMW, p. 164

Eg keureyth Hewel e mae hyt eguerth pedeyr keynnyauc e uot en lleyder guerth; o henne allan e uot en eneyt uadeu. Ereyll a dyweyt o pob anyueyl petwartroedyauc a dyccer en lledrat, nac oen na myn na porchell, e uot en eneyt uadeu; eyssyoes dyogelhaf yu hyt pedeyr keynnyauc.

In the law of Hywel, he is a sale thief up to the value of fourpence, and from there on his life is forfeit. Others say that for every four-footed animal which is stolen, whether lamb or kid or piglet, his life is forfeit; nevertheless it is safer to say from fourpence.

37. Three Columns of Law. Lllor, §115/6, LTMW, p. 165

Eg keureyth Hewel e bu tal ac eyl tal am ledrat, ac odyna e symudus Bledyn uab Kenuyn am uot en dygaun talu e dyn y gollet urth y damdug.

In the law of Hywel there was payment and second payment for stolen property; and thereafter Bleddyn ap Cynfyn changed it, so that it was enough to pay the person his loss according to his sworn appraisal.

The Growth of Law in Medieval Wales, c.1100–c.1500

38. Three Columns of Law. Lllor, §116/12, LTMW, p. 169

[Ereyll a deweyt nat mwy reyth lledrat en e byt no devdeg wyr ac e mae devdeg wyr a watta lledrat, a'r neyll hanner en wyr not a'r llall en wyr dynot: ac evelly e gwedyr lledrat llosc, kanys mwy breynt e lledrat no breynt e llosc.]¹
¹ *From* C

Others say that no compurgation in the world for stealth is more than twelve men, and that it is twelve men that deny stealth, one half being designated men and the other undesignated men: and so burning by stealth is denied, since the status of the stealth is greater than that of the burning.

39. The Value of Wild and Tame. Lllor, §122/1–2

[Ereyll a dyweyt am ebavl panyw pedeyr keynnyavc kyvreyth ew y werth...]¹
¹ *From* C

Others say for a foal that it is four legal pence that is its value...

40. The Value of Wild and Tame. Lllor, §127/9–10, LTMW, p. 175

[Ereyll a dyweyt panyw kymeynt ac a vo eyssyev o'r llestyr o'r llaeth, y vrthvryt o werth e llaeth y'r nep pyeyffo e wuch: os hanner e llaeth, hanner e gwerth; os trayan e llaeth, trayan e gwerth. A hvnnv ew e dvll gorev.]¹
¹ *From* C

Others say that however much is wanting from the vessel of milk, so much of the value of the milk shall be returned to him who owns the cow: if half the milk, half its value; if a third of the milk, a third of its value; and that is the best style.

41. Value of Equipment. Lllor, §139/1, LTMW, p. 190

Llyma e gueles e doethyon¹ bot en grynno escryuennu guerth e tey a'r doodreuyn, ac am kyuar a llugyr yt, ygyt a'r Llyuer Prauf.
¹ doethyon] Yorverth vap madavc vap rahavt C; yoruerth am madauc E; yoruerth vab madauc A

Here the wise men saw that it would be useful to write the value of the houses and the equipment, and about *Cyfar* and Corn Damage, together with the Test Book.
¹ wise men] Iorwerth ap Madog ap Rhawd C; Iorwerth am Madog E; Iorwerth ap Madog A

42. Value of Equipment. Lllor, §144/1, LTMW, p. 195

Rey a dyweyt am y dyllat panyu damdug ysyd arnadunt; ereyll a dyweyt panyu y dull hun esyd arnadunt, nyt amgen ...

Some say of clothes that it is sworn appraisal which applies to them. Others say that it is this arrangement which applies to them, to wit ...

Appendix: 'Rei a dyweit'

43. Cyfar. Lllor, §151/3, LTMW, pp. 200–201

O deruyd bot amrysson am eredyc, [a'r neyll en mennu eredyc][1] em pell ac arall en agos, a henne erug deu kyuaruur, e kyureyth a dyweyt[2] na deleant uynet en lle na alloent er ychen kyrhaydu eu budelu ac eu gued en wan ual en gadarn en e kymut.
[1] From A
[2] e kyureyth a dyweyt] nyny a dywedun E, A

If it happens that there is a dispute about ploughing, [and one insists on ploughing][1] afar off and other ploughing near at hand, between two joint-ploughing partners: the law says[2] that they are not bound to go to a place so that the oxen cannot reach their tying-posts and their team when weak as when strong, within the commote.
[1] From A
[2] the law says] we say E, A

44. Cyfar. Lllor, §152/3, LTMW, p. 201

Puybynnac a wnel kyuar a guedy henne kyuaru ac arall, e kyureyth a dyweyt[1] deleu bot er ychen henne en e kyuar kyntaf, a chet gunel cant kyuar guedy henne, deleu ohonau kynnal pen er yeu em pob lle e gunel.
[1] e kyureyth a dyweyt] nyny a dywedun E, A

Whosoever makes a joint-ploughing contract, and after that contracts for joint-ploughing with another, the law says[1] that it is right that those oxen be in the first joint-ploughing, and though he should make a hundred joint-ploughing contracts after that, he is bound to support the end of the yoke everywhere he has made a contract.
[1] the law says] we say E, A

45. Cyfar. Lllor, §152/4, LTMW, p. 201

Puybynnac a wnel kyuar ac na del en hywed y eredyc, na dyd na deu y bo hep dyuot, e kyureyth a dyweyt,[1] nac o'y uod nac o'y gymhell y del ef, hyt na dele ef dym o'r a arder hepdau.
[1] e kyureyth a dyweyt] nyny a dywedun E, A

Whosoever makes a joint-ploughing contract, and does not come readily to plough, whether it be one day or two that he fails to come, the law says[1] that, whether he comes of his own will or under compulsion, he is not entitled to anything of what is ploughed without him.
[1] the law says] we say E, A

46. Cyfar. Lllor, §152/6, LTMW, p. 201

O deruyd y den kyuaru ych, a duen er ych en lledrat, e kyureyth a dyweyt[1] na dele ef dale pen er yeu, ac na dele enteu kaffael er eru.
[1] e kyureyth a dyweyt] nyny a dywedun E, A

If it happens that a person puts an ox into joint-ploughing and the ox is stolen, the law says[1] that he is not bound to support the end of the yoke and that he is not entitled to have the acre.
[1] the law says] we say E, A

47. Cyfar. LlIor, §152/7, LTMW, p. 201

O deruyd e den kyuaru ych a bot en well gan e den dody arall en y le, e kyureyth a dyweyt[1] na dele ef e symudau ef hep ganhyat y kyuarwyr.
[1] e kyureyth a dyweyt] nyny a dywedun E, A

If it happens that a person puts an ox into joint-ploughing and that the person prefers to put another in its place, the law says[1] that he is not entitled to move it without the leave of the partners.
[1] the law says] we say E, A

48. Corn Damage. LlIor, §154/11–14, LTMW, p. 203

En e keureyth e bu huch o'r moch, neu o'r man escrybyl rydywedassam ny uchot, keny bey namen try llyden onadunt, un. Sef achaus oed henne ... Odyna e symuduyt ...

In the law there used to be a right to a pig from the pigs; or from the small livestock we have named above, though there might be only three head of them, there was a right to one. This was the reason for that ... From that it was changed to ...

Llyfr Damweiniau

49. From E, p. 100; cf. AL IV.iii.2

Rey a dyweyt panyu dyn amdyuenhedyc, yu kyuarch kyfyll. Ereyll a dyweyt panyu derwen a ladher yn agkyuarch ar trew tat pryodaur, a dylyu dody mantell arnau o'y gudyau rac y welet, a bot yn waratwyd y'r trew tadauc y welet. Jorwerth uab Madauc eyssyoes a dyweyt panyu hun yu kyuarch kyfyll yn yaun: sew yu hynny, pan ...

Some say that when a man has been cut off from everything, that is *cyfarch cyffyll*. Others say that it is when an oak is felled without permission on the patrimony of a proprietor, a mantle ought to be put on it to hide it from sight, and that it is an insult to the patrimonial to see it. Iorwerth ap Madog however states that it is this that is rightly a *cyfarch cyffyll*: that is, when ...

50. From E, p. 102; cf. AL IV.iv.2

Am uorỏyn gwreyc: gwedy roder y ur a hytheu yn uoruyn, a hep gysgu genthy, ot darfey duyn treys arney, rey a dyweyt na dylyey cowyll. Ereyll a dyweyt y dylyey. Nyny eyssyoes a dywedun puy bynnac a dorro moruyndaut gwreyc dylyu ohanaỏ talu ydy y chowyll.

Regarding a virgin wife: after she has been given to a man and she is a virgin, and has not been slept with, if it happens that she is raped, some say that she is not entitled to *cowyll*. Others say that she is entitled [to it]. We however say that whoever takes the virginity of a woman is the one who ought to pay her *cowyll* to her.

Appendix: 'Rei a dyweit'

51. From E, p. 105; cf. AL IV.iv.18

O deruyt y dyn uynet yn uach, a chyn teruynu yr haul y uynet yn clauur neu yn uynach neu yn dywyll, ny tybyco ef dylyu ohanau atep. Nyny a dywedun dylyu ohanau kywyrau a edewys tra uo byu.

If it happens that a man becomes a surety, and before the claim is finished he becomes leprous or a monk or blind, he might suppose that he does not have to answer. We say that he ought to complete that which he promised while he is living.

52. From E, p. 106; cf. AL IV.iv.30

Puy bynnac a dyco creyryeu y dadleỽ ac eu ceyssyau o'r pleyt arall a oed yn y erbyn y creyryeu a doeth canthau ew; nyny a dywedun na dyly ew y creyryeu hynny yny darfo y dadleu ...

Whoever brings relics to pleadings and the other party who was against him seeks the relics which he brought; we say that he is not entitled to those relics until the pleadings are finished ...

53. From E, p. 189; cf. AL V.ii.36

Or deruyd geni dyn ac aelodeu gỽr a rei gỽreic ganthaỽ, ac yn petrus o ba vn yd aruerho; Rei a dyweit panyỽ herỽyd y mỽyaf yd aruerho y kerda y vreint. Os o bop un yd aruerha ynteu, kyfreith a dyweit dylyu ohonaỽ kerdet ỽrth y breint uchaf.

If it happens that a man is born with male members and female ones, and it is uncertain which he uses; some say that his status is defined according to the one he uses the most. If he uses all of them, the laws says he is entitled to be defined by the highest status.

54. From D, p. 209; cf. AL V.ii.108

Rei a dyweit na ellir torri amot; kanys ual gouunet yỽ amot, a phop gouunet kyt torrer, iaỽn yỽ dyuot idi drachefyn a'e gadỽ o newyd. Ac ual hynny am amot gan dieissiwaỽ y neb y torrer ac ef. Kyfreith a dyweit, pỽy bynnac a ymỽrthotto a pheth yn kyfreithaỽl yr meint y ymrỽyn ac ef nac amot vo na pheth arall; nat oes haỽl idaỽ ar hỽnnỽ trachefyn, kan torres y rỽym, a bot yn ỽrthot ar amot y dorri.

Some say that a contract cannot be broken; because a contract is like a vow, and every vow although it is broken, it is right to return to it again and keep it anew. And so it is for a contract by compensating whoever is broken with him. The law says, whoever refuses a thing lawfully whatever the amount into which he is bound, be it a contract or another thing; that he has no right to that afterwards, because he broke his bond, and it is a rejection of a contract to break it.

55. From D, pp. 216–217; cf. AL V.ii.129

O deruyd bot peth ygkyt y rỽg deudyn, a mynnu o bop un onadunt y rannu, ac amrysson onadunt pỽy a ranho, pỽy a dewisso; kyfreith a dyỽeit dylyu onadunt ell deu rannu yn deu hanner yn gyntaf, ac odyna rannent pop vn onadunt yn deu hanner y ran ry del attaw, ac odyna dewiset baỽp vn ar y ran a rannaỽd y llall. A honno a elwir ran kyfreith kyttundeb. Ereill a dyweit panyỏ y ieuaf bieu rannu a'r hynaf dewissaỏ, ony byd uch breint y ieuaf. O deruyd na wyper pỏy uchaf pwy issaf y vreint, pỏy hynaf pỏy ieuaf, kyhyded a vyd y rygthunt ac yna y dyly y rann a dywedassam ni uchot.

If it happens that there is something jointly between two men, and each of them insists on dividing it, and there is a dispute among them about who is to share, who is to choose; the law says that they are both to divide into two halves first, and then let them each of them divide the share which comes to them into two halves, and then let each of them choose from the share which the other divided. And that is called the division in the law of agreement. Others say that it is the youngest who is to divide and the eldest to choose, unless the status of the youngest is higher. If it happens that it is not known who is the highest and who is the lowest in status, who the eldest who the youngest, there will be equality between them and then it is to be the division which we stated above.

Part II

A New Approach to Cyfraith Hywel

4

'ALL ADDITIONAL AND LATER MATTER': THE 'ANOMALOUS LAWS' AND THE LAWTEXTS

The ANOMALOUS or WELSH LAWS constitute an important portion of the Work. Under this head are given such anomalous chapters as are respectively found in those Manuscripts which afforded the text for the regular Codes, and also all additional and later matter, wherever found.[1]

In Part I, much attention was given to the historiography of the lawtexts. The working methods of the medieval lawyers were shown to have had a major effect on the way the texts were being produced. But a second, huge, influence on the way the lawtexts are viewed has its origin in Aneurin Owen's work, *Ancient Laws*. That work was shown to introduce a division of the material which may not necessarily reflect the organisation of the material at the time of creating the lawtexts.

In examining the extant manuscripts, early editors – Owen included – focused on attempting to recreate an original 'Book of Hywel', or tracing the texts back to an early archetype. While there is some evidence that there may well have been an early written tradition of Welsh law, attempting to recreate that in the form of a book, working from the law manuscripts that have survived, creates new problems. One of those issues that arose as a result of attempting to refashion an early or original lawbook is that the material that has survived is varied in date. As a response, far more emphasis was placed on 'early' sections of the lawtexts, and the 'later' sections were disregarded, because they could not be fitted into the imagined form of the 'original' lawbook, being later creations. This is not a criticism of looking for early or pre-Norman elements in Welsh law per se. Care must be taken, however, in emphasising, and indeed over-valuing, the early sections of law simply for being early, as may have been done by early editors; this could mean that the passages that are dated to a later period are disregarded as evidence.

Aneurin Owen, as was shown, divided the material in this way. His division was severe, into two parts,[2] the first containing Owen's concept of the three versions of Hywel Dda's book, and the second containing later laws, which are, to this day, seen as 'additional', even though Owen himself conceded that they were no less important.[3] The effects of his editorial decisions have been far-reaching, colouring attitudes

---

[1] Owen, AL, Introduction, xx.

[2] AL was published in a large folio edition as well as in the quarto edition. In the quarto edition, the division is clear since the work was published as two volumes for practical reasons. The title page of the book, in both versions, does show the division: 'Ancient Laws and Institutes of Wales; comprising Laws Supposed to be Enacted by Hywel the Good ... and Anomalous Laws ...'. The two parts are in a larger font than the other material. See Fig. 1, 132, below.

[3] Owen, AL, Introduction, xx.

towards the legal manuscripts even today and causing several genres of legal texts to be viewed as secondary. Many of these texts have not been edited more recently and are only accessible through Owen's second volume.

This chapter will offer a new reading of the legal texts, and will focus particularly on certain genres of material found in Owen's second volume. It will argue that these texts are in no way 'additional', but are an intrinsic part of the legal compilations from medieval Wales. The relationship between the material in the first volume of *Ancient Laws* and that in the second will be discussed, but a focus will be placed upon the motive and purpose of the material in Owen's second volume. None of the texts from the law manuscripts, including in the manuscripts that are collections of distinct materials from separate exemplars, occur as stand-alone booklets, for example, which would mean that they could have been inserted in the law manuscripts at a later date; nor are they preserved anywhere other than in law manuscripts. Since their link to the law manuscripts is so clear and indisputable, it is difficult to describe this material as 'additional'.

None of the legal material or the genres examined are optional extras to the texts in the first volume of *Ancient Laws*. Instead, the argument here is that the genres found in the second volume should be viewed and treated like any other legal material found in the law manuscripts, such as the better-known tractates found in the redaction texts.[4]

The Division of the Lawtexts

As has been shown, Aneurin Owen had a very organised system for dealing with the legal material. He separated the material with which he was dealing according to his own opinion of those that formed the 'core' texts of Welsh law. This designation is still used to a great extent, and many of the published editions of law manuscripts still present the material from the first volume of *Ancient Laws*.[5] However, Owen's second volume organised the remainder of the texts in a systematic and practical way. His main method was to organise the material by genre, or by the manuscript(s) in which it was contained. This is in contrast to *Ancient Laws* I, as the tractates found there are organised by subject, and it is the genre organisation that gives the material in *Ancient Laws* II the appearance of being chaotic and disorganised, but this is not the case. While *Ancient Laws* II has received less attention than the first volume – for example, there are newer editions of each of the three redactions found in *Ancient Laws* I, in addition to studies of individual tractates including modern editions of those texts[6] – this lack of attention to the second volume is not necessarily because

---

[4] The triad form is a well-known genre in the lawtexts and, like the material discussed in this chapter, triads often occur in collections. Triads are not presented as a book in the Anomalous Laws, but were included by Owen as collections within other legal material. Triads are not 'additional material', and a collection of triads form a tractate within the main Blegywryd and Cyfnerth redactions. I intend to discuss the way triads have been viewed and the evidence of the triads in the development of the legal texts at another time.

[5] There are, of course, exceptions. An early example is Wade-Evans, 'Text of Pen. MS. 37', which presents the *damweiniau* from manuscript U; more recently, *ALD*, is a full edition of manuscript H, which was only used in AL XIV.

[6] Cyfnerth: *WML*, and *Pomffred*; Iorwerth: *LlIor*; Blegywryd: *LlBleg*, and *J(ed.)*; the Latin texts: *LTMW*. The tractate studies are: *WLW*; *LAL*; *WKC*; *TCC*; and *LT*.

of the way Owen separated the material, but may have more to do with its complex nature. This chapter will focus on the material that Owen organised by genre.

Thomas Charles-Edwards points out that there are two genres included in the Anomalous Laws that are 'of outstanding importance': the *damweiniau*, and *cynghawsedd*.[7] *Damweiniau* are a collection of legal provisions, many of which have the opening formula *O derfydd* ('If it happens'). *Cynghawsedd* comprises collections of model pleadings. Both genres are sometimes described as 'Books', that is, as *Llyfr Cynghawsedd* or *Llyfr Damweiniau*, and they are closely linked to the Iorwerth manuscripts. The question that will be asked here is whether *damweiniau* and *cynghawsedd* were simply further tractates, or a less formally organised section that could be added to or included within other legal material, since both genres are found in other manuscripts from other redactions as well. The same questions will be asked of other genres discussed in this chapter.

A further consideration with the *cynghawsedd* and the *damweiniau* is whether they were books that existed separately from the law manuscripts, and this might impact the way that they are viewed. The same is true of other texts found in the 'Anomalous Laws' – *holiadon* ('interrogatories') are genre-based collections, as are the plaints. The argument has also been made of triads, a well-known genre in the lawtexts, which, like other material discussed in this chapter, often occur in collections. Triads are included in the Anomalous Laws as collections within other legal material, and as separate chapters in the books, e.g. AL X.vii, presenting excerpts from the extended triad collection from Q. Triads are not 'additional material', and a collection of triads form a tractate within the main Blegywryd and Cyfnerth redactions, and triad collections are a feature of Owen's DC and GC as well as in the Anomalous Laws.[8]

The final 'anomalous' collection under discussion is different. *Llyfr Cynog* ('the Book of Cynog') was a titular lawbook, attributed to St Cynog, and that contained different types of material – this is not a subject-specific book, or a genre-based collection.[9] If the material circulated as a separate book of law, but contained different laws to those in the other lawbooks, then its purpose and nature may be very revealing on the subject of 'additional' material. In all cases, however, there is no solid evidence from any other source to suggest that any of these texts did exist separately.

(a) Damweiniau

Damweiniau are sentences outlining particular situations – if a certain event occurs, then a particular result follows – and many of the examples in the collections open with the formula *O derfydd* ('if it happens').[10] The purpose or function of the *damweiniau* is less clear. They may simply be a stylistic tool to present legal material; or they may have an educational purpose. They may even show development of the Welsh laws and legal discussion or even philosophy, as they present situations not dealt with anywhere else in the laws: in other words, they were a medium for thinking outside the box. Charles-Edwards argues that the *damweiniau* were 'odd

---

[7] Charles-Edwards, *The Welsh Laws*, 49.
[8] Despite being a genre, triads were not afforded a separate book in the Anomalous Laws and so are excluded from the discussion in this chapter. See also n.4, above.
[9] Elias, '*Llyfr Cynog* of *Cyfraith Hywel*'.
[10] Charles-Edwards, *The Welsh Laws*, 49.

bits that the compiler could not integrate and yet would not sacrifice', and that the existence of *damweiniau* allowed Iorwerth to be systematic and tidy, since the *damweiniau* became a repository for the things 'which did not fit into the structure of the tractate'.[11] However, since some tractates in the first part of the Iorwerth manuscripts are followed by a section of *damweiniau*, Charles-Edwards assumes some reworking and editing of an earlier lost version of Iorwerth.[12]

The *damweiniau* are an area of the Welsh laws that have not been studied in full, although recent work by Robin Chapman Stacey, on the textual development of the collection of *damweiniau*, has advanced the topic a considerable amount.[13] Stacey considers the two collections of *damweiniau* in *Ancient Laws* and in *DwC* – *Damweiniau* I and *Damweiniau* II – calling both collections '*Llyfr y Damweiniau*'.[14] She also shows that *Damweiniau* I was earlier and better known, and in her focus on the text in *Damweiniau* I she argues that the collection was in fact very logically structured, rather than being an untidy and disordered repository for random things.[15] There is strong evidence for splitting the *damweiniau* into two collections, and Aneurin Owen may have spotted the division, since *Damweiniau* I is found in Owen's Book IV, and *Damweiniau* II forms his Book V.

Llyfr Damweiniau is attested either in full or in part in twelve surviving manuscripts, and is known to have been in a further lost manuscript (the Llanforda manuscript).[16] This, arguably, makes *damweiniau* the text that is attested in the highest number of manuscripts, excepting the main redaction texts. It also occurs in manuscripts of each redaction, and in early manuscripts as well as later ones.

Table 4.1: Manuscripts containing Llyfr Damweiniau

Manuscript	Date	Redaction	Damweiniau
A, NLW Peniarth MS 29	$s.\text{xiii}^{\text{med}}$	Iorwerth	*Damweiniau* I
Col, NLW Peniarth MS 30	$s.\text{xiii}^{\text{med}}$	[Iorwerth]	*Damweiniau* I + II
Llanforda MS, now lost	$s.\text{xiii}^{\text{med}}$	Iorwerth	*Damweiniau* I + II
E, BL Add. MS 14931	$s.\text{xiii}^2$	Iorwerth	*Damweiniau* I
G, NLW Peniarth MS 35	$s.\text{xiv}^1$	Iorwerth	*Damweiniau* I
U, NLW Peniarth MS 37	$s.\text{xiv}^1$	Cyfnerth	*Damweiniau* I
J, Jesus Oxford MS 57	$s.\text{xiv/xv}$	Blegywryd/ Iorwerth	*Damweiniau* I, II [*extracts*]
D, NLW Peniarth MS 32	$c.1404$	Iorwerth	*Damweiniau* I + II
Q, NLW Wynnstay MS 36	1440s	Blegywryd	*Damweiniau* I + II + III
Ep, NLW Peniarth MS 258	$s.\text{xv}^2$	Blegywryd	Copy of Q

---

[11] *Ibid.*, 49–50.
[12] *Ibid.*, 50.
[13] Stacey, 'Legal Writing in Medieval Wales'.
[14] *Ibid.*, 63. Stacey calls the book '*Llyfr y Damweiniau*', using the definite article, as does Dafydd Jenkins in his edition. The definite article is not found in the title in the manuscripts: see *DwC*, viii. The use of the definite article implies a complete collection and, since this is not the case, the form will be used throughout without the definite article, as *Llyfr Damweiniau*.
[15] *Ibid.*, 71.
[16] Jenkins, 'Llawysgrif Goll Llanforda', 93.

F, NLW Peniarth MS 34	s.xv^2	Non-redaction	*Damweiniau* I + II
K, NLW Peniarth MS 40	>1469	Iorwerth	*Damweiniau* I + II + III
Lew, NLW Peniarth MS 39	s.xv^{med}	Iorwerth	*Damweiniau* I [*not in full*]

As noted by Stacey, and demonstrated in Table 4.1, above, *Damweiniau* I occurs in 11 manuscripts, and *Damweiniau* II in seven. Of the seven manuscripts containing *Damweiniau* II, all but one precede the collection with *Damweiniau* I, but J's *damweiniau* comprise a small block from Damweiniau I on pp. 206–207, and then a main collection on pp. 264–270, from *Damweiniau* II but not including all of the latter.[17] The relationship between the texts of *Damweiniau* I and II is a subject for study in itself; but the texts of D, F, G, K, Q and U of *Damweiniau* I seem to share readings that are different to those in A; Col tends to side with the other manuscripts against A. U may have copied G for its text of *Damweiniau* I, and the manuscripts are in the same hand.[18] Dafydd Jenkins noted that the textual relationships of the manuscripts for *Damweiniau* I and *Damweiniau* II were not necessarily the same (and they could be different to the main Iorwerth text too).[19] It is interesting that Llanforda and U have a heading marking the opening of *Llyfr Damweiniau*, U marked the end of *Damweiniau* I, and Llanforda marked the end of *Damweiniau* II, but there are no headings or colophons in the other manuscripts. It is therefore difficult to determine how the manuscript redactors viewed the *damweiniau*, whether *Llyfr Damweiniau* was generally viewed as an entity, and whether *Damweiniau* I and II were viewed separately, although it appears in the case of the latter issue that the collection was simply viewed as one.

Robin Stacey also acknowledges that there was 'what ought probably to be considered yet a third collection', presented in Owen's Book VI, and taken from only two manuscripts, K, a Iorwerth manuscript, and Blegywryd Q.[20] As Stacey notes, some of the material is also found in the *damweiniau* in Colan, and *Damweiniau* III is only partly extant in manuscript Q.[21] However, while the material is presented as a collection in *Ancient Laws*, it is not together as a consecutive block of material in either Q or in K. Rather, the *damweiniau* in AL Book VI have been filtered out of the extended *Damweiniau* II collection in those manuscripts, and while some blocks are consecutive, there is other material, found in other manuscripts containing *Damweiniau* II, mixed in with the 'different' *damweiniau* in AL Book VI from Q and K. The order and content of the full *damweiniau* collection in Q and K is very similar – *Damweiniau* II tends to vary in order across the manuscripts, but the (extended) text of *Damweiniau* II copied into both Q and K is a close text and the order of the *damweiniau* is the same on the whole. The nature of the presentation in *Ancient Laws* is misleading and makes the *damweiniau* look like a neat collection.

This is not the only instance of manuscripts K and Q sharing a portion of text that is not found elsewhere. They also share the alternative triad collection, which, with the *damweiniau*, a plaint, and *holiadon*, form the whole of the non-Iorwerth part of manuscript K. There are striking similarities in the way the two manuscripts treat this triad collection and *Damweiniau* III. The manuscripts were clearly getting material

---

[17] J(ed.), 100.9–19; 128.22–131.6.
[18] Stacey, 'Legal Writing in Medieval Wales', 61.
[19] *DwC*, ix.
[20] Stacey, 'Legal Writing in Medieval Wales', 63 n. 27.
[21] *Ibid.*, 63 n. 27.

from a source unavailable to other redactors, and perhaps even copying exemplars that only contained one source or genre, such as a collection of *damweiniau* or triads.[22] This third text of *damweiniau*, like the separate collection of triads, has a different textual development to the main collections of *damweiniau* already discussed. The *damweiniau* and the triad collection in Q and K may have been created from existing collections, but with some new additions. Why these 'new' collections were created is more puzzling, and impossible to answer without knowing where they originated. The collections were certainly circulating in south Wales, and the triad collection was also copied into manuscripts S and Tim (related to each other and by the same scribe), but it seems that the *damweiniau* collection was only copied into K, in full, and selectively into Q.

Charles-Edwards, in an examination of the Iorwerth manuscripts, noted the contrast between the Iorwerth redaction and Blegywryd and Cyfnerth, and this may help determine whether *damweiniau* are 'additional' or not. 'The other lawbooks appear to have remained within a tradition in which all of Hywel's law was expounded within Hywel's Book'; Iorwerth, however, had *Llyfr Damweiniau* as a potential repository for material that was more didactic and with a less formal structure, with Iorwerth and *Llyfr Damweiniau* being complementary texts, 'system as against heterogeneity'.[23] This would not explain why *Llyfr Damweiniau* or parts of it were copied into other, non-Iorwerth manuscripts. One possible answer is that the non-Iorwerth manuscripts included the section of *Llyfr Damweiniau* as a way of incorporating Iorwerth concepts that were different from the material they already had, but did not involve copying Iorwerth tractates. In addition, the *damweiniau* may have had a different purpose or intention, and certainly took a different form, which meant that they were including 'new' or 'different' material to that which was already in their text.

Can the *damweiniau* really be viewed as additional material, or were they seen as being a part of the lawbooks? There are two considerations here: the *damweiniau* linked to the Iorwerth redaction, and the collections that are linked to manuscripts of other redactions. The manuscripts of the Iorwerth redaction form a close group, and the texts divide into three parts: the Laws of Court, the Laws of Country, and the Test Book. The Test Book is the third part and is often attributed to Iorwerth ap Madog himself. It contains the Three Columns of Law, the Value of Wild and Tame, and also tractates on agricultural topics – *Cyfar* (co-tillage), and Corn Damage. While the Test Book has a prologue in every Iorwerth manuscript apart from B (which deliberately removed the prologue),[24] it has no end marker in most of the Iorwerth manuscripts. The text of Corn Damage ends, and either the text moves to *damweiniau* or other material (in A and D), or there is a loss (C and E).[25]

B alone has a note marking the end of Corn Damage (*ac yuelly e teruynyr am lugyr yt*, 'and so it ends regarding Corn Damage'), but the end of the Test Book is not marked, and B is one of only two Iorwerth manuscripts that does not have *damweiniau*. Manuscript C has no *damweiniau* but the manuscript is incomplete and has lacunae; it appears that there would be *damweiniau* in the manuscript

---

[22] See *LT*, 32–34. I intend to deal with this material more fully elsewhere.
[23] Charles-Edwards, *The Welsh Laws*, 53.
[24] Charles-Edwards, 'The Textual Tradition of Llyfr Iorwerth', 42.
[25] At this point E seems to have a leaf missing; the Corn Damage section continues up to the last word of f. 46v, which is 'Puybyn–', the first word of *Lllor*, 158/9; the text on f. 47.1 is the last six words of *DwC* 17, and the text continues with *DwC* 18 onwards. The opening of *Damweiniau* I is not in E, and there seems to be one missing folio in E. C is laconic throughout.

were it complete.²⁶ Manuscript B has deliberately removed the *damweiniau* and has included *cynghawsedd* instead.²⁷ There is nothing to suggest, in the Iorwerth texts, that the *damweiniau* or the *Llyfr Damweiniau* were viewed as additional or optional, but rather they appear to have been a part of the basic Iorwerth material. They may have travelled separately to the Iorwerth texts at some stage although there is little evidence for this within the Iorwerth manuscripts; the existence of *Llyfr Damweiniau* or parts of it in other, non-Iorwerth manuscripts, may be evidence in favour of this, but it is difficult to prove. Either way, most of the Iorwerth manuscripts do not view *damweiniau* as being additional material – although the compiler of B chose to omit the book in its entirety. But even if *Llyfr Damweiniau* were optional at an early stage, they became part of the Iorwerth text, at least in a group of manuscripts from thirteenth-century Gwynedd, linked to the circle of Iorwerth ap Madog, fl. *c*.1240–*c*.1268. The inclusion of the *damweiniau* collection in these early Iorwerth manuscripts shows that a collection of *damweiniau* was an acceptable thing to have as part of a Iorwerth lawbook, and it had gained ground as Iorwerth material. The problem, perhaps, is B, which does away with the *damweiniau*, which might suggest that they were therefore disposable. B however excised all references to Iorwerth ap Madog in his text, and was consciously adapting the manuscript that he was using.²⁸ The addition of *cynghawsedd* instead of *damweiniau* does suggest that something was needed after the Corn Damage section, and B appears to be replacing to keep his text 'whole' rather than omitting for the sake of it. It suggests that *damweiniau* were an intrinsic part of the Iorwerth redaction, at least in Gwynedd manuscripts, by the thirteenth century, and something that was expected following the Corn Damage tractate.

To the compilers of the other manuscripts containing a large collection of *damweiniau* it was simply another text available to copy, rather than having any special status. The separate collection of *damweiniau* found in K and partially in Q is the only collection of *damweiniau* that may be viewed as 'additional' or indeed optional, but it is no different to *Damweiniau* I and II. The manuscripts containing *Damweiniau* III are both fifteenth-century manuscripts. Q dates from the first half of the fifteenth century and is an important manuscript since it presents a re-editing and reorganisation of the legal material; several exemplars were used, and some of these – such as the one for the *damweiniau* and for the separate triad collection – are not widely attested. The *Damweiniau* III collection is only attested in one other manuscript: K, in the hand of Lewys Glyn Cothi, *c*.1420–1490, and so K is likely to be a little bit later in date than Q.²⁹ K is not a copy of Q, although there are other similarities between the two manuscripts. *Damweiniau* III may have been a special composition for inclusion in the new and reorganised version of the laws in Q. The extant manuscript Q is a fair copy of an earlier and complex work, but if *Damweiniau* III were created for this new edition in Q, they may have been written down and subsequently made available to the scribe of K, who copied the entire text, whereas the scribe of Q was more

---

[26] Charles-Edwards stated as much in a discussion after a paper given at Seminar Cyfraith Hywel; the paper was published as Charles-Edwards, 'The Textual Tradition of Llyfr Iorwerth', but does not include a discussion on *damweiniau*.

[27] On the editorial work and omissions in B, see Charles-Edwards, 'The Textual Tradition of Llyfr Iorwerth'.

[28] *Ibid.*, 42.

[29] On K, see Owen, 'A Fifteenth-Century Lawbook'; Antur, 'I Mewn Hen Ysgrifen Gron', 11–12.

selective (as was his wont).³⁰ The fact that several items from this *Damweiniau* III collection appear to be based on ones from the main collection suggests that this too is an integral part of the lawtext tradition, not 'additional' or 'anomalous' material. While it may have originated in a different way, it too is still firmly based in the textual context of the law manuscripts. It is unlikely that it was ever intended as a composition separate to the law manuscripts: it was made to be incorporated.

(b) Cynghawsedd

Another important genre for consideration is *cynghawsedd*, model pleadings, a guide on how to present a legal case in a court, sometimes including direct quotations for various legal stances, or with references from the lawtexts.³¹ *Cynghawsedd* texts make up Books VII–IX of *Ancient Laws*.

Table 4.2: Ancient Laws *and* Cynghawsedd

Book	Manuscripts in AL	Other manuscripts	Notes
VII	B, BL Cotton Titus MS D II G, NLW Peniarth MS 35 J, Oxford, Jesus College MS 57 (for 43–47)	Q, NLW Wynnstay MS 36 F, NLW Peniarth MS 34	'*Llyfr Cynghawsedd*'
VIII	F, NLW Peniarth MS 34 G, NLW Peniarth MS 35	*No other manuscripts*	Individual sections of *cynghawsedd*
IX	As, NLW Peniarth MS 175 Z, NLW Peniarth MS 259B Mor, NLW Peniarth MS 36C	H, NLW Peniarth MS 164	North-east Wales *cynghawsedd*

The *cynghawsedd* collections in *Ancient Laws* were put together in a similar way to the *damweiniau*: there is a section of material presented in Book VII, which is known as *Llyfr Cynghawsedd*, attested in B and G, and some parts of *Llyfr Cynghawsedd* also occur in J, Q and F.³² Book VIII has more *cynghawsedd*, mainly taken from manuscript G but with some sections also found in F, Q, B and Z. This is not found in the manuscripts as a consecutive collection, but is individual sections of *cynghawsedd* found throughout the manuscripts, but that do not fit into the other collections. The other collection of *cynghawsedd*, from north-east Wales, is a uniform and well-structured collection that further splits into two parts. It is presented in AL Book IX and found in manuscripts As (which has little if any other material in it), and Mor. These manuscripts may preserve a specific book of *cynghawsedd*. The same collection is also in Z, and parts of it are in H: these are the north-east Wales manuscripts.³³

---

[30] Roberts, 'Creu Trefn o Anhrefn', 416. If this is the case, then questions need to be asked about the separate triad collection in Q, S and Tim, and K; however, the scribe of Q copied the triad collection selectively, which suggests that it was not created for that manuscript. K is likely to be slightly later than Q.

[31] Charles-Edwards, '*Cynghawsedd*'; Stacey, 'Learning to Plead'; Charles-Edwards, *The Welsh Laws*, 53–67; and *ALD*, xxxv–lxvi.

[32] Charles-Edwards, '*Cynghawsedd*', 191. J was used for AL VII, but Q and F do not appear to have been used for the *cynghawsedd*.

[33] See *Pomffred*, 39–41.

The *cynghawsedd* material in AL II appears to be discrete recognisable sections, one of which is a known book, *Llyfr Cynghawsedd*. However, far from being anomalous or extraneous material, *cynghawsedd* as a form – as with the *damweiniau* – is also found in the main text of the Iorwerth manuscripts.[34] In the Land Law section of Iorwerth, there is a lengthy account of what should happen in a land suit, and two forms of the same word are given: *cynghawsedd*, and *cyngheusaeth*.[35] In Iorwerth, the term *cynghawsedd/cyngheusaeth* is used for the formal statement of the legal position, and the sharing of the case between the litigant and his *cyngaws* (someone who would present the case for the litigant) and *canllaw* ('guide', probably an advocate),[36] but the meaning also widened to cover the genre of writing.[37]

Cynghawsedd and *damweiniau* occur as part of the subject-specific tractates in the Iorwerth texts, and were included by Owen in his 'Venedotian Code'. As well as the lengthy piece of *cynghawsedd* in the Land Law tractate in the Iorwerth text, there are similar sections (but lacking the name *cynghawsedd*) in the Suretyship and Theft tractates in Iorwerth.[38] As these sections of *cynghawsedd* occur within the 'main' tractates in Iorwerth, *cynghawsedd* in general can hardly be called 'additional' material – rather, it was simply another way of writing law. The Iorwerth tractates are united by subject, but the *cynghawsedd* and *damweiniau* collections are united by form or genre.[39] It has already been argued that a *damweiniau* collection was part of the original material in the Iorwerth lawbooks, but the *Llyfr Cynghawsedd* was not. If the *cynghawsedd* was gathered together to form a book, which was then added to some Iorwerth manuscripts, specifically in B instead of the *damweiniau*, then it is less certain where this material originated. It may have been composed especially, or was part of the oral training of lawyers, at least in north Wales, since it provides models of speech for a court setting.

Another feature of *cynghawsedd* which makes it stand out from the other genres in AL II is that the material largely occurs in manuscripts that are linked to the Iorwerth redaction. As 'additional material' goes, *cynghawsedd* is very much a northern phenomenon, with some rare exceptions, and there are different collections of it in the law manuscripts. Leaving aside the *cynghawsedd* found in the Land Law tractate in Iorwerth, which also occurs in some Blegywryd manuscripts as it travelled with the Iorwerth Land Law section, the focus here will be on the separate collections of *cynghawsedd*.

Six of the eight Iorwerth manuscripts are similar in order and content, and they form a close group.[40] The remaining two manuscripts are more mixed and, while they contain Iorwerth material, they may not have a complete text and they also have other material incorporated. G and Lew also unfortunately have disordered binding. Lew contains *damweiniau* and some *cynghawsedd* along with some parts of the

---

[34] See for example *LlIor*, §§72–79, which presents a detailed case for land, including the seating plan for the personnel involved, and quotations of what was to be said: *Lyman esyd yaun y'r haulur y deweduyt* ('and this is what it is right for the claimant to say'); the word *kygheusaeth* is also used.

[35] Charles-Edwards, *The Welsh Laws*, 54–56.

[36] Ibid., 58; *LTMW*, 331, 322.

[37] Charles-Edwards uses the form *cyngheusaeth* 'for the senses given to the word in IOR', and *cynghawsedd* for the wider meaning and the genre: Charles-Edwards, *The Welsh Laws*, 60.

[38] Charles-Edwards, '*Cynghawsedd*', 190.

[39] See also discussion on triads, below.

[40] Charles-Edwards, *The Welsh Laws*, 17–18.

Iorwerth redaction, plus other material that appears to have a south Wales origin – the manuscript was created in south Wales. Hand I of G is similar, in that it also has parts of a Iorwerth text, *cynghawsedd, damweiniau* and more limited south Wales material, but G also has parts of the Book of Cynog, which is discussed below.[41] Also linked to the Iorwerth redaction but usually classed as an 'anomalous' or non-redaction-based manuscripts is F. Like G and Lew, F does have some portions of a Iorwerth text – far more limited than G and Lew, as it has some of the Three Columns material, and a small section of material on suretyship – *damweiniau, cynghawsedd*, and some south Wales material. All three manuscripts, and perhaps F in particular, are under-studied texts deserving of more attention, in particular the link between the Iorwerth redaction and the material circulating in south Wales.

(i) Llyfr Cynghawsedd

Llyfr Cynghawsedd, titled as such and with its end marked, is appended to Iorwerth B, and this is presented in AL VII, with variants from G, and J and Q as well for one piece of text. This material also occurs in manuscript G, there is a partial copy in F, and some of it occurs in the Blegywryd manuscript J, but in the latter, Iorwerth part of that manuscript.[42] Another manuscript from the Blegywryd redaction that has some Iorwerth material in it is Q, and it also has the same section of *cynghawsedd* that is found in J, but J and Q are close at times and have the same material.

Llyfr Cynghawsedd as presented in AL VII follows B as the base text. The same text is also found in G, following the same order as that in B and in *Ancient Laws*, but G is not a copy of B, although they may be copying the same exemplar. G also has AL VII.i.43–47 in a different sequence to B.[43]

Table 4.3: Llyfr Cynghawsedd *as presented in* AL *VII*

Section	Content	Notes
VII.i.1–8	General on land claims	G
VII.i.9–21	Land claims – proprietorship	G, 10–19, 21 in F
VII.i.22–23	Land claims – *Ymwrthyn* (contention)	G, 22 in F
VII.i.24–25	Land claims – *Mamwys* (mother-right)	G, 25 in F
VII.i.26–29	Land claims – *Dadannudd*	G, 26–28 in F
VII.i.30–40	The role of the justice	G, 33, 36–39 in F
VII.i.41–42	Setting boundaries	G
VII.i.43–47	Claiming property taken by force/ surreption	J, Q; G, 46–47 in F
VII.i.48–51	Land claims – *cyfran* (division)	G, 48–49 in F
VII.i.52–53	Land claims – loan; general on loans	G

---

[41] I would like to thank Professor Thomas Charles-Edwards for kindly letting me see a copy of his unpublished article 'NLW Peniarth MS 35 (G) and the Textual Tradition of *Llyfr Iorwerth*'.
[42] *J(ed.)*, 101.14–106.35, which is also found in AL VII.i.43–47.
[43] See Wiliam, 'Llyfr Cynghawsedd', 74–75.

This book of *cynghawsedd* opens with a text that follows the same *O derfydd* ('if it happens') form which makes up the *damweiniau* – this may point to a recognisable pedagogical technique. These sections present general procedural notes on a claim in Land Law, with short sentences on matters to be dealt with *ene dyd kentaf* ('on the first day'), clearly starting in the beginning. There is an awareness that the text is linked to the lawtexts – *ac ena e mae iaun eyste en kyfreith 6el e deweyt leuyr Hewel* ('and then it is right to sit in law as is stated in the book of Hywel').[44] This appears to be a reference to the instructions given in the Iorwerth redaction, and the statement seems to separate this material from 'Llyfr Hywel', suggesting that this material is different. The redactions may have had a special identity, if not status, of their own, and the *cynghawsedd* may not have originally been part of the redactions.[45] It may be the case that the purpose of the *cynghawsedd*, or the audience for it, was different; it is possible that the *cynghawsedd* was intended as a practitioner's handbook for a *cyngaws*, something that is even suggested by the term *cynghawsedd*. This does not have to diminish the value of any material – such as the *cynghawsedd* – that may not originally have been part of the redactions, and the cross-references suggests that the person using the *cynghawsedd* would also have at his disposal a version of 'Llyfr Hywel', a text of the laws containing the section of Land Law found in Iorwerth; the reference to it does not suggest that the *cynghawsedd* would work as a text separate from the law manuscripts. The *cynghawsedd* may be later than the early Iorwerth redactions behind the extant manuscripts – this is highly likely – and perhaps the *cynghawsedd* with the reference to 'Llyfr Hywel' was self-consciously separate, as it was not included in that book, but it certainly used 'Llyfr Hywel' and was linked to it.

The case gets going, the paragraphs becoming much longer by AL VII.i.9, and the subject matter focuses on a claim of proprietorship. This is followed by *ymwrthyn* ('contention', two people claiming proprietorship or rightful claim to the same piece of land), and then a claim by mother-right. AL VII.i.26 introduces *dadannudd*, a claim that is discussed fully in the Iorwerth Land Law tractate, and lists the three *dadannudd* actions, and goes through each one but with more detail in the first section since the remaining two follow the same process.[46] AL VII.i.30 moves away from the model pleading format and gives various short rules and procedural matters largely focusing on the role of the *ynad* (justice), again using the '*O derfydd*' formula.

There is another model pleading from AL VII.i.41 on setting boundaries, which ends with a closing sentence: *A honno yu haul teruyn* ('and that is a claim of boundary'). The subject then changes and a new *cynghawsedd* begins, on claiming property taken by force, and by surreption, from AL VII.i.43–47. This section is also found in J, and in Q – the texts are very similar and most likely from the same exemplar – and is an isolated piece of *cynghawsedd* in those manuscripts, followed by *holiadon* (question-and-answer sentences) in both of them, although it is not the same collection in the two manuscripts. The *cynghawsedd* is very self-contained, has regular references to what the law says, and is very self-aware, with references to *y gynghawsedd hon*

---

[44] Quotation taken from manuscript G, NLW Peniarth MS 35, 53r16–17; see *LTMW*, 85; the instructions form part of the 'procedure in an action for land', which is *cynghawsedd*: LlIor, §73.

[45] Charles-Edwards, *The Welsh Laws*, 59.

[46] *LTMW*, 261; *dadannudd* is a way of claiming land that had previously been held by the claimant's ancestors but that had been occupied by someone else. '*Dadannudd*' means uncovering a fire banked up overnight, and the *dadannudd* action for land is a symbolic action of uncovering the ancestor's fire, which had been extinguished for some time. *LTMW*, 261; Charles-Edwards, *Early Irish and Welsh Kinship*, Chapter 6 'Welsh *Dadannudd*', 274–303.

('this pleading'). Its inclusion in the two Blegywryd manuscripts, and the fact that it is not on Land Law, unlike the other material in *Llyfr Cynghawsedd*, suggests that *Llyfr Cynghawsedd* is less circumscribed than it appears – this particular *cynghawsedd* may be a text that was circulating separately but was brought in to *Llyfr Cynghawsedd* perhaps by the editor of B or G, or was in their exemplar. Both B and G contain this section, but it is in a slightly different position in the sequence in the two manuscripts. It then travelled south and was available for the scribe Hywel Fychan to copy it into J, and the scribe of Q to copy into his text; J and Q share several texts. The fact that it is followed in both of the southern manuscripts by *holiadon* again suggests a pedagogical origin, perhaps from legal schools, for practical purposes.

The remainder of *Llyfr Cynghawsedd* turns back again to Land Law, and looks at *cyfran* ('division'), and then loans and borrowing. B marks the end of *Llyfr Cynghawsedd*: the section ends with *Ac e uel henne e dadleuyr am uenfyc* ('And so a loan is to be argued/pleaded'), and *Ac euelly e teruyna llyuer kyghaussed* ('And thus ends *Llyfr Cynghawsedd*'). G has neither of these sentences but is clearly ending something since it has a Latin colophon: *Dextra scriptoris careat grauitate doloris. Jn nomine dei amen.*

Llyfr Cynghawsedd was clearly a recognisable book, containing a particular genre of text. As a book of model pleadings, this text may have originated in a pedagogical environment, and may have been a handbook, teaching a would-be practitioner, a *cyngaws* perhaps, how to plead a legal case. This emphasis on purpose is important if we consider the concept of the model lawbook – material for teaching or learning the law is usually rejected as not being part of the 'model lawbook', the original 'Book of Hywel' (whatever that may be). *Llyfr Cynghawsedd* is also seen to be later in date than the Iorwerth redaction – although it should be kept in mind that it is found in manuscript B, dating from the late-thirteenth century and also containing a text of the Iorwerth redaction, and so this collection of *cynghawsedd* may be within a generation of the earliest extant Iorwerth texts, if not of a date with them. But its lack of antiquity has also led to its being dismissed and indeed under-studied.

Rather than dismiss *Llyfr Cynghawsedd* as 'something additional', because it is not likely to be part of the original and early 'model lawbook', a new way of viewing this material should be sought. *Llyfr Cynghawsedd* presents law that was current in the thirteenth century at least, and it is likely to be older than the earliest book that contains it. The self-conscious references to it being a book suggests that this was not a hastily assembled selection, and it was already known in legal circles before it was incorporated into manuscript B. And finally, while it may not have been part of the early 'model lawbook', it was considered important enough to be included in manuscript B, a manuscript containing a version of the Iorwerth redaction. The act of including *Llyfr Cynghawsedd* with the legal text in B certainly makes the material look as if it were part of the Iorwerth redaction, but the reference to 'Llyfr Hywel' in the *cynghawsedd* maintains its distinctiveness, yet is also a nod to the fact that the two books work together. Had *Llyfr Cynghawsedd* been treated differently by the redactor, it may have remained a book circulating separately, if that was how it started out – the self-conscious references to it being a book may point to this, or may alternatively be an attempt to make the text more 'official' and formal, which again shows importance placed on the text. The Iorwerth text referred to as 'Llyfr Hywel' in *Llyfr Cynghawsedd* certainly had a different status, if not pre-eminence, and it was an essential text for anybody wishing to use *Llyfr Cynghawsedd*; but the inclusion of *Llyfr Cynghawsedd* in B means that the text was considered important, and was linked to the Iorwerth redaction; the difference may lie in the purpose behind the text.

The 'Anomalous Laws' and the Lawtexts

(ii) Other Cynghawsedd

AL Book VIII offers more *cynghawsedd*. AL VIII.i–v uses F as the base text and gives variants from G only for some of AL VIII.i–v, since G has a missing folio from the beginning of the first quire and the surviving folio has a large piece torn away. The remainder of AL VIII was taken from G, a Iorwerth manuscript, and the end of the book is said to be taken from *Llyfr Cynog*, the Book of Cynog: *Ac y uelly teruyna llyuyr Kyna6c* ('And so ends the book of Cynog'). A small portion of this material is found in manuscript Y, which is largely Blegywryd but with Laws of Court from Cyfnerth and much other material combined with the Blegywryd text, and the Blegywryd manuscript Q also has a section of *cynghawsedd* that is found in AL Book VIII. Neither Y nor Q were used for variants in *Ancient Laws*.

Table 4.4: The cynghawsedd *in AL VIII*

Section	Content	Notes
VIII.1–5	Suretyship, testimony, procedure	Some variants from G
VIII.6–11 (end)	Various, marked 'miscellaneous'	No variants

The first five sections in AL VIII, taken from F (because of the lost and damaged first folios in G), are on the subject of surety and debtor. The first one stands alone as it has its end marked: *Ac uelly y mae teruyn ar y gyghavssed honno* ('And so that *cynghawsedd* ends'), and the next three sections are intended as a set, with the second and third example in the discussion marked. The remainder of Book VIII, using G as a base manuscript, is on various topics including some *cynghawsedd* but also other interesting material, and some of this is taken from the Book of Cynog.[47] The scribe of G copied another law manuscript, the Cyfnerth text in U (including a collection of *damweiniau*), and also the important collection of prose texts in Peniarth 45.[48] The *cynghawsedd* from G – AL VIII.vi–x – seems to have been taken from another book, and is a working copy of some sort giving examples, and with notes on the source. Rather than presenting the rules in the way found in the tractates in Iorwerth, for example, this *cynghawsedd* in G seems to indicate that this was a lawyer's notebook, in which the lawyer jotted down sections of law, perhaps as part of his study. This may even have included rewriting sections of law – the *cynghawsedd* on *sarhaed* may be the basis for a plaint, which will be discussed later – or even composing new sections or dealing with unfinished matters found in his exemplar or in practice. AL VIII.viii–x are examples of *cynghawsedd*:

> Ac yna y mae teruyn ar y gyngha6ssed. Ac yn y bra6t lyuyr y mae y ura6t a dylyir am y gyngha6ssed honn. Llyma gyngha6ssed arall.

> And here ends the *cynghawsedd*. And the judgement which ought to be for this *cynghawsedd* is in the judgement book. Here is another *cynghawsedd*.[49]

> Y gyngha6s honn nyt oes ura6t ym bra6t lyuyr ymdeni. A chanyt oes, reit y6 y barnu yma. A llyma mal y dylyir am hynny ...

---

[47] Elias, '*Llyfr Cynog* of *Cyfraith Hywel*', 31–32.
[48] *RWMS*, Scribe X87.
[49] Manuscript G, 8r7–10.

For this *cynghawsedd* there is no judgement in the judgement book. And because there is not, it must be judged here. And this is how that ought to be ...[50]

Both examples refer to the source from which the lawyer drew his material, including, in the first case, the *brawd*, decision; in the second case there was no decision or judgement in his source book, and so he wrote out his own judgement in his working book, manuscript G.[51] This book is called *brawdlyfr*, a book of judgements. As was discussed in Chapter 3, part of the justices' work was to choose the best judgement in a legal case, and their decisions could be appealed as 'wrong judgements', but this would need to be proven by reference to a better written judgement. It is likely that this '*brawdlyfr*' would be a collection of these decisions, and that the book was used to create G, a working book for a justice. However, there is a possibility here that the '*brawdlyfr*' may be a Iorwerth text: the *cynghawsedd* in the examples from G corresponds to the provisions on claiming an animal found in *Lllor* §§113–114, with the animal here specified as a sheep; the Value of Wild and Tame tractate outlines grounds for claiming other animals too.[52] Once again, the *cynghawsedd* texts, and indeed practitioner texts such as G, are linked to the Iorwerth redaction texts, and this may explain why G also has parts of a text of that redaction in the working book along with the *cynghawsedd* texts.

The remainder of AL VIII is more miscellaneous and is labelled as such by Aneurin Owen. It appears that the first chapters in Owen's Book VIII are more organised, an intentional text, perhaps regarded as linked to the redaction portion of the manuscripts containing the same text, but the latter part of AL VIII does not fit the same format. However, the reason for this may be simple – the latter part of AL VIII was taken from manuscript G, which is itself not organised or neat (indeed, the quires have been disarranged before binding), and the scribes included sections as and when they came up, with no intention of creating a unified text, at least not at that stage. As it happens the *cynghawsedd* in AL VIII is taken from manuscripts that also have a copy of all or parts of *Llyfr Cynghawsedd*, but AL VIII is not a tidy collection of a single genre, unlike its neighbours AL VII and AL IX.

Both *Llyfr Cynghawsedd* and the *cynghawsedd* presented in AL VIII appear to have had a limited circulation, and very little of the material is repeated, but the importance of manuscript G for the study of *cynghawsedd* is clear. Neither collection was copied in full into any other law manuscript.

(iii) North-East Wales Cynghawsedd

The third collection of *cynghawsedd* in AL IX is taken from manuscripts As and Mor, manuscripts mainly comprised of this *cynghawsedd*. Z, a Cyfnerth manuscript but with added material from other exemplars also has the same collection of *cynghawsedd* but it is in a different order in Z, perhaps due to a loose-leaf exemplar.[53] This *cynghawsedd* then is not contained within Iorwerth manuscripts as such, but it retains its northern connections, since all these manuscripts are from north-east Wales, as is H, which has some similarities and also has parts of this *cynghawsedd*.

---

[50] Manuscript G, 8v17–20.
[51] The use of lawbooks in legal practice in medieval Wales is discussed in Chapters 6 and 7.
[52] With thanks to Thomas Charles-Edwards for suggesting this.
[53] *Pomffred*, 40.

Charles-Edwards notes that *cynghawsedd* originated in north Wales, but travelled south in the fourteenth and fifteenth centuries. Parts of this *cynghawsedd* material are also found in S, which is a Blegywryd manuscript and southern – although the correspondence between S and As/Mor/Z is not particularly close.[54] However, Charles-Edwards points out that there are some aspects of the *cynghawsedd* in AL IX that may have a 'southern domicile'.[55] That said, the three main manuscripts that used the exemplar – and it does appear that each of the manuscripts were using the same exemplar – are all linked to north-east Wales, which does not preclude Charles-Edwards's suggestion, but it does show that the exemplar was located in north-east Wales for some time even if the material was not originally created there.[56]

Table 4.5: The cynghawsedd *and organisation of* AL *IX*

Section	Content	Notes
IX.i-xvi.21	Theft, related subjects – *cynghawsedd*	First Collection
IX.xvi.22–35	Notes on procedure in legal cases	Not *cynghawsedd*
IX.xvii	Crosses	Not *cynghawsedd*
IX.xviii	*Naw Tafodiog* (Special witnesses)	Not *cynghawsedd*
IX.xix	*Wyth Pynfarch* (Eight Pack-Horses)	Not *cynghawsedd*
IX.xx-xxii	Nine abetments of *galanas*, theft, fire	Not *cynghawsedd*
IX.xxiii	Lord's entitlement to man's property	Not *cynghawsedd*
IX.xxiv	*Galanas* questions and answers	Not *cynghawsedd*
IX.xxv	Crosses	Not *cynghawsedd*
IX.xxvi-xxxvii	Land law – *cynghawsedd*	Second Collection
IX.xxxviii	*Holiadon*, question-and-answer sentences	Not *cynghawsedd*
IX.xxxix	'The Law of the Court'	Not standard version, local

The *cynghawsedd* texts from north-east Wales separate neatly into two collections: the first is on theft and other related subjects, and the second collection is concerned with Land Law. There are three manuscripts that contain all this material, As and Mor, from the second half of the fifteenth century, and Z, a sixteenth-century manuscript of several exemplars some of which date from the mid-fourteenth century onwards. None of the three manuscripts label the collection as *cynghawsedd*, but the first portion starts with the heading *Llyma y gyniver fford y gwhana dyn a'i dda* ('These are the many ways by which a man is separated from his property') and then lists the 11 topics that are dealt with in that order in the text that follows. The topics are theft, followed by how to make a charge of theft and the punishment for theft; violence, including violence in absence; surreption or borrowing without consent; loans; deposits; lending, hiring; exchange; negligence; impounding; and unlawful removal.[57] The way the text

---

[54] Charles-Edwards, '*Cynghawsedd*', 197; *ALD*, lix.

[55] Charles-Edwards, '*Cynghawsedd*', 197. His argument is that the second collection in AL IX shows northern, Iorwerth elements, but also southern versions of legal procedures. I would argue, however, that this 'curious mixture' is more redolent of the nature of the texts, and their likely Marcher origin and use.

[56] *ALD*, lvi; Mor, lvi-lvii, and H: cxii–cxv; and also Roberts, 'Law texts and their Sources', 55–57.

[57] See the notes in *Pomffred*, 336–343.

is presented does suggest that this had a particular purpose, either pedagogical or for use in court, but most likely the former. The first section on theft is long and detailed, giving the definition of theft and the two kinds of theft, theft where the object is present and where the object is not present, and details on things that are not to be treated in the same way, and it also gives procedural details, for example on how to object to a justice.[58] It includes direct quotations:

> Ac yna govyned yr ynad i'r amddiffynwr 'pwy dy gyngaws a ffwy dy ganllaw?', ac yna dyweded ynte pwy i gyngaws a ffwy i ganllaw, a dangosed wynt. Ac yna govyned yr ynad 'a ddodi di koll a chayl yn ev pen hwy?', ac yna dyweded ynte 'dodaf heddiw drosof a thros vy nevnyddie'. Ac yna govyned yr ynad 'a gymerwchi koll a chayl yn ych pen?'. Dywedent wyntav 'kymerwn yn oed y dydd heddiw'.

> And then let the justice ask the defendant 'who is your pleader and who is your *canllaw*?', and then let him say who his pleader and who his *canllaw* is, and let him show them. And then let the justice ask 'do you place loss and gain in their mouths?', and then let him say 'yes I will place it today on my behalf and on behalf of my matters'. And then let the justice ask 'do you accept loss and gain in your mouths?'. Let them say 'we accept it in the set time today'.[59]

After the opening section, which sets the scene and discusses the details of theft, it turns to topics linked to theft: how to make a charge of theft against someone, a list of punishments, and other details on theft, which takes up several manuscript pages. This very lengthy text is a full treatment of how to deal with theft – presumably in a court situation – and how to bring a case to its full conclusion. The level of detail, including discussing unusual or non-standard cases of theft, means that this text stands alone to a great extent: it is the ultimate detailed handbook on dealing with theft in legal pleadings.

By contrast, the sections that follow, and the remainder of the text, devote short paragraphs to each legal topic discussed. Little detail is given for the other topics, and some of the sections are very short indeed – hiring and exchange, for example, have three or four lines each, with no detail on procedure.[60]

> Val hyn y dyleir am gyffnewid.
>
> Kymrvd mach ar bob kyfnewid, kanid kyfnewid heb vach, onid tlyssav rredegawc nid raid mach arnaddvnt. Nid amgen, gwregis a chay a chyllell kyfreith, oni chair ev goddiwes wrth I anilyssv.
>
> This is how it ought to be concerning exchange.
>
> A surety is to be taken for every exchange, because it is not an exchange without a surety, apart from worthless trinkets which do not need a surety for them. Namely, a belt and a bracelet and a legal knife, unless they are caught up with so that ownership can be reclaimed.[61]

---

[58] *Pomffred*, 1874–1963; AL IX.i.1–32.
[59] *Pomffred*, 1897–1900; AL IX.i.12.
[60] *Pomffred*, 2072–2076; AL IX.x.1.
[61] *Pomffred*, 2075–2077; AL IX.xi.1.

There is no need for the finer detail on pleading the case, since the general procedure for setting up the courtroom and establishing the extent of the claim has already been dealt with in full under theft, which is the guide to pleading a case. The sections after theft do not stand alone, and only provide specific details for that topic. Anybody wishing to plead a case of exchange, for example, would need to refer to the procedure set out for theft and adapt that case.

The form that this *cynghawsedd* takes reflects the purpose of the book. This seems to be a handbook on how to hold a legal case on various topics, with the full procedure given at the outset, and the main action in all the pleadings following largely the same format but with slight differences in detail, related to the subject matter. It is possible that this was intended for use in court, perhaps by someone who was involved in administering the law, such as a *cyngaws*. However, it may be that the lawyer would need to learn beforehand, rather than using the actual quotations from the handbook in a real legal case. This is an important legal collection, as it may show the continuation of Welsh law in north Wales, after the conquest, and perhaps in an area outside the Cyfraith Hywel heartlands – for example in the March, where a lawyer could have been called upon to take on a case from a legal system with which he was not fully familiar.

After the first collection of *cynghawsedd* dealing with theft, there is non-*cynghawsedd* material in the manuscripts – it occurs in As, Mor and Z give or take short lacunae – and these are texts on procedural matters, such as how to carry out a land claim using a cross. The sections are short, and tend to give bare rules or simple lists, and one of the sections has question-and-answer sentences on *galanas*. While not *cynghawsedd*, this material interspersed with the *cynghawsedd* in the north-east Wales manuscripts again appears to have a specific purpose – this has the air of notes for the use of someone who would want to act as a lawyer in a court situation.

The second collection of *cynghawsedd* from north-east Wales is largely on Land Law and, like the first, starts out with a long section – on stating the extent of a claim – but unlike the first collection it has no introduction or explanation of what is going to be covered. It is only the change in topic (to Land Law) and the separation of the material in Z that suggests that this can be divided into two. The second part is less well-organised than the first, and is not all 'pure' *cynghawsedd* – the majority of the *cynghawsedd* deals with land cases, but there are 'interruptions' to the *cynghawsedd*: a piece on the nine tongued-ones, and a set of the abetments for the Three Columns of Law.[62] After a discussion on crosses in land cases, there is a short introduction on ways of claiming land – kin and descent, *dadannudd*, contention, mother-right, division, equal division and final division. These sections each have a full discussion although the latter sections on the different kinds of division are shorter than the first discussions. While not as obvious perhaps as the first set of *cynghawsedd* in this collection, this again points to a text to learn how to proceed in a legal case.

The *cynghawsedd* collections in the manuscripts from north-east Wales then may have been copied into these manuscripts in the fifteenth century because they were of practical use, and were a ready reference work for a lawyer to use in court. In her study of manuscript H, which has some of this north-east Wales *cynghawsedd*, Angharad Elias states that the texts represent post-1282 developments in *cynghawsedd* – and to that it could be added that rather than being of antiquarian interest, there was still some useful value to models of legal procedure at least in the fifteenth century

---

[62] *Pomffred*, 208–213, sections 1706–1787; see AL IX.xviii–IX.xxi.

in north-east Wales.[63] The actual manuscript of H is small, portable and scruffy, and was not produced to a library standard.[64] It is likely that the form of these procedures were already fixed by the fourteenth century, as the subjects are closely linked to the law manuscripts, but they were still in use in the fifteenth century, at least in some regions of Wales or the March.

The collection found in the north-east Wales manuscripts may have travelled separately from the law manuscripts but, like the other *cynghawsedd* collections, it did not have a wide circulation. Given the useful nature of the *cynghawsedd* it is surprising that there is not more of it around, but it may be the case that its very nature and purpose meant that this was not a text that needed to be circulated widely but was something that only lawyers needed to know, for practical application in their work. Alternatively, rather than learning the knowledge formally, the lawyers may have become familiar with the information naturally, while practising their craft.

The *cynghawsedd* in *Ancient Laws* is, despite first appearances, organised and uniform, like the *damweiniau*, and the way that Aneurin Owen presented the material, divided into books and further into chapters, shows that he had a grasp of the distribution of the material, based on the manuscripts that were available to him. Even though the genre-focused material did not fit into his scheme in the first volume, his treatment was sensitive and, on close examination, it can provide the basis for further work on the textual relationship of these sections.

(c) Llyfr Cynog

As noted, Book VIII of *Ancient Laws* contains some *cynghawsedd*, but the majority of the material is taken from manuscript G and the colophon to the non-*cynghawsedd* material in G states that it is from *Llyfr Cynog*, 'The Book of Cynog'.[65] This has been discussed more fully elsewhere.[66] It seems to have originated in south Wales, although it is uncertain whether it had a fixed form or whether the title was applied to heterogeneous bodies of material. References were made to it in the Blegywryd and Cyfnerth redactions, and in Latin B and Latin D, which may point to a discrete book of law of some repute.[67] In any case parts of it were copied into G, and it occurs in other manuscripts, including Z, which has a clear north-east Wales link.[68] Unlike other sections that Aneurin Owen included in his 'Anomalous Laws', *Llyfr Cynog* is certainly elusive and indeed 'something of an enigma'.[69]

Other than G, the latter part of Z includes sections that may be from *Llyfr Cynog*, and there are two explicits in Z that name *Llyfr Cynog*. Both of these are problematic and unclear. The first explicit is split over two lines: *Llyma dervyn Llyfr Praw / A Llyfr Cynog* ('Here ends the Test Book / And *Llyfr Cynog*').[70] It is not clear whether

---

[63] *ALD*, xlix.
[64] Manuscript H is discussed in full in Chapter 7.
[65] Charles-Edwards, *The Welsh Laws*, 21.
[66] See Wiliam, *Llyfr Cynog*; Elias, '*Llyfr Cynog* of *Cyfraith Hywel*', 27–47; Wiliam, 'Restoration of the Book of Cynog'; *Pomffred*, 26–27, 30–32; see also Elias, 'Dr Morfydd E. Owen'.
[67] Elias, '*Llyfr Cynog* of *Cyfraith Hywel*', 29–31.
[68] Wiliam, *Llyfr Cynog*, ii, xiii. Manuscript G has a quire given to *Llyfr Cynog* material.
[69] Stephenson, *Medieval Powys*, 211.
[70] *Pomffred*, 26–27.

this marks the end of both the Test Book and *Llyfr Cynog*, or is marking the end of the Test Book and the beginning of *Llyfr Cynog*. Some of the material preceding this first explicit also occurs in the *Llyfr Cynog* quire in G.[71] The second explicit is clearer and marks the end of *Llyfr Cynog*: *Yma y tervyna Llyfyr Kynawc* ('Here ends *Llyfr Cynog*').[72] The end of *Llyfr Cynog* is marked far more often than its beginning in the manuscripts. If the first explicit is taken to be marking the beginning of *Llyfr Cynog*, it is followed by the Seven Bishop-Houses of Dyfed, which is also found in other versions of *Llyfr Cynog*, including in G where a reference to *Llyfr Cynog* is followed by the Seven Bishop-Houses.[73] The Seven Bishop-Houses in Z is a different version, shared with Mor, but Mor has a clear incipit marking the start of *Llyfr Cynog*.[74]

Recreating the contents of *Llyfr Cynog* then is hugely problematic. Its end is marked in G, and probably in Z, and its beginning is marked in Mor. Parts of the material said to be from it are found in Q, and in F, which is linked to G.[75] *Llyfr Cynog* was quoted in other manuscripts as having a text on *adnau* ('deposits'); but in Mor, the text *preceding* the incipit of *Llyfr Cynog* is on *adnau*, which adds further confusion to the matter.[76] *Llyfr Cynog* appears to have been a Welsh lawbook, and Elias states convincingly that it 'originated in southern Wales, that it was written in Welsh and ... that it was compiled no earlier than the twelfth century'.[77] She also argues that, because of the attribution to St Cynog, it was produced in Brycheiniog, perhaps in Merthyr Cynog.[78] Stephenson, however, argues that it may have been copied or kept at Merthyr Cynog, but it may not have been compiled there originally – and the many references to Powys, coupled with the link to the Iorwerth redaction, support this view.[79] There is of course no Powys lawbook, but there are many references to Powys in the lawtexts, confined to the Iorwerth redaction.[80] The link between *Llyfr Cynog* and Bleddyn ap Cynfyn (the ancestor of the twelfth- and thirteenth-century rulers of Powys) also gives *Llyfr Cynog* a Powysian flavour, and it also gives it an early origin or back-story at the very least.[81] Stephenson does not go as far as to state that *Llyfr Cynog* 'was a Powysian lawbook', but the evidence is interesting and tantalising, and Powys is the missing link in the geographical picture of the Welsh lawtexts.[82]

---

[71] *Pomffred*, 27.

[72] *Pomffred*, #1611.

[73] Wiliam, *Llyfr Cynog*, ix–x, and viii–ix; see also Charles-Edwards, 'The Seven Bishop-Houses', and the discussion below.

[74] *Pomffred*, 30.

[75] Elias, '*Llyfr Cynog* of *Cyfraith Hywel*', 36.

[76] Wiliam, *Llyfr Cynog*, viii, x.

[77] Elias, '*Llyfr Cynog* of *Cyfraith Hywel*', 36–37.

[78] *Ibid.*, 46.

[79] Stephenson, *Medieval Powys*, 210–211.

[80] Charles-Edwards, *The Welsh Laws*, 44; Stephenson, *Medieval Powys*, 210. Although Bleddyn ap Cynfyn was king of Gwynedd at a time when Gwynedd encompassed much of Powys, as the 'progenitor of the dynasty that ruled the kingdom and subsequent lordships of Powys in the twelfth and thirteenth centuries', Stephenson, *Medieval Powys*, 28, he was seen in the middle ages as the founder of the kingdom of Powys, and this sentiment may be reflected in *Llyfr Cynog*. See also Chapter 3.

[81] Stephenson, *Medieval Powys*, 213.

[82] *Ibid.*, 213.

Whatever it represents, *Llyfr Cynog* is an important part of Aneurin Owen's Anomalous Laws, and is one of the very few texts in that work that may point to a separate book of law with a different origin to the majority of Cyfraith Hywel texts. It may be earlier than the Cyfraith Hywel material – St Cynog was after all earlier than Hywel ap Cadell, and linking a book to Cynog may point to its antiquity, real or assumed. The laws in *Llyfr Cynog*, while linked to Iorwerth, may be 'other' laws, in a way in which the genre-based material in the second volume of Ancient Laws is not. Saying that, the subjects covered in the extant sections said to be from *Llyfr Cynog* are all law and exist in parallel to the other law manuscripts – the concepts are not, on the whole, brand new, or 'additional' to the existing lawtexts. As with other texts included in AL II, *Llyfr Cynog* complements and occasionally supplements existing law, and does so in a recognisable format; the surviving sections may have been excerpted for that reason. The answer may be that *Llyfr Cynog* was a recognisable Cyfraith Hywel book of law that was intended for circulation in a particular region, perhaps Powys. This would mean that it was not 'additional' in any way, but a specially-created text that appears to take a different format. But the very nature of *Llyfr Cynog* makes it extremely problematic and difficult to deal with – it is highly likely that it did have a fixed form, but it is impossible to date that form, or make confident suggestions as to its place of origin.

(d) Plaints

Book XII of *Ancient Laws* is also genre-based, presenting plaints, a subject that has been treated fully elsewhere.[83] Plaints are sections that are linked to *cynghawsedd*, and a plaint was the original statement explaining what had happened and initiating the legal procedure, which would then be followed by *cynghawsedd*.[84] The plaints occur in collections, and are models, similar to the *cynghawsedd* – they are attested in a small number of manuscripts, and are a rare survival. Aneurin Owen placed the plaints together in Book XII, forming another genre-specific book but following the manuscript-specific Books X and XI, from Q and S respectively.[85]

Table 4.6: Plaints in Ancient Laws

Source Manuscript	Plaint Number in Book XII
Q, NLW Wynnstay MS 36	I–X
Ep, NLW Peniarth MS 258 (*copy of* Q)	I–X
Dd, *a copy of the lost* White Book of Hergest	II, VI–X, XI, XVI
Bost, NLW MS 24029A	XI
K, NLW Peniarth MS 40	XI
'The Book of Trev Alun'	XII–XV, XVII

The first collection of plaints is a set of ten, taken from Q, with variant readings from another manuscript – a manuscript that contained material other than law.[86] A

---

[83] Roberts, 'Plaints'; Roberts, 'More Plaints'.
[84] Roberts, 'Plaints', 223.
[85] *Ibid.*, 219.
[86] *Ibid.*, 225, 229–230.

The 'Anomalous Laws' and the Lawtexts

single plaint is found in K, and also in Bost.[87] The remaining plaints were found in a manuscript called 'The Book of Trev Alun', now lost, although there are later copies of it – this manuscript may also have included material other than law.[88] This immediately raises a new issue – given that much of the so-called 'additional material' is not 'additional' in a true sense, since it is all legal material and it all occurs in law manuscripts – for the plaints we have a rare example of a genre of law texts included in manuscripts that are not purely legal. This may point to legal material that was circulating separately to the law manuscripts, or was at least available separately and was copied into mixed genre manuscripts. But the plaint form needs to be considered to suggest an explanation for this.

Plaints do appear to have been models for use by a lawyer – and indeed, in some of the copies, they may have been 'working material' for a lawyer, with blank spaces left so that the lawyer or legal presenter could fill in the relevant details.[89] The plaints from Q appear to be more literary in form, but this may be deliberate – the redactor of the plaints may have formalised the text and even made it appear 'more Welsh'.[90] Some of the Q plaints also occur in Dd, a copy of the lost White Book of Hergest (said to be in the hand of Lewys Glyn Cothi, *c*.1420–1490, and so a little later than Q)[91] and these omit place names and personal names – which means the plaints could be adapted for use in different places.[92] The relationship between Q and Dd is uncertain, particularly as there are plaints in Q that are not in Dd, but there may be a common exemplar behind the texts. The Dd plaints may show how the redactor of Q did tidy up his texts, and that the form was originally intended to be adaptable and useful.

In contrast, the Book of Trev Alun plaints have a more workaday air about them. They may be examples of actual cases, although to date no recorded cases from north-east Wales have been found that match these plaints. In that sense, the practical usefulness of the plaints may have been the reason why they were copied into manuscripts that contained other, non-legal material, although this argument is weakened by two factors. First, the plaints are a very rare survival – if they were so useful and necessary, it would be expected that there were many more of them around. Secondly, the plaints are not the only Welsh legal practical material – *cynghawsedd* also has the same function, as model pleadings. The plaints differ to the *cynghawsedd* in that they would initiate the legal proceedings, much like a claim form or an English writ, and not all cases would reach the full conclusion and require the full pleading as presented in the *cynghawsedd*. However, the two forms of the word, *cynghawsedd* and *cyngheusaeth*, discussed above, may point to the plaint and the *cynghawsedd* being, at one stage, the same thing: in the Iorwerth Land Law section, *cyngheusaeth* is limited to two things: 'the formal statement of a position and offer of proof made by plaintiff and defendant, and the sharing of the conduct of a litigant's case between himself, his *cyngaws* and his *canllaw*'.[93] The former is very similar to what is found in the plaints, and it may be that the term '*cwyn*', if not the forms discussed here, show the development of the legal process and the firming up of a process shown in

---

[87] Roberts, 'More Plaints', 183–187.
[88] *Ibid.*, 173–176.
[89] Roberts, 'Plaints', 227.
[90] Roberts, 'What's Yours is Mine', 9.
[91] Roberts, 'Plaints', 229.
[92] *Ibid.*, 227. The place names in Q may support the theory that these were not copies of actual cases; 'Plaints', 225.
[93] Charles-Edwards, *The Welsh Laws*, 58. See also 111, above.

an earlier form in the Iorwerth *cynghawsedd*.⁹⁴ This is also supported in the use of the definite article, *y gyngha6ssed*, in the texts in G quoted above.⁹⁵ The same view of *cynghawsedd* is also attested in the discussion in *Lllor* where the statement *ac wedy y darfo udunt eu due kygheusaeth ual y dywedassam ny uchot* ('and after they have finished their two *cyngheusaeth* as we stated above') refers to the previous section, where the claimant and defendant state in turn the legal position and the events that have occurred, also familiar as a plaint.⁹⁶

In addition, the plaints are short, and the *cynghawsedd* texts are long, which makes copying a text less attractive and more labour intensive. Finally, the plaint form may be more common, while the *cynghawsedd* was probably confined to legal practitioners and needed some expertise and training to be usable. It is also worth noting that the number of manuscripts containing *cynghawsedd* is relatively low, and compares well with the number of manuscripts containing plaints.⁹⁷ The plaints appear to be a Marcher text, and both collections have clear Marcher links.⁹⁸

The form and content of the plaints have been discussed fully, but one plaint in particular is deserving of particular attention – the singleton represented in Bost and K, and also in Dd, a copy of the lost White Book of Hergest. The plaints are closely linked to *cynghawsedd*, and the subject matter of the plaints is limited to the same subjects as the *cynghawsedd* – land actions, and property, but few personal actions, although there are differences between the collection in Q and that in The Book of Trev Alun.⁹⁹ The singleton in Bost and K, however, is on the subject of *sarhaed* (despite having the title *galanas*, homicide, and a very serious injury with an open head wound, the victim does not die).¹⁰⁰ The plaint is similar to a section of *cynghawsedd* in manuscript G, given in Book VIII of *Ancient Laws*, and may well be modelled on it or reworked from it, but at a remove of at least one exemplar.¹⁰¹ The copy of the plaint in Dd is closer to the *cynghawsedd* in G than the version in Bost and K.¹⁰² As the style of the plaint is different to that of the other extant plaints, it may be that this was not intended as a plaint at all but was a section of *cynghawsedd*, including the opening plaint (the section states that it is a plaint: *Llyma g6yn Ieuan ap Dafydd ap Howel ...*, 'This is the plaint of Ieuan ap Dafydd ap Howel ...') and the descriptive section is a surprising piece of prose, full of gruesome detail and alliterative phrases, but it is also matched in the *cynghawsedd* in G.¹⁰³ As a survival,

---

⁹⁴ *Ibid.*, 58; Charles-Edwards states that in the *cynghawsedd* found in the Land Law tractate in Iorwerth, 'it is not at all clear, however, that this genre of writing is yet called *cyngheusaeth* or *cynghawsedd*'. This development and refining of the terminology and indeed of the form may have happened later, perhaps in the post-conquest period.

⁹⁵ Manuscript G, 8r7.

⁹⁶ *Lllor*, 76.1.

⁹⁷ Roberts, 'Plaints', 219. There are three manuscripts containing *Llyfr Cynghawsedd* – B, G and F, which only has a partial copy – and the north-east Wales collections of *cynghawsedd* is also extant in three manuscripts (with some of the material in H). It is rare to get a high number of manuscript witnesses to *cynghawsedd* be it in collections or as individual sections.

⁹⁸ Roberts, 'What's Yours is Mine', 8–9. The Q plaints show clear links to the Marcher lordship of Cantref Bychan, whereas the Trev Alun plaints are located in Dyffryn Clwyd.

⁹⁹ Roberts, 'Plaints', 223–224; Roberts, 'More Plaints', 178–180.

¹⁰⁰ *Ibid.*, 183, 185.

¹⁰¹ *Ibid.*, 185–186; AL VIII.vii.1–6; also edited in Wiliam, *Llyfr Cynog*, 17–19.

¹⁰² Roberts, 'More Plaints', 186.

¹⁰³ *Ibid.*, 187.

The 'Anomalous Laws' and the Lawtexts

this plaint is an important piece of evidence, both in itself due to the scarcity of plaints, but also in connection with *cynghawsedd*, as it is so closely linked to the model pleadings. In addition, it once again highlights the importance of manuscript G as a source for legal material that is not found elsewhere, and the survival of the practical forms in Welsh law.

(e) Holiadon

Found primarily linked to manuscripts of the Blegywryd redaction, there was a further collection of genre-based material, called *Holiadon* (or 'Interrogatories') by Aneurin Owen. His label is found in his Book IX, which has As as its base text, although the title is not found in that manuscript, or apparently in any other manuscript either, so it appears that it was created by Owen.[104] The Welsh word is strange, grammatically, but it is a useful label.

Table 4.7: Manuscripts containing Holiadon

Manuscript	Notes
L, BL Cotton MS Titus D IX	Blegywryd
Bost, NLW MS 24029A	Blegywryd
J, Oxford, Jesus College MS 57	Blegywryd
S, BL Add. MS 22,356	Blegywryd
Y, NLW MS 20143A	Primarily Blegywryd
Q, NLW Wynnstay MS 36	Blegywryd
E, BL Add. 14931	Iorwerth; *holiadon* on final page, different hand
K, NLW Peniarth MS 40	Iorwerth but parts sharing exemplar with Q
G, NLW Peniarth MS 35	Iorwerth but mixed material
Z, NLW Peniarth MS 259B	Latter part north-east Wales
As, NLW Peniarth MS 175	North-east Wales, linked to Mor
Mor, NLW Peniarth MS 36C	North-east Wales, linked to As

The material takes the form of question-and-answer sentences, quizzes, or as Stacey calls them, 'Instructional Riddles'.[105]

> A oes un alanas ny dylyo bot affeith idi? Oes: or deruyd i aniueil llad dyn, hwnnw yw y llofrud.
>
> A oes un dyn a vo mwy gwerth y law no'e eneit? Oes: caeth.[106]
>
> Is there one *galanas* for which there should be no abetment? Yes: if it happens that an animal kills a man, that one is the homicide.
>
> Is there one man whose hand is worth more than his life? Yes: a slave.

---

[104] AL IX.xxxviii.1–16. 'Interrogatories' is an English law term.
[105] Stacey, 'Instructional Riddles'.
[106] *J(ed.)*, 91.

As well as being testing devices, the *holiadon* are numerical in style (as are several other sections in the laws). They concentrate on the number one, listing the sole exceptions to the rules discussed in the main text of the laws. The *holiadon* occur as a collection in several manuscripts: they are found in the third part of the Blegywryd manuscripts L, Bost and J, and are also found in several other manuscripts: S, Q, Y, G, As, Mor and Z. The focus in this section will be on the textual nature of the genre, but the manuscripts and their relationships is the focus of a discussion later on, in Chapter 7.

Robin Stacey, in her excellent article on these 'instructional riddles', emphasises the importance of the *holiadon* – they may well have been questions for interrogating candidates for the office of justice, and one title that is found in the manuscripts is *Profi ygneid 6eithion* ('Now testing judges').[107] The title, with the words *profi ygneid*, may also be a firm link to the Iorwerth Test Book, although the *holiadon* are not included in any of the Iorwerth manuscripts or within the Test Book itself as it appears in the extant Iorwerth texts.

The Test Book in Iorwerth claimed to be what every jurist needed to learn and to know well in order to become a justice, and it contains the Three Columns of Law (homicide, theft and arson), the Value of Wild and Tame, and some other useful material.[108] The title found in S supports Owen's suggestion that they are tests for lawyers who were required to remember the exceptions to the rules. Christine James states that some manuscripts contain material used for training lawyers, suggesting that much of their learning was oral; this includes the triads, *damweiniau*, and the unique cases found in question-and-answer form, the *holiadon*.[109] It may be the case that these *holiadon*, perhaps like the triads, or the Test Book in Iorwerth, were part of the large corpus of material that the lawyers would have to remember.[110] It is striking that certain triads are found in the collections of *holiadon* in L, Bost and J, and triads are also found close to the *holiadon* – preceding or following them – in other manuscripts too. The triads in L, Bost and J go well with the *holiadon*, since three of the four triads commonly found in the collections of *holiadon* discuss *galanas* and *sarhaed*, the subject of several of the *holiadon* themselves. However, the significant difference between the *holiadon* and the triads is that triads often expand on the subject, or three subjects, found in the heading.[111] There is rarely any expansion on the rules given in the *holiadon*: what we have is the simple question, then the answer, 'yes there is', and sometimes a short sentence giving the briefest information possible about the one exception in the question. This may be further evidence supporting the fact that these *holiadon* were, at some stage, used as mnemonics – just as the original triads were probably the simple type, extremely short with the briefest or no explanation.[112] The teacher would explain these points orally, and the difficult nature of the questions would be a way of exercising the mind of the learner. Also, the single exception could be a memory-trigger, a way of remembering several rules: the

---

[107] Title taken from manuscript S. See Stacey, 'Instructional Riddles', 339.

[108] Jenkins, *Cyfraith Hywel*, 11, 99.

[109] *Machlud*, xiii–xiv.

[110] Owen, 'Gwŷr Dysg', 49.

[111] In the short collection of *holiadon* material in E, one of the *holiadon* asks a question – 'which three wild birds should nobody kill on another's land without permission, and if they are killed there will be *dial* (revenge, reparation)?' – and the same material is found as a triad in the Blegywryd collections, including the extension stating what the fine would be.

[112] *Machlud*, xiv.

The 'Anomalous Laws' and the Lawtexts

lawyer's memory would take him from one of the *holiadon* to the relevant passage in the lawbooks. However, as is the case with triads, in the *holiadon* found in later manuscripts such as S and Q, more of an explanation is given and the form is extended.

The question-and-answer format may also suggest some form of group learning, the question being asked by someone more senior, and the answer given by a pupil or learner, but the *holiadon* are not firm evidence for law schools. They could equally be exercises for an individual. The title in S gives the plural form, *ygneid*, justices; perhaps it suggests a group of lawyers competing to be the first to give the correct answer.[113] Alternatively, this could be the test that a would-be justice was required to pass before taking office. Indeed, it could be both.

It is striking that much of the material in the *holiadon*, the test questions for would-be lawyers, is common to that found in the Test Book. Of the 37 *holiadon* that occur across the law manuscripts, 16 of them are on topics found in the Three Columns of Law, such as *galanas*, and theft cases, although there are none on fire; a further six are on matters of status or life value (including two on slaves), which is linked to the Three Columns. Over half of the *holiadon*, then, are on topics that can be linked to the Three Columns. The next biggest subject is children and inheritance, with six *holiadon* on this topic. Land law is the topic of four of the *holiadon*, and two of those are on the very specific subject of using crosses to claim land, something that is not found in the lawbooks as such.[114] Four *holiadon* concern animals. The Test Book as it exists in the extant Iorwerth manuscripts comprised the Three Columns of Law, The Value of Wild and Tame, and linked subjects, Corn Damage and *Cyfar*, the co-tillage contract. Children and inheritance occurs directly before the Test Book in Iorwerth, but Land Law is not part of the Test Book – although arguably there was an emphasis on land since the two tractates on *Cyfar* and Corn Damage focus on specific actions relating to land. It could be argued that the *holiadon* on Land Law may not have been drawn from the Test Book itself, but they may have been matters that the jurists in medieval Wales needed to know – it would be hard to imagine, given the focus on Land Law in the law manuscripts in general, that it would be possible to be a jurist in medieval Wales without a good working knowledge of Land Law. Another point to note in passing is that much of the material found in Owen's Anomalous Laws, and/or sections sometimes classed as 'Additional Material', focus on land disputes. The matter of the *holiadon*, confined to subjects of use in everyday transactions and not taking in subjects such as the Law of the Court, again emphasises the practical nature of this material, the possibility that it was law that was current and in use, and that it also had a strong Marcher link.[115]

Stacey notes that the material is found in 'the non-lawbook writings of the period', and is 'another non-lawbook genre' like the *cynghawsedd*.[116] The *holiadon* genre – like the *cynghawsedd* – is actually not found separately to the lawbooks, and Stacey's view is based on the traditional division of the Welsh law material into the Redactions (Owen's Codes), and the Anomalous Laws. It should also be noted that a collection of *holiadon* is found in L, Bost and J, in material that Owen included in his Dimetian Code (Blegywryd), and not in his Anomalous Laws.[117] Having said that, the *holiadon* collection is a surprising one in that it occurs in several places: in the

---

[113] Williams, *Detholion*, xiii.
[114] Roberts, 'What's Yours is Mine', 10–11
[115] *Ibid.*, 8.
[116] Stacey, 'Instructional Riddles', 338.
[117] AL DC III. See Chapter 5.

third part of the Blegywryd manuscripts in L, Bost and J; in the latter part of other manuscripts that contain more varied material, such as S and Q; and also in other manuscripts that are linked to the Iorwerth redaction or that are non-redaction texts. The reoccurrence of the *holiadon* may point to the popularity of the form.[118]

The *holiadon* occur in collections, but there was more than one separate collection circulating, probably in south Wales. Examples of the genre occur quite soon after the *Arferion Cyfraith* introduction in L, Bost and J, and as such they are included in AL DC III. The collection in *Ancient Laws* is not an exact copy of the collection in L, but is instead augmented by insertions from the fuller collection found in S. Manuscripts Q, J, L and S were used for variant readings. This collection will be discussed further in Chapter 5. However, a collection of *holiadon* that appears to be linked to *Llyfr Cynog* needs particular attention here.

The earliest manuscript containing *holiadon* is Iorwerth E. On the final page of the manuscript there is a short text, 17 lines, filling the second half of the page and breaking off mid-sentence; it is in a different hand to that of the rest of the manuscript, an unusual and old-looking hand. The material is also unusual and not found elsewhere – there are three sentences that follow the *A oes* ('Is there') form, but a further three use *Mae* ('Where is/are') as the interrogative, and one of the sentences asks *Pa tri ederin* ('which three birds'). Not all of the *holiadon* here have answers, and there is other material towards the end of the section, on the punishment for shaving a man's head while he is asleep. This is a strange collection, and it is difficult to reach any firm conclusions on it because of its brevity. Other than this material in E, the next oldest collection of *holiadon* is also linked to the Iorwerth redaction: it occurs in manuscript G, which dates to the first half of the fourteenth century. The main hand of G is the same as that of Cyfnerth U.[119] He also stated that this manuscript is called *Llyuyr Kyna6c*, and Aled Rhys Wiliam used G to form his version of *Llyfr Cynog*.[120] Furthermore, in this collection in G, the material typically conveyed in the *holiadon* format mostly does not appear in the usual question-and-answer form. There are two regular *holiadon* on f. 70 (first hand) of the manuscript, but in the same section there are a number of sentences, plain statements, beginning with *Vn lle* ('One place'). Of the total of 11 sentences, the sixth and seventh are the only ones that follow the *A oes* formula. However, all of the other sentences are found as *holiadon* in the other manuscripts, mainly in S and Q. The sentences in G appear to be in note form, or at least a simplified form. This again seems to imply that G was a lawyer's handbook, and indeed a source for later legal reworking.

There are two possible reasons why the question-and-answer formula does not appear in G. The formula may have been a recognised one already, and the scribe therefore wrote it out once or twice, but for most of the *holiadon* he left it out although it was inferred; the reader was expected to recognise that these are formulaic sentences. The only fault with this is the fact that the two sentences including the formula are found right in the middle of the collection, and not at the beginning as a sort of key or memory jogger. Had he given the formula at the beginning and omitted

---

[118] In her study of the *holiadon* Stacey notes that there are similar passages in English Common Law literature, and the parallels are striking as she says; this may point to borrowing and knowledge of a parallel legal tradition, as well as an indicator of legal education in both England and Wales. Stacey, 'Instructional Riddles', 341–342.

[119] *RWMS*, Scribe X87; he was also the scribe of Peniarth 45, a prose collection. The second hand is the scribe of a version of the Welsh Brut.

[120] Wiliam, *Llyfr Cynog*.

it from then on, it would be clearer for the reader that all this type of sentence should fit into the question-and-answer form. The second possibility is that the sentences in G were formed before the formulaic question-and-answer was made general; in other words, what we have in G are the raw materials used to make a series of *holiadon*, in the same way as was seen with the material originally presented in G, which reoccurs but presented as a plaint.[121] Again, the two formulaic sentences in the middle of the collection raise problems with this theory. As it stands, this could easily be a small collection of numerically arranged material, similar to the triads, but using the number one instead – apart from one of the pair of question-and-answer statements all of the sentences start with 'Vn'. What may have started off as a numerical collection could have been transformed into the *holiadon* as one or two sentences from the collection did not fit into the 'Vn' formula, although it is clear that they are all *one* exception to the rule. The change may also have taken place because of the repetitive or familiar action of copying the same form repeatedly – (over)familiarity, and indeed boredom, can lead to a scribe making variations in the wording.

Two of these sentences in G begin with *Pa* ('Which'), and both are found in the Dimetian Code collection of *holiadon* with the other formula – it seems that the lawyers were keen to have this question-and-answer formula, but at this stage they had not settled on the question form: there is no need for a corresponding answer form for the *Pa* type question, but they are referring to one exception to the rule, like the more common *holiadon*. One of these sentences has been transformed from a *Pa* question with three sections, into a simple triad in Q, again highlighting the links between the *holiadon* and the triads.[122] Most of the *holiadon* in G are also found in Q or S, the later manuscripts, rather than in L or J. S has the largest collection of *holiadon*, so it is not surprising that there is overlap. The *holiadon* found in G may have been, as noted earlier, a possible numerical group that was changed to a different formula or the raw material for the questions and answers in the later *holiadon*. The fact that they are included in the later manuscript in their other form is interesting, particularly as Q includes two of the *holiadon* without the question-and-answer formula. The *holiadon* may have been found towards the end of the original *Llyfr Cynog*, following some triads. Most of the references to *Llyfr Cynog* concern *adnau* ('deposits'), but it is striking that the material found at the end of the book, triads and *holiadon*, are of practical use in memorising sections of law.

Apart from the manuscripts discussed above, there are some *holiadon* in manuscripts that are not linked to a redaction text, although the form of the *holiadon* in this case is very different from those previously discussed. These are found in manuscripts As and Mor. Apart from their occurrence in these specific legal manuscripts, the *holiadon* have an added interest in that they move away from the traditional form as seen in the other collections, and they present *holiadon* that have a negative answer.

Turning to *Ancient Laws*, the *holiadon* are included in this work in two sections; in AL DC III, and also in the Anomalous Laws, in AL IX.[123] The base manuscript used for Book IX was As, with variants from Mor, and IX.xxxviii.1-9 is a section comprised of ten of these alternative *holiadon*. Mor seems to miss some *holiadon*, but resumes at the fourth in As. Z is also used for variant readings for the rest of Book IX but has a hiatus at this section. The *holiadon* in this book are not found in any of the other collections. The subject matter is different, as they are all discussing *galanas* or

---

[121] Roberts, 'More Plaints', 186.
[122] Wiliam, *Llyfr Cynog*, 56.
[123] See also Table 4.4, above.

sarhaed. A further oddity occurs in Book IX; chapters xx, xxi and xxii are given each to the nine abetments of *galanas*, theft and arson, respectively. Arson, xxii, is very short, comprised of an introductory sentence and a triad only. Both xx and xxi are a little longer; each has an introductory sentence, then each has a short discourse on *galanas* and theft, in question and answer form. However, these are not *holiadon* as found in Blegywryd, as the verb varies: we find *a dyleir ... dyleir* ('should there (be) ... there should'), *paham ... llyma paham* ('why ... this is why'), and *pwy* ('who'), and as well as positive answers, we also find negative answers. These are very brief sections, relating to the Three Columns of Law; men wishing to be jurists in medieval Wales needed to know the Three Columns of Law and the Value of Wild and Tame (the contents of the Test Book) in order to practice.[124] These question-and-answer sections may be a more informal form of the *holiadon* preserved in the formal written Blegywryd lawbooks, and the closest we can get to the training undertaken by medieval jurists. The *holiadon* appear to have an obvious educational function, and show similarity to the wider European tradition, as well as having what appear to be close English parallels.[125] The *holiadon*, however, stand alone in the Welsh legal tradition in terms of their genre and style – while other parts of the law may perhaps have an instructional purpose or had originated as learning material, the existence of the *holiadon* may be a rare insight into medieval Welsh legal training.

Conclusion

The texts examined in this chapter have been, to some extent, relegated to a secondary status. Most have been neglected: editions of some of these texts are available but in an early form, and are often difficult to obtain.[126] The *holiadon* and *cynghawsedd* remain unpublished as single studies.[127] Accessible texts of all of the genres in *Ancient Laws* II are problematic, and it is unlikely that modern editions of the texts in their own context – as has been done for various tractates of other parts of the laws – will be made in the near future. The main focus on edited texts of the laws are recognisable tractates, and, more rarely, single-manuscript editions.[128] This situation has clearly occurred as a result of the presentation in *Ancient Laws*.

---

[124] *Machlud*, xiv.

[125] Stacey, 'Instructional Riddles', 340–343.

[126] For example, the *damweiniau* from Col were edited by Dafydd Jenkins in an edition that he stated was in a '*ffurf amatewraidd*' ('an amateurish form') with the intention of publishing the work rather than letting it slip, but the work has never been re-edited: *DwC*, vii. *Llyfr Cynog* was published by Aled Rhys Wiliam in a pamphlet series that was intended 'to make available, without excessive delay, work which has been given some publicity, but is not necessarily in definitive form', and the series was 'prepared for limited circulation': note on the *Pamffledi Cyfraith Hywel* series printed in the back of some of the pamphlets. The note also adds that 'Readers are particularly requested not to cite this material in print without previous consultation with the authors', which suggests that the pamphlets were personal notes rather than publications.

[127] Both genres have only been edited if a manuscript that contains them happens to have been edited: for example, the *holiadon* collection in S can be found in *Machlud*, 64–66; and those in J in *J(ed.)*, 89–91. The north-east Wales *cynghawsedd* was edited in *Pomffred*, but the text is disordered in manuscript Z.

[128] Both *Machlud* and *ALD* were originally PhD dissertations and studies and editions of individual manuscripts – the importance of these works should not be underestimated.

All of the genres discussed in this chapter have been designated 'additional' by scholars, and have not been afforded the attention that they deserve. But on the whole, calling these genres 'additional' is inaccurate. These texts are different from the redactions, but this may have more to do with the context of their writing. The lawyers who were creating texts of *cynghawsedd* or collections of *damweiniau* were aware of the redaction texts, and may have intended their work to sit alongside other texts that were standard accounts of Cyfraith Hywel: the reference to 'Llyfr Hywel' reveals this awareness. The text of Iorwerth created by Iorwerth ap Madog was intended to be a superior account of the laws, and it became known as the standard version; but Iorwerth ap Madog made use of earlier texts similar to those found in the *damweiniau* and *cynghawsedd* collection. These texts cannot exist without the redaction texts, but the redaction texts were originally from the same legal tradition as these genres that are sometimes classed as 'additional'.

If we move away from the concept of the material in *Ancient Laws* II as being 'additional' or 'anomalous', how then should it be viewed? Perhaps the new approach should be to see this material on its own terms, and in its own context. Regardless of its position in a law manuscript, or its occurrence in any given law manuscript, perhaps the focus should be moved to the nature and purpose of this material. Firstly, the lengthy collections of *damweiniau* and *cynghawsedd*, and the shorter collections of *holiadon* and plaints, should be viewed in the same way as other tractates, such as Suretyship or the Law of Women. The difference between the other tractates is that they are organised by subject, whereas the *damweiniau, cynghawsedd, holiadon* and plaints are all sections that are organised by genre. If we treat the collection of triads found in all of the redactions in the same way, then the model already exists in the 'main' redactions, the parts of the lawbooks that have been given pre-eminence, for a tractate that has varied subjects within it but is united by form.

In addition, another factor that this material has in common is that it may have a different purpose to the legal rules expounded in the first volume of *Ancient Laws*. Several of these sections would be essential knowledge for a practising justice, necessary for him to be able to speak in legal cases. Others have a didactic or training origin, and again they would have had practical application. This should elevate the material to a primary position. Rather than call the genre-based material in the second volume of *Ancient Laws* 'additional', separating them out from the main redactions, a better approach would be to examine the texts as functional prose, and look instead at the nature and purpose of the material, as well as the context of the manuscripts in which it is contained. The material is all united by its usefulness, its application for a working lawyer and, as such, it may represent living law – arguably more so than other sections of the laws, the Laws of Court being an obvious, but not isolated, example. A new examination would erase the old established divisions that separates out these sections of law – and that are separated since they do not always follow the format of the better-known tractates and the redaction texts – but instead give them their due as texts intended to serve a purpose and, furthermore, reveal a great deal about the working of the law in medieval Wales.

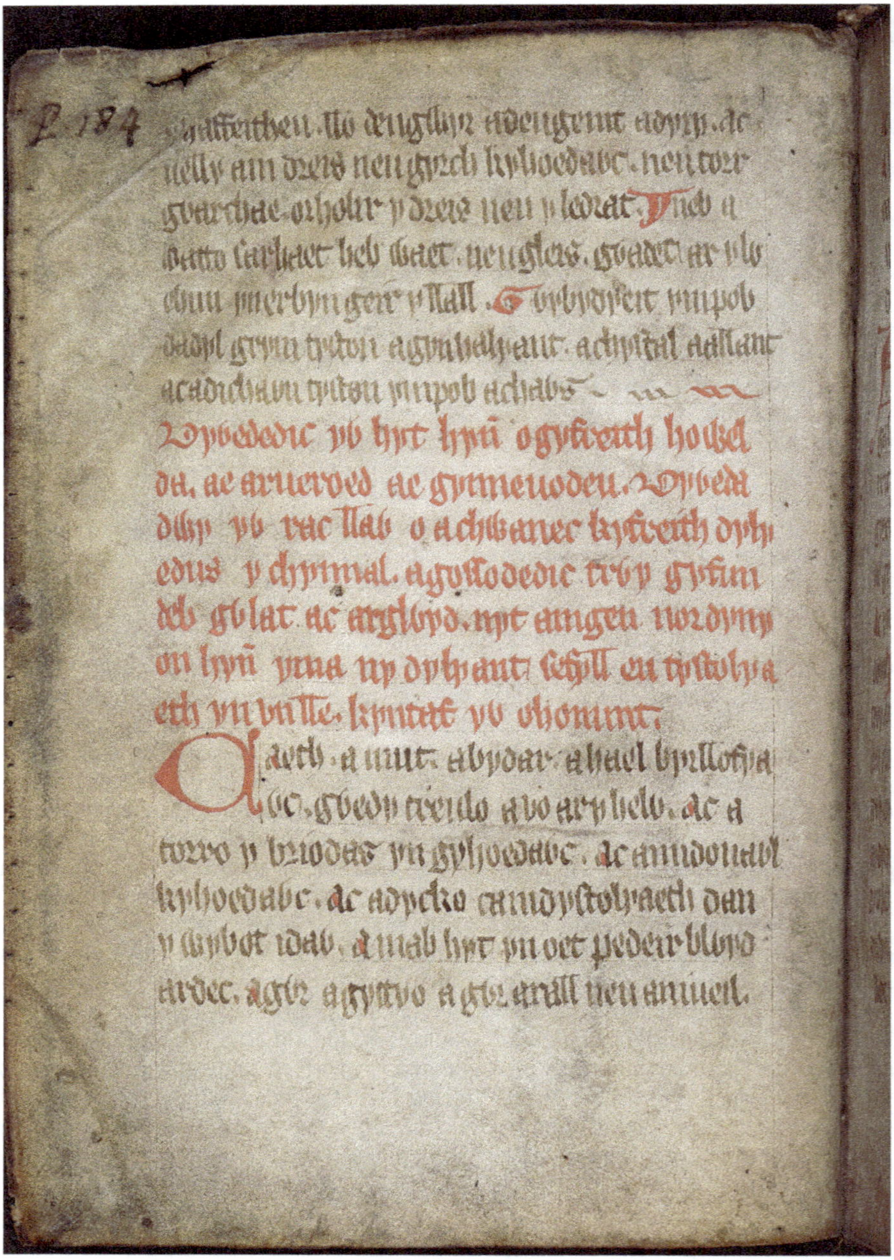

gasserthen. llo deugllyn adeugemt adyui. ac
uelly am dreis neu gwch kyboedauc. neu torr
gwarthae. oholur y dreis neu y lewat. Neb a
watto carlbeet beb wact. ueugbers. gwadet ar vlo
cbuu merbyn geir y llall. Orbyorsen ympob
dadyl gwyn tyston a gymhelyant. achystal adllant
acaducbaun tyston ympob achabs. ~ m ~
Ypbedeoic yb hyt hyn ogystveth hotsel
da. ac aruervoes ae gymneuodeu. Ypbeda
diby yb rac llau o achbaner kystveth dyhi
edus y chytynal. agostodeoic trwy gystim
deb gblat. ac arglbyd. nyt amgen nordymy
on hyn ytna up dyh aut sesyll eu tystolya
eth yn vn lle. kyntaef yb ohonunt.
Aeth a nut. a by dar. a bael by ellofia
oc. gbedy treiclo a vo ary belv. ac a
torro y briodas yn gybioedauc. ac amdouawl
kyhoedauc. ac adycko cauudystolyaeth dan
y cauvot iday. a mab hyt yn oet pedeir blyo
ardec. agbr a gystvo a gbr arall neu amuerl.

Figure 2: Oxford, Jesus College MS 57, p. 184. By kind permission of Jesus College, Oxford.

5

'ACHWANNEC KYUREITH DYLYEDUS Y CHYNNAL': THE BLEGYWRYD REDACTION

Dywedadwy yw rac llaw o achwannec kyureith dylyedus y chynnal a gossodedic trwy gyuundeb gwlat ac arglwyd.[1]

Henceforth will be spoken of additional law which ought to be maintained and which is set by the agreement of country and lord.

The aim of this chapter is to examine the Blegywryd redaction and its structure, and compare it to the Iorwerth redaction and its tripartite structure. *Arferion Cyfraith* ('Practices of Law'), which is said to be a third part of the Blegywryd manuscripts, will be examined, as will the long-held idea that some manuscripts, particularly Blegywryd manuscripts, have 'tails' of 'additional material' appended to a main text of the laws. This chapter will present the argument that this so-called 'additional material' is no less important than the preceding text and should not be separated or given less attention. This follows on from the discussion in the previous chapter, primarily focused on the material in the Anomalous Laws, and the genre-based books such as *damweiniau* and *cynghawsedd*, which were often appended to the text of a Iorwerth manuscript. These Iorwerth books are very rarely described as being 'tails' – perhaps because of the organised appearance of their material, or because of their connection with the well-structured Iorwerth version. On the other hand, several Blegywryd manuscripts are seen to have 'tails' of additional material, and this is often ascribed to the manuscripts being later in date: they have absorbed later compilations of law but appended them to an existing text rather than incorporating the material into relevant points in the preceding text. As will be shown, this may not be a valid way of viewing these complex texts.

Manuscript Tails

Manuscript J is a beautiful law text in the hand of Hywel Fychan, one of the scribes of the Red Book of Hergest. Melville Richards's edition of J in 1957 was an important step in the study of the legal manuscripts.[2] Apart from the printed edition, it has been digitised.[3] It has a Blegywryd text, similar to that found in L, which was

---

[1] AL DC III.ii.pr, taken from L.

[2] J(ed.).

[3] J, Oxford, Jesus College 57, has been digitised by the Bodleian Library, Oxford, and can be viewed at <https://digital.bodleian.ox.ac.uk/objects/91819125–25f1–4533–9fdd-99a4d1c84491/>, accessed 30/11/21.

used as the base manuscript for Owen's Dimetian Code, followed by material largely from another redaction, Iorwerth. The introduction to the 1990 edition of the work, by Daniel Huws, Morfydd E. Owen and Thomas Charles-Edwards,[4] gave the entire manuscript the attention it deserved, and considered the Blegywryd manuscripts as a group. This drew heavily on the work undertaken by Christine James in her study of manuscript S, a complex Blegywryd manuscript, much expanded. In the published edition of J, the text was organised by mirroring the various sections of *LlBleg* for the first half of the manuscript, while the remainder of J was called a 'tail'.[5]

The concept of a 'tail' can be seen as a development of the idea of 'additional material'. It is common to see the lengthier law manuscripts, primarily Blegywryd ones, described as having a 'tail', or as containing 'additional material'. But this immediately invites the question – additional to what? The answer is that it is supposedly additional to material given pre-eminence following an early editorial decision tied in with a concept of basic legal material. However, this division between basic and additional material is not reflected in the manuscripts. The division into 'Code' and 'tail' owes its existence to Aneurin Owen, once again, as is made explicitly clear by Morfydd Owen in the introduction to the 1990 edition of J:

> Like most manuscripts of Cyfraith Hywel, the Jesus College LVII manuscript, or J, includes a form of one of the Versions along with a tail of mixed material. Usually, the Version corresponds broadly to one of the Versions published by Aneurin Owen in the first volume of *Ancient Laws and Institutes of Wales*, and the tail, mostly, to material which is in the second volume.[6]

Had it not been for the enduring influence of the editorial mindset of Aneurin Owen and his *Ancient Laws*, perhaps the standard approach would have been closer to that adopted by Morfydd Owen, who looked at the manuscript and asked whether there was any obvious dividing line in the text itself.[7] The material in the second part of these Blegywryd manuscripts is said to come '*o ffynhonnell sydd yn annibynnol ar lyfrau'r Deheubarth*' ('from a source independent of the Deheubarth books [of law]').[8] In the context of J, this may mean that one of the sources is a northern, Iorwerth manuscript.

The 'tails' of the Blegywryd manuscripts have been viewed in the light of Aneurin Owen's division of the laws into Codes and Anomalous Laws. Owen saw the 'tails' of the Blegywryd manuscripts as being in the Anomalous category, even though the manuscripts with a 'tail' attached could represent the Blegywryd code as well; he presented sections of the 'tail' of Q and S in Book X and Book XI respectively.[9] But several other manuscripts have a 'tail' of additional material in the same way: Cyfnerth Z has a long and mixed tail; J has a 'tail' largely consisting of Iorwerth

---

[4] *J(ed.)*, 'Preface', vii, notes that Huws was responsible for the discussion of the manuscript, and the discussions on Blegywryd and Iorwerth were by Owen and Charles-Edwards respectively.

[5] *J(ed.)*, xiii.

[6] *J(ed.)*, xiii. 'Fel y rhan fwyaf o lawysgrifau Cyfraith Hywel, y mae Llawysgrif Coleg yr Iesu LVII, sef *J*, yn cynnwys ffurf ar un o'r Dulliau ynghyd â chwt o ddefnydd cymysg. Fel rheol, y mae'r Dull yn cyfateb yn fras i un o'r Dulliau a argraffwyd gan Aneurin Owen yng nghyfrol gyntaf *Ancient Laws and Institutes of Wales*, a'r gwt, gan mwyaf, i ddefnydd sydd yn yr ail gyfrol.'

[7] *J(ed.)*, xvi–xvii.

[8] *J(ed.)*, xvi.

[9] He did however use the Iorwerth second half of manuscript J for variant readings in his Venedotian Code.

material; and L and Bost have material that has been called a short tail.[10] Owen was aware of the 'tail' of L, but did not use the Boston manuscript since it had gone to the US by the nineteenth century.[11] Since Owen used L as his base text for the Blegywryd redaction, his Dimetian Code, he did not distinguish between the material forming the main text in L and the material forming the short tail, other than putting the latter into his Book III of the Dimetian Code. While it is sometimes said that the sections with titles in *LlBleg* form the 'core' Blegywryd text, or the 'traditional' Blegywryd material, and that other material is additional, this is an idea based on the divisions and editorial decisions made by Williams and Powell in 1942; the existence of a short 'tail' in L, Bost and J may point to a more flexible view of how the lawyers saw their lawtexts and how they intended them to be used.[12] In other words, this is not a tail at all, not material appended to the text. Rather, it is the continuation of the Blegywryd text, but its form may be different because of its particular purpose.[13]

Arferion Cyfraith

The majority of the Blegywryd manuscripts, with some caveats regarding editing and rearranging, end with a section known as *Arferion Cyfraith*, which opens with an extended triad.[14] However, on careful consideration it can be seen that this is not a 'tail' or any anomalous material, but rather that this section is a standard and integral part of Blegywryd texts.

Arferion Cyfraith is the heading applied to the section by the editors of *LlBleg*, but it is not found in the manuscripts; there the word *arfer* or plural *arferoedd* is used, and this was translated as 'practices' by Aneurin Owen.[15] *Arfer* can have different senses, but here it means 'practice' and, as Jenkins notes 'the tractate sets out rules of procedure appropriate to various classes of cases'.[16] It is not entirely clear what exactly comprises *Arferion Cyfraith*. There appear to be several short sections towards the end of a Blegywryd redaction manuscript (assuming that it is complete) that occur in the same, or in a similar, order. The argument here is that the Blegywryd redaction has a tripartite structure, as outlined in a triad,[17] and that *Arferion Cyfraith* is comprised of these short sections towards the end of a Blegywryd manuscripts, with all of the sections collectively forming the third part of Blegywryd.

Jenkins states that *Arferion Cyfraith* is 'rather more than four pages', and half of the tractate is commentary on the triad.[18] Of course, it is entirely possible that the section is simply the extended triad on *Arferion Cyfraith*, but since several tractates within the Blegywryd redaction are introduced by a triad or take a triadic form, and

---

[10] *J(ed.)*, xvii.
[11] On the Boston manuscript, now NLW 24029A, see Owen, 'Llawysgrif Gyfreithiol Goll'; the manuscript has been digitized and there is a further discussion on its history and contents on the National Library of Wales' website: <https://www.llgc.org.uk/index.php?id=6466>, accessed 26/11/21.
[12] *Machlud*, xl–xli.
[13] See the discussion below.
[14] *LT*, 230–233, Triad Q242.
[15] *LlBleg*, 127; AL, 'Table of Contents'.
[16] Jenkins, 'Custom', 427.
[17] *J(ed.)*, 86.6–10, and quoted below.
[18] Jenkins, 'Custom', 427.

then continue with more material on the same theme, it is entirely possible that the *Arferion Cyfraith* triad opens the section, and the following sections also make up the *Arferion Cyfraith* tractate.[19]

It is perhaps of note that the *Arferion Cyfraith* triad is not found in the Iorwerth or Cyfnerth redactions, or in any other collections of legal triads, again supporting the idea that it is a triadic opening for the longer section. While the Iorwerth manuscripts divide into three distinct sections – the Laws of Court, the Laws of Country, the Test Book – it is generally assumed that this is not the case with the Blegywryd manuscripts (or the Cyfnerth manuscripts for that matter) and the division is far less clear. Several of the Blegywryd manuscripts have a section at the end called *Arferion Cyfraith*, and the complete manuscripts also have a short explanation, dividing the lawbooks into three, in a triad that usually precedes *Arferion Cyfraith*:

> Teir rann yw awdurdawt Howel Da a'e gyfreitheu, nyt amgen, kyfreith y lys peunydyawl, a chyfreith y wlat, ac aruer kyfreithawl o bop un ohonunt.
>
> Dywededic yw hyt hynn o gyfreith y llys a chyfreith y wlat. Dywedadwy yw rac llaw o'r arueroed.[20]
>
> Three parts is the authority of Hywel Dda and his laws, namely, the law of his daily court, and the law of the country, and the legal practice of each of them.
>
> Hitherto has been spoken of the law of the court and the law of the country. Henceforth the practices are related.

The preamble or rubric is a familiar dividing point between the main divisions of a lawtext and the different or new section that then follows. The Blegywryd manuscripts often have a short preamble to the Laws of Country:

> O hynn allan y treithir o gyureith y wlat a'r swydogyon dywededic; ac yn gyntaf o teir colofyn kyfreith, nyt amgen ...[21]
>
> From now on will be treated the law of the country and the aforementioned officers; and firstly the three columns of law, namely ...
>
> Hyt yma y dywetpwyt o swydogyon llys y brenhin ac eu kyfreitheu. Rac llaw, trwy nerth Duw, y dywedir o swydogyon kyffredin yssyd rwng yr arglwyd a gwyr y wlat.[22]
>
> Up to now the officers of the king's court and their laws have been spoken about. From now, by the strength of God, the ordinary officers which are between the lord and the men of the country will be stated.

These kinds of rubrics are commonly found in narrative prose and in other texts too, which links the Cyfraith Hywel texts to the wider context of prose writing in middle

---

[19] *LT*, 9. Jenkins refers to a second triad within the section, *Tair gosodedigaeth* (three ordinances), which is on a similar subject and follows the *Tri arfer cyfraith* triad; Jenkins, 'Custom', 427.
[20] *J(ed.)*, 86.6–10.
[21] *LlBleg*, 29.26–28.
[22] *J(ed.)*, 23.9–11.

Welsh and, indeed, other languages.[23] The Iorwerth manuscripts often have rubrics marking sections and, in general, the Iorwerth texts have more titles or preambles and colophons. This is particularly the case with manuscript C, the product of a trained scribe, but less so of A and E – but this may reflect the more organised nature of the Iorwerth texts.[24] The Blegywryd texts usually only have rubrics for the main divisions of the lawtexts – but that in itself may make the *Arferion Cyfraith* preamble more striking.[25]

The *Arferion Cyfraith* that follow the preamble appear, at first sight, to comprise a relatively short section in a triadic form. In a complete text, the triad on *Arferion Cyfraith* is then followed by several shorter sections on various loosely related topics (see Table 5.1). The *Arferion Cyfraith* section occurs in most Blegywryd manuscripts, but also, importantly, in Latin D. A manuscript version of Latin D, but not the extant manuscript, was translated to form the Blegywryd redaction.[26] Since the *Arferion Cyfraith* section is also in Latin D, that factor suggests it has been carried over from the original Latin into Blegywryd. *Arferion Cyfraith* does not occur in M, N, R or T, but all these manuscripts have their end wanting. O is also lacking *Arferion Cyfraith* but also has something odd happening on its final pages – the text breaks off and then changes to something else, which suggests a lacuna in the text being copied. So it can be seen that *Arferion Cyfraith* is best viewed as a section that ought to be in all standard Blegywryd manuscripts, and so it does not seem appropriate to view the section as additional material.

It is also striking that, given that the Blegywryd manuscripts are purportedly divided into three sections, of which *Arferion Cyfraith* is the third, the section is so very short. The Laws of Court and the Laws of Country are far longer and encompass a great deal more material. So, for example, in Aneurin Owen's edition, the Dimetian Code is presented as three books, with the Laws of Court subdivided into thirty-one chapters, and the Laws of Country into thirty-six chapters; *Arferion Cyfraith* do not have a title given by Owen, and AL DC III has only six chapters, with the first one comprised of *Arferion Cyfraith*. The third part of Owen's Venedotian Code, known as the 'Test

---

[23] With thanks to Ceridwen Lloyd-Morgan for her insight on this matter.

[24] For example: *Ac euelly e teruynha e Lleuer Llys* ('And so ends the Court Book'); *Eman e dechreun ny o kyureythyeu e guraged ... Ac uelly e teruena keyreyth e guraged* ('Here we begin on the laws of women ... And so ends the law of women'); *Eman y dechreuant keureythyeu e wlat* ('Here begin the laws of country'); *Am haul uach a chynogen* ('On a claim of debtor and surety'); *Am dadleu tyred yu henn* ('This is on pleadings for land'); *Ac yuelly e teruyna teyr kolouen keureyth* ('And so end the three columns of law'); *Am llugyr yt ... Ac yuelly e teruynyr am lugyr yt.* (On Corn Damage ... And so it ends on Corn Damage.). *LlIor*, 43.13; 44.1, 55.15; 56.1; 58.1; 72.1; 120.7; 154.1, 160.9. The latter ends *LlIor* and the standard Iorwerth manuscripts; but it is not a final ending to the laws as it would be possible to include another tractate or more material following the discrete Corn Damage section. The Test Book, the third part of Iorwerth, is marked as follows: *Llyma e dechreu e Llyuer Prauf. Sef yu henne, teyr colouen keureyth a guerth guyllt a dof ac a perthyn arnadunt. ... Ac yuelly e teruynha e Llyuer Prauf.* ('Here begins the Test Book. That one is, the three columns of law and the value of wild and tame and that which pertains to them. ... And so ends the Test Book.'); *LlIor*, 104.1–2; 138.14. The colophon occurs at the end of the list of values of trees and woods; the rest of Iorwerth continues with the extended Value of Wild and Tame section and the list of equipment and tools and their values, and other sections.

[25] It should be noted that the Latin texts, in particular Latin D from which the Blegywryd redaction was translated, have titles for clear sections. The Cyfnerth texts are striking in the absence of markers, titles, preambles or colophons – only the Laws of Court are distinguished from other sections in this way. The Cyfnerth texts tend to finish with the triad collection.

[26] *LT*, 29; Emanuel, 'Llyfr Blegywryd', 28.

Book', is quite short, with twenty-five chapters compared to forty-three in the Laws of Court and thirty-one in the Laws of Country, and yet it is still a significant and notable section – unlike the third book of the Dimetian Code.[27] Given that it is stated quite clearly that the Blegywryd redaction divides into three sections, and that the third section is *Arferion Cyfraith*, it is surprising that such a short section is given such prominence; it was, however, important for legal theory.

Table 5.1: Arferion Cyfraith *and other connected sections*

Section (opening words)	AL	LlBleg	J(ed.)
Cynefodau [Customs]	II.xxxvi.1–3	*107.9–16	[91] 85.29–36
Cyfraith Anysgrifenedig [Unwritten Law]	II.xxxvi.4	126.19–25	[92] 85.37–86.5
Tair rhan yw awdurdod [Three parts is the authority]	II.xxxvi.5	126.26–29	86.6–8
Dywedadwy yw rhag llaw [Up to now has been stated]	II.xxxvi.5	126.30–32	86.9–10
Tri Arfer Cyfraith [Three Practices of Law]	III.i.1–5	127.1–27	[93] 86.11–32
Amser tystu [Time to testify]	III.i.6	127.28–128.5	86.33–87.2
Llysu tystiolaeth farwol [Objecting to dead testimony]	III.i.7–8	128.6–14	87.3–9
Galw gwybyddiaid [Calling knowers]	III.i.9	128.15–18	87.10–12
Gwrthneu gwybyddiaid [Objecting to knowers]	III.i.10	128.19–28	87.13–21
Amser ymwystlo â brawd [Time to gage for judgement]	III.i.11	128.29–129.5	87.22–28
Pwy bynnag ni wypo arfer cyfraith [Whoever does not know the practice of law]	III.i.12	129.6–7	87.29–30
Tair gosodedigaeth [Three ordinances]	III.i.13	129.8–25	87.31–88.5
Ni saif neb amddiffyn [No defence stands]	III.i.15–16	129.26–130.2	88.6–12
Pwy bynnag a ddywedo ar y brenin [Whoever says of the king]	III.i.17	130.3–10	88.13–19
Gwadu [Denial]	III.i.18–26	130.11–131.10	88.20–89.4

As can be seen, there are several sections that follow the *Arferion Cyfraith* triad. There are also preceding and introductory sections – the set of triads on *Cynefodau* ('Customs') appears to be linked, but it is placed before the triad tractate in *LlBleg*, the edition taken from manuscripts from the Blegywryd group which do not have Laws of Court and have rearranged some sections.[28]

---

[27] AL, 'Table of Contents'. The Gwentian Code is divided into two sections, 42 and 41 chapters respectively.
[28] *Machlud*, xxx.

Another interesting point about the *Arferion Cyfraith* section is that the very short texts jump from subject to subject. The phrase *arferion cyfraith* is translated as 'practices of law' by Melville Richards, following Aneurin Owen's example.[29] But looking at the section, 'usage of law' would be an appropriate (although less elegant) translation, and *arfer* has another meaning of 'what is usual'.[30] The extended triad of *Tri arfer cyfraith* ('The three practices of law') first examines the timing of holding law courts and cases, and appropriate times for legal action; the second limb is on the mode of holding a legal case, with an extension on the record of the court; and the third limb looks at lawful timings, including the time for testifying.[31] The text then follows on without a break with further material on testimony, and defunct testimony, then a short discussion on witnesses, objecting to witnesses, and mutual pledging to a judgement. A possible end for the section – although the triad seems to have finished some time earlier – is the sentence that demands that the lawyer must know *Arferion Cyfraith*:

> Pwy bynnac ny wypo aruer kyfreith, ny dichawn aruer o gyfreith.[32]
>
> Whoever does not know the practice of law, he is not able to practise law.

In all editions, and in the complete manuscripts (ranging from the Gwilym Wasta manuscripts from the early fourteenth century to the fifteenth-century manuscripts), there then follows a triad on the three statements or pronouncements in Welsh law: *Tair gosodedigaeth* ('Three ordinances'), on dealing with opposing views and 'to complete the law and its practices perfectly'.[33] Further sections follow this triad, on defence and denial. In all, this only takes up a few manuscript pages (and four or so pages in a printed book), and is a miscellaneous part of the law manuscripts, although the material is all on a similar theme – the practice of law, or rather, use of the law or legal procedure. There does appear to be a clear thematic grouping here, and perhaps calling the material miscellaneous is inappropriate – several well-known tractates also jump around in a similar way, but with the theme of the section as a unifying factor for the material.

The suggestion here is that *Arferion Cyfraith* is the third branch of the Blegywryd texts, and it was a full tractate, 'a book or literary work treating of a particular subject',[34] on legal procedure and actual practice – something upon which the other tractates are often silent, being focused on legal rules. The section may be short, but there was also an opportunity for development into a longer text. This development did not occur in most of the extant Blegywryd manuscripts – they are shorter texts, and may have their end wanting. The development may be seen in the longer Blegywryd texts that contain more material – procedural, with an emphasis on legal practice – following the *Arferion Cyfraith* opening, making the third section much longer.

---

[29] Richards, *The Laws of Hywel Dda*, 116; see also Jenkins, 'Custom', 427.
[30] Jenkins, 'Custom', 427.
[31] *LT*, 230–233, triad Q242.
[32] *J(ed.)*, 87.29.
[33] *LT*, p. 229, triad Q238.
[34] OED, q.v. tractate, 1.a.

The Tripartite Division

It is not just the Blegywryd texts that have three sections where the third section has material relating to the practice and practicalities of the law. It is a structure found in Iorwerth manuscripts, with the Justices' Test Book, and in Cyfnerth manuscripts, with collections of triads. Iorwerth manuscripts famously have a tripartite division. The first two sections are the same as those in Blegywryd, but the third part is the Justices' Test Book, said to have been created at least in part by Iorwerth ap Madog (fl. ?1240–?1268).[35] In his study of the make-up of the Welsh law manuscripts, Charles-Edwards sets out the main divisions of a Cyfnerth manuscript, Mk, versus the Iorwerth manuscripts.[36] Unfortunately, Charles-Edwards does not present a parallel analysis of Blegywryd, since he is concentrating on establishing a clear contrast between the more primitive Cyfnerth and the developed Iorwerth manuscripts. Charles-Edwards also divides the Cyfnerth text in Mk into three, giving triads as the third part: there is a collection of triads at the end of several extant Cyfnerth manuscripts.[37]

Table 5.2: The Tripartite Divisions

Iorwerth	Cyfnerth	Blegywryd
Laws of Court	Laws of Court	Laws of Court
Laws of Country	Laws of Country	Laws of Country
Test Book	Triads	*Arferion Cyfraith*

In his discussion, Charles-Edwards explains that the distinction between Aneurin Owen's division of the texts into the Versions (Codes) and the Anomalous Laws 'lies in the existence of a certain pattern according to which it was thought that a wide-ranging account of the Law of Hywel ought to be constructed. The pattern was not immutable ... Nonetheless it existed and lawyers knew when they were making a significant change to the pattern ...'.[38] Aneurin Owen also saw this pattern, and he felt that his 'Codes' represented it; by contrast the material in AL II, the Anomalous Laws, was material that he deemed as not conforming to the pattern. Charles-Edwards goes on to say that 'The shift to the new pattern in IOR may be described as a move to a three book arrangement.'[39] The 'new' section in Iorwerth, possibly created by Iorwerth ap Madog and certainly in thirteenth-century Gwynedd, would be the Test Book, which is indeed a distinct entity, entitled as such.[40]

The purpose of the Test Book in Iorwerth is clear, and it is said to contain the material that the lawyers needed to know, and the material in the Test Book includes the things listed in Cyfnerth as the essential basic knowledge for the justice: the Value of Wild and Tame, and the Three Columns of Law. While Charles-Edwards

---

[35] Charles-Edwards, *The Welsh Laws*, 23–24; 29–30. See Chapter 3.
[36] Ibid., 27–28. Charles-Edwards numbers the Prologue as the first part of the manuscripts, giving four sections.
[37] Ibid.
[38] Charles-Edwards, *The Welsh Laws*, 26–27.
[39] Ibid., 29.
[40] Ibid., 30. Only the Test Book is called a 'book'; the Laws of Court and the Laws of Country are sections, *cyfreithiau* (laws) or collections of *cyfreithiau*.

states that 'the reasons behind this shift to a three book arrangement can only be guessed at', one possibility is that the tripartite arrangement reflected the love of the number three in all Middle Welsh didactic literature.[41] However, it should be noted that the tradition of dividing legal tracts into three is one that is found in Roman law: Gaius's *Institutions* was divided into three sections looking at persons, things, and actions, and this was followed by Justinian; this 'Institutional scheme' is the basis for the organisation of many legal systems even today.[42]

It was also not unique to the Iorwerth manuscripts. Although the way the material may have been edited and some material moved around is special to Iorwerth, the arrangement in three parts, with the third part emphasising the practice of law, seems to have been a general trend in Welsh lawbooks.[43] The Test Book was very much a novel creation for Iorwerth, but a similar thing, if not as obvious, was also occurring in the Blegywryd manuscripts, and the tripartite division of the laws was even made explicit in a triad in Blegywryd.[44]

The Cyfnerth redaction does not have a clearly marked tripartite division; rather, the Laws of Court and the Laws of Country form two sections. The Cyfnerth texts are early, and it is difficult to assign clear patterns to them – their manuscripts do not match so closely as their Blegywryd and Iorwerth counterparts. However, looking at the last part of some of the manuscripts does show some interesting things. Manuscripts V and W are linked, sharing the same scribe, and both manuscripts end with a collection of triads. The material preceding the triad collection is different in V and W, but both manuscripts have a section on trees, included in the Iorwerth Test Book; they also have sections on procedure – in W, the 'ninth days' (on time allowed to do certain things), and on judgement, and in V a section on witnesses, which is also found in Blegywryd. These sections have the same procedural feel to them as the material in the Iorwerth Test Book and in *Arferion Cyfraith* in Blegywryd.[45] Mk ends with triads, but before the triads it has sections that are also found in *Arferion Cyfraith* in Blegywryd texts. Manuscript U is perhaps the most interesting. It has a collection of triads near the end, which is preceded by a section on the *rhingyll*, a local enforcement officer. But after the triads, U has a collection of *damweiniau*

---

[41] The triad form was popular in Welsh literature in general, and is also found in Irish literature, including law. *LT*, 1–2. Narrative sources often use incremental repetition in threes and this may be a feature of oral presentation, and the popularity of the triad form may also link the lawtexts to oral use. *LT*, 5–6.

[42] With thanks to Professor Thomas Watkin for discussing this – and other matters – with me. See also Birks and McLeod, *Justinian's Institutes*, 13, 16, and for the influence of the Institutional Scheme on modern legal systems see 19–26.

[43] This again may reflect the Institutional Scheme and the division into people/things/actions: the Laws of Court discusses the people of the court; the Laws of Country considers things, including property; and the Test Book in Iorwerth can be seen as considering legal actions, and legal practice. Birks and McLeod, *Justinian's Institutes*, 13.

[44] One Cyfnerth manuscript, U, also has a clear and marked tripartite arrangement: preceding the collection of *damweiniau* at the end of the manuscript is a sentence stating *Hyt hyn y traethassam k'theu llys a chyfreitheu yr gwlat. O hyn allan or damweineu* ('Up to now we discussed the laws of court and laws of country. From now on the *damweiniau*.') This may be a back-formation following other texts. U is an early manuscript, from the first half of the fourteenth century, it shares a scribe with G, and both manuscripts have a very similar text of *damweiniau*.

[45] Parts of the Iorwerth Laws of Country are also focused on procedure e.g. the procedure in a land case included under Land Law, and parts of the suretyship tractate.

('eventualities'), which are more commonly linked to the Iorwerth redaction and that follow the Test Book material in those manuscripts.

Charles-Edwards argues that triads form the third part of the Cyfnerth texts.[46] The argument has already been set out that the collection of triads in Blegywryd and Cyfnerth should be seen as a tractate, but here looking at the purpose of the material may be helpful. If the triads were mnemonic devices, for learning the law, then that brings the large collection of triads forming the third part of the Cyfnerth manuscripts closer to the practitioner-led material in Iorwerth and also in Blegywryd. Having triads near the end of the manuscript, and the nature of the other material near the end of the Cyfnerth manuscripts, with its emphasis on legal procedure and practice, suggests that the idea of having a tripartite division, with the third part devoted to legal practice, had already been started in the Cyfnerth texts, albeit in an embryonic form. Manuscript U with the *damweiniau* is particularly important.

Looking at the Latin texts may also support this theory of the tripartite division of the Welsh lawtexts. The inspiration for the necessary learning for a justice in Iorwerth, moved, edited and renamed the Test Book, may have originated from an earlier Latin text, similar to the Latin A manuscript. That manuscript, at the end of the Laws of Court and as a preamble to the Three Columns of Law, states:

> Nemo debet iudicare nisi sciat illa tria que dicuntur *teyr colouyn kefreyth*, et pretium hominum, et animalium que usui hominum sunt necessaria. Sunt autem hec tria: *nau affeyth galanas, nau affeyth than, nau affeyth lledrat*.[47]

> Nobody ought to be a justice unless he knows the three things which are called *teyr colouyn kefreyth*, and the value of men, and of the animals which are necessary for the use of men. Those three are: *nau affeyth galanas, nau affeyth than, nau affeyth lledrat*.

The manuscript for Latin A is similar in date to the earliest Iorwerth manuscripts, the mid-thirteenth century, but a corresponding piece of text is not found in the other Latin manuscripts. A similar sentence, listing the material that became the Iorwerth Test Book, is also found in the Cyfnerth manuscripts, in the justice's section in the Laws of Court.[48] Latin A does not have a tripartite arrangement and does not end with triads, but it ends with the Value of Wild and Tame and Corn Damage, those sections that a justice needed to know, and which are found in the Iorwerth Test Book. This may be significant.

The Latin manuscripts are not closely related, and Latin C is not complete. Latin B and Latin E are linked, however, and Latin E seems to be a tidier version of Latin B. Latin B has, like Latin A, the Value of Wild and Tame near its end, which is followed by the triad collection. This may link to the Cyfnerth positioning of triads, as legal learning materials, in the third part. But the most significant thing about Latin B – a factor shared with Latin E – is that the manuscript has material that is not found elsewhere after the triads, and some of this material once again has a procedural bent – there are *damweiniau*; material referring to Powys;[49] there is a

---

[46] Charles-Edwards, *The Welsh Laws*, 27–28.
[47] *LTWL*, 121.
[48] *Ny dyly neb varnu ar ny 6yppo teir colofyn kyfreith a g6erth pop aneueil kyfreitha6l* ('Nobody ought to judge without knowing the three columns of law and the legal value of every animal'). *WML*, 16.13.
[49] See Chapter 3, 81–84.

text on the local officials, the *maer* and the *cynghellor*; and there are Irish canons. This is miscellaneous material but, as with the other redactions of law, several of the sections hint at material for a practical purpose, for the administration of law, perhaps for the use of practitioners. Neither the Cyfnerth manuscripts, or Latin A, B, C, and E, have a clear tripartite division, nor do they have a Test Book or *Arferion Cyfraith*. But the manuscripts, in the material found near the end, may show the first seeds for the development of the tripartite arrangement and the third section focused on legal practice.

Dating this tripartite arrangement is a further issue. Previously, the tripartite arrangement was attributed to the Iorwerth manuscripts alone. The Iorwerth manuscripts are earlier than those of Blegywryd – the earliest Blegywryd manuscripts date from the first half of the fourteenth century,[50] versus the Iorwerth manuscripts from the thirteenth century.[51] While the exact text that was used as the basis of the Blegywryd manuscripts is no longer extant, Latin D in Bodleian Rawlinson MS C 821 is similar, and that manuscript dates from the late thirteenth century, which is closer in date to the mid-thirteenth-century Iorwerth manuscripts. The triad stating that the laws are divided into three parts is found in Latin D, towards the end of the manuscript, along with the preamble to *Arferion Cyfraith* that is found in the Blegywryd manuscripts:

> Tres autem sunt partes auctoritatis Howel Da de legibus: scilicet, lex curie, et lex patrie, et usus utriusque. Huc usque de legibus curie et patrie dictum est. Amodo de usu utriusque legis dicendum est.[52]

> There are three parts of the law with the authority of Hywel Dda: namely, the law of court, and the law of the country, and the legal practice of each of them. Hitherto the discussion has been of the laws of court and of country. Henceforward the discussion should be about the practice of each law.

This is then followed by the material found in the *Arferion Cyfraith* section at the end of the Blegywryd manuscripts, ending with the material found before the next division of the text in J and related manuscripts, although with an additional sentence which is not found in the Blegywryd redaction, and a poem.[53] This dates the tripartite division of Blegywryd around two generations (at most) after the Iorwerth innovations. What is uncertain is whether the Blegywryd texts and their preceding Latin version were aping the Iorwerth Test Book, or whether it was an independent or parallel development. A third possibility is that this was an inherited element, and that the Iorwerth redaction and Latin D took the tripartite division from a common source but reacted to it in different ways. This may mean that the innovation is earlier than the first manuscripts of the laws – we have no direct evidence that predates the

---

[50] The scribe of three early Blegywryd manuscripts, Gwilym Wasta, is dated to Dinefwr in 1302–3; Owen and Jenkins, 'Gwilym Was Da', 429. See also Russell, '*Canyt oes aruer*', 173.

[51] Blegywryd N, O, R and Tr are dated to the first half of the fourteenth century, with I, J, L, M, T, Bost and Y from the mid- to late-fourteenth century. In contrast, Iorwerth A and C are the earliest Welsh law manuscript, from the mid-thirteenth century, and B and E are also thirteenth-century manuscripts.

[52] *LTWL*, 394.

[53] *Ibid.*, 396–397, corresponding to *J(ed.)*, 89.2, with the final sentence: Si vero *saraed* hominis, ut dicitur uxore eius abuti, negabitur, iuramento quinquaginta hominum negetur. This does not appear to be included in the Blegywryd texts.

thirteenth century – but the first steps for this arrangement are visible in Cyfnerth texts and in Latin A and B. It may have been a parallel development in Blegywryd, but one that was not as noticeable because the Blegywryd texts are not as organised as the Iorwerth texts.

Legal Practice

The redistribution and rearrangement of the material in Iorwerth may not completely change the focus of the exposition. If the purpose of the Test Book was 'to assemble together a body of material which it was thought particularly important that lawyers should know',[54] then this may simply have been achieved by moving more sections into the third part of the manuscripts, while keeping the essential material together. In the same way, the *Arferion Cyfraith* appears to have accommodated the practical parts of the Blegywryd manuscripts, with a heavy emphasis on procedure as opposed to academic rules of law. It may be that Iorwerth ap Madog, who is given credit as being the compiler or editor of at least part of the Iorwerth Test Book, created his tripartite book by keeping the Laws of Court and the Laws of Country in his Iorwerth text as presenting the laws, and then put the essential knowledge that a justice needed to know to practise law in his third section. But the same thing was done for the Blegywryd redaction, and that before the text was translated from the Latin into Welsh. And further support to the idea that the third part of Blegywryd had a similar theme to that of Iorwerth is found in the statement within *Arferion Cyfraith* that states that *this* is what the justice must know in order to practice: *Pwy bynnac ny wypo aruer kyfreith, ny dichawn aruer o gyfreith* ('Whoever does not know the practice of law, he is not able to practise law').[55] The singular form of *arfer* as opposed to the plural *arferion* is useful in that statement – a justice would need to know how to practice law; it would not be enough to simply know the law. The plural form *arferion* used as the title for the section in printed editions does appear to be a modern construct, as the preamble refers to *arferoedd*; the meaning 'the practice of law' makes more sense in the context, as opposed to a nominal sense of things which would be called 'practices of law'.

The Iorwerth Test Book has an unusual title, which is also difficult to explain, and the exact meaning of 'Test Book' has been under discussion in the past. Aneurin Owen translated 'Llyfr Prawf' as 'The Proof Book', which is equally difficult. The title '*Llyfr Prawf*' is found in all Iorwerth manuscripts that contain a copy or partial copy of it, and at the beginning of the section it is named as a book: *A'r llyfr hwn a elwir y llyfr praw* ('And this book is called the test book'); in manuscript B, its start point is marked and named: *Llyma e dechreu e Llyuer Prauf* ('Here begins the Test Book').[56] The use of '*Prawf*' to describe the book is rather difficult to explain. The word also occurs in the set of question-and-answer sentences found in some manuscripts: '*Profi Ynadon*', or *holiadon*, a section that is discussed in Chapter 4. These sentences are tests, questions posed with a single answer, and so the use of '*Profi Ynadon*' for such a genre makes sense – although it occurs for the first time in a fifteenth-century text, and is not found in the earlier collections. It may also be

---

[54] Charles-Edwards, *The Welsh Laws*, 30.
[55] *J(ed.)*, 87.29.
[56] *LlIor*, §104.

influenced by the 'Llyfr Prawf' title in that manuscript. For the Test Book, the third part of the Iorwerth manuscripts, it may be that the title emphasises the necessity for every lawyer to learn and know the Test Book well, and the suggestion that it was used as a measure to see whether a would-be justice was learned enough to become a professional justice.

> Whosoever wants to take up justiceship, thus it is proper for him: to know this book so that it is worthy for him to take justiceship: and when his teacher sees that he is worthy, let him send him to the Court Justice, and it is for the Court Justice to test him ....[57]

This prologue is found in three Iorwerth manuscripts and refers clearly to knowing the contents of the Test Book, but without stating what those contents were; the main introduction to the Test Book does list the contents, the Three Columns of Law and the Value of Wild and Tame and what pertains to them. While the Test Book in Iorwerth is very specific, and named, there is a similar section in Blegywryd, which equally lists the same things – the Three Columns and Wild and Tame – as being essential for a would-be justice to know, but there is no reference to the test in the Blegywryd text.[58]

The Development of the Blegywryd Material

Having concluded that *Arferion Cyfraith* is an integral part of the structure of Blegywryd manuscripts rather than being a mere tail section to more important parts, we need to look at what it actually contains, how it developed and whether it can be thought of as possessing a tail of its own.

The *Arferion Cyfraith* section in Blegywryd may not be complete in most manuscripts, nor indeed in the printed text of *LlBleg*. It occurs at the end, where manuscripts typically suffer loss. *Arferion Cyfraith* is not found in M, N, O, or R, but each of these manuscripts have hiatuses. It is found in I, Llan, Tr, and T, but in all of these cases the end of the manuscript is wanting; Tr has the colophon naming Gwilym Wasta as the scribe of the manuscript, but the preceding section, part of *Arferion Cyfraith*, stops mid-sentence. The scribe may have added his colophon at the end of the material he had. The *Arferion Cyfraith* section is in an edited form in Q and its copy Ep (P, the other copy, breaks off mid-way through the triads and ends there); it occurs in S and Tim, but a section has been moved in S, and also in I, which is very close to S at that point; it occurs in full in Tim and is followed by more material as it is not at the end of the manuscript. Sections of *Arferion Cyfraith* also occur in Y, Mk and Mor, but the complete section is not in any of those manuscripts. Importantly, the section occurs at the end of Latin D, but the final sentence on *gwybyddiaid* as found in the edition in *LlBleg*, taken from L, which is also the final sentence of the particular section in the edition of J, is missing in Latin D. Instead, there is a poem written at the end of the manuscript. Having *Arferion Cyfraith* at the end of a Blegywryd manuscript was a practice started early on in the textual history of Blegywryd, as it is found in Latin D, although the Blegywryd text continued to develop in its Welsh form.

---

[57] *LTMW*, 141, taken from manuscript C, but the same section also occurs in D and K.
[58] *LTMW*, 142.

The Growth of Law in Medieval Wales, c.1100–c.1500

Table 5.3: Arferion Cyfraith in the Blegywryd manuscripts

Manuscript	Arferion Cyfraith
Latin D	*Arferion Cyfraith*, short, followed by poem
I, Peniarth 38	*Arferion Cyfraith*, relocated
J, Oxford, Jesus College 57	*Arferion Cyfraith*, followed by other material
L, Cotton Titus D IX	*Arferion Cyfraith*, followed by other material
M, Peniarth 33	No *Arferion Cyfraith*, hiatus/end wanting
N, Peniarth 36B	No *Arferion Cyfraith*, hiatus/end wanting
O, Peniarth 36A	No *Arferion Cyfraith*, hiatus/end wanting
P, Peniarth 259A	No *Arferion Cyfraith*, hiatus/end wanting
Q, Wynnstay 36	*Arferion Cyfraith*, rearranged, long 'tail'
R, Peniarth 31	No *Arferion Cyfraith*, hiatus/end wanting
S, BL Additional 22,356	*Arferion Cyfraith*, relocated, long 'tail'
T, Harleian 958	*Arferion Cyfraith*, end wanting
Tim, Llanstephan 116	*Arferion Cyfraith*, relocated, long 'tail'
Tr, Cambridge, Trinity College O.7.1	*Arferion Cyfraith*, end wanting
Bost, MS 24029A	*Arferion Cyfraith*, followed by other material
Llan, Llanstephan 29	*Arferion Cyfraith*, end wanting
Ep, Peniarth 258	*Arferion Cyfraith*, rearranged, long 'tail'
Y, NLW 20143A	Sections of *Arferion Cyfraith*

Three manuscripts remain, which need particular mention in this context. L, J and Bost, are complete, and have *Arferion Cyfraith* in full, but they also have other sections at the end. Each carries on where other manuscripts – and the edition in *LlBleg* – stop, and each has the same material by and large. The *LlBleg* edition was taken from manuscript Tr supplemented from L. Tr is the source for *Arferion Cyfraith* in the edition apart from the last sentences, which are taken from L.[59] An editorial decision was made to stop at a particular point, since there is more material in L than there is in the edition in *LlBleg*, and the decision was probably made on the basis of a colophon to *Arferion Cyfraith*:

Dywededic yw hyt hynn o gyureith Hywel da, a'e arueroed, a'e gynneuodeu.[60]

Hitherto has been spoken of the law of Hywel Dda, and its practices, and its customs.

Since the closing sentence is found at the end of *Arferion Cyfraith*, the expectation is that the closing sentence given above would only occur in a manuscript that also contains a complete text of *Arferion Cyfraith*. So in manuscripts without a full text of *Arferion Cyfraith* or manuscripts with the end wanting, this closing sentence would also naturally be lost. The sentence is followed by a further explanation:

---

[59] *LlBleg*, 131.1–10.
[60] AL DC III.i.26, taken from L.

'*Achwannec kyureith dylyedus y chynnal*': The Blegywryd Redaction

Dywedadwy yw rac llaw o achwannec kyureith dylyedus y chynnal a gossodedic trwy gyuundeb gwlat ac arglwyd. Nyt amgen no'r dynnyon hynn yma ny dyly eu tystolyaeth seuyll yn vnn lle.⁶¹

Hitherto has been spoken of additional law which ought to be maintained and which is set by the agreement of country and lord. Namely of these men here whose testimony ought not to stand in any place.

The explanation states what is coming next, in the case of manuscripts that contain further material – *Dynion na ddylai eu tystiolaeth sefyll* ('men whose testimony should not stand').⁶² This colophon to *Arferion Cyfraith* is rare in the manuscripts, due to the fact that they often peter out before the end of *Arferion Cyfraith*, but it occurs in three significant manuscripts, each containing what has been called a 'short tail': L and Bost, and J, which has the same 'short tail' but develops it further.⁶³ In L and Bost, significantly, the colophon is written in red ink. It looks as if the colophon concludes the main lawtexts or, at the very least, it concludes *Arferion Cyfraith* and the other linked sections. However, even if it does conclude *Arferion Cyfraith*, the use of *dywededig yw hyd hyn* ('stated up to now') implies that the texts were open to having more material added to them. *Dywededig yw hyd hyn* is based on the Latin *dictum huc usque*, which was used in manuscripts to mark the end of one text; the manuscript may continue but not with the same text before the *dictum huc usque*. In L and Bost, although this is a colophon, written in red ink, it is not closing the law in a final sense, and an appropriate frame was in place for adding more material if necessary.

The exact wording of the colophon deserves attention. The first part explains that the text was simply Welsh law, in a general way, with special mention given to '*arferoedd*' and customs. *Arfer* (pl. *arferoedd vel sim*) as a noun means 'usage, practice, habit, custom' according to *GPC*, and Jenkins notes the non-technical use, 'what is usual', and 'the technical use for "practice", i.e. procedure' – with an emphasis on the practical nature of the material again.⁶⁴ It then continues stating that what will follow will be *achwannec kyureith dylyedus y chynnal* ('further law which ought to be maintained'), and the emphasis on the agreement of the country and the lord may be with the aim of giving this material equal status with the preceding material, even though this was not seen to be part of Hywel Dda's work, but something that came later. The section that follows is on men whose testimony is invalid, on a similar theme to the material found with *Arferion Cyfraith*.

Looking at the extended Blegywryd manuscripts, the colophon is not found in S, but there is no closing sentence to *Arferion Cyfraith* in S (which is not at the end of the manuscript in any case), and the *Dynion na ddylai* section has a different preamble. Tim is missing its *Arferion Cyfraith*, as well as the *Dynion na ddylai* section. Q and Ep have a different order due to editing work in those manuscripts: the *Arferion Cyfraith* section is found as a number of shorter sections, placed at relevant points in the main text, and so there is no natural point for the closing sentence; the *Dynion na*

---

[61] AL DC III.ii.pr, taken from L

[62] i.e. a list of 15 men who are not permitted to give testimony, either because they are disabled (deaf or mute), or disallowed for another reason such as being underage or have been found guilty of a serious offence. Homosexuals are included on the list.

[63] The same material is not found in Latin D, which has a Latin poem at the point where the colophon is in L, Bost and J, and the manuscript ends with closing words. *LTWL*, 397.

[64] *GPC2*, arfer¹; Jenkins, 'Custom', 427.

ddylai section is found in a different location – as the *Arferion Cyfraith* section has been moved around – and so it does not have a preamble and it follows on from the previous section (a part of *Llyfr Damweiniau*).

Therefore, what can be said about this 'short tail' of material, with the colophon to *Arferion Cyfraith*, is that it occurs in a certain form in three manuscripts only: L, J and Bost, although the material is attested in other manuscripts.[65] All three manuscripts have the full collection of material presented in AL DC III, in the same order as in that edition, which is taken from L; and in L the manuscript finishes at that point. There is clearly a link between L, J and Bost through this particular material.

Table 5.4: Ancient Laws: *Dimetian Code Book III*

DC III	Section Number and Title*	Manuscripts
i.1–26	93 Arferion Cyfraith	L I J Q S Bost Ep Tim P Llan Tr T Y Mor Lat D Mk
ii.1–17	94 Dynion na ddylai eu tystiolaeth sefyll	L J Q S Bost Ep [Not Tim]
iii.1–48	95 Profi Ynadon	L J Q S Bost Ep Tim G K Y Mor
iv.1–11	96 Oedi Cyfraith	L J Q S Bost Ep Tim Y G
v.1–7	97 Lle y dylai ceidwaid fod	L J Q S Bost Ep Tim U As
vi.1–26	98 Pethau sydd unfraint â lledrad yn llaw 99 Amodau, etc	L J Q S Bost Ep Tim

*Taken from *J(ed.)*.

As can be seen from the table, AL DC III is comprised of *Arferion Cyfraith*, other linked material that follows it, and then the 'short tail' of L, also found in Bost and J. Despite this being additional material in the sense that it is appended to the manuscript, and in particular the material following the colophon – which only occurs together in three manuscripts (two in Owen's edition as he did not use Bost); and despite the material appearing to be marked as different or additional in the manuscripts themselves, Owen did not separate it or deem it 'anomalous' and therefore suitable for his second volume. It is not entirely clear why – perhaps he wanted to maintain a tripartite division – but there are points in favour of this material being treated with the main Blegywryd text as Owen did. It may be an added text (particularly so if it is taken as law that was agreed by everybody, after the time of Hywel Dda's lawmaking activities), and the material does appear to be more miscellaneous in nature. But if it is viewed as a subject-specific section, united by being material on procedure and practice of law, then it is less random. It also has a title, like many of the well-known tractates. The colophon at the end of *Arferion Cyfraith* may point to the material that follows as being 'additional', but it may also simply be a tractate subdivision within the third part of the Blegywryd manuscripts, *Arferion Cyfraith*. Even if it is 'additional' in some sense, or later – it does not occur in Latin D, which represents the basis of the Blegywryd redaction – it is a deliberate and unified text. Seeing the material as 'additional' often equates it with being secondary, but even if it is additional in some sense it is still an informative and relevant part of the *Arferion Cyfraith* section of the Blegywryd manuscripts instead. It deserves to be viewed for its own value, and with a focus on its purpose.

---

[65] There is a discussion of the material in other manuscripts below, on 155–156.

'Achwannec kyureith dylyedus y chynnal': The Blegywryd Redaction

Leaving *Arferion Cyfraith* aside, there are five other sections to consider in AL DC III (see Table 5.4). Owen notes that the base manuscript is L, and also refers to J, Q and S as other manuscripts containing the sections. To these manuscripts, for all of the sections, should be added Ep and Bost, which were not used by Owen, while Tim contains all but one section: Tim is related to S and shares much of the same material, but is not a copy of that manuscript. Ep is a copy of Q, and has the same material in the same order, so when reference is made to Q, it also includes Ep. So, we have seven manuscripts – L, J, Bost, S, Tim, Q, and Ep – containing almost all of this material, although they used the material differently in some cases.

First we must consider the nature of these sections. All of the sections bar one, *Profi Ynadon*, are relatively short, and several of them are lists. Section 94, *Dynion na ddylai eu tystiolaeth sefyll*, is a list, with the first item numbered, although the subsequent items are unnumbered, and it considers a question of evidence, those whose evidence is invalid. The section on delays in law, 96, *Oedi Cyfraith*, is again a short list with a brief explanation at the end; 97, *Lle y dylai ceidwaid fod*, on maintainers and evidence, is a very short section and a numbered list of four. The final section in AL DC III is lengthier, and combines two sections (98 and 99) in the edition of J, with two titles that reflect the themes of the sections; from 98, *Pethau sydd unfraint â lledrad yn llaw*, starting with things equal to theft in hand, the section continues with more varied material. All of this material comprises short sentences, sometimes on a similar topic, and it includes a triad, a numbered section (*saith gynneddf*, seven qualities), and ends with sentences summarising situations, all starting *Sef yw* (this is [what X is]).[66] While this appears to be more miscellaneous in nature, and less organised than *Arferion Cyfraith*, it is similar to the way material is presented in some of the tractates in the Laws of Country in Blegywryd – it is united by being under one basic theme, but it may jump around and almost dissolve into the form of notes within the tractate itself. The material included is all procedural – and that means that it fits well under the *Arferion Cyfraith* section heading – and discusses the practical side of dealing with the law – swearing oaths, giving evidence, people whose testimony may be invalid, and occasionally definitions of particular things. Aneurin Owen did not consider this material to be Anomalous, and he may have been right to do so, if this material as it occurs in L, Bost and J is simply part of *Arferion Cyfraith*.

The Blegywryd Continuation

This fuller third section of Blegywryd is preserved in three manuscripts, and the three manuscripts deserve consideration individually before examining the relationship between them. L (*s.* xiv^{med}) was used by Aneurin Owen as the basis for his Dimetian Code, and he considered it to be the oldest of the Blegywryd manuscripts, and 'the nearest affinity to the original compilation sanctioned by Howel' (which says a great deal about the way Owen considered the material at the end of that manuscript).[67] The manuscript is now dated to the mid-fourteenth century, and may be in the same hand as Scribe A of the White Book of Rhydderch; if so, it is associated with Strata Florida abbey.[68] After *Arferion Cyfraith* and other sections, L has the colophon written in red

---

[66] *J(ed.)*, 92–94.
[67] AL, Introduction, xxx.
[68] Huws, *Medieval Welsh Manuscripts*, 234–239. Cardiff 2.7, *s*.xv^2, is a copy of L, by Scribe X81: *RWMS*.

ink, and contains all the material found in AL DC III. At this point, the manuscript ends, leaving half a page blank, but with the last few words, *y dyn o'e da* ('the man from his goods') in an odd display hand; it seems that this was all that L had.

Bost (*s*.xiv^2) is similar in date to L, or a little later, and it is also textually close to L. The material following *Arferion Cyfraith* in Bost starts on f. 90r, l. 16, and continues in the same way as that found in L, but including some material that is not in L. The textual and codicological history of Bost is a little more complicated than that of L. The manuscript was for a long time kept at the Massachusetts Historical Society's library in Boston, Mass., but in 2012 it came up for sale at Sotheby's, and was bought by the National Library of Wales. Following the acquisition, much conservation work was done on the manuscript, which included taking its binding apart. This revealed an interesting aspect to its collation, something that would not be revealed under other circumstances. Towards the end of the manuscript, a separate gathering[69] of six leaves, ff. 94–99, had been inserted between the pages of the existing manuscript, and then subsequently bound with the remainder of the manuscript, giving the appearance of one continuous book.

Table 5.5: The Third Section of Bost, with the inserted gathering marked by shading

Section	Bost	Notes	Scribe
93 Arferion Cyfraith	88r1–90r15	Also L, J	A
94 Dynion na ddylai eu tystiolaeth sefyll	90r16–90v10	Also L, J + colophon in red	A
95 Profi Ynadon	90v11–93r6	Also L, J up to *J(ed)* 91.27	A
Portion of non-legal text, different hand	93r7–93r16	Scribe B	B
95 Profi Ynadon	93v1–14	Also L, J *J.ed* 91.28–92.3	C
96 Oedi Cyfraith [INTERRUPTED]	93v15–24	Also L, J Up to *J(ed.)* 92.11	C
95 Profi Ynadon [REPEATED]	94r1–94r22	starts at *J(ed.)* 91.24	D
96 Oedi Cyfraith	94r23–94v13		D
97 Lle y dylai ceidwaid fod	94v13–94v19		D
98 Pethau sydd unfraint â lledrad yn llaw 99 Amodau, etc	94v19–96r18		D
Lladrad	96r18–96v17	Ior 113.10–113.16	D
Cwyn	96v18–98r1		D
Emyn Curig	98r2–99v23		D
96 Oedi Cyfraith [CONTINUED]	100r1–100r4	Also L, J starts at *J(ed.)* 92.11	C
97 Lle y dylai ceidwaid fod	100r4–100r9	Also L, J	C

---

[69] 'A gathering, or quire, in a manuscript or printed book is a discrete group of leaves, a series of which units sewn together makes up the volume.' Beale, *Dictionary of English Manuscript Terminology*, q.v. scribal errors.

98 Pethau sydd unfraint â lledrad yn llaw	100r9–101r21	Also L, J	C
99 Amodau, etc		Also L, J; L ends	
Lladrad	101v1-end	Ior 113.10–113.18 Also J	C?

The material in the additional gathering in Bost is very interesting indeed. It contains a version of the end of the Blegywryd text that was already in Bost before the gathering was inserted, and was also in L and J: this is the basis of AL DC III, taken from L. Legal texts already in Bost are repeated in the inserted gathering, and in the same order. This includes a Iorwerth section on theft that fits well with the previous sentence on theft in hand (which is the final sentence in L). Then other material is added: a plaint, which is also found in manuscript K; and a non-legal text, an incomplete copy of *Emyn Curig*, a prayer.[70]

There are four hands in this manuscript, with the main scribe, A, dated to the second half of the fourteenth century.[71] Scribe A copied the bulk of the manuscript, up to the end of the *Profi Ynadon* section on f. 93r6. His work ends at this point, and he had left much of the page blank. Scribe B copied a non-legal text on the second half of f. 93r; the text is now difficult to read. The main text continues on the next folio, f. 93v, but in the cursive hand of Scribe C, who was the scribe of the final pages of Bost: f. 93v1, and ff. 100r1–101r21. The material on ff. 94r–99v is by Scribe D, and this is the inserted gathering. The plaint in the hand of Scribe D has a date in it, 1401, which means that the text cannot be earlier than the beginning of the fifteenth century.

What we have in Bost is a continuous text by two hands. Scribe A finishes, leaving half a page blank; this was filled in by Scribe B. Scribe C then takes up, starting on a new page, and continues the text from the point Scribe A left off. The inserted gathering was put between two pages, in Scribe C's portion. The nature of this inserted gathering is important, particularly because it repeats the text in the main manuscript. Considerations include why this gathering was placed between the pages of Bost – and it is tempting to wonder whether it was the exemplar copied by Bost, or vice versa. The origin of this gathering also needs to be discussed.

Daniel Huws states that this material is 'a quire of six leaves, wanting text at both beginning and end, evidently taken from another manuscript'.[72] If this was a legal manuscript, the gathering could have been a quire from a manuscript most likely containing a full Blegywryd text – this would probably be the final quire. It may have been circulating as loose quires. However, the existence of *Emyn Curig* means that the material is not purely legal, although often non-legal material could be added to empty pages at the end of a manuscript – another example of that occurs in Bost, on f. 93r. But the material found in this gathering need not be part of a longer lawtext or manuscript: it could have been legal texts circulating separately to the main manuscripts, and was available to copy: much of it is also found in L and J, and in other manuscripts such as S, Tim and Q. The plaint was also copied into K, but the other material in this gathering was not, and the plaint is only witnessed in K and this gathering in Bost.

Given that the inserted gathering is a repeat of the text copied in part by Hand A and finished by Hand C, one question is why it was inserted in the manuscript. On

---

[70] On the plaint, see Roberts, 'More Plaints'. On *Emyn Curig*, see Roberts, 'Rhai swynion Cymraeg'.

[71] *RWMS*.

[72] *Ibid*.

the basis of the date in the plaint, 1401, the gathering is later than Main Bost, but was it perhaps a copy of Main Bost? The text of this inserted gathering starts towards the end of the *Profi Ynadon*, and it may be copied from the same text as the *Profi Ynadon* in the main hand of Bost, as it shares some similarities, but it is difficult to form a judgement on the basis of a few lines. However, the next part of the text in the inserted gathering is also in Bost, as the work of Scribe C. The same text is also found in L, and J. We therefore have four manuscript witnesses for most of this material: L, J, Main Bost, Bost inserted gathering.

Looking at the text, there are similarities between the text in L, J, and the Main Bost version, but the version in the inserted gathering has some differences not shared in the others. Looking at section 97, *Lle y dylai ceidwaid fod*, the texts separate significantly. The text in Main Bost and in L are very close indeed, and contain six items in the same order, with only slight differences in orthography. The text in the inserted gathering is a little different, and the items are in a different order, which may suggest that it was copying a different text. J only has four items, although the text is similar to that in L and Bost; the first three items are in the same order as those in L and Bost, and there may be a case of eyeskip[73] in J or in the text it was copying, with an attempt to correct it.[74]

Main Bost and L (Text from Main Bost)

Llyma y lleoet y dyllyant geitweit vot kyntaf yw catw tir a dayar gan dyn eil yw cadw kyn coll[75] Trydyd cadw gwesti pedweryt yw geni a meitryn pymet yw cadw breint whechet yw cadw alltudaet gan dyn.

These are the places where maintainers ought to be: first is to maintain land and earth for a man; second is keeping before loss; third is keeping a guest; fourth is birth and rearing; fifth is maintaining status; sixth is maintaining alien status for a man.

Manuscript J

Llyma y lleoed y dylyant y keitweit vot kyntaf yw cadw tir a daear gan dyn eil yw cadw kynn coll trydyd yw cadw gwestei pedwyryd yw cadw alltutyaeth gan dyn.

These are the places where maintainers ought to be: first is to maintain land and earth for a man; second is keeping before loss; third is keeping a guest; fourth is maintaining alien status for a man.

Bost inserted gathering (94v13)

Yn hyn o leod yseyd keitueit vn yỽ kado tir a dayer gan dyn. Eil yỽ kado kyn koll. Trydyd yỽ geni a maeithrin. Petweryd yỽ cado gỽestei. Pymhyt yỽ kadỽ breint. Y chwechede yỽ kadỽ alltudyaeth gan dyn.

---

[73] 'eyeskip (*homoioteleuton*): when a scribe moves back to the wrong point in his exemplar after his eye has wandered, commonly when the last word copied occurs again lower down on the page and he mistakenly jumps to that point, omitting the intervening words'. Beale, *Dictionary of English Manuscript Terminology*, q.v. scribal errors.

[74] For a similar case in J, see *LT*, 309.

[75] Bost reads *coyl* here but this is likely to be a misreading of *coll*, which is in all the other manuscripts.

In these places there are maintainers: one is to maintain land and earth for a man. Second is keeping before loss. Third is birth and rearing. Fourth is keeping a guest. Fifth is maintaining status. The sixth is maintaining alien status for a man.

In the section that follows this, there is a case of eyeskip in the inserted gathering in Bost: the scribe jumped from the first instance of the word *llaw* (hand) to the next, missing a short portion of text.[76] This error is not shared by any of the other manuscripts. This inserted gathering may have been copying a different exemplar, but it could also be a looser copy of an exemplar used by L and Bost Scribe C (and possibly J also), who were all copying closely and more faithfully. The final possibility is that it was indeed a copy of Bost Scribe C's text, but not a close copy; if so, the copy was placed between the pages of its exemplar and preserved that way. This would raise interesting questions about the text preceding the surviving portion in this inserted collation, and also the material in the collation that is not in the main Bost manuscript.

The plaint and *Emyn Curig* ('The Hymn of Curig') are not found in the other three manuscripts, including the Main Bost text. Plaints are rare occurrences in the law manuscripts, but they have a practical purpose. The plaint in the Bost gathering comes after a Iorwerth section, the same one in Main Bost and in J, although it ends earlier in the gathering.[77] This suggests that there was also a section of Iorwerth, if not a complete manuscript, circulating with the third part of the Blegywryd texts – the section is taken midway through the long discussion of theft in Iorwerth. Looking at plaints in general, very few survive – fewer than 20 – including a collection of ten in Q, this singleton in the inserted gathering in Bost (shared with K), and a collection in the lost Book of Trev Alun, which was copied from the lost fifteenth-century manuscript known as the White Book of Hergest, and that was a more varied collection.[78]

The other item in the inserted gathering is *Emyn Curig*. It would be tempting to suggest that this non-legal piece was written on blank leaves at the end of a quire, although there is no way of telling and it does take up several leaves. It appears to be complete, ending with an Amen on the final page of the inserted gathering and it is followed by another religious text that breaks off. (The inserted gathering appears to have been missing some of its outer leaves since the text on the first page is mid-sentence, and the end of the text following *Emyn Curig* is wanting.) *Emyn Curig* is a prayer of defence or protection and the vocabulary has legal touches occasionally. The first reference to it is by the poet Lewys Glyn Cothi.[79] He was also a scribe: he copied part of the White Book of Hergest, which included plaints as well as a copy of *Emyn Curig*; and a law manuscript, K, which contains a copy of the plaint that precedes *Emyn Curig* in this inserted gathering.[80] Lewys Glyn Cothi may have either seen this inserted gathering with the plaint and *Emyn Curig*, or an exemplar, which included *Emyn Curig* as well as the plaint, which he copied.[81] He did not copy *Emyn Curig* into K.

---

[76] The text in J reads '*kystal yw hwnnw a lledrat yn llaw; trydyd yw, kaffel lledrat yn llaw dyn, neu ar y geuyn*', J(ed.), 92.21–23, but the text in the Bost collation misses out '*trydyd yw, kaffel lledrat yn llaw*'. See Charles-Edwards's discussion on eyeskip in 'The Textual Tradition', 33.

[77] *LlIor*, 113.10–113.16; Main Bost continues to *LlIor*, 113.18 to the end of its final page. J continues with a longer Iorwerth text.

[78] See Roberts, 'Plaints', 219–261.

[79] Roberts, 'Rhai Swynion Cymraeg', 202.

[80] *Ibid.*, 203.

[81] Roberts, 'More Plaints', 183–187.

Of the other manuscripts, L is the first of the manuscripts to end, as it does not have the Iorwerth material found following *Amodau* (section 99 in *J(ed.)*) in the other manuscripts. The Bost inserted gathering has a copy of material corresponding to *LlIor* 113.10–113.16, but then switches to the plaint. The same material is also found on the final page of the main Bost manuscript, but it continues to the end of the page, corresponding to *LlIor* 113.10–113.16; it then breaks off mid-sentence. But the most interesting factor is that this same material is found in manuscript J, and it continues where the other two texts in Bost end.

The striking point about all of this material is that it has a practical purpose – as with the other material in the third part of Blegywryd.[82] J is described as being a composite manuscript, starting with a Blegywryd redaction text and the second part comprised of Iorwerth material – the Iorwerth text is said to start on p. 94.3 of the edition, with section 100, *Lledrad* ('Theft').[83] It is highly significant that *Lledrad* is also found in Bost, in the same position (following the same material), in both the inserted gathering and in Main Bost. This suggests that what was happening in J was also happening in other manuscripts around the same time. The difference with J is that the text continues where Main Bost breaks off, so there is no telling how far it went. In J, further material is added: Iorwerth material, *cynghawsedd* (model pleadings), and *Damweiniau* ('eventualities').[84] The Iorwerth material in J focuses on areas of law that continued after the Statute of Rhuddlan, post-1282, and it comprises texts that are not generally found in the Blegywryd manuscripts.[85] For example, J has a complete text of *Cyfar* ('Co-tillage'), which is a Iorwerth text; but the sister text, the revised Iorwerth version of Corn Damage,[86] is not found with the Iorwerth material in J, since it had already been included as a Blegywryd version, in the Blegywryd portion of the manuscript. Otherwise, much of the material is on Land Law, and *cynghawsedd* and the collection of *Damweiniau* is also represented: material which would often be found with Iorwerth texts.

Table 5.6: The Second Part of J[87]

Section	Page – MS	J(ed.)	Other Edition
Lladrad (Theft)	193.12–197.16	94.3–96.4	*LlIor*
Cyfar (Co-tillage)	197.17–203.3	96.5–98.30	*LlIor* 148.1–153.3
Briwio Anifail (Animal injury)	203.3–205.16	98.31–100.2	*LlIor* 57.1–57.6
Trais (Violence)	205.17–206.1	100.3–100.8	*LlIor* 115.21
Damweiniau II	206.2–207.9	100.9–100.34	
Gwerth Aelodau (Value of Limbs)	207.9–207.16	101.1–101.7	*WML* 43.4–7
Profi Ynadon (Testing Judges)	207.16–208.1	101.8–101.13	
Cynghawsedd	208.2–219.12	101.14–106.35	

---

[82] *J(ed.)*, xxii.

[83] *J(ed.)*, xiii.

[84] *J(ed.)*, xx.

[85] *J(ed.)*, xx.

[86] See Chapter 3, 68–71.

[87] Based on the 'Conspectws Argraffiadau' made by Dafydd Jenkins for the printed edition: *J(ed.)*, 147–162.

Profi Ynadon (Testing Judges)	219.11–220.8	106.35–107.16	
Cyfraith Tir (Land Law)	220.9–237.19	107.17–119.3	*LlIor* 72.1–88.7
Mesurau cyfreithiol (Measurements)	244.20–247.18	119.4–120.21	*LlIor* 90.1–18
Cyfraith Teulu (Family Law)	247.19–256.12	120.22–124.27	*LlIor* 97.1–103.4
Damweiniau II	256.12–257.12	124.28–125.15	
Dadlwriaeth (Disputing)	257.12–258.2	125.16–125.26	AL Book X
Damweiniau II	264.9–268.21	128.22–130.30	

This material may not have been taken from a full Iorwerth manuscript – there is no extant manuscript from which J appears to have been copying[88] – but was instead material on certain aspects of Welsh law that had a specific use, and that was intended to form the third part of the Blegywryd manuscripts, and was also incorporated into the Iorwerth manuscripts. There seems to be less of a case for the compiler of J doing something revolutionary (since the first part of the material is also found in Main Bost, and in the inserted gathering), and little evidence for selecting parts from a full Iorwerth manuscript. Material may have been appended to the third part of Blegywryd, but only material that was of practical use and on the practice of law. It may be the case that, rather than viewing this material as 'additional', or as a 'tail' or appendix, the material should be viewed as a full third section of useful material in Blegywryd forming *Arferion Cyfraith*. It has only survived in full in J, but there is no telling whether other manuscripts – Bost, for example – had, or were intended to have, much more of the material found in J. Where the Iorwerth manuscripts have copies of *damweiniau* or *cynghawsedd* with the main law text, the Blegywryd manuscripts may have been open to the possibility of having such material, but we have no surviving evidence.

The Blegywryd Continuation in Later Manuscripts

The material in AL DC III is uniform in order and content across the four witnesses, L, Bost, J and the partial text in the inserted collation in Bost. Table 5.4 noted that much of the content of continuation is found in other manuscripts too, but these manuscripts do not have the texts in the same position or the same form in which it occurs in L, Bost and J. It has been incorporated into the second part of those manuscripts in a different way, not as a continuous block of text.

Table 5.7: The LBostJ texts in other manuscripts

Section	Manuscripts and Notes
Dynion na ddylai eu tystiolaeth sefyll Men whose testimony should not stand	S: *similar to LBostJ. Partial and garbled version of the colophon* Q: *heavily edited text; may account for differences* [Tim: *Lacuna at this point – the text may be lost*]
Profi Ynadon Proving/testing judges	Q, S, Tim, G, K, Y, Mor *All appear to be independent collections*

---

[88] J(ed.), xxi.

(Table 5.7 continued)

Section	Manuscript and Notes
Oedi Cyfraith Delay in law	Q S Tim Y G *All very similar, from same source?*
Lle y dylai ceidwaid fod Places where maintainers ought to be	*Three versions* U: *similar to LBostJ, same source* S, Q, Tim: *similar texts, same source* As, Z: *similar, from same source*
Pethau sydd unfraint â lledrad yn llaw Things of the same status as theft in hand	Q S Tim *Long section, only parts in each of the manuscripts. Not possible to determine sources.*

These manuscripts deal with the texts in different ways and, on the whole, they do not form sub-groupings of texts. Q and its copy Ep have most of the continuation, but without the colophon, but Q is a heavily edited text and may have omitted it deliberately.[89] *Arferion Cyfraith* has been divided and placed at different points in Q, but it may have had an exemplar containing the whole of *Arferion Cyfraith* plus the continuation texts. S and Tim are by the same scribe but are not identical, although they share some texts. The *Dynion na ddylai* text in S is very similar to the version in L, Bost and J, and opens with a partial and slightly garbled version of the colophon found in those manuscripts.[90] Tim may well have had this section but there is a lacuna at the relevant point in the manuscript. Tim has a colophon,[91] but in Tim the reference to *Arferion Cyfraith*[92] has been superseded by a reference to *Rhol Dafydd Llwyd* (Dafydd Llwyd's Roll), and other parts of the sentence have been amended. The Roll is said to be the most important and necessary things for a justice, similar to the Test Book in the Iorwerth manuscripts.[93]

These manuscript witnesses to some of the texts in the Blegywryd continuation show that the material was still circulating, and perhaps still relevant, but there was flexibility in the treatment of it. The manuscript compilers did not feel that they had to copy or present their texts in a particular fixed format, at least not concerning the latter part of Blegywryd, but could pick and choose the sections they wanted, and include them at different points in their longer texts.

Conclusion

The Blegywryd redaction has been viewed traditionally as the redaction whose manuscripts are most likely to have 'additional material' appended to them. This concept is heavily coloured by the early edition of the redaction made in *LlBleg*, which divided the material into 91 (titled but unnumbered) sections, and which led everything else to be seen as 'additional' or 'a tail' of material added. But this division is not apparent in Aneurin Owen's edition of the Dimetian Code – which has a Book

---

[89] Roberts, 'Creu Trefn o Anhrefn', 416.
[90] See the text on 169–170.
[91] Lewis, *Llanstephan MS. 116*, 42.
[92] *J(ed.)*, 86.10.
[93] *Machlud*, xviii–xxix. On *Rhol Dafydd Llwyd*, see Chapter 6, 170–172.

III comprised of further material found in three witnesses – or indeed by looking at the manuscripts. A detailed consideration of the manuscripts shows that many of the Blegywryd texts have their end wanting, some finishing mid-way through the section known as *Arferion Cyfraith*, but that three manuscripts, L, Bost and J, have the same continuation. This came to be known as the 'short tail'. As the inserted gathering in Bost also preserves a fourth witness to this material (found in AL DC III) then there is a textual subgroup within the Blegywryd manuscripts, all containing this so-called 'short tail'. This does not mean that these manuscripts started a trend of adding a 'tail' of 'additional material'.

It is likely that these three manuscripts, L, Bost and J, share an exemplar, and are from the same legal tradition or grouping. The manuscripts are from south Wales and are fourteenth century in date, L being one of the earlier of the Blegywryd texts, but whether they were produced in the same place is more difficult to determine. It may be more likely that the exemplars or material included in them was circulating in a particular region and was available for creating law manuscripts. The readings are close enough on the whole to suggest that they all shared an exemplar at least for the second part of Blegywryd. In terms of the Blegywryd redaction, Bost, L, and J form a sub-group of manuscripts with material in common. It is also possible to state, tentatively, that the Iorwerth-type second part of J may not have been unique; the final page in Bost suggests that the material was available to other redactors, notably to the redactor of Bost. It is impossible to say whether the material would also have been included in L, and there are no clues in the manuscript – no torn or missing pages, but the scribe left half a page blank, and it is possible that he copied all that he had in his exemplar.

Consideration should be given to the way material could be incorporated into manuscripts. David Daube discusses this in his study of the legal codes in the Pentateuch. His discussion centres on how new provisions would be added to an existing code of law: while a logical method would be to add the new rule (or section in our case) between other material on the same subject, in Daube's text and the example from the *lex Aquilia*, 'The existing code is left undisturbed, and the new rule simply tacked on at the end'.[94] This means that the text developed in a certain way, and leads to 'a quite unsystematic arrangement'.[95] This may go a long way to explaining the situation with our legal texts, and may also be the key to the problems faced by Aneurin Owen (and others) in dealing with texts that appear to be disorganised and miscellaneous, and that have different layers of texts from different periods travelling as one whole. Daube suggests some reasons for placing new material at the end: it was less trouble to do so; amalgamating new provisions into existing law involved a more advanced technique; the fact that law sometimes circulated as oral tradition; and ancient codes were often written on stone, literally, so it would be difficult if a lot of material needed to be added.[96] But perhaps the most interesting argument focuses on the importance of tradition, which meant that the writers or amenders left the existing code alone and added their new material at the end 'rather than squeeze the fresh provisions anywhere into the established, almost holy, text'.[97] The cross-references in the Welsh law text to certain 'established' sections suggest that the latter plays an important role – there were recognisable sections that were known to lawyers, if not

---

[94] Daube, 'Codes and Codas', 74.
[95] *Ibid.*, 75.
[96] *Ibid.*, 75–77.
[97] *Ibid.*, 77.

to a wider audience. Daube advises caution in automatically assuming that the later part of the code is later in date, and this is also true of the Welsh lawtexts where material from different periods would be included in the latter part of a manuscript.[98] The 'final redaction' of the lawtext, however, would involve texts from different periods, arranged perhaps in an unsystematic manner, but it would then travel as an entirely new statute. In his conclusions, Daube considers the importance and authority bound up with adding provisions to existing codes; he notes that a private reader would be more likely to add comments at the relevant point in the text, perhaps as glosses, but,

> when we find additions that are not inserted in this ruthless fashion, when ... the older part of the code left intact and the fresh rules put right at the end, the presumption is (of course, it is no more than a presumption) that these rules have been added authoritatively, by the official guardians of the law. It is they who will think twice before interfering with the traditional text.[99]

This is certainly true of the Welsh lawtexts, where the work on the laws was carried out by lawyers and, as a result, none of the material should be afforded less importance because it is less recognisable than the well-known texts of the laws.

The suggestion that Blegywryd also has a tripartite division is clear in the texts themselves, with an early witness in Latin D, but it may be that this division has been overlooked in lieu of the colophon in the last part of L, Bost and J, and that too much has been made of this sentence, which is merely a dividing point in the text rather than marking the beginning of a 'tail'. If that is so, *Arferion Cyfraith* would be the third part of the Blegywryd text, and it would be practical material, essential for a man wishing to practice law, as the title suggests. This brings the Blegywryd redaction much closer to the Iorwerth redaction with its Test Book. The occurrence of the sections making up the extended *Arferion Cyfraith* section in other Blegywryd manuscripts, S, Tim and Q, gives further credence to the idea that the Blegywryd text divided into three, with a practical third part, although the form of the material has been changed in those manuscripts. They will be examined in the next chapters, but at this point we might bear in mind the idea that the third part was open-ended, and further practical material could be added to it.

The final question is what were the redactors of the Welsh law manuscripts attempting to do by collating and bringing together this material? The answer will vary from manuscript to manuscript, as the context of the codex is crucial in any such discussion. Some manuscripts were created for a specific purpose, and the material included in particular collections of lawtexts could be tailored according to need or usefulness. But the important point regarding this material in the third part of the Blegywryd redaction is that it had a practical application, and the material continued to be copied; this will be discussed more fully in the following chapters. It was something that may well have been current and necessary during the time of the compilation of these law manuscripts, including the majority of the Blegywryd manuscripts, which are post-conquest in date. The collation and compilation work in these manuscripts may have been started earlier, in an exemplar that was at least at one remove from the extant texts, but the later manuscripts continued to add and copy material, including the texts discussed in this section; and the majority of the material was practical, which again highlights the usefulness of the text. While most

---

[98] *Ibid.*, 82–83.
[99] *Ibid.*, 97.

of the law manuscripts did not leave out sections – with the exception of the Laws of Court, which were omitted in some manuscripts – it seems that the concept of a book of law included certain sections, giving rules and the general themes of the law, but it was a flexible entity and the practical material went hand-in-hand with the other material. It is often thought that not many manuscripts have a so-called 'tail' of 'additional' material, but rather it may be the case that all Blegywryd manuscripts could have had this extended text, were they complete. In sum, the material in the third part of the Blegywryd section deserves fuller attention as a critically important part of the Welsh legal codices.

6

'O GYUREITH HYWEL DA, A'E ARUEROED, A'E GYNNEUODEU': THE DEVELOPMENT OF THE REDACTION MANUSCRIPTS

Dywededic yw hyt hynn o gyureith Hywel Da, a'e arueroed, a'e gynneuodeu.[1]

Up to now has been spoken of the law of Hywel Dda, and its practices, and its customs.

The arguments in this work have led to a rejection of the possibility that material found towards the end of certain Blegywryd manuscripts is 'additional' or forms a 'tail'. It argues instead for a flexible interpretation of what constituted a lawbook. The emphasis here is on the textual history, not dealing with the status of the text as law but its status within the textual tradition; the approach is to view the material on its own terms – as material derived from various exemplars, sometimes shared with other manuscripts, sometimes not – and to consider its nature and its context. This means looking at each text as a text, rather than separating out 'additional material' which is not related to the first portion of the material in the same manuscript. Both the material and its textual history have their own value, and the reoccurrence of the material in other manuscripts (if not in the same precise location) warns us not to let it be overshadowed by the 'additional' designation, or to submerge it into a 'tail'.

The law manuscripts contained law, and the compilers treated all law in the same way, regardless of its origin or nature. This may explain the problems that the early editors of Welsh legal texts had in trying to create a uniform basic text of Welsh law. This is not something that can be easily solved – Welsh law manuscripts do have considerable variation in order and content, and it is not the purpose of this work to redraw the 'core text' of medieval Welsh law; rather, it is to reject the notion of the basic code with anything deviating from that text being dismissed as 'additional'.

However, it cannot be denied that there are some manuscripts that are completely different in form to the other manuscripts. Some of the manuscripts in this class start with a recognisable text of one of the law redactions (usually Blegywryd, but also Cyfnerth in one example), which has a close affinity to other texts from the same redaction, but the manuscript then continues with different material not found in other manuscripts. Often, the material collected together forms a single collection not repeated in the same form elsewhere, which has led to it being called a 'tail' – although much of the material itself is generally not unique to one manuscript.

This chapter will, in the first place, examine the material from numerous exemplars found in manuscripts that open with a text of the laws found in the Welsh law redactions. As has been noted previously, most Welsh law manuscripts have a text that fits

---

[1] AL DC III.i.26, taken from L.

into one of the three Welsh redactions, but they also have other material that may be found in other manuscripts too. In the case of the Iorwerth manuscripts, the material 'added' to the redaction text is usually shared in other manuscripts of the same redaction, and it takes a fairly standard recognisable form – *damweiniau*, and *cynghawsedd*.[2] For the Blegywryd and Cyfnerth redaction manuscripts, the non-redaction material is less uniform and is not always shared by a number of other manuscripts.

The Composite Law Manuscripts

A further division of the law manuscripts can be seen when turning to some of the lengthy composite law manuscripts. These contain material that Aneurin Owen categorised as being 'anomalous', i.e. not fitting in with the pattern that he saw in the legal texts, although most of the manuscripts under discussion also include a full copy of one of the redaction texts, usually Blegywryd. Owen had a clear idea of what was Anomalous and what was not, and he certainly had a definite idea of what the basic text of Welsh law should look like – his Codes. But the manuscripts themselves are far less clear-cut in their division of the material. The manuscripts, on the whole, do not distinguish the 'redaction' text from what follows. Also, several of the redaction texts have material embedded within them that Owen would have classified as 'anomalous'. This suggests that the lawyers themselves did not see this material as fundamentally different.

Manuscript U, for example, marks the point where the collection of *damweiniau* begins – there is a statement that says that it is now turning to look at customs.[3] But most of the manuscripts, including the lengthier texts with considerable material that formed Owen's Anomalous Laws, have no such marker or dividing point. AL IV–IX, and AL XII, contain material from the same genre: *damweiniau*, *cynghawsedd* and plaints, respectively. Some of this material is grouped together, as collections, although Stacey notes that *Damweiniau* I, the focus of her study, also has other material (primarily triads) interspersed so it is not a 'pure' genre-based collection.[4]

However, while collections do occur, neither *damweiniau* nor *cynghawsedd* are confined to the collections that were included in the law manuscripts. The same is true of triads, which occur both as a large collection in the Cyfnerth and Blegywryd manuscripts, but can also be found interspersed throughout the tractates in the law-texts, as a literary form. *Damweiniau* as a form are also attested within the Iorwerth redaction, for example in the Surety tractate, or parts of the Law of Women.[5] A large part of the Land Law tractate in Iorwerth is the legal case for land, which is basically model pleading, otherwise known as *cynghawsedd*. The fact that the form is well-known makes this material less separate than Owen's division makes it seem. It also muddies the waters to see the material in the Anomalous Laws as later in date – some of it is undoubtedly later, but the forms or genres are not, since they occur in

---

[2] See Chapter 4.
[3] Charles-Edwards, *The Welsh Laws*, 26.
[4] Stacey, 'Legal Writing in Medieval Wales', 63–64.
[5] *LlIor*, §§61–62, §64; §§49–50, §§52–57. In the Laws of Country in Iorwerth, *damweiniau* really do seem to be a way of writing law, and may contrast to the negative *ny dyly* (it is not permitted). The form even occurs in 'runs' that could be called collections. Col in particular has a fondness for the form, and it appears there that triads have been refashioned as *damweiniau*. Col also has a long collection of *damweiniau* at the end of the text, published separately as *DwC*.

the Codes as well. This is particularly true when considering the *damweiniau* and the *cynghawsedd*, which occur in the Iorwerth texts – since parts of those lawtexts are seen to be broadly contemporary to the date of the manuscripts – and also calls into question to what extent these two genres should be treated separately.

A final point on the genre-based books of *Ancient Laws*: the material is very well organised. It usually occurs as a collection, bringing similar material together, in the manuscripts themselves. One might perhaps expect that 'anomalous' material would have a degree of randomness, but that is not the case in the manuscripts. This is not a miscellaneous collection of legal material, and the fact that it occurs in manuscripts containing other legal material suggests that there should be no division, or hierarchy, between the different parts.

The first books of AL II, organised by genre, were the focus of Chapter 4 in this study. The remaining books of *Ancient Laws*, Books X, XI and XIV, are based on manuscripts: Q, S and H respectively. H does not contain a redaction text, but Owen took his material from it selectively, omitting any part that showed a similarity to anything already included in *Ancient Laws*, such as triads found in his Dimetian Code, or *cynghawsedd* in AL VII–IX. In the case of S, much of the material in Book XI was taken – again selectively – from the second half of the manuscript. The same is not true of Q, which is a heavily edited manuscript, where material from various sources was brought together to form tractates organised by subject. Manuscript Z also has considerable material added to its Cyfnerth text, although Z was barely used by Aneurin Owen.

Owen's division of the material and his concept of the Codes was perhaps one of the most enduring parts of his work, and the division had a significant impact on later editions of the laws. *LlBleg*, for example, was based on O and Tr, with lacunae filled from L, but the editors omitted the material at the end of manuscript L, although it was the final part of Owen's Dimetian Code.[6] Aled Rhys Wiliam, the most recent editor of a Iorwerth manuscript,[7] omitted the *cynghawsedd* that was included in his manuscript, B; and, likewise, in his study of Col, Jenkins divided the manuscript into a main text, published as *LlCol*, and published the *damweiniau* separately as *DwC*, '*yn y ffurf amatewraidd hon*' ('in this amateurish form').[8] This is not a division that is reflected in the manuscript itself. Even in the important edition of J, although the entire manuscript is edited, there is still an emphasis on the earlier organisation of the Blegywryd redaction into the 91 titled tractates in the edition, and the remaining material in J is called a 'tail', or 'additional material'.[9] Here, these manuscripts, the composite texts, will be considered in detail, and the focus will be on a new reading prioritising the context and purpose of the texts.

In the first part of this discussion, the two Blegywryd manuscripts with an extensive collection of non-standard material will be discussed: they are S and Q, both dating from the mid-fifteenth century. The manuscripts are also linked to others of the Blegywryd redaction: S is connected to Tim, Llanstephan 116, another

---

[6] AL DC III. Enoch Powell of course had his own ideas of what was included in the original lawbook: see *LlBleg*, xxxix–xlvi. For a discussion on Powell's 'Floating Sections' theory see *LT*, 11–15.

[7] No editions of complete Iorwerth manuscripts have been published since *LlIor* in 1960. Earlier versions of Iorwerth texts are Aneurin Owen's 'Venedotian Code' in AL; and Lewis, 'Copy of the Black Book of Chirk'.

[8] *LlIor*; *LlCol*; *DwC*, vii.

[9] *J(ed.)*, xiii.

fifteenth-century Blegywryd manuscript that has an incomplete Blegywryd text but shares some material with S in its second half, also incomplete; Tim is not a copy of S or vice versa, but both share the same scribe.[10] Q, dating from the 1440s, has two near-contemporary copies: P, Peniarth 259A, from the second half of the fifteenth century, is a close copy of Q, even reproducing the *mise-en-page*, but it breaks off midway through the extended triad collection and therefore does not include the latter part of non-Blegywryd material found in Q.[11] Ep, Peniarth 258, also from the second half of the fifteenth century, was a copy of Q made fairly soon after Q had been completed, and is a complete one; it preserves a gathering of four leaves that was lost when Q was rebound – the text from the missing leaves preserved in Ep happens to include some material not found elsewhere.[12] Manuscript Z is important since it is a Cyfnerth manuscript, a sixteenth-century copy of an earlier text, and it was neglected by Aneurin Owen (largely due to it being rather difficult to reconcile with his other texts).[13] These manuscripts will be given attention here but in the wider context of the law manuscripts that are related to them.

Z, NLW Peniarth MS 259B

Manuscript Z is a sixteenth-century paper copy, made by Richard Longford and his amanuensis, of a full (earlier) Cyfnerth text, followed by a second half of the sort of material more commonly linked to the Blegywryd redaction.[14] It has been studied in full, and while there are some issues with the binding of the manuscript, the material in the second part separates into clear sections or tractates, which may have been from a number of different exemplars, and it all appears to be material that was current in north-east Wales.[15] Furthermore, it had a specific purpose – it was practical, and had a strong element of raising funds for the lord. Included in the latter part of Z was the north-east Wales collection of *cynghawsedd*, which was also copied into manuscripts Mor, As and (parts of it) into H, all three dating from the second half of the fourteenth century; H and Z also share other material.[16] The *cynghawsedd* in Z, As and Mor appears to have been all copied from the same exemplar.

Z could be seen to be a typical example of a basic text of Welsh law to which material was then added, and it is interesting that the basic Cyfnerth text in Z has a close relationship to the text of the mid-fourteenth century manuscript X, possibly the most straightforward copy of the Cyfnerth text, showing little or no development or additions. In that sense, manuscript Z may preserve the clearest example of a Welsh law manuscript with a lengthy and miscellaneous collection of material added at the end, but all with a specific purpose in mind.

---

[10] *Machlud*, xli.
[11] Roberts, 'Creu Trefn o Anhrefn', 402.
[12] *Ibid.*, 402–403.
[13] *Pomffred*, 20.
[14] See Huws, 'Yr Hen Risiart Langfford', 308–309.
[15] *Pomffred*, 23–26.
[16] *Pomffred*, 39–41; for the relationship between these manuscripts see Roberts, 'Law Texts and their Sources'. See also Elias, 'Llawysgrif Peniarth 164', 40–41, 44, 50; *ALD*.

Q, NLW MS Wynnstay 36

A re-examination of the nature of manuscript Q by Daniel Huws considered the way the manuscript had been produced, and the quality of the materials, the labour and the texts used. There is no question that Q was produced to a very high standard, using high-quality parchment, good ink, and in 'the best hand of the fifteenth century'; Huws describes it as the 'most majestically ambitious [manuscript] of the fifteenth century'.[17] As Huws noted, this law manuscript would have been produced for someone who had access to the best quality material and most skilled scribes, and the contents point to someone who was knowledgeable about law and interested in it. This led Daniel Huws to the persuasive suggestion that this manuscript was produced for a powerful person: Gruffudd ap Nicolas (fl. 1415–1460) was an 'esquire and a leading figure in the local administration of the principality of South Wales in the middle of the 15th century',[18] and is perhaps famously remembered as being influential in government in west Wales, but also for his unscrupulous and somewhat lawless behaviour.[19] He had 'a career unequalled in the history of West Wales during the fifteenth century', but this meant that he would have been in a position to commission a Welsh law manuscript, and his position in society also brought the wealth to be able to pursue his cultural interests.[20] He was able to gain the support and praise of the poets, particularly after he had organised the Carmarthen eisteddfod, probably held at Dinefwr, between 1451 and 1453, and it appears that he saw himself as a traditional ruler and powerful patron.[21] If manuscript Q was produced for Gruffudd ap Nicolas – and there is no better candidate as the commissioner of this extraordinary lawtext – then this would mean that it was probably created in Carmarthenshire, and around the 1440s, since Gruffudd ap Nicolas was then at the height of his power, before his political circumstances changed as a result of the increase in power of the House of York.

Manuscript Q – and throughout, the same is true of its full copy, Ep – has a complete Blegywryd text as given in *LlBleg* for example, but the material has been re-edited and reorganised to some extent, with an attempt at keeping material on the same theme together, but taking it out of other tractates.[22] The editing work can be best seen in the *Tair Colofn Cyfraith* ('Three Columns of Law') section, where scattered sections on *galanas* (homicide) were moved to a position immediately after the *Naw Affaith* ('Nine Abetments'); triads on *galanas* were moved from the triad collection to the new *galanas* section, material on *galanas* that is not found in other Blegywryd texts was added, and some sections of *Arferion Cyfraith* discussing *galanas* are also moved. The same is done with theft, and also fire.[23]

One effect of this reorganisation is that *Arferion Cyfraith* in Q has been split into sections, which makes examining the third part of Blegywryd in Q in the context of the material in L, Bost and J very difficult. A further effect is that 'additional' or

---

[17] Daniel Huws, Paper at Seminar Cyfraith Hywel, 8 October 2016.

[18] Jones, 'Gruffudd ap Nicolas (fl. 1415–1460)', *Dictionary of Welsh Biography*.

[19] On Gruffudd ap Nicolas see Griffiths, 'Gruffydd ap Nicholas and the Fall'; and Griffiths, 'Gruffydd ap Nicholas and the Rise'; see also Griffiths, *The Principality of Wales*.

[20] Griffiths, 'Gruffydd ap Nicholas and the Fall', 213; Griffiths, 'Gruffydd ap Nicholas and the Rise', 257.

[21] Griffiths, 'Gruffydd ap Nicholas and the Fall', 230.

[22] Roberts, 'Creu Trefn o Anhrefn', 404–408.

[23] *Ibid.*, 404–405.

unexpected material is found throughout the main Blegywryd text, and therefore it is difficult to follow a given text in Q alongside any another Blegywryd manuscript. It also means that the division between the idea of a 'tail' of additional material and the Blegywryd text is not at all clear cut. This suggests that the compiler of Q did not consider the material to be 'additional'. Manuscript Q may have edited the material heavily, but it was done sensibly, bringing similar thematic material together, and blurring the lines between the concept of a 'basic' or 'core' Blegywryd text and any 'additional' material: to the compiler of Q, *galanas* was *galanas*, Land Law was Land Law, and so forth. This heavy editing, adding more material on the same topic, including Iorwerth material where such was available, was carried out for the Three Columns, Suretyship, Land, and Women; in contrast, the Value of Wild and Tame appears to have been copied as it was, and the Laws of Court are also a straight Blegywryd text with no editing. There is no Iorwerth triad collection as such,[24] but the main Blegywryd triad collection in Q has an additional collection added to it, as well as triads taken from *Llyfr Damweiniau* and other places.[25] But as well as weaving his material into the existing Blegywryd text that he was copying, some material was also appended to the Blegywryd text for the latter part of the manuscript.

Once the recognisable sections of the Blegywryd text in Q peter out, around f. 99r, it could be said that the 'tail' starts in earnest, although it is important to note that there is nothing to mark this out in the manuscript and this is in no way a 'tail', simply law that is not part of the Blegywryd text. Most of the material in the latter part, more than two-thirds of the so-called 'tail', is comprised of *damweiniau*. In addition, there are Iorwerth sections on the Three Columns – it is not certain why these are here and not in the edited version of the Three Columns earlier on in Q. There is also material that is presented in AL X, and is not found in most other manuscripts, although some of it is shared with S.[26] This is clearly legal material that was circulating in south Wales – in contrast to what was found in north-east Wales. Among it is the collection of ten plaints, which was not copied into the other manuscripts of Welsh law.[27]

This section of Q shows us, to start with, that there was a considerable variety of material circulating in this region of Wales. There was certainly a Blegywryd redaction text, and there were parts at least of a Iorwerth redaction text. Other material is not found in the earlier redactions – much of the non-redaction material is likely to be later in date, perhaps contemporary with the manuscripts in which it is included, so of late fourteenth century date at the earliest. There was clearly a need for new legal material to reflect the needs of the region at that time – texts on matters of administration, or reflecting legal procedures that are not discussed in the lawbooks; and this material was deemed important enough to be written, and also to be included in compilations of laws. It also seems to mark a difference in attitude between the redaction texts and the later material. All of the legal compilations discussed in this chapter included a redaction text, often with the prologue and the Laws of Court, with the other material. The Iorwerth texts show an awareness of different legal practices in another region, and arguably a belief that those practices could be useful, so

---

[24] See Roberts, 'The Iorwerth Triads'.
[25] Roberts, 'Creu Trefn o Anhrefn', 408–409.
[26] *Ibid.*, 412–413.
[27] Roberts, 'Plaints', 224. Two of the plaints appear in a slightly different format in Dd, a copy of the lost White Book of Hergest. The relationship between the plaints in Q and the two also in the White Book of Hergest is unclear, but they may have shared a common exemplar; plaints are a very rare occurrence in the lawtexts, however.

that it was deemed necessary to have a copy of them in the law manuscripts. It may be the case that to the compilers the redaction text was what made their books of law into proper, official, Cyfraith Hywel books, but the texts and the exemplars they drew upon adapted those books to make them useful and current. It would be interesting to know how much use was made of the redaction texts in actual legal practice, or whether the focus was on the latter part of these manuscripts. But, by combining the material, no distinction was made by the compilers between the different exemplars, the texts that they used – they were all included, and no part of the book was intended to be more (or less) important than others.[28]

The compiler of Q had a collection of triads that were similar to the triads found in the main Blegywryd triad tractate, and these triads included some of the same content as the triad tractate in Blegywryd, but usually with different wording.[29] The triad collection was copied selectively by the redactor of Q, and the version of this collection in S and K may better reflect its contents. It also occurs in the same position in both S and K, following the same material (on denying a son), and it is almost identical in S and K, which suggests that they shared an exemplar.[30] Sections of the triad collection also occur in Tim, and it may have been complete in Tim as well at one point.[31] This appears to have been a triad collection that was formed from the main Blegywryd triad tractate, and it may have been circulating separately from the law manuscripts – something akin to Enoch Powell's imagined 'Book of Triads'.[32]

The collection of *damweiniau* that is shared by Q and K is not found in any other manuscript. It was copied selectively into Q, and several of the *damweiniau* also occur in *Damweiniau* I, but with different wording, and with other *damweiniau* interspersed. The similarity to the additional triad collection in Q and K is striking and, again, this may have circulated separately from the law manuscripts.[33] The reasons behind such compositions are obscure to us now, but it appears that there was someone working with existing collections of triads and *damweiniau* to create new collections in a certain region. The *damweiniau* collection was not copied into S, unlike the triad collection – which may suggest that they were not bound together as one manuscript and supports the idea that they existed as separate, independent texts.

The compiler of Q also had a Iorwerth text that was used, although it may not have been a complete Iorwerth text – he did not appear to have the Iorwerth Laws of Court at his disposal (or may have disregarded them), but most other sections were copied. There is a very close relationship between the material in J and in Q,[34] and in the Iorwerth sections the texts are so close that they are almost indistinguishable. J

---

[28] The exception to this in Q may be the Laws of Court: the compiler simply copied the Laws of Court without attempting to re-edit or move material around. This may indicate that the Laws of Court had less practical importance to him, although since they were not omitted altogether they had a function in the lawbook, and are acknowledged as one of the three divisions of the Blegywryd lawbook. It is possible that the Laws of Court were needed to make a lawbook recognisable as part of the tradition.

[29] *LT*, 32.

[30] *LT*, 33.

[31] *LT*, 33.

[32] *LT*, 32–34.

[33] Stacey, 'Legal Writing in Medieval Wales', 71, and the discussion in Chapter 6.

[34] Roberts, 'Creu Trefn o Anhrefn', 410–412.

is the earlier of the two manuscripts, from the late fourteenth/early fifteenth century, and is in the hand of Hywel Fychan, one of the scribes of the Red Book of Hergest. Q is unlikely to be a copy of the latter part of J, since one or two of the Iorwerth sections in Q and J appear to be from a different source. There are also more Iorwerth sections in Q than there are in J, and there is one section in J which ends midway through a text, but the same text continues in Q. This implies that Q and J may have had the same exemplar, but both are very close copies, almost identical in spelling and even punctuation.

The relationship between Q and K also needs to be reconsidered. K is in the hand of Lewys Glyn Cothi, fl. 1447–1489, and was made sometime after 1469.[35] K is a Iorwerth manuscript, with the additional triad collection and the *damweiniau* shared with Q. A natural assumption would be that the Iorwerth material in Q is close to that in K, but this is not the case – it is similar, but not as close as the relationship between Q and J for the Iorwerth texts. Q, J and K may have shared the same Iorwerth exemplar, but that exemplar may not have included the Laws of Court – none of the manuscripts have a Iorwerth text for the Laws of Court, and it would be surprising if all chose individually to omit it. The fact that there are more Iorwerth sections in Q and in K than there are in J supports the idea that J was copying selectively, but there seems to have been one southern Iorwerth exemplar available in the region, used by Q, K, Tim and S.[36] It would also accord with the Iorwerth material in J being from a different source to the other Iorwerth manuscripts – it is not a copy of an extant Iorwerth text.[37] All this suggests that the Iorwerth material must have had a use in south Wales. It also implies that to the compilers, the redactions and their textual history were not the critical issue but the usefulness of the material, regardless of its origin. That the Iorwerth text originated in thirteenth-century Gwynedd may have been immaterial in fifteenth-century south Wales. There were however different preoccupations in different regions and at different times: in the south in the fifteenth century, written lawbooks had high authority, but in the thirteenth-century north, the prestige of the author and whether a particular rule was authoritative in Gwynedd (and, in some cases, in Powys) mattered more. In Q, the Iorwerth material is not marked out as being different in any way; it is simply more material on a particular topic. The same is true of other manuscripts but with a less organised structure.

There is no question however that the compiler of Q had some material available to him which was not available to most other Blegywryd manuscripts as far as we can tell. The plaints occur as a collection of ten model plaints in the manuscript, and are practical, procedural material, similar to – and linked with – *cynghawsedd*.

S, BL Add. MS 22,356

Another manuscript with a Blegywryd text as well as a substantial amount of non-redaction material is S, and S is closely related to Tim in some aspects. Both S and Tim are fifteenth-century manuscripts by the same scribe. S was the subject of Professor Christine James's doctoral thesis, developed into a monograph – the ground-breaking research presented by James is a masterful contribution to this subject, and made the

---

[35] Antur, 'I Mewn Hen Ysgrifen Gron', 1–2.

[36] *J(ed.)*, xx–xxi.

[37] *J(ed.)*, xxi.

present work possible.³⁸ In discussing manuscript 'tails', James notes that the process of creating a 'tail' was started in L and Bost, and expanded in J to create a tail of Iorwerth material, although see the discussion above.³⁹ From there, the nature of the material had changed and it had become disorganised and broken, changing themes regularly, and the 'tail' found in L, Bost and J is found in Q and S but scattered and divided – it is not presented as a coherent run of material in the same way.⁴⁰ The organisation of the material in L, Bost and J is not the main concern, but the content, and so the rearranging of the material in Q and S, makes sense if the material existed as stand-alone tractates under the broad theme of *Arferion Cyfraith*, or was included in a collection of practical and/or procedural material, rather than being a tractate with a certain form (as in L, Bost and J). Dafydd Jenkins stated that the redactors, when creating 'tails', would *'[b]wrw i mewn bopeth nad oedd yn cofio ei fod eisoes yn y llyfr, ond dichon hefyd iddo ychwanegu'r pethau a oedd o'r gwerth ymarferol mwyaf yn ei gyfnod ef* ('throw in everything he had not remembered was already in the book, but perhaps he also added the things which were of the greatest practical value in his time').⁴¹ James concedes that the 'tail' in Q is not at all disorganised, and that the material was incorporated thematically; I would say that the same is also true of the latter part of Z, where the material is incorporated according to the sources available, but with the unifying aim of collecting practical material. James notes that Q represents the end of the process that was started in L.⁴² However, although she states that the L/Bost 'tail' is not in S, Tim or Q, I would modify that: the material is there, just not in the order it is found in the earlier manuscripts.⁴³

The 'tail' of S is stated by James to start on ff. 60, and there is a colophon that could be said to mark the end of the Blegywryd text and the beginning of the new texts that follow.⁴⁴ However, the colophon is followed by *Arferion Cyfraith* and some of the sections connected to it, which suggests that there is something else going on here. Looking at the sections in this part of S, on ff. 59r6–59v27, before the colophon, there are sections that are not from the main Blegywryd text as presented in *LlBleg*, but are found variously in AL VC (so Iorwerth material), AL VIII (*cynghawsedd*), or in no other manuscript except Tim, which is linked to S.⁴⁵ Then, the aforementioned colophon is presented:

> Kyn no hyn y deɓesbɓyd o soɓydogyon llys benydyaɓl y brenhin a chyfreitheu y llys benydyaɓl. Bellach y deɓedir o sɓydogyon y ɓlad a'r gyfreith gyffredin a ossoded o bleid y brenhin rong y brenhin a'e ɓyr ymhop gɓlad o'e deyrnas. Nyd amgen sɓydogyon a ossoded ym pob llys o dadleuoed kɓmɓd neu gantref yGɓyned a Phoɓys: maer, kyghellaɓr, righill, offeiriad u yssgrifenu dadloeoed, ac vn braɓdɓr o vreint sɓyd; a phedɓar sɓydoc megis y rei kyntaf ymhop llys o dadleuoed kɓmɓd neu ganteref yNeheubarth, a llyaɓs o vraɓdɓyr o vreint tir, nyd amgen no phob perchen tir megis yd oedynt kyn Hyɓel Da herɓyd kyfreith Dyfynɓal.

---

³⁸ *Machlud*. This was published online in 2013 and is forthcoming as a printed book.
³⁹ *Machlud*, xl–xli.
⁴⁰ *Machlud*, xli; see also Chapter 5, 155–156.
⁴¹ Jenkins, Review of *J(ed.)*, 106.
⁴² *Machlud*, xli.
⁴³ *Machlud*, xli.
⁴⁴ *Machlud*, xii.
⁴⁵ *Machlud*, Conspectus pp. 169–170.

Previously has been treated of the officers of the king's daily court and the laws of the daily court. Hereafter will be treated of the officers of the country and the intermediary law set forth on behalf of the king between the king and his men in every country of his kingdom. These officers were placed in every commote or hundred court of pleadings in Gwynedd and Powys, namely: a *maer*, a *canghellor*, a summoner, a priest to write pleadings, and one judge by virtue of office; and four officers like the former in every commote or hundred court of pleadings in Deheubarth, and many judges by virtue of land, namely every land owner as they were before Hywel Dda according to the law of Dyfnwal.[46]

This could be said to be an introduction to the 'tail' of S, but rather, in the light of the third part of L, Bost and J, this looks to be a revised version of the introduction to the Laws of Country in other Blegywryd manuscripts. James notes that it does not sit comfortably at this point in the manuscript.[47] S does not have the Laws of Court, and it has what may be a fudged sentence to explain the omission, stating that they are no longer in use.[48] The adapted sentence in S refers to the local officials that are dealt with in Blegywryd, but outside the Laws of Court; it may be the case that the sentences that appear to be introducing the 'tail' are, rather, an attempt to cover a gap in the manuscript, and that the scribe has rewritten and adapted an existing introduction to the Laws of Country. Far more important, however, is the explanation that occurs at the same point in manuscript Tim, a manuscript that is closely linked to S at this point:

Teir ran yỽ aỽdyrdaỽd Hyel Da a'e gyfreitheu, nyd amgen: kyfreith y lis bennydyaỽl, a chyfreith y ỽlad, ac aruer kyfreithaỽl o bob vn ohonunt. Dyededic yỽ hyt hyn o gyfreith y llys a chyfreith y ỽlad, yr hon a elỽir yr aỽdyrdaỽd diledef; ereill a geilỽ y braỽdlyfyr. Dỽetaỽy yỽ rac llaỽ o Rol Dauid Llỽyd, sef yỽ honno, seretein o pyngkeu yssyd gyfreidiol y pob gỽr o gyfreith ỽrthynt pob amser.[49]

The authoritative text of the laws of Hywel Dda is in three parts, namely: the law of his daily court, and the law of the country, and the legal practice of each one of them. Up to now has been spoken of the law of the court and the law of the country, that which is called unwavering authority; others call this the *brawdlyfr* (lawbook). What is to be treated of next is from Dafydd Llwyd's Roll, namely certain topics which are essential for every man of law at all times.[50]

In this interesting passage, the tripartite organisation of the lawtexts is maintained: the Laws of Court, the Laws of Country, and the legal practice of each one. The first two have been dealt with, and the text now turns presumably to the third, and *Rhol Dafydd Llwyd* here may represent the 'legal practice' part of the lawbooks. However, the text is difficult to interpret on the distinctions that are being made. The Laws of Court and Laws of Country are called 'unwavering authority', as they are the text of unwavering authority, and 'others' call it the *brawdlyfr* ('judgement book', cf. OE *dōmbōc*). The text seems to say that the first part is called both things – unwavering

---

[46] Text and translation from James, 'Dafydd (Llwyd)', 155–156.
[47] *Machlud*, xxi; see also *J(ed.)*, 23.9–11.
[48] On an alternative explanation for the absence of the Laws of Court, see Russell, 'Canyt oes aruer', 176, 183. See also *Machlud*, 2–3.
[49] *Machlud*, xxi; from NLW Llanstephan MS 116, f. 21v.
[50] See also James, 'Dafydd (Llwyd)', 156.

authority by some, judgement book by others. Both descriptions emphasise authority, and the Laws of Court and Laws of Country have always been authoritative, since the time of Hywel Dda, but that does not mean to say that the following part, from *Rhol Dafydd Llwyd*, has *less* authority; that is said to be necessary now for every man of law. Linking *Rhol Dafydd Llwyd* to the first two parts of the law gives it authority, and it is also a named book of law, like others, and linked to a well-known jurist.

James notes that the tail of S divides into two – the first part, up to §2236, is also shared with manuscript Tim, and is likely to be a version of *Rhol Dafydd Llwyd*.[51] Dafydd Llwyd was a *dosbarthwr*, a 'mediator' or 'arbiter', a man who worked with the law and had a practical use for a law manuscript.[52] It is, of course, uncertain how much of this part of S was copied from the Roll, whether the Roll provided only the first portion of the material, or all of the first part of the 'tail' of S and Tim, up to §2236 in the edition. If the Roll was a fairly sizeable document, then it may have travelled as one source, and it is likely that it contained the material found in the third part of Blegywryd, as well as *Arferion Cyfraith* that is found towards the beginning of this section of S, not long after the introductory sentence. In S, the material found following this introduction is not found in the other Blegywryd manuscripts, but it is found in Q, which may have had most or all of the Roll as well, and copied it selectively. The bulk of the *Rhol Dafydd Llwyd* material in S and Tim is material that is not found in the main Blegywryd, Iorwerth or Cyfnerth tradition, presented in AL X (from Q) and AL XI (based on S). There are also some *damweiniau* in this section.[53]

The compiler of Lew, a mid-fifteenth century Iorwerth manuscript that is more mixed, and that contains an incomplete Iorwerth text, Damweiniau I and some sections from other redactions, may have seen some of the Roll as well. Lew is in the hand of Lewys Ysgolhaig, who was working in south-west Wales in the mid-fifteenth century,[54] and is said to have been written *o ddethol y llyfrev gorev ac a gauas ef* ('from selecting the best books which he obtained').[55] Manuscript Lew was not known to Aneurin Owen. The binding is disordered, and the first two quires are defective, but they contain material that is also found in S and Q: most of the material is found in Q and the reading is closer to Q than it is to S; however, the material is not in the same order as the material in Q, or that in S, so it is difficult to determine what Lew was copying – it may be that he was copying single manuscript, or perhaps several smaller texts.

The material in this part of S can all be said to have a practical purpose, for administering the law, and it may be an extension of other material found in south Wales, linked to the Blegywryd tradition. It could be tentatively suggested that *Rhol Dafydd Llwyd* was also derived from the Blegywryd tradition, and may have been a version of *Arferion Cyfraith*, or the third and practitioner-focused part of the laws. Looking at this section of S, allegedly *Rhol Dafydd Llwyd*, there is a striking parallel

---

[51] *Machlud*, xxi, xlviii.
[52] *Machlud*, xxi–xxv; it is possible that he is the 'Dafydd Llwyd ap Gwilym' who held various official roles in Cardiganshire between 137/8–1428/9: James, 'Dafydd (Llwyd)', 157, 164.
[53] *Machlud*, Conspectus, 170–189; the *damweiniau* are found towards the end of what James calls the first half of the 'tail' of S: §§2147–2236. They may have been included in the exemplar since they are shared with Tim and both manuscripts appear to have been copying the same exemplar at this point.
[54] Antur, 'I Mewn Hen Ysgrifen Gron', 15.
[55] Evans, *Report*, Vol. I, Part II – Peniarth, 373.

to the material in the other 'practical' manuscript, Z, which was material from northeast Wales, useful to a practitioner.

The remainder of S has material that may be independent of Tim, and is mostly derived from other redactions, mainly Iorwerth; Tim has hardly any unique material in its second half.[56] The relationship between S and Tim shows that there was a body of material circulating in south Wales, and the scribe added this material to a traditional version of the law, but S and Tim have a different Blegywryd text. James points out that this suggests that neither version of Blegywryd was more valued than the other.[57] But it also hints at the extent of the material available in the region at that time, to that scribe. Apart from two separate Blegywryd texts, there was an independent work, *Rhol Dafydd Llwyd*, which may have been formed from several texts, some perhaps gleaned from the Blegywryd tradition; and also portions of a text from the Iorwerth tradition. And all of this material would be useful to practitioners, which fitted in with the third part of the Blegywryd text as exemplified in L, J and Bost – this shows the development of the Blegywryd redaction in south Wales, and of law in Wales in general, with a move towards the practical, useful aspects of medieval Welsh law.

Beyond *Llyfr Blegywryd*

In general, the manuscripts of the Blegywryd redaction that have not already been dealt with are 'standard' manuscripts, often incomplete, and they follow the Blegywryd pattern set in *LlBleg*, and contain no material extra to that. No reference to these manuscripts are found in AL II since the material within them is all contained in AL DC. The manuscripts are R, M and P, which have all lost their end, as are N, T, and Llan, which are also generally laconic. However, two Blegywryd manuscripts do have a small amount of material that is not included in *LlBleg*, and they will be discussed next.

Tr, Cambridge, Trinity College MS O.7.1

Tr and O were used for *LlBleg*; both date from the first half of the fourteenth century, and both of have some material that was omitted from the edition. Manuscript L was used to fill any lacunae in O and Tr and supplied the Laws of Court, absent in both O and Tr.[58] The editors chose the three earliest Blegywryd manuscripts, and their aim was to attempt to recreate the exemplar of these manuscripts.[59] The three manuscripts used by Williams and Powell all end rather differently. *LlBleg* ends on p. 131.10, with the sentence preceding the *Dywededic yw hyt hyn* colophon: the decision to end *LlBleg* at that point was probably made on the basis of the colophon in manuscript L.[60] L continues with the text found in AL DC III.

---

[56] *Machlud*, xliv.

[57] *Machlud*, xli.

[58] *LlBleg*, xl.

[59] *LlBleg*, xxxix. O and Tr are dated to the first half of the fourteenth century; N, Peniarth 36B is also from the same period and is in the same hand as O and Tr, and R, Peniarth 31 is in a different hand but is contemporary with the other three. L is slightly later, dated to the mid-fourteenth century, but is a fuller text.

[60] See above, 146.

O ends first, at *LlBleg* 123.15, midway through the triad collection.[61] Tr has most of the remainder of the text of *LlBleg*, only missing the ten final lines on p. 131; Tr ends mid-sentence at the bottom of a verso folio, which suggests that further pages have been lost.[62] The following folio in Tr has the Gwilym Wasta colophon, and then, in a different hand, there is a text on the *Deuddeg Annoeth* ('Twelve Unwise'); this may have been left out of the edition since it is in a different hand.

The *Deuddeg Annoeth* is a list that derives from a seventh-century Irish text, *De duodecim abusiuis saeculi*, quoted by the *Collectio Canonum Hibernensis* (an Irish collection, in Latin, of Continental canon law, dating from the late seventh and eighth centuries), and it was a popular text in Europe. It belongs to the genre of wisdom-texts, which 'contain general statements expressing early Irish views on the society's structure and ethos',[63] and its inclusion in the Welsh law manuscripts is an example of a text that is extremely old in origin – as well as being known in the wider European tradition – included in the law manuscripts.

This section on the *Deuddeg Annoeth*, found after the Gwilym Wasta colophon in Tr, echoes several other parts of the laws, but the section does not occur generally in any of the redaction texts. However, it is found in two other manuscripts, and the text from Q was presented in AL II X.ix, preceded by a section on the Nines of Law, and followed by *Llyfr Cynyr ap Cadwgan*, another section that is numerically ordered. In Q, the section is called *Deudec peth yssyd yn llugru y byt* ('Twelve things which corrupt the world'), but the opening text in *Ancient Laws* has been amended to *Tridec peth* ('Thirty [sic] things'), which should read '*tri ar ddeg*', thirteen, since 13 items are listed. The section also occurs in manuscript G from the part of that manuscript which is said to be taken from *Llyfr Cynog*.[64] The three versions are reproduced here, along with the Latin version.

De Duodecim Abusivis Saeculi.

Sapiens sine operibus bonis; senex sine religione; adolescens sine oboedientia; dives sine elemosyna; femina sine pudicitia; dominus sine virtute; Christianus contentiosus; pauper superbus; rex iniquus; episcopus neglegens; plebs sine disciplina; populus sine lege.

The wise man without good works; the old man without religion; the youth without obedience; the rich man without almsgiving; the woman without modesty; the abbot-nobleman without virtue; the contentious Christian; the poor man who is proud; the unrighteous king; the negligent bishop; the sect without discipline; the people without the law.[65]

Tr, Cambridge, Trinity College O.7.1, 68r7–17

Deudec anoyth yr in oys oyssoyd, nyt amgen: ignat heb weythredoeth, a brenhin creulaὸn, ac argl6yth g6an, ac escob heb enmyned, a g6lad heb gyureyth, a tlvyth heb

---

[61] O however has a further page of other triads, discussed below.
[62] The text of Tr in *LlBleg* ends with the first word on 131.1, 'a'; the remainder of p. 131 is from L.
[63] Kelly, *A Guide to Early Irish Law*, 2–3.
[64] Wiliam, *Llyfr Cynog*, 48.
[65] Text and translation from Goodman, 'In a Father's Place', 73, which is based on Aidan Breen's edition.

gosb, a hen heb greuyth, a yeanc heb vuylltaud, ac echena6c ryuug6s, a christaun kynhennus, a gureic heb gywylyd, a goludauc heb alwyssen.[66]

The twelve unwise things since the beginning of time, namely: a justice without actions, and a cruel king, and a weak lord, and a bishop without patience, and a country without law, and a retinue without discipline, and the old without religion, and the young without good sense, and the arrogant needy, and a quarrelsome Christian, and a woman without shame, and the rich without charity.

Q, Wynnstay 36, 53r30a–53r14b

Deudec peth yssyd yn llugru y byt a byth y bydant ynda6, ac ny ellir byth y g6aret ohona6; sef y6 y rei hynny: brenhin en6ir, a g6ann argl6yd, ac ygnat cam6eda6c, ac offeirat g6reiga6c, a chy6eithyd hep reol, a phobyl hep dysc, a g6lat hep kyfreith, ac escob hep 6ybot, a hen heb greuyd, a ieuanc hep vuyllta6t, a goluda6c kebyd, ac aghena6c syber6, a lleidyr kynena6c yg6lat.

There are twelve things which corrupt the world and they will always be in it, and it is not possible ever to be rid of them; those ones are: an unjust king, and a weak lord, and an unjust justice, and a married priest, and a company without rule, and people without learning, and a country without law, and a bishop without knowledge, and the old without religion, and the young without good sense, and the miserly rich, and the proud needy, and a contentious thief in a country.

G, Peniarth 35, 19v12–19

Deudec peth yssyd yn llygru y byt a byth y bydant ynda6, ac ny ellir byth eu gwaret ohona6; sef y6 y rei hynny: brenhin enwir, a gwan argl6yd, ac ygnat camweda6c, ac offeirat g6reiga6c, a chyweithyd hep reol, a phobyl heb dysc, a g6lat hep k*yfreith*, ac escop heb enmyned, a hen heb greuyd, a jeuanc hep uuyllta6d, goluda6c kybyd, ac ychena6c syber6, lleidyr kyneuodic yg g6lat.

There are twelve things which corrupt the world and they will always be in it, and it is not possible ever to be rid of them; those ones are: an unjust king, and a weak lord, and an unjust justice, and a married priest, and a company without rule, and people without learning, and a country without law, and a bishop without patience, and the old without religion, and the young without good sense, and the miserly rich, and the proud needy, and a habitual thief in a country.

Comparing the texts of the three Welsh versions, it is immediately clear that the text in Tr reflects the source more closely than the other Welsh versions. The similarities in Q and G are shared innovations, and even the orthography is similar; they may derive from a common hyparchetype. The only difference is the description of the bishop: *hep 6ybot* ('without knowledge') in Q, but *heb enmyned* ('without patience') in G, which matches Tr including in the unusual spelling of *enmyned*. Both Q and G have 13 items in the list, despite claiming to have 12, although the final item – which does not compare with any of the 12 items in Tr – may be an addition to the list, perhaps to make it more 'legal' in nature. The version in Tr has 12 items, has a different and more concise title, and the order of the items are different to the order in Q and G. Putting aside the final item in Q

---

[66] See also the discussion of the section and a transcript in Powell, 'The Trinity College Manuscript', 122.

and G, three of the items in the list in Tr do not compare with any of the items in Q and G: neither *Christaun kynhennus* ('a quarrelsome Christian'), or *gureic heb gywylydd* ('a woman/wife without shame') is found in Q and G, but the version in those manuscripts do have *offeirat g6reica6c* ('a married priest'), *cyweithyd hep reol* ('a company with no order'), and *pobyl heb dysc* ('people with no learning'). The replacement of the 'woman without shame' with the 'married priest' is evidence of revision of the text in the wake of church reform, and the movement against married clergy in the twelfth and thirteenth centuries. The other item in Tr that has no parallel in Q and G is complex – it seems to be *tlvyth heb gosb* ('a retinue without discipline'), although the manuscript is difficult to read. This may be a loose parallel to *cyweithyd hep reol* ('a company/retinue without rule') and is in a similar vein, but Powell did not equate the two.[67]

The *Deuddeg Annoeth* does not have a clear parallel anywhere else in the laws, although it is found in the wider European tradition, and it is an example of a numbered list with the items within it all having a moral air, with more than a little Christian influence on the things listed. This is often a feature of wisdom-texts, and it is less 'legal' in theme, although moralising and controlling behaviour might be relevant to a legal system, and the addition of the 'habitual thief' in Q and G's version may be an attempt to make the piece fit better with legal material.[68] There are other examples of numbered lists in the laws, which means this does not stand out as unusual, but the fact that it has been copied on the last page of Tr, in a different hand, suggests that this was a short section that was not in Gwilym Wasta's exemplar.

It does not appear that there was a relationship between Tr and the other two manuscripts, Q and G. Both Tr and G are earlier than Q and date to the first half of the fourteenth century, and Q is dated later, to the early fifteenth century, but both Q and G contain sections of *Llyfr Cynog*, and this may be the origin of this text in those manuscripts.[69] The text in Tr may have been drawn directly from the Latin original or from a translation of that. The main scribe of Tr, Gwilym Wasta, was a burgess in Dinefwr, Carmarthenshire, which is presumably where he wrote his manuscripts, but little is known of Tr's movements from the Tywi valley.[70] The hand of the *Deuddeg Annoeth* is said to be contemporary to the date of the manuscript. It is impossible to suggest an origin for this piece in Tr, other than it does not seem to derive from the *Llyfr Cynog* material. It is not copied from any extant law manuscript, and tells us very little about the origin of the material or the circumstances of writing.

O, NLW Peniarth MS 36A

As discussed, there are three Blegywryd manuscripts in the hand of Gwilym Wasta: O, Tr and N, all from the first half of the fourteenth century. Each of these manuscripts have lacunae and all three are wanting their end. O ends earlier than Tr does, with the text breaking off towards the end of the triad collection: the words *Tri ryw amdiffyn yssyd* ('There are three defences') are found at the bottom of f. 70v (in the older foliation); there is no f. 71; and a different text starts on f. 72r, continuing from a missing folio.[71]

---

[67] Powell, 'The Trinity College Manuscript', 122.
[68] Kelly, *A Guide to Early Irish Law*, 2.
[69] See Chapter 4, 120–122, on *Llyfr Cynog*.
[70] *RWMS*, forthcoming in 2022; Daniel Huws has always been extremely generous in sharing his work with scholars, and this comment was taken from the 2010 draft of the work.
[71] See *LlBleg*, 123.16, where O ends and the triad collection continues from Tr.

Table 6.1: Quire 10 of O, fol. 74–76

Folio	Opening words	Cross-reference
f. 74r1–5	Tri meib yssyd ny dylyant gyfran o tir	*LlBleg*, 112.11–16; *LT*, Q74
f. 74r 5–6	Tri defnydd hawl	*LlBleg*, 119.19–20; *LT*, Q120
f. 74r 7–10	Teir golwc a dygir yg kyfreith	*LlBleg*, 119–21–3; *LT*, Q121
f. 74r 10–13	Tri geir kylus	*LlBleg*, 119.24–6; *LT*, Q122
f. 74r 13–23	Tri ryw wallawgeir	*LlBleg*, 119.27–120.3; *LT*, Q123
f. 74v1–9	Tri chof gwedy brawt	*LlBleg*, 120.19–26; *LT*, Q128
f. 74v9–16	Teir tystolyaeth marwawl [no closing sentence]	*LlBleg*, 121.6–12; *LT*, Q121
f. 74v17–75r1	Teir gwraged a dyly eu meibion	*LlBleg*, 111.5–11; *LT*, Q78
f. 75r2-v2	Pedeir taryan yssyd	*LlBleg*, 44.8–28
f. 75v2–9	[Pan d]echreuer kynhenn am teruyn	*LlBleg*, 70.17–26
f. 75v9–24	Pwy bynhac a ofynho datanhud	*LlBleg*, 71.24–72.11
f. 76r1–5	Ac vrth hynny y dywedir ny eill	*LlBleg*, 73.2–7
f. 76r5–11	Megys y mae brawt	*LlBleg*, 75.19–24
f. 76r11–24	Os keitwat a gyll	*LlBleg*, 46.4–16
f. 76v	Neb a uo mach dros dyn arall	*WML* 86.13–87.4

It is clear from the older foliation of the manuscript that there is a leaf missing, since f. 72r follows f. 70v.[72] Following the lost leaf, f. 72r opens with the final five lines of a triad and follows with several other triads that are normally found in the Blegywryd triad tractate, repeating triads already given in O (as the triad tractate occurs earlier in the manuscript). The text jumps around giving some 'runs' of triads in order, but skipping several – it is not therefore a direct copy of the triad tractate as it appears in most of the Blegywryd manuscripts, and does not appear to be a copy of the triad tractate found earlier in O. The text, however, is continuous, as the last of these triads ends on the first line of f. 75r, and is followed by other Blegywryd sections, all continuous with no marker to show gaps or omissions: *gwarant* ('warranty'), Land Law, and *adnau* ('deposits'). All of these sections are also repeats of texts found earlier on in the manuscript. They are different to the versions of the same text that were included earlier on in O – for example, the triad *Tri defnydd hawl* ('Three substances of a claim') has the items in a different order – but neither do the texts show close similarity to any of the other extant versions of the same texts. The final section in the manuscript, on f. 76v, is also found in Cyfnerth, and is a part of the Suretyship tractate. The same section is also found in manuscript Q, and thus is in AL X, appended to an extended triad called *Tri balog fechni* ('Three buckle suretyships'), found in several manuscript sources.[73] However, the text in O is not from the same source as that in Q and, while it is closer to W and Mk, it is not close enough to be certain that it shared an exemplar with either of these manuscripts.

---

[72] The manuscript has older foliation, and newer pagination, but both of these skip the lost leaf, which must have been lost after the manuscript was foliated/paginated. See also <http://www.rhyddiaithganoloesol.caerdydd.ac.uk/en/ms-page.php?ms=Pen36A&page=71r>, accessed 30/11/21.

[73] *LT*, 319 and Q196.

These repeated texts appear to have been taken from a different source to the main exemplar of O, and added at the end of the manuscript; although why the scribe did so is difficult to determine. The texts are not close to that of any of the extant manuscripts and, in addition, the order of the triads, and also of the other texts, suggests that they were not taken from a complete Blegywryd manuscript. Rather, it is more likely that this was a section of legal material that was available to be copied into the manuscripts at a particular locality – this has been seen time and time again with material in the law manuscripts, and is a feature of S, Y, and Z, for example. The subject matter of the sections could be said to be of use to a practitioner, either to be used in court (e.g. model pleadings), or as part of a legal education or training. The triads are on claims, testimony and Land Law, and the non-triadic sections are again on Land Law and also on warranty and deposits. It may be that these sections were brought together from another source to preserve the texts, but there does not appear to be any deliberate motive behind this action of copying, unlike the other examples that have been discussed.

Y, NLW MS 20143A

One final Blegywryd manuscript needs attention as it too contains material that is not found in the edition in *LlBleg*. Although the situation is far more complex and unlike the manuscripts discussed above, it does not contain a Blegywryd text followed by other material. Manuscript Y, dating from the second half of the fourteenth century, was used by Aneurin Owen, but it proved a problem to him – he was able to give variants from it from the Laws of Court in AL GC, up to the end of the description of the officers, but he then stated that 'The remainder of this book is not in Y'.[74] In that, he was accurate; Y is a composite manuscript, in two hands. Hand A was responsible for the Cyfnerth Laws of Court and, at the end of the section, half a page was left blank at the end of the second quire.[75] The remainder of the manuscript is the work of Hand B, belonging largely to Blegywryd.[76] However, the Blegywryd portion of the manuscript is not at all straightforward. While it starts out as a Blegywryd text of the Laws of Country, other redaction material is then found interspersed. For example, the first part, the Three Columns of Law, combines the Blegywryd text with sections from both Iorwerth and Cyfnerth, and the tariff of values of body parts has a great deal of Cyfnerth material with some Blegywryd material.

Table 6.2: The Three Columns of Law in Y

Text	Reference	Redaction
Opening section on *galanas*	20r1a–22r14b	Blegywryd
Opening section on *galanas*	22r14b–22v16a	Iorwerth
Opening section on *galanas*	22v16a–23r7a	Blegywryd
Opening section on *galanas*	23r7a–23r14b	Iorwerth
Opening section on *galanas*	23r14b–24r2a	Blegywryd

---

[74] AL, pp. 670–671, note 21 (quarto edition).
[75] Huws, 'National Library of Wales MS 20143A', 420.
[76] Owen, 'The Laws of Court from Cyfnerth', 430.

(Table 6.2 continued)

Text	Reference	Redaction
Opening section on *galanas*	24r3a–24r14a	Cyfnerth
Sarhaed, *galanas*, values	24r15a–26v15a	Blegywryd
Value of the body	26v15a–26v13b	Blegywryd
Value of the body	26v14b–27r4a	Cyfnerth
Value of the body	27r4a–27r11b	Blegywryd
Value of the body	27r11b–27r16b	Cyfnerth
Value of the body	27r16b–28r12a	Blegywryd
Sarhaed, *galanas*, values	28r13a–28r17b	Blegywryd
Opening section on theft	28r17b–28v9a	Blegywryd
Paying land for *galanas*	28v9a–28v1b	Cyfnerth
Two men whose *galanas* cannot be claimed	28v1b–28v15b	Cyfnerth
Selections from triad collection	28v15b–29v5a	Blegywryd
Cynghawsedd	29v5a–29v1b	Other
Selections from triad collection	29v2b–29v19b	Blegywryd
Opening section on fire	30r1a–30r18b	Blegywryd
Accidental fire	30r18b–30v3b	Blegywryd
Opening section on fire	30v4b–31r16a	Iorwerth

As can be seen from Table 6.2, in the Three Columns of Law, the basic text appears to be Blegywryd, with sections from both Cyfnerth and Iorwerth interspersed. But the method was not to copy the whole Blegywryd section and then change to another redaction; it was to select and reorganise. In this, Y is different to Q – Q tended to copy the whole of the section from one redaction exemplar before adding other sections from other sources. Manuscript Q proceeds in this way throughout, although towards the end of the manuscript there is a block of non-redaction material, following *Arferion Cyfraith*. However, the general organisation of Y is atypical, and in reality it does not fit into the scheme of presenting a redaction text in full followed by material from other non-redaction sources, particularly since the Laws of Court are from a different redaction to the remainder of the manuscript and are in a different hand.

The Laws of Court aside, the majority of the second part of Y, by Hand B, belongs to the Blegywryd redaction. The Blegywryd texts usually appear first in any section, which suggests that the scribe was starting with Blegywryd and the material from other redactions and sources were intended to supplement his Blegywryd text. This second part of the manuscript opens with the Three Columns of Law, stating that *galanas* will be dealt with first (as is standard), but does not include any preamble explaining that these are the Laws of Country. The Blegywryd sections in manuscript Y suggest that Hand B had a complete Blegywryd text to copy, and it seems that most of it was copied into his work; there are some missing sections, but it appears that all of the expected tractates are represented here if not copied in full. The Blegywryd text in Y shows some similarities to manuscripts I, and also to S, which is linked to

The Development of the Redaction Manuscripts

I,[77] although the order of manuscript Y is different. Hand B also uses some short sections taken from a Blegywryd version of the Laws of Court. These sections discuss the role of the Justice, and they are commonly included in manuscripts such as S which lack the Laws of Court, since they are useful sections presumably meant for the user of the manuscript. But their inclusion in Y may suggest that the Blegywryd text that was being copied had a full text of the Laws of Court; the Laws of Court in Y had been copied by Hand A from his Cyfnerth exemplar, and so there was no need for Hand B to repeat this lengthy section. As a composite manuscript, it seems that Hand A and Hand B had different working methods, and perhaps different texts to copy; whether they worked together in any way is difficult to determine.

The Cyfnerth portion of Y is also interesting.[78] The Laws of Court are close to those in manuscript X and appear to be a complete text in Y.[79] Daniel Huws states that the text of this part of Y is 'an unadulterated Cyfnerth text', but two short sections – a sentence and a few lines – are included in this version of the Laws of Court whereas they occur in the Laws of Country in all other Cyfnerth manuscripts.[80] This may have been the case in the text that Y was copying as well, since the sections are on falcons' nests, which fits with the sections on hunting in the Laws of Court, and a very short sentence on the value of a king's pet animal, which again has a link to the royal court.[81] It is difficult to ascribe any editing to the Laws of Court in Y, since the text of the Laws of Court in general was very stable, and was rarely edited or moved around (although it could sometimes be omitted). However, Hand B for the second part of the manuscript seems to have been the active editor, and Hand A's role is less clear.[82]

Hand B may also have had a fuller Cyfnerth text and, if that was the case, then the editing and organising of the material is even more selective than it first appears. This seems to be deliberate selection and editing. Most of these Cyfnerth sections in the Laws of Country, which number 14 in total, are very short, some of them single sentences, but there is one longer piece in the collection – a section on suretyship. One issue that needs to be considered in relation to Hand B's Cyfnerth sections is whether the text is related to manuscript X, as Hand A's Cyfnerth Laws of Court seem to be similar to X.[83] This is not the case – all the short Cyfnerth sections in Hand B's part of Y, with the exception of the extract on suretyship, are closer to W.[84] Hand B was not copying W directly, but the text he was copying has more in common with W than it does with X or U. This means that the two parts of manuscript Y, in two different hands, may have been drawing on different sources and perhaps even had a different purpose. The second part was clearly based on a Blegywryd text with sections of Iorwerth and Cyfnerth added at various points, but the Laws of Court

---

[77] *Machlud*, xxxviii–xl. I and S are more similar to each other than Y is to either manuscript.

[78] Owen, 'The "Cyfnerth" Text', 180.

[79] Huws, 'National Library of Wales MS 20143A', 422. Huws points out that the last leaf of the second quire is missing, but it may have been blank in any case.

[80] *Ibid.*, 420.

[81] NLW MS 20143A, ff. 11va12–11vb14; 17va4–17va6: *punt y6 g6erth llet6egin brenhin* ('the value of a king's semi-tame [animal] is a pound').

[82] Huws, 'National Library of Wales MS 20143A', describes scribe A as 'more old-fashioned than B, perhaps an older man', 421.

[83] Owen, 'The "Cyfnerth" Text', 431–432.

[84] The exception is *Pum allwedd yngneidiaeth* ('Five Keys of Justiceship'), which is different in Y, W, Z and Mk, with variety in the order of the list in the manuscripts. On this text, see Emanuel, 'The Seven Keys of Wisdom'.

were taken from a different source or text. Hand B does not appear to have been working with Hand A, but it may be that it was convenient, and less time-consuming, to use the Laws of Court that had already been copied by Hand A in order to start the manuscript in the usual way, and then work through the Blegywryd text, adding material as he felt would be useful.

The sections that have been taken from the Iorwerth redaction are the smallest in number. There are 12 sections in Y that belong to the Iorwerth redaction. On the whole, all but two of the Iorwerth sections are short, but they seem to have been taken from a longer text, and the tendency in Y is not to copy a complete tractate or even a complete text on a particular theme. The first of the longer Iorwerth portions is on Corn Damage, not the complete tractate but a part of it, and it begins midway through the section in the complete Iorwerth manuscripts. The second is found towards the end of Y and it discusses theft, specifically claiming an animal taken through theft, so it is material that may have had a use as a guide to procedure for a practitioner.

The Iorwerth sections in Y are close to two other manuscripts: D, c.1404, and K, after 1469, but they are not a copy of either manuscript. The closest affinity is with K, although there is a section of the Law of Women in Y, and K does not contain the Law of Women. It is difficult to be certain whether Hand B of Y had a complete Iorwerth text. Y has sections taken from the Laws of Country, including the Law of Women, and the Test Book, but nothing from the Iorwerth Laws of Court.[85] If Hand B did have a complete Iorwerth text, then his selection of the sections he included was done very carefully, and suggests a thorough knowledge of the text he copied. He may well have chosen sections that he felt were of use, or perhaps were current.

Manuscript Y seems to move away from its Blegywryd text towards the end of the manuscript. It does not have the colophon found in L, Bost and J, but it has a triad collection at the end of the manuscript instead, something that happens in several Cyfnerth manuscripts and in the Gwilym Wasta Blegywryd manuscripts. Several of the Blegywryd continuation texts occur in Y, but again they are ordered into subject-specific sections. This suggests that Hand A had a full Blegywryd text, perhaps including the Blegywryd continuation material. There are also some triads in the continuation material, some of which occur in *Llyfr Damweiniau* or with the *holiadon* collection (also in the continuation). Two of these triads in Y, however, are only otherwise found in manuscript Q, but the version in Y is different, so the redactor of Y was not copying Q (or vice versa) and they may not have been copying the same text either. It seems that the final part of Y is a collection of triads and other practical material, and it follows the working method of Hand B: gathering similar material together.

The Iorwerth sections included in Y suggest a different purpose than that of the mixed sections in Q, for example. In Q, the scribe or collator would gather together tractates on a common theme and list first his Blegywryd text, then his Iorwerth text, and other material on the same subject. The aim of that manuscript was to bring similar material together. In Y, the selection from the different tractates may be because there is a sentence or a short text that is useful; the scribe was not copying everything that he had on any particular topic. Manuscript Y is clearly complex, and was drawing on several texts. Some of the material incorporated into Y can be found in the miscellaneous collection in the Blegywryd continuation, labelled *Pethau sydd unfraint â Lladrad yn Llaw* ('Things which are of the same status as Theft in Hand'), but as is often the case with that material, it is distributed throughout the manuscript

---

[85] See above on the Iorwerth text circulating in south Wales, 167–168.

and does not occur as a unit. Y is particularly significant as it is a manuscript that has been made up of several texts. There is the Cyfnerth Laws of Court, which stands alone as a tractate to fill the first two quires of the manuscript. The Laws of Country are based on Blegywryd but draws together material from other sources: Iorwerth and Cyfnerth – apparently a different text to the one providing the Laws of Court – and some other sources perhaps, if not an extended Blegywryd manuscript. The material is not confined to procedural explanations or material that would be of use to a practitioner, as is the case with the material in the second part of Z for example, and the gathering together of the material from different redactions or sources is similar to the tidy editing in manuscript Q; however, Y is better classed as an expanded Blegywryd text (for the second part) rather than some reorganisation of the laws. In any case, the manuscript is highly important because of the reorganisation and inclusion of sections from other redactions.

K, NLW Peniarth MS 40

The final manuscript that needs to be considered in this chapter is K, in the hand of Lewys Glyn Cothi and copied after 1469.[86] Unlike most of the manuscripts discussed previously, K belongs to the Iorwerth redaction, despite Aneurin Owen wrongly categorising it as a Blegywryd manuscript, perhaps due to its similarity in places to Q. Like Q, K opens with a calendar and, because of this, it was called Kalan by William Maurice, which inspired Aneurin Owen's siglum K for it.[87] However, K is a later Iorwerth text, and it has material towards the end that does not occur in any other Iorwerth manuscript. It is a modified text, with a southern origin, as was shown by Morfydd Owen in her important study of K.

In a 'standard' Iorwerth lawbook, the Test Book would be the third part, with the Laws of Court taking the prominent position for various reasons, including to give the lawbooks a purported royal and ecclesiastical link. K does not contain a section on the Laws of Court, however.[88] This strongly appears to be a deliberate omission, but this is a topic of debate among scholars of Welsh law.[89] By the time Lewys Glyn Cothi came to write K in the mid-fifteenth century, almost 200 years after the conquest of Wales, it seems that there was no need to defend the Welsh laws from external criticism, or elevate their royal provenance.[90] Rather than opening with the royal Laws of Court, in K, prominence has instead been given to the Test Book. This appears to be a deliberate act, placing an emphasis on the practical use to which the manuscript was to be put. Once again, the context of the creation of the manuscript is crucial in explaining the material contained within it.

Following the calendar, it opens with the preface to the Test Book, and is then followed by sections from the Three Columns of Law, as would be expected in the Test Book, and as is stated at the end of the preface: *sef y6 hynny tair colofyn k[yfreith]*

---

[86] Antur, 'I Mewn Hen Ysgrifen Gron', 1–2.
[87] Owen, 'A Fifteenth-Century Lawbook', 77. This work is indebted to that study.
[88] *Ibid.*, 88.
[89] See for example Russell, '*Canyt oes aruer*'.
[90] See Brand, 'An English Legal Historian', particularly 37–56, on the application of English law in the conquered territories.

('that is, the Three Columns of Law').[91] Then follow several sections of Iorwerth redaction law, but not an entire text. The second half of the manuscript is given to the collections of triads and *damweiniau* shared with manuscript Q; a collection of *holiadon* (question-and-answer sections); the final item in the manuscript is a plaint. As Morfydd Owen notes, the material in the second half of K is 'concerned with the procedure of the courts'.[92] Opening the manuscript with the Test Book preface may be a tidy and convenient way of omitting the less current Laws of Court, and the preface itself is a useful opener. Nevertheless the Test Book was important in its own right: as stated in the preface of K, it was the book that every lawyer needed to know before he could take up office.

Morfydd Owen demonstrated that K was made for Ieuan ab Phylip, the Constable and Receiver of Cefnllys, who probably used it in court; it is a firmly Marcher text.[93] In the March, Welsh law and English laws and practices were combined and, on a day-to-day level, in the courts, practitioners and officials would need to have a working knowledge of Welsh law, and procedures in particular – or perhaps access to a source of information on the topic. In this case, K appears to be similar to another Marcher text, Z, where material was selected for the second half of that manuscript due to its importance and usefulness. The compiler of Z added material from a variety of exemplars available locally to supplement an older, Cyfnerth, text of Welsh law. For K, Lewys Glyn Cothi, working in Radnorshire, used an older text, a Iorwerth-type law manuscript, but selected the relevant sections from his exemplar and omitted other sections.

The Iorwerth text in K is similar to that in Q and J, which are very close texts, and Tim is another close text: they all probably share an exemplar. S may be a fourth manuscript in the group, but there is more variation in the text in S, although this may be due to scribal adaptation. These connections are shown in Charles-Edwards's revised stemma of the Iorwerth texts, and they form a separate branch to the text in D.[94] Despite the exemplar(s) that Q and K share (the collections of triads and *damweiniau*), the Iorwerth sections in Q are closer to J than they are to those in K, but all are likely to be from the same sub-archetype, if not from the same exemplar. This again suggests that there were certain texts circulating separately, in south Wales. This includes a Iorwerth text, and the collections of triads and *damweiniau* that both occur in Q and K; the triads and *damweiniau* may have been bound together and were probably the work of the same man. Q is likely to have originated in Carmarthenshire, produced for Gruffudd ap Nicolas,[95] and is closely linked to the Red Book of Hergest. K is unlikely to have been from the same place, but texts circulated, and the separate collections of triads and *damweiniau* may have travelled. The triad collection was also copied into S and Tim, but the *damweiniau* do not seem to have been, perhaps because of the similarity of the collection to the other copies of *Llyfr Damweiniau*; or perhaps because the *damweiniau* text is long and labour-intensive to copy. The same Iorwerth text was available to the scribes of K, Q, J, Tim and possibly S as well. This suggests a southern Iorwerth exemplar available in a limited

---

[91] Text from K, NLW Peniarth MS 40, p. 23. The Test Book preface is lengthy and a text and translation (ending before the sentence quoted above) from C, BL Cotton Caligula MS A iii is presented in Russell, *The Prologues*, 40–41. A translation from C is given in *LTMW*, 141.
[92] Owen, 'A Fifteenth-Century Lawbook', 89.
[93] Owen, 'A Fifteenth-Century Lawbook', 82.
[94] Charles-Edwards, 'The Textual Tradition', 44–45.
[95] See above, 165.

region. K is the witness to the largest part of this Iorwerth text, using it as its base text, and it is followed by Q, and then J which has a limited selection. S and Tim have some sections, but they also have Iorwerth Law of Women sections, where K has none of the Law of Women.

K does not present a 'standard' Iorwerth text, although it has many elements of a Iorwerth redaction text. As noted above, it opens with the Test Book preface, which is long and includes the story of Hywel Dda and the creation of the law: this was interchangeable with the more familiar main prologues to the law manuscripts. The preface in K ends by stating the contents of the Test Book, and the *Naw Affaith* ('Nine Abetments') of *galanas* follows (usually found in the Test Book), with a decorated initial. As well as the Three Columns, the manuscript has the Value of Wild and Tame and the values of houses and equipment list, followed by *Cyfar*, and Corn Damage, all part of the Iorwerth Test Book. The Laws of Country come after the Test Book in K.

The Iorwerth text in K is a near-complete text, but there are three obvious omissions: apart from the Laws of Court, the first two tractates in the Laws of Country are absent. In most Iorwerth manuscripts, the Laws of Country open with *Y Naw Tafodiog* ('the Nine Tongued-Ones'), listing special witnesses whose testimony is to be believed in all cases. Then follows the Law of Women, a fairly long tractate with its beginning and end marked.

In Iorwerth B, the Law of Women comes immediately after the Laws of Court, and is followed by the *Naw Tafodiog* section, with its Laws of Country preface. Manuscript C, from the mid-thirteenth century, has several lacunae and as such is missing both the *Naw Tafodiog* and also the Law of Women, and starts the Laws of Country with a section on injuring an animal's foot. K has the same start to the Laws of Country, but this is likely to be a coincidence rather than evidence of K copying C – it is not known when C lost parts of the text, and K preserves other sections of the Iorwerth text, for example in the Value of Wild and Tame, which are absent in C. It is, however, very interesting that K does not have any part of the Law of Women, or its preceding section that included the Laws of Country introductory sentence. The *Naw Tafodiog*, which is not in K, usually has a sentence of introduction stating that it is the start of the Laws of Country.[96] The next section, which Jenkins called 'Injury to Animals', is found as the first section after the Test Book in K.

The omission of the first part of the Iorwerth lawbook, from the Laws of Court to the section after the Law of Women, is interesting; it does appear to be a deliberate omission rather than due to K having a partial exemplar for the first part, because the introduction to the suretyship section is included, and the text does not start mid-way through a section. However, the absence of the Law of Women is difficult to explain. In the second part of manuscript Z, for example, there was an interest in the Law of Women section since there was a potential income from it, but it had most probably been superseded by English law by the fifteenth century.[97] This would mean that the Law of Women was not used in its original form by the compiler of Z, but some sections could be applied or exploited for financial gain – Z is a Marcher manuscript and such practices did take place in the March. This is unlikely to be the case for K, though. The Law of Women was also a stand-alone section in the Iorwerth text, labelled at the start and end, and in manuscript B it may not have been part of the

---

[96] See *LTMW*, 45–62.

[97] Z is a sixteenth-century copy of an earlier text, which perhaps dated from the mid-fourteenth century: *Pomffred*, 15–17.

Laws of Country – the section on the Nine Tongued-Ones is the one that is stated as starting the Laws of Country.[98] This section, also absent from K, is an old and probably obsolete section. Morfydd Owen is likely to be correct in saying that K contained practical, procedural material that would have been necessary and in use in the Marcher courts in Cefnllys, Maelienydd.[99] This useful Iorwerth redaction material was combined with other material that was circulating in south Wales and had been included in at least one other manuscript – a collection of triads, and a collection of *damweiniau*. This makes manuscript K an interesting parallel to manuscript Z, which combined a Cyfnerth redaction text with specially selected material copied from exemplars available in north-east Wales; but in the case of K, the Iorwerth text appears to have been deemed to be still useful. This was not likely to be the case with the Cyfnerth text in Z. It also means that K compares very well with other manuscripts containing Iorwerth material – in particular Q, and manuscript J, which has a Blegywryd text as its first half, and sections of a Iorwerth text as the second half. But, as Morfydd Owen notes, K stands alone with its special social and legal background, and to that can be added that the text is also highly significant in telling us how the manuscripts reflected the social and legal context.[100]

Conclusion

In all these lengthier or composite texts there is nothing to mark out any parts of the manuscripts as being different, or 'additional', in any way. The manuscripts studied here all include a redaction text, but alongside other material that is not matched by the majority of the other manuscripts of the same redaction. Christine James describes this phenomenon: the manuscripts contain '*nid yn unig brif destun yn perthyn i un o'r tri dull ... ond hefyd atodiad o ddeunydd arall*' ('not only a main text belonging to one of the three redactions ... but also an appendix of other material').[101] Such descriptions of the manuscripts as having a 'tail' have led them to be viewed in a way that may not accurately reflect how or why they were compiled. The material certainly originated in different and various exemplars, but there is no suggestion in the manuscripts themselves that the material was viewed in divergent ways. Some of the material deemed 'anomalous' or 'additional' may be later in date, but some is not, and there is considerable variety in the dating of the different tractates in the 'main' redaction texts too. The same phenomenon has affected the *damweiniau*: Robin Stacey calls them 'the poor stepchild' of Welsh law, and she also describes *damweiniau* along with other texts as being 'legal writings situated outside the lawbooks proper', and 'non-lawbook legal texts'.[102]

Instead, a new, more flexible view needs to be taken when looking at these longer manuscripts. First, several of the Blegywryd manuscripts have their end wanting, which means that the latter half of the manuscripts are curtailed – but there is no way of knowing how much material was lost, or indeed whether any material was lost. If the new way of viewing the lawtexts is to see the lengthier texts as simply bigger

---

[98] *LTMW*, 61.
[99] Owen, 'A Fifteenth-Century Lawbook', 89.
[100] *Ibid.*, 90.
[101] *Machlud*, xii.
[102] Stacey, 'Legal Writing in Medieval Wales', 59.

collections of legal material, with nothing marking any of it out as being additional or appended to other parts of the law, then these manuscripts do not reflect a different organisation of the material, but perhaps reflect an incorporation of the legal texts available to a compiler, and the selection of texts.

The purpose of the lawtexts is the crucial factor here. Q was created as a 'perfect' legal text, organising the material into subject-specific sections, and bringing material on the same subject together. It also has a heavy emphasis on short legal dicta – triads, *damweiniau* and proverbs feature highly in Q. It organised the material in a highly sophisticated way, and this library manuscript is likely to reflect the needs of the patron, perhaps with heavy influence from the collator. The scribe had considerable material at his disposal, but it was all treated equally. Y has a similar organisation, and again it does not separate the material in any way. S, along with its sister manuscript Tim, is comparable to Z. These manuscripts first present the redaction text, and then follow with material that may have still been in use. James showed that S was probably created for a *dosbarthwr* (a legal practitioner), and Z is highly likely to have been for the same purpose or the same class of person.[103] Owen demonstrated that K was also probably been made for – and used by – a specific patron who practised law.[104] As was shown in the previous chapter, and as is evidenced in manuscript J, another manuscript with considerable practical material included,[105] there was nothing to prevent the scribes from adding any necessary material to create a large book of highly useful legal rules and notes.

Rather than viewing these manuscripts as composite books, anthologies, main text plus tail, or later versions of the laws, perhaps they should be viewed instead with an open mind. Yes, many of them share the same tractates, sometimes the same 91 tractates presented in *LlBleg*, or the 93 tractates in *J(ed.)*, although complete manuscripts with all of those tractates are rare.[106] Most of the earlier Iorwerth manuscripts, A–E, contain the 160 sections printed in *LlIor*, but they also contain a large collection of *damweiniau*, and the separation of *damweiniau* is not something that is reflected in the original manuscripts.[107] The Blegywryd manuscripts, particularly the lengthy ones, are later in date than the Iorwerth manuscripts, but it may not have had a major impact on the organisation of the text. Perhaps the Blegywryd redaction text was intended as a starting point, and it could be followed with anything that was useful or practical, with no limit. The material could be taken from the northern versions of the law – as in J, but also in Y, Q and S – and there was seemingly a Iorwerth text developed in south Wales that included *damweiniau*, but perhaps not the Laws of Court. The material included could also be material from the courts, such as *Rhol Dafydd Llwyd* in S and Tim, and the plaints in Q. And it could be all of those things together. If *damweiniau* are fully included as part of the early manuscripts in the Iorwerth redaction – and there is nothing to suggest that they should not be – then anything that is not in *LlBleg* should be treated in the same way for those manuscripts containing a Blegywryd text. Rather than viewing the manuscripts as showing development in the writing of legal text as time went on, perhaps they should be seen as

---

[103] *Machlud*, xvi–xxv.

[104] Owen, 'A Fifteenth-Century Lawbook', 90.

[105] *J(ed.)*, xx–xxi.

[106] *LlBleg* has 91 unnumbered sections from the Prologue to *Arferion Cyfraith* at the end; *J(ed.)* has numbered sections, and *Arferion Cyfraith* is section 93, on page 86.

[107] Stacey, 'Legal Writing from Medieval Wales', 63. *Llyfr Damweiniau* was not really united in form, despite first appearances.

demonstrating a way of writing law in a particular region, primarily south Wales in the case of the Blegywryd redaction, and the law was seen as a highly flexible and useful tool. The manuscripts do not reflect different types of material, separating some sections out as being 'additional' or 'later', but rather they were flexible and inclusive books that contained law, and treated all of it the same.

7

'MUCH MATTER NOT ELSEWHERE TO BE FOUND': THE NON-REDACTION LAWBOOKS

Much matter, not elsewhere to be found, has been collected from this volume.[1]

In his description of manuscript S, one of the 'composite' manuscripts described in the previous chapter, Aneurin Owen noted that he found in that manuscript material other than the redaction material that made up his 'Codes'. These unique texts from S were presented in AL XI, and other non-redaction material in S was used for variant readings in AL X. This final chapter will consider several manuscripts that contain large amounts of legal material which is not found 'elsewhere', material and texts which do not form part of the redaction texts, some of it unique to individual law manuscripts. As was noted in Chapter 6, the composite manuscripts contain a redaction text as well as other material that defies categorisation into a redaction, and Owen's treatment of these manuscripts was discussed there. The manuscripts under consideration in this chapter were even more problematic for Owen, since many of them do not contain a redaction text at all. Some he assigned into a category of 'anomalous' manuscripts; others were used very little in his work. One or two were 'not collated' by Owen (although he was clearly aware of their existence), and these were not included in his list of sources in the introduction to his work. To give Aneurin Owen his due, his contribution to the field in general was enormous, and his categorisation of the material was done in part out of a practical necessity, as well as being led by his view of the nature of the law. This makes *Ancient Laws* a product of its time, but it must be acknowledged that Aneurin Owen made great strides in making the contents of the legal manuscripts accessible in a way in which they had not been before.

Perhaps as a result of this, the manuscripts that will be studied in this chapter have not received much attention from scholars. Of the eight in question, only two have benefitted from a full edition.[2] Very few parts, if any, of the remaining six have been edited or published, and very little attention has been paid to them, either individually or as a group. This study, then, will focus on these neglected texts, will look at what is contained within them, and examine the contents without the constraints of attempting to fit them into any scheme. Rather than put all the weight on the redaction texts, the emphasis here will be on the texts actually presented in these manuscripts, where it may have originated, and the nature of the material. This may suggest a context for them, one that may not necessarily conform with ideas of Hywel's Book or the origins of Welsh law, but may instead reveal a great deal about the nature of the law in medieval Wales, and the kind of texts that the lawyers needed or wanted as practitioners in certain milieus.

---

[1] AL, Introduction, xxxi.
[2] Col in *LlCol,* and H in *ALD*.

Aled Rhys Wiliam is perhaps best known as the editor of the only modern edited text of a Iorwerth redaction manuscript, *Llyfr Iorwerth* (1960).³ However, his interests in Welsh law were wide-ranging, and he had a particular interest in *Llyfr Cynog* ('the Book of Cynog'), discussed in Chapter 4; this he described as 'a medieval Welsh digest'.⁴ It is likely that it was his work on *Llyfr Cynog* that led him to reconsider the so-called 'anomalous' manuscripts and to explore the contents of AL II, and his study of some of these manuscripts advanced the subject considerably; it was published as a journal article, 'Y Deddfgronau Cymraeg', in 1953.⁵ The title of the work is a label that Wiliam applied to some of the Welsh law manuscripts, but he took it from an earlier work. William Maurice created his compilation of the Welsh lawtexts in Wynnstay 37 and 38, and the second volume was titled *Deddfgrawn* (a collection or corpus of laws); this title that Maurice gave to his own, late collection of laws was deemed by Wiliam to be appropriate for certain of the lawtexts that he was considering.⁶ Wiliam stated that most of the manuscripts contained a copy of one of Aneurin Owen's three 'Codes' (redactions),⁷ but that several of them also contain other material from the Anomalous Laws: '*Y mae gennym hefyd dystiolaeth bod i'r defnydd pwysig hwn ei draddodiad dogfennol ei hunan a'i fodolaeth annibynnol y tu allan i lawysgrifau'r* Dulliau.' ('We also have evidence that this important material had its own documentary tradition and its independent existence outside of the manuscripts of the *Codes*').⁸ In this study he focused on particular manuscripts that did not fit as well into the 'standard' organisation of Welsh law manuscripts – F and G – and as such his work on these manuscripts remain the fullest study of each of the manuscripts that has been published to date. Both manuscripts will be discussed in more detail in this chapter.

Wiliam's concept of the legal compilation, the *Deddfgrawn*, has been adopted by Christine James as a useful label for manuscripts that are included in the 'anomalous' category, as well as for the longer manuscripts that contain both a version of one of the 'Codes' and other material found in AL II.⁹ However, James notes – in what is a critically important section of her study for the present discussion – that Aneurin Owen's division of the material, driven as his textual decisions were by his own concept of the nature of Welsh law, had '*effaith andwyol o wahaniaethol ar astudiaethau ym maes Cyfraith Hywel am dros ganrif wedyn*' ('a ruinous discriminating effect on studies in the field for over a century afterwards'), including the neglect of manuscripts taking a less 'standard' form, with a focus on the 'Code' manuscripts.¹⁰

---

³ *LlIor*.

⁴ Wiliam, *Llyfr Cynog*; and see also Wiliam, 'Restoration'; see also 120–122, above.

⁵ Wiliam, 'Y Deddfgronau Cymraeg'.

⁶ Jenkins, 'Deddfgrawn William Maurice', 33–36.

⁷ Wiliam's work was early – *LlIor* was based on his doctoral thesis, which he started in 1949, and, despite recognising that Owen's names for his 'Codes' were not accurate, Wiliam was still bound to a great extent to the ideas and categorisations set out by Owen in AL. He still referred to the manuscripts that he was using as 'Venedotian' (although he was fortunate in that the description was not inaccurate for his particular redaction), and also maintained the use of the word 'Codes'. *LlIor*, xvii–xxiii.

⁸ Wiliam, 'Y Deddfgronau Cymraeg', 97.

⁹ *Machlud*, xii. She included S and Tim as '*Deddfgronau*', and goes as far as to call *Deddfgronau* a 'genre' of text, but notes that while manuscript S has a clear division into two parts, the dividing line between the two sections is more complex than her summary suggests.

¹⁰ *Machlud*, xi.

James emphasises that it is the division of the material that caused the most problems – leading to a lack of studies of the historical development of the latter part of these law manuscripts.

The manuscripts labelled *Deddfgronau* or 'anomalous' manuscripts – although neither title is wholly appropriate to describe these texts – will be the subject of the following discussion, and the nature of these texts and their importance in the manuscript tradition will be given detailed attention. The manuscripts will be examined with a focus on their contents, before concluding by setting them in their wider context.

Aneurin Owen's Categorisation of the Manuscripts

Aneurin Owen adopted a sensible *modus operandi* for classifying the manuscripts: if a particular manuscript contained a 'recognisable' text, such as the Laws of Court, or a well-known tractate from one of his three 'Codes', then that manuscript was assigned to that redaction. This method worked fairly well. Of the 30 (or so) manuscripts viewed and categorised by Owen, only four are misplaced. Y was grouped with the Cyfnerth manuscripts, but only the Laws of Court in Y belong to the Cyfnerth redaction, and Owen noted as much and did not use it after the Laws of Court.[11] F and H were both assigned to the Iorwerth redaction, though they do not have a substantial Iorwerth text. K was classed as Blegywryd, probably due to a triad collection that occurs in it, but it is in fact a Iorwerth redaction manuscript.[12] That three of these misplaced manuscripts are Iorwerth ones may be telling; while the Iorwerth redaction text presented in *LlIor*, and also in Owen's *Venedotian Code*, is fairly uniform in the manuscripts that contain it (A–E, with some caveats), there is a distinction between the Iorwerth redaction and the Iorwerth tradition. The Iorwerth tradition was more flexible, and could include material that formed part of the Iorwerth redaction, but several manuscripts include Iorwerth tradition material without a redaction text, such as F, G, and Col.[13] B presents Iorwerth redaction material for many tractates, but in the case of *Naw Affaith Galanas* ('The Nine Abetments of *Galanas*') a different version of the text was substituted,[14] from the Iorwerth tradition.

Owen also listed four manuscripts as 'anomalous', in that they defied his categorisation. One of the four was misplaced, since Ep is a copy of the Blegywryd Q. It is likely that Owen had not seen the manuscript himself.[15] As and Mor are sister

---

[11] 'As Y. henceforward agrees more with the Dimetian form, and Z. is carelessly transcribed and has many chasms, they will only be noticed when important variations or new matter occur.' AL, 686–687n (quarto edition). On Y, see Chapter 6.

[12] See the discussion on K in Chapter 6. K is a southern Iorwerth text, and the manuscript includes a collection of *damweiniau*, which would be a Iorwerth feature. However, the collection of *damweiniau* is shared with manuscript Q, as is the triad collection, which may show that Owen had undertaken detailed comparative work on the two texts.

[13] The Iorwerth tradition material in J, Q and other composite texts is also relevant; this material was discussed in Chapter 6.

[14] In AL, the alternative version of the *galanas* material in B was included, but at the bottom half of the page with a separating line: AL III.1.11–38, and pp. 220–241 in the Quarto edition. For a full discussion see Charles-Edwards, 'The *Galanas* Tractate'.

[15] His description of the manuscript is suspiciously brief, which may be because he had not seen the manuscript himself: 'Є. The designation of collations from a manuscript formerly in the Sebright collection, in Wotton's schedule styled S. 3'; AL, 'Introduction', xxxii. He used Ep for variant readings for the Plaints in AL XII, but may have taken these readings directly from *Leges*

manuscripts, and they contain a collection of *cynghawsedd* as well as other material, but no redaction text.[16] Dd contains a variety of material, including non-legal texts, but was used by Owen for its collection of plaints.[17]

There is evidence that Owen saw or used other manuscripts that he did not list. Some of his plaints are said to be from 'The Book of Trev Alun', apparently in the hand of Gutun Owain, though it is likely that Owen used a later copy of it.[18] Owen's unlucky Book XIII was taken from a mystery manuscript, which was in fact a convincing forgery from the hand of Iolo Morganwg.[19] There is evidence that Owen used An, but again he did not include it in his list of manuscripts.[20] Charles-Edwards's list of manuscripts in his *The Welsh Laws* corrects Owen's organisation of the three redactions, and the group titled there 'Anomalous Laws' comprises seven manuscripts.[21] Ep is still in this list, although in later studies it is correctly included in the Blegywryd list.[22] One more manuscript, which was only recently assigned a siglum, An, is also in this group.[23] To the list of non-redaction manuscripts can be added Col, which is a manuscript of the Iorwerth tradition, but does not present a Iorwerth redaction text. The composite manuscripts divide into two groups: those linked to the Iorwerth tradition, and those less easily linked to a redaction. They are listed in Table 7.1, and they will be discussed in chronological order in their group.

Table 7.1: Manuscripts designated as 'anomalous'

Siglum	Manuscript Call Number	Date	Notes
Composite manuscripts linked to the Iorwerth tradition			
Col	NLW Peniarth MS 30	*s.*xiii^{med}	Known to Owen but not listed
G	NLW Peniarth MS 35	*s.*xiv^1	Iorwerth redaction with other material
Lew	NLW Peniarth MS 39	*s.*xv^{med}	Not known to Owen
F	NLW Peniarth MS 34	*s.*xv^2	With Iorwerth MSS in *Ancient Laws*

Wallicae rather than from the manuscript itself. Ep was probably originally owned by Edward Lhuyd, and passed to the library of Sir John Sebright – it was there when Williams and Wotton were compiling *Leges Wallicae*. It had been bought by the Hengwrt library following the sale at Sotheby's in 1807, but it may not have joined the others in the libraries that Owen used. Rees and Walters, 'The Dispersion', 173. Owen himself made a catalogue of Hengwrt manuscripts in 1834 and this suggests that the manuscripts, including Ep, were kept at Rûg.

[16] On the *cynghawsedd* in these manuscripts, see Chapter 4.

[17] On the plaints, see Chapter 4. Dd is said to be a copy of the lost White Book of Hergest, and the extant manuscript has a considerable amount of important non-legal texts, including *Trioedd Ynys Prydein* and *Y Bibyl Ynghymraec*. As such, this is the only example of legal material in a non-legal manuscript or vice versa: generally, legal material is confined to law manuscripts, genre specific, and it does not (or has not) made its way into other manuscripts. Manuscript K contains poetry as well as law, although it is a substantial legal text.

[18] See Chapter 4, and the discussion of The Book of Trev Alun in Roberts, 'More Plaints'.

[19] Iolo Morganwg was a Welsh scholar and poet, a collector of manuscripts, and a successful and convincing forger. He was eccentric and a heavy laudanum user. On Iolo Morganwg see Jenkins, *A Rattleskull Genius*.

[20] An is discussed in more detail below.

[21] Charles-Edwards, *The Welsh Laws*, 99–102.

[22] See *J(ed.)*, xv.

[23] This siglum was decided by Seminar Cyfraith Hywel at the meeting on 8 October 2016, and was added to the new sigla list: <http://cyfraith-hywel.org.uk/cy/seminar.php>.

Other composite manuscripts

H	NLW Peniarth MS 164	$s.\text{xiv}^2$	With Iorwerth MSS in *Ancient Laws*
As	NLW Peniarth MS 175	$s.\text{xv}^2$	Anomalous in *Ancient Laws*
Mor	NLW Peniarth MS 36C	$s.\text{xv/xvi}$	Anomalous in *Ancient Laws*
An	NLW Peniarth MS 166	$s.\text{xvi}^1$	Known to Owen but not listed

Col, NLW Peniarth MS 30

Dafydd Jenkins was responsible for one of the earliest modern published editions of a Welsh law manuscript and, to some extent, his *Llyfr Colan*, published in 1963, marks the start of a new era of scholarship on the Welsh laws – though Jenkins stated that he had actually started working on Col from 1938.[24] Given the lack of other editions, the comparative work undertaken by Jenkins was remarkable.[25] Jenkins was fully aware of the importance of this thirteenth-century law manuscript, usually described as a revised version of Iorwerth, and stated that it was most probably the last medieval Welsh law text to be created in an independent Wales.[26] The manuscript is not complete, and it was examined in two parts by Jenkins – the second part of the manuscript contained a text of *Llyfr Damweiniau* that is different in nature to the legal tractates in the first part.[27] The most significant aspect of Col for this study is that, although it is a 'revised version' of Iorwerth, it is actually contemporary with the early manuscripts of Iorwerth, from the mid-thirteenth century.[28] Col is a crucial manuscript when it comes to considering the development of the law, since it implies that not even Iorwerth, despite the considerable uniformity across the early Iorwerth manuscripts, was a fixed and stable text. There was room for manoeuvre, editing and adapting the laws for particular purposes.[29]

Col was used by William Maurice, who named it 'Col-ên', a combination of *colofnog* ('in columns') and *hen* ('old') '*am ei fod yn golofnog ei lythyr yn hên anawdd ac yn ddierth*' ('because it is columnar, its words old, difficult and unfamiliar').[30] Aneurin Owen revealed that he was familiar with the manuscript and had even viewed it, but called it 'a later MS., not collated' and made very little use of it,

---

[24] *LlCol*, vii. Jenkins stated that his work, and the edition of Col, had been finished before *LlIor* had appeared, although he would have had access to Aled Rhys Wiliam's thesis. Jenkins, 'Ail Olwg ar Lawysgrif Colan', fills some of the gaps and answers some questions that remained after the publication of *LlCol*.

[25] This is particularly true of his discussion of the Latin manuscripts, since the edition of the Latin texts only appeared in 1967: *LTWL*.

[26] *LlCol*, xxxiii.

[27] *LlCol*, xvi. The subtitle of the volume makes it clear that this is a study of the first part of the manuscript, and the *damweiniau* collection that is also contained in Peniarth 30 was edited in a separate publication. On the *damweiniau* see Chapter 4.

[28] Charles-Edwards, *The Welsh Laws*, 21.

[29] This is also shown by B, which is a Iorwerth redaction manuscript in parts, but that also adapts the text, linking it to the wider Iorwerth tradition.

[30] *LlCol*, xv.

making only two references to it.³¹ Owen was clearly aware that there were different readings in the manuscript, but may have decided against 'collating' the manuscript in his text since it was so problematic, for Owen's scheme. Dafydd Jenkins's study of Col and his two publications on it have moved the subject on considerably, and a summary of the main conclusions will be presented here.

The manuscript is not simply a rewriting of a Iorwerth text, since there is material in Col that is not in the Iorwerth manuscripts – although the text of *Llyfr Damweiniau* in Col is close to the other versions of that book.³² Col also drew on Latin manuscripts available to the compiler: Jenkins noted that the compiler used a manuscript similar to Latin B, and to Latin D, but his conspectus draws on Latin A and Latin C as well.³³ Col was not drawing on any of the extant manuscripts of Iorwerth (or indeed the extant manuscripts of the Latin texts), but may have been using an exemplar of those manuscripts, and this was a written exemplar.³⁴ Jenkins notes that the compiler of Col (who was not likely to be the scribe of the extant manuscript) was particularly interested in the legal explanation of matters rather than in general rewriting, and was willing to leave out background information; this may reveal the compiler's purpose in creating the text.³⁵ He suggests that since the lawbooks give the option of choosing the best judgement in order to reach a conclusion in a legal case, perhaps this was the purpose of Col – the compiler was trying to create the most accurate and useful lawbook possible, combining material from the other lawbooks he had at his disposal.³⁶ In that sense, I would disagree with one aspect of Jenkins's later conclusions. In his contribution to Daniel Huws's *Festschrift*, Jenkins attempted to work out what was missing in the defective Col manuscript, by comparing it with the Iorwerth texts. He concluded that the Laws of Court may have been intended to fill the first two quires, now lost, and then would be followed by the beginning of the Law of Women, and the *Naw Tafodiog* ('Nine Tongued-Ones', a list of special witnesses).³⁷ Given what is known about the nature of the Laws of Court, and the purpose of Col as suggested by Jenkins, I would suggest that perhaps the Laws of Court were never included in Col, and it may be that less of the manuscript is missing than Jenkins suggested. The Laws of Court were considered to be out-of-date in thirteenth-century Gwynedd, although they were adapted for the Iorwerth texts; they also show the royal court in a festive nature rather than administrative, and would be less relevant for a legal practitioner. The Laws of Court are also not the same kind of law as that found in the Laws of Country and the Test Book; they are explanations of how things are to be done (for a social situation that had ceased to exist) but were unlikely to be the subject of debate in courts of law. Manuscript K is an example of a later Iorwerth text that does not have the Laws of Court, and several Blegywryd manuscripts also

---

[31] AL I, p. 325 (quarto edition), has a note pointing out a variant reading in Col but it is as a footnote and not included in the apparatus since Owen had not assigned a siglum to Col; in AL II, p. 50 (quarto edition), the reading from Col is included in the apparatus but it is called 'A MS. not collated'.

[32] *LlCol*, xv.

[33] Jenkins, 'Ail Olwg ar Lawysgrif Colan', 69, 71, 75–78.

[34] *LlCol*, xxx.

[35] *LlCol*, xxvii.

[36] *LlCol*, xxxiii.

[37] Jenkins, 'Ail Olwg ar Lawysgrif Colan', 67.

lack them. I suggest that the compiler of Col took a similar pragmatic attitude and abandoned the Laws of Court.

Col provides clear evidence that the Iorwerth redaction was a work in progress, or rather perhaps that legal texts in Gwynedd in the thirteenth century were open to discussion and adaptation. Jenkins calls the Iorwerth texts 'revised editions', and also notes that they did not have the status of an authorised book, linked to the royal court of Gwynedd, and therefore could be edited, adapted or changed.[38] The Iorwerth redaction itself was a revised version of the laws, with an innovation that was carried into several manuscript versions of the text – the Iorwerth redaction divides the laws into three parts, and the third part, the Test Book, is viewed as a novel introduction, perhaps originating from Iorwerth ap Madog.[39] The Test Book's agricultural tractates on *Cyfar* (Co-tillage) and Corn Damage certainly seem to have been rewritten from earlier sources for the special purpose of making the Iorwerth redaction.[40] It would be tempting to suggest that Col originated from the same place as the work of the editor of the Iorwerth sections, or even that it was the work of the same editor, but the existence of a revised Iorwerth version of *Cyfar* and Corn Damage in Col – and a better version of *Cyfar* according to Jenkins – makes that idea less plausible.[41] However, since *Cyfar* and Corn Damage were probably fairly new tractates at the time of the creation of the Iorwerth redaction manuscripts, it does show that the redactor of Col had the latest texts available to him, and he was also working with very current law, at the forefront of legal activity in Gwynedd.

While Col is not an 'anomalous' manuscript in the same way as some of the other manuscripts discussed in this chapter – it is firmly linked to the Iorwerth redaction, for one thing – it is still an appropriate manuscript with which to open this discussion of these understudied but highly important lawbooks. Like Iorwerth, Col was created from earlier texts. It shows a living law, and the compiler's interest in the legal aspects and the practical applicability of the text, along with perhaps an attempt to create the best possible – and most useful – version of the laws from the material that he had to hand. We may have little evidence of legal texts being used in a court setting or in any practical way, whether being quoted as an authority in the court, or serving as preparatory training for a *cyngaws* or *canllaw* preparing to argue a case; but that such intentions lay behind our lawbooks is clear from Col.

G, NLW Peniarth MS 35

G is a composite Iorwerth manuscript. From the second half of the fourteenth century, it is in the same hand as Cyfnerth U, and Peniarth 45, a manuscript containing non-legal prose texts.[42] It contains parts of a Iorwerth text, but also has other material, including sections of *Llyfr Cynog*. It has been studied in some detail by Thomas Charles-Edwards, but his work has not yet been published, and Aled Rhys Wiliam discussed G in his study of the *Deddfgronau*, calling it a '*Deddfgrawn ar hanner*

---

[38] *LlCol*, xxvi.

[39] Charles-Edwards, *The Welsh Laws*, 29–30; Dafydd Jenkins notes, in a footnote in *LlCol*, that he had a hunch that Iorwerth ap Madog was only responsible for what he termed the 'Test Book Appendix'. *LlCol*, xxv, n. 18. See also Chapter 3 on the work of Iorwerth ap Madog.

[40] See the discussion on this subject in Chapter 3, 68–71.

[41] *LlCol*, xxvii.

[42] *RWMS*, Scribe X87.

ei gyfansoddi' ('a *Deddfgrawn* which is halfway through being composed').[43] He also stated that there are seven documents included in this one book, but that they were not all part of the same text, and this is supported by Charles-Edwards who notes that material by one of the scribes of the manuscript may not belong with that of the other hands.[44] The exact breakdown of Wiliam's seven texts is not clear, but he seems to be counting each Iorwerth section separately – G has Land Law, Suretyship and some Three Columns material – and then counts *damweiniau*, *cynghawsedd*, *Llyfr Cynog* and the 'miscellanea' as individual items. G therefore does not have a complete Iorwerth text and it is lacking the prologue and Laws of Court, although it has enough sections from the Iorwerth tradition – *damweiniau*, *cynghawsedd* – for it to be classified as part of that redaction.[45] In addition, it has a quire said to be from *Llyfr Cynog*, labelled as such, mainly comprised of *cynghawsedd*, and it also has the *holiadon*, which may have been in *Llyfr Cynog* if that book had a fixed form of any kind.[46]

The material in G purporting to be from *Llyfr Cynog* is shared with some other manuscripts, including Q and K; this material is different to that which forms the non-Iorwerth portions of Lew. G has some unique *cynghawsedd*, and there is a connection between G and F in some *cynghawsedd*, as is demonstrated in AL VIII. The link between G and K is particularly striking when looking at the plaint that is in K. This singleton plaint, on the subject of *galanas*, is in K but in a different hand to the main text. A version of it is also in the inserted gathering in Bost, and there is a slightly different version in Dd, a manuscript in which the only legal material is some plaints, where this is included in a collection.[47] The plaints were discussed in Chapter 4, but the text of this plaint is unlike the others: it is a remarkably dramatic composition, and it also includes a date, which may link it to an actual case.[48] However, there is a striking similarity between the plaint in K and Bost, and a section of *cynghawsedd* that is unique to G. The plaint may well be modelled on this bit of *cynghawsedd*.[49] The use of a section in G as a possible source for a plaint created from an existing legal text is another suggestion that G was intended as a practical lawbook, and was used.

G stands out among Iorwerth texts because it dates to the first half of the fourteenth century, and is thus late; moreover, it also has some affinity with the earliest Cyfnerth and Blegywryd manuscripts, and the inclusion of *Llyfr Cynog* in G may show that it was created for a special purpose – this was not intended simply to be a Iorwerth text. The manuscript itself has marginalia and notes and this shows that it was used; this all suggests that G was a practical text, one that stands at the boundary between the early Iorwerth manuscripts and the later Blegywryd manuscripts.

---

[43] Wiliam, 'Y Deddfgronau Cymraeg', 100.
[44] *Ibid.*, 100.
[45] G is listed with the Iorwerth manuscripts in Charles-Edwards, *The Welsh Laws*, 100, and is not under doubt as a Iorwerth manuscript; both F and G are included in the discussion of the text of Iorwerth in *LlIor*, xxiii–xxxvii, but neither are included in the Conspectus of Texts, xlii–xliv.
[46] On these manuscripts see Chapter 6; also Charles-Edwards, *The Welsh Laws*, 21.
[47] Roberts, 'More Plaints', 183–185.
[48] *Ibid.*, 185. The two manuscripts give a different date: K has March 1468–March 1469, while Bost has September 1400–September 1401, both given as regnal years; this is problematic.
[49] *Ibid.*, 185–186. The third version of the plaint, in Dd, may be the version which was composed from G or the exemplar of G.

Lew, NLW Peniarth MS 39

Lew was not studied by Aneurin Owen, and he makes no reference to it – although, as is often the case with Peniarth manuscripts, it was in the Hengwrt library originally and he would probably have been aware of it since it was listed in the catalogue. William Maurice did use Lew for his compilation of the laws, but it is uncertain to what extent Owen used Maurice's work. Lew is a later Iorwerth manuscript, from the mid-fifteenth century, written in the hand of Lewys Ysgolhaig ('Lewys the Scholar').[50] There are gaps in the text, but it includes most of a Iorwerth text, and parts of *Llyfr Damweiniau* and *Llyfr Cynghawsedd*, which further link this material with the Iorwerth redaction. Despite this, Aled Rhys Wiliam did not use it for his edition in *LlIor*, although he referred to the *damweiniau* in the manuscript and included it in his scheme.[51] There has been no full discussion of Lew and, while the manuscript has only been mentioned in passing in studies of the Iorwerth texts, it is relevant to discussions of *damweiniau* and *cynghawsedd*. The way Lew fits into the scheme of the Iorwerth texts has been dealt with fully elsewhere, mainly by Thomas Charles-Edwards,[52] but here it is the composite nature of Lew that will be examined, including the material it shares with the later Blegywryd texts, Q and S.

Lew is a disorganised manuscript, and the first Iorwerth section occurs on f. 10r, mid-way through a sentence, indicating that material is missing. However, the preceding folios include material that is not usually found in the Iorwerth redaction, but rather is found in the southern manuscripts Q and S. Maurice wrote *coll mawr* ('a large loss') above the first words of the manuscript, and the text starts part of the way through a sentence in the *Tair gorsedd dygynull* ('Three specially convened sessions') section, a very lengthy triad on court procedure; it is not complete in Lew.[53] The other lengthy triad and related sections on *Argaeëdigaeth dadl* ('bars to a case')[54] are also here in Lew, again not complete. These sections on procedure and conducting sessions are included in AL X, all taken from Q with variant readings from S: in Q and S they are included in some of the later practical material on procedure and conducting sessions, which would have been of use to practitioners of law.[55] The version in Lew is very similar to Q and S, although Lew has one sentence that appears to have been omitted through eyeskip in Q and S, which places those texts closer to each other; S and Q do not appear to be copies of each other, so there seem to be two textual groups here: Lew and QS. After these texts, found on the first pages of the manuscript although it starts some way into the first of the long triads, the text in Lew turns to Iorwerth, with sections from the Test Book.

The second portion of non-Iorwerth material in Lew is similar. It occurs on f. 72v, after the end of the Iorwerth *Cyfar* text and an isolated *damwain* that is found in the *damweiniau* collections. The section is an individual triad on three men who receive tithes, and it outlines the payment for a justice – it may well have been included here if the book was created for someone who may have been called upon to practice law

---

[50] On Lewys Ysgolhaig see Antur, 'I Mewn Hen Ysgrifen Gron', 15.

[51] *LlIor*, xxviii–xxix.

[52] Charles-Edwards, 'The Iorwerth Text', 137–138. Lew was used as the base manuscript for the edition in this work.

[53] *LT*, 210–215.

[54] *LT*, 222–227.

[55] The material has been discussed more fully above, in Chapter 6, in the discussion on Q and S.

and could claim such a payment. The triad is followed by a section of *cynghawsedd* that appears to be unique.

This material in Lew, combined with a Iorwerth text, shows how Iorwerth texts could develop, and in that sense it compares well with F. Useful material was being included with the Iorwerth texts, material that may have been practical and necessary for men who were called upon to act as justices, but who may not have had the traditional training of a justice that is hinted at in the thirteenth-century Iorwerth texts.

Lew itself is a small book, written in a neat hand attributed to Lewys Ysgolhaig and, according to William Maurice:

> Y llyver hwnn a beris Ho' ap Gr' Lloyd y Lewys ysgolheic a Lann vynnydd y ysgriuennv o ddethol y llyfrev gorev ac a gauas ef.[56]
>
> Hywel ap Gruffudd Lloyd had Lewys Ysgolhaig of Llanfynydd write this book from a selection of the best books which he could find.

Lewys Ysgolhaig was presumably a paid scribe, although the epithet 'ysgolhaig' (scholar) may suggest that he was a cleric or in holy orders; he was from (or was residing in) Llanfynydd in Carmarthenshire, south Wales.[57] Little is known at present about his patron or employer, Hywel ap Gruffudd Lloyd, but he may not have been from Llanfynydd. However, the similarity of Lew to the work of *dosbarthwyr* and other patrons and parties interested in Welsh law in the same broad region is striking. S and its sister text Tim were both created from several exemplars, as was Q; these are southern texts from a similar date, and they may even share some of the same exemplars used by Lewys Ysgolhaig for Lew. The main difference between S and Q on the one hand and Lew on the other is the nature of the manuscripts themselves – S and Q are larger than Lew. Lew is very small indeed, roughly 12 x 9cm, a true pocket-sized book. It may have been intended for use in a court situation, perhaps by Hywel ap Gruffudd Lloyd himself.

F, NLW Peniarth MS 34

G and Lew fit into the Iorwerth tradition to a great extent, but both also include material that is not linked to the Iorwerth redaction. Along with F, these manuscripts reflect the later development of the Iorwerth material, and also point to the origin of material that was included in later Blegywryd manuscripts, the southern texts that are composite manuscripts.

Originally assigned to the Venedotian group by Aneurin Owen, F is linked to the Iorwerth redaction but has not been studied in great detail, and no edition of it currently exists.[58] It is a fifteenth-century manuscript and is in the same hand as

---

[56] Lew, NLW Peniarth MS 39, f. 74v.

[57] I intend to discuss Lewys Ysgolhaig in more detail elsewhere; see also Antur, 'I Mewn Hen Ysgrifen Gron', 15.

[58] Some work on the manuscript was carried out by Aled Rhys Wiliam, published as Wiliam, 'Y Deddfgronau Cymraeg'. This has been superseded by an important article by Charles-Edwards, 'The *Galanas* Tractate'. Charles-Edwards also includes the *galanas* text from F in full in Appendix 2 of his work.

Cardiff 2.7, which is a copy of Blegywryd L.[59] There are a small number of Iorwerth sections in the manuscript, and it also has a prologue that links it to the Iorwerth redaction, but it is nowhere near being a full Iorwerth text. It also contains *damweiniau* and *cynghawsedd*, and Aled Rhys Wiliam described it as the manuscript with the fullest collection of 'additional' material.[60] Wiliam probably stated this since there is a near-complete version of both *Llyfr Damweiniau* and *Llyfr Cynghawsedd* in F, which means it is important in the context of those books, but he makes the assumption that *cynghawsedd* and *damweiniau* are both 'additional' texts, which is not the stance taken in the present work.[61]

Wiliam describes F as disordered, and he set out the list of contents in the correct order in his article. Before it was disordered, F opened with a prologue that is a version of the Test Book prologue in Iorwerth, and followed with the Three Columns of Law, starting with *galanas*.[62] This was followed by triads, *damweiniau*, and Surety sections from Iorwerth, with some triads in between; the manuscript ended with a copy of *Llyfr Cynghawsedd*, which has its end wanting. There is nothing to suggest that there was other material in the manuscript that has been lost.

The Three Columns of Law material and the preface to the Test Book in F have received some attention. The version of *galanas* in F is shorter than in the other Iorwerth manuscripts, and Wiliam suggested that this was because it was from an earlier source.[63] However, this has been disproved by Charles-Edwards, who states that while F has one of the four versions of the Iorwerth *galanas* tractate, it does not have the original *galanas* material; instead, it has omitted the material other than the *Naw Affaith* list.[64] In addition, the same is not true of theft and fire in F, which are Iorwerth versions of the tractate. The Test Book preface in F refers to the 'old book of the White House', which again has made some scholars suggest that this was an early text and an exemplar of other manuscripts, but this again is disproved because of Charles-Edwards's observations on the *galanas* material in F.[65] The Test Book in F may have been a collection of texts that were circulating separately to the Iorwerth texts, and that were reorganised (some of this work perhaps done by Iorwerth ap Madog), and there are references to it in Z and H as well as in F.[66]

The treatment of suretyship in F has not been studied, and F was not included in the study of the Suretyship tractate in *LAL*.[67] This material is linked to the Iorwerth redaction again, and it includes much of the Iorwerth Suretyship text. The *damweiniau* in F are similar to those in other manuscripts: this seems to have been a fairly uniform collection.[68] The *cynghawsedd* in F is likewise part of the Iorwerth *cynghawsedd* tradition.[69] The Iorwerth sections, and then the *damweiniau* and

---

[59] *RWMS*, Scribe X81.
[60] Wiliam, 'Y Deddfgronau Cymraeg', 97.
[61] See the discussion on both genres in Chapter 4.
[62] Wiliam, 'Y Deddfgronau Cymraeg', 97–98.
[63] *LlIor*, xxxii.
[64] Charles-Edwards, 'The *Galanas* Tractate', 92, 101, 104.
[65] Jenkins, 'Llawysgrif Goll Llanforda', 95; Charles-Edwards, 'The *Galanas* Tractate', 97–103. See also *Pomffred*, 27–30.
[66] *Pomffred*, 29.
[67] *LAL*.
[68] See the discussion on *damweiniau* in Chapter 4.
[69] See the discussion on *cynghawsedd* in Chapter 4.

cynghawsedd, establish that F fits in with other manuscripts containing Iorwerth tradition material that was probably circulating in north Wales. If we discount the idea that *cynghawsedd* and *damweiniau* were 'additional' and instead take as our basic situation that the *damweiniau* at least were part of the Iorwerth redaction (if not part of the Test Book), then this means that F is less 'anomalous' than it appears at first – it is instead a later compilation that belongs to the Iorwerth tradition, though it does not have all the expected Iorwerth material. Wiliam states that 'the immediate archetype of F was a digest of useful legal information compiled from several sources by a man who had no interest in the outdated parts of the laws'.[70] He also noted that it is an oversimplification to focus on the three redactions (he uses the word Codes) when a more accurate approach would be to take into consideration these so-called 'hybrid texts' such as F, which contain material from the Codes but in a different form, and combined with material that is less familiar as part of a redaction text.[71] F appears to be firmly rooted in the Iorwerth tradition, and most of its contents are not unusual if viewed in the Iorwerth context.

However, there is some material within F that does not fit in with the Iorwerth tradition, although this is a small percentage of what is in the manuscript. Two of these sections are very short pieces (one is barely a sentence) that were listed under '*damweiniau*' in Wiliam's list of contents, although they are not found in the main collections of *damweiniau*. The section on wildfire is also found in J and Q. None of these three texts is a copy of one of the others, but they may share an exemplar: one word, '*amgu/aragu/arwar*' was clearly in the exemplar, but none of the scribes understood it and each of them offered a different interpretation.

F, Peniarth 34, 77.2–77.9

O deruyd llosci ty o walltan, ef a dyly talu ty o pop parth idav or lloscant gantaỏ, ac ny thal y rei hynny y tey nessaf vonnt vynteu kyt lloscont ganthunt, kanys tan gỏyllt vyd yna, ac ny ellyr y amgu, ac vrth hynny ny dylyant vynachadv y tan hvnnv na thalu dros y weythret.

If it happens that a house burns through accidental fire, it ought to pay for a house on either side of it if they are burnt by it, and those ones do not pay for the next houses to them[?] even though they are burnt by them, because then it is a wild fire, and it cannot be [?], and because of that they ought not to [?]keep that fire or pay for its activity.

J, *J(ed)*, 145.8–12.

O deruyd llosgi ty o wall tan, ef a dyly talu ty o bop parth idaw or lloscant gan y dan ef, ac ny dyly y tei hynny talu y tei nessaf udunt wy kyt lloscont ganthunt, kanys tan gwyllt yw, ac na ellir y aragu,[72] ac wrth hynny ny dylyant wynteu na chadw y tan hwnnw na thalu y weithret.

If it happens that a house burns through accidental fire, it ought to pay for a house on either side of it if they are burnt by its fire, and ought not to for the houses next to them even though they are burnt by them, because it is a wild fire, and it cannot be [?], and because of that they ought not to keep that fire or pay for its activity.

---

[70] *LlIor*, xxxii.
[71] Wiliam, 'The Welsh Texts', 21.
[72] Corrected to *arafu* ('slowed') in the printed text. *J(ed.)*, 145.

Q, Wynnstay 36, f. 126ra

O deruyd llosci ty o 6alltan, ef a dyly talu ty o pob tu ida6 or lloscant ganta6 ef, ac ny dyly y tei hynny talu y tei nessaf vdunt h6y kyn llosco gantunt h6y, canys tan g6yllt y6, ac na ellir y ar6ar, ac 6rth hynny ny dylyant 6ynteu na chad6 y tan h6nn6 na thalu y 6eithret.

If it happens that a house burns through accidental fire, it ought to pay for a house on either side of it if they are burnt by its fire, and those houses ought not to pay for the houses next to them even though they are burnt by them, because it is a wild fire, and it cannot be [?], and because of that they ought not to keep that fire or pay for its activity.

There is a sentence in F, on denying a dog or a bird, which is found in other texts, but the (incomplete) version in F seems to be a unique rendering of it; another potentially unique section, a short piece on women and suretyship, echoes material found in a Iorwerth triad on the three useless suretyships.[73] None of these sections is completely unknown, but the versions in F are different, and are either reworked or are from an exemplar not used by any other extant manuscript.

The triads that are listed by Wiliam as part of the contents of F are more interesting. A triad collection is not a regular feature of the Iorwerth texts, and the two triad collections in F do not originate in the Iorwerth redaction.[74] Neither are they taken from the recognisable Blegywryd triad tractate. Rather, with one exception, they are found in other manuscripts that have been said to contain 'additional material'. The triads are also found in S and in Q, although one of them is unique to F. These triads in F do not show a close similarity with the same triads in Q or S; there may be a common source or exemplar for the triads, but it is possible that the redactor of F selected particular triads from this source and reorganised the material, presenting it in a different way. The triads in F are part of the material with an emphasis on legal procedure, which was copied into several later south Wales manuscripts, although the majority of the other material in F has a clear northern origin. Ownership notes in the manuscript indicate that it was owned by individuals in north-east Wales, including two members of the Eyton family linked to Wynnstay near Rhiwabon.[75] The manuscript may have originated in north Wales, but the material that it shares with the southern manuscripts is not part of the Iorwerth tradition; it may however have originated in the north and moved south later on.

H, NLW Peniarth MS 164

H is a unique and complex manuscript, one of four from north-east Wales.[76] It dates from the second half of the fourteenth century. This manuscript, which stands alone in the context of the Welsh lawtexts, has been edited in full by Angharad Elias, bringing this crucial material to the forefront of the discussion on the Welsh law manuscripts.[77] The present discussion draws heavily on Elias's valuable work, and I am much indebted to Elias for her discussions of H.

---

[73] *LT*, 118–119, 290.
[74] See Roberts, 'The Iorwerth Triads'.
[75] Evans, *Report*, Vol. I, Part II – Peniarth, 367.
[76] The other three are As and Mor, discussed below, and Z, examined in Chapter 6.
[77] *ALD*.

Owen had originally placed H in the Iorwerth redaction (his Venedotian Code), but his reasons for doing so are unclear, since there does not appear to be any large enough corpus of Iorwerth material in the manuscript to justify its position within that group. Owen pointed out that the text had been ruined by the application of 'a chemical process'; he did not use H for variant readings, but it was the basis of his AL XIV.[78] The manuscript was at one stage bound with A, The Black Book of Chirk; since this was the case when Owen was working with the manuscripts it may have influenced him to place H in the Iorwerth redaction. H is in no way a Iorwerth text, and Owen himself admitted as such: apart from stating that it was not possible 'to admit at present any possibility of any further reference', he also described it as being 'the only existing version of what appears to have been intended by the compiler as illustrations of Welsh laws and customs digested into the form of triads'.[79]

The manuscript itself has an interesting history. It is not dated to the sixteenth century, as was stated by Aneurin Owen, but rather to the mid-fourteenth century, or perhaps the early fifteenth century.[80] It has been badly stained with gall, and is only partly legible, but John Jones of Gellilyvdy made a copy of it when it was in a slightly better condition than it is now, extant as Llanstephan 121. The neat manuscript by Robert Vaughan of Hengwrt, Peniarth 278, is a copy of John Jones's transcript.[81] Aneurin Owen used Peniarth 278 for his text in *Ancient Laws*, since he deemed the original manuscript to be too badly damaged, but he appears to have seen the original. The manuscript was probably illegible even before the gall was applied by John Jones, and both his copy and Vaughan's copy of that are missing parts.[82] Gwenogvryn Evans seemed to think that this was no great loss: 'the text is one of the later numerous compilations which have no apparent value except in so far as they may illustrate changes in law and procedure introduced into Wales during the XIVth century'.[83]

The manuscript may not be complete, but while Evans stated that it was missing its beginning and its end, in fact the beginning may be intact.[84] Evans may have felt that it was missing its beginning as it does not open with a prologue, as many of the other law manuscripts do; H opens with triads, and is mainly a collection of triads.[85] There are almost 500 of them, the largest number of legal triads in any manuscript, and a large proportion are independent of those in the redaction texts, although others do occur elsewhere. Z shares some material found in H, including triads that are unique to these two.[86] Some of the triads in H may be based on ones found in the Blegywryd redaction or other versions of the laws, but they are not direct copies, and the triads in H are often ordered by subject. Elias suggests that the compiler of H was

---

[78] AL, Introduction, xxix.

[79] AL, Introduction, xxix.

[80] Elias, 'Llawysgrif Peniarth 164', 50. This important article examines manuscript H in full and is a critical aspect of the work on the manuscript.

[81] Roberts, 'Law Texts and their Sources', 41–42.

[82] Evans, *Report*, Vol. I, Part II – Peniarth, 956. Gwenogvryn Evans states incorrectly that it was Robert Vaughan who applied the gall 'unsparingly', so that much of the text 'is now practically illegible'.

[83] *Ibid.*

[84] Roberts, 'Law Texts and their Sources', 42.

[85] Elias, 'Llawysgrif Peniarth 164', 38.

[86] *Ibid.*, 39, 40–41.

an innovator, changing the wording of texts or adding material to triads, and putting his own personal stamp on them.[87]

There are also sections of law that are not in triadic form in the manuscript, although they cannot be linked to the main 'Codes' as set out by Owen and others. Some of these non-triadic sections were included in AL XIV, which suggests that he could not find any parallel to them in his Codes.[88] Other sections in H were not included in AL XIV because they are similar to texts presented in the Codes, but Owen did not use H for variant readings in his 'Codes' as the texts in H are too different to be cited for variants. There are sections of a Blegywryd text in H, but none of the Blegywryd triads are found.[89] The second part of H is largely non-triadic law, and some of the longer prose sections are *cynghawsedd* from the north-east Wales collections presented in Owen's Book IX, the same texts found in As, Mor and Z.[90] Elias states that the fact that this material is also shared with Z again highlights the relationship between H and Z; H contains the earliest version of this *cynghawsedd* from north-east Wales.[91] She also points out that the *cynghawsedd* is likely to be post-conquest, noting its focus on Land Law and theft, subjects that were critical in post-conquest Wales.[92] In addition to the north-east Wales *cynghawsedd*, H also contains *cynghawsedd* that is found in *Llyfr Cynghawsedd*, AL VII,[93] and some sections of *cynghawsedd* that are unique to H. This heavy emphasis on *cynghawsedd* may point to the useful nature of the manuscript, and the interest in the practical aspect of pleading legal cases, and this is backed up by the other non-triadic material in the manuscript.[94]

The links between these manuscripts, particularly between H and Z, are striking, and point to legal material circulating in a particular area, north-east Wales.[95] In addition, the nature of the manuscripts and their contents may tell us a great deal about the purpose of these manuscripts, and that purpose may reflect the development of law in post-conquest Wales, and particularly the situation of law in the north-east. Z contains a Cyfnerth text, but also includes further material from various exemplars, all with a similar purpose or focus; most of the material in the latter part of Z has a practical bent, with an emphasis on Land Law, procedure in court, and fines for various matters. The manuscript would have been useful to anybody who wished to make money from applying the Welsh laws: the material includes lists of fines, which would be income to the lord, and various renders to the lord, along with sections on rights to land, including fishing, unlawful ploughing, setting boundaries, and measurements.[96] This would perhaps be relevant in a Marcher lordship, where the Lords Marcher had the power to create their own laws, and there is evidence that they exploited the Welsh laws (and indeed the Welsh people) for their own financial gain.[97]

---

[87] *Ibid.*, 39–40.

[88] Roberts, 'Law Texts and their Sources', 48.

[89] *Ibid.*, 48–49.

[90] *Ibid.*, 50–51, and see below. Linguistic evidence also places the manuscript in north Wales; see Elias, 'Llawysgrif Peniarth 164', 35.

[91] *Ibid.*, 44.

[92] *Ibid.*, 44.

[93] *ALD*, xl–xlviii.

[94] Elias, 'Llawysgrif Peniarth 164', 44.

[95] Roberts, 'Law Texts and their Sources', 55–57.

[96] *Pomffred*, 22.

[97] Davies, *Lordship and Society*, 158: 'the amercements that were due by Welsh law ... were no doubt attractive to the lord'; see 150–151 for a discussion on the yield of courts.

The *cynghawsedd* and other material in manuscripts As and Mor all shows considerable interest in how the law would be upheld, perhaps in north-east Wales or the March. Manuscript H shows a similar emphasis: H was from the same region as As and Mor, and the compiler of H had similar interests. Elias points out that H – and therefore As and Mor – may emphasise the importance of the administration of law in late medieval Wales.[98] There were developments in pleading in English law, but the *cynghawsedd* setup in Wales was different, and in regions where the two legal systems ran concurrently these differences may have been very obvious; manuscript texts to explain procedures would have been useful, if not necessary. This would have been especially the case in the March, where there were both Welsh and English courts in operation.

In addition, Elias considers the compiler of H, and the way his text may reveal his interests to us. H is a personal text, and unique, but it is organised in its own way, and it was a deliberate literary creation.[99] The compiler was flexible in the way that he dealt with his sources and, while the manuscript appears messy and disorganised, this may reflect a practical book that would have been used for study or even in court. If this is the case, then H, as well as Z, As and Mor, need to be considered in the context of interest in Welsh law in the Marcher lordships, and that explains the different style and format of these manuscripts.

As, NLW Peniarth MS 175 and Mor, NLW Peniarth MS 36C

As and Mor are also from north-east Wales, and both suffered the double misfortune of being categorised by Aneurin Owen as 'anomalous' manuscripts and being assigned as sigla 'other characters taken from the Saxon alphabet', which made it difficult to render them on modern word processors.[100] As may be the earliest of the two, dated by Huws to the second half of the fifteenth century, and Mor is late fifteenth or early sixteenth century. The manuscripts are very closely related, and both have a collection of *cynghawsedd* that was presented in AL IX (discussed above in Chapter 4). The same *cynghawsedd* collections were also copied into manuscript Z, but it is uncertain whether either As or Mor was the exemplar for the text in Z, or whether As, Mor and Z all shared a common exemplar. As and Mor appear to be sister manuscripts, very close in their readings, and Aneurin Owen stated that Mor 'agrees nearly verbatim' with As.[101] While this is true, it is difficult to determine whether one is copied from the other, or whether they share the same exemplar.

As was given a date of 1429 by Aneurin Owen on the basis of a text that no longer survives in the manuscript;[102] Daniel Huws suggests that it may have been written on a flyleaf now lost, although the date itself does occur in Mor:

---

[98] Elias, 'Llawysgrif Peniarth 164', 44.

[99] *Ibid.*, 45–46.

[100] AL, Introduction, xxv. The manuscripts have since been given new sigla by Seminar Cyfraith Hywel, using As for Peniarth 175 following its designation in the Hengwrt catalogue; and Mor for Peniarth 36C, in honour of William Maurice who used it.

[101] *Ibid.*, xxxii.

[102] Owen stated that manuscript Z dated from 1480, 'from a date occurring incidentally in the matter', but this date is no longer in the manuscript, if ever it was; *Pomffred*, 20. Owen also notes that there is a date – 2 Henry IV – in the 'pleadings' in Q, but this is also not so: AL, Introduction, xxx. In this case, Owen may have confused As and Mor – the manuscripts are very similar.

A hono y sy varn Tudur ap Jeuan goch anno regni Henrici sexti septimo in curia de Issalet.[103]

And that is the judgement of Tudur ap Ieuan Goch the seventh year of the reign of Henry VI in the court of Isaled.

J. Gwenogvryn Evans stated that there was nothing to suggest that the manuscript was incomplete: 'there is nothing to indicate that the MS. is imperfect, nothwithstanding [sic] the note of the Editor of the Welsh Laws'.[104] Evans refers to Owen's note, at the end of AL IX.xxxviii.16, which states that 'The remainder of A[s] is lost'. This may simply be the end of the text, and Mor continues with a different text under a new heading in AL IX.xxxix. Evans also quotes a note in the manuscript that states that there are 44 folios in it ('*Pedair dolen adevgayn yn y llyvyr hwn*'); and the note occurs on the final page.[105]

Mor is longer, and while As and Mor contain much of the same material, Mor is not complete and is missing leaves towards the end of the *cynghawsedd*: f. 28v ends midway through a sentence. It resumes on f. 29r with the same text found near the end of As, and then continues with further material that does not occur in As. As appears to be complete and is a collection of *cynghawsedd* material from one source only, and so the further material in Mor may show that it was a broader legal collection, including material from other sources, rather than being a book of *cynghawsedd*. There were already lacunae in Mor when William Maurice used the manuscript in 1662–1663, and the pages have been disordered in the binding. It was at one stage bound together with O and M.

Table 7.2: Manuscript Mor and its contents

Text	Mor	Notes
Cynghawsedd	22r3–28v20	Also in As, Z. Lacuna in Mor
Holiadon	29r1–29r12	Also in As
Laws of Court	29r13–29v20	Not a redaction text
Land Law	30r1–30v21	Iorwerth
List of personal names	31r	
Dead House	31v.1–31v3	Also in Z
Damweiniau	31v.1–31v9	Also in *Damweiniau Colan*
Women	31v10–32r14	
Llyfr Cynog	32v1–32v14	Also in Z
Land law	33r1–33v14	Iorwerth
Women	34r1–36r5	Blegywryd
Violence	36r6–36v9	Also in Z

---

[103] The note appears twice in Mor, on f. 37r with a reference to Tudur ap Ieuan Goch but with no date or location; and including the date and Is Aled on f. 37v. An earlier version of the same note, including the date, also occurs in Latin E, Cambridge, Corpus Christi College MS 454, f. 58v.

[104] Evans, *Report*, Vol. I, Part II – Peniarth, 970.

[105] *Ibid.*; Peniarth MS 175, f. 44v. It should be noted that the manuscript is badly gall-stained, which makes the text difficult to read.

(Table 7.2 continued)

Text	Mor	Notes
Holiadon	36v9–36v17	Also in J
Laws of Court	37r1–37r14	
Land Law diagram	37v1–37v8	
Three Columns of Law	37v.9–19	Iorwerth
Slaves	38r1–38r11	Cyfnerth, also in Z
Customs, Arferion Cyfraith	38r11–41r15	Blegywryd
Pope Anastasius	41v1–42r11	Similar text in Z
Triads	42r11–42r14	Blegywryd
Damweiniau	42v1–42v13	Also in *Damweiniau Colan*
Land Law, Justices	43r2–44v13	Blegywryd

The material that is in Mor but not in As comprises legal texts, from various sources. Some of this material in Mor is also found in Z, a manuscript from the same region, and that also had access to the *cynghawsedd* collection also in As and Mor. This may point to the exemplars being available in north-east Wales, and may even suggest that Z and Mor were from the same place. Other parts of Mor are Iorwerth, including sections on Land Law, and one section on *sarhaed*, and short texts from the *damweiniau* collections. Blegywryd texts are also included, on customs and other procedural matters. In addition, Mor contains some sections that are linked to the enigmatic *Llyfr Cynog*, and it has a note that states '*Llyma dechreu Llyfyr Kynawc*' ('Here begins the Book of Cynog'), followed by the Seven Bishop-Houses of Dyfed text.[106] The Seven Bishop-Houses in Mor is very close to that in Z, since both manuscripts share the same error and, like Mor, Z is also said to contain sections of *Llyfr Cynog*, but the incipit preceding the Seven Bishop-Houses in Mor is absent in Z.[107] The material that Mor and Z have in common may all be from *Llyfr Cynog*. Portions of that text – or indeed all of it, if it were in book form – appear to have been in north-east Wales at some point. Z and Mor were not copied from the same exemplar, it seems; but the problem is the nature of *Llyfr Cynog*, which is enigmatic, and may not have been an organised text set out as a book, which makes it difficult to know how much of the material from either manuscript, and which parts of it, was actually linked to *Llyfr Cynog*.[108]

The mixture of material in Mor has the common theme of being procedural and practical once again, and this may point to the manuscript being used in court, or compiled as a reference book for a lawyer. The record of a legal case is particularly interesting in that sense, since it may have come from a local source in north-east Wales. As, on the other hand, has collections of *cynghawsedd* but very little material other than that; perhaps it was intended as a separate book of *cynghawsedd*. It is also tempting to suggest that As was the exemplar for the same collections of *cynghawsedd* in Mor and Z, but there is not enough evidence to be able to prove that suggestion.

---

[106] *Pomffred*, 30.
[107] *Pomffred*, 30–31.
[108] *Pomffred*, 30–31.

An, NLW Peniarth MS 166

An is the latest addition to the corpus of Welsh law manuscripts, although it was known as a law manuscript for some time. The manuscript has benefited from a detailed study by Angharad Elias, and much of this discussion will be drawn from her conclusions in that work.[109] An is a sixteenth-century text of the laws, and it contains some material that is not found elsewhere, although other parts of the manuscript link it to the redaction texts, particularly to the Blegywryd redaction or to later manuscripts from that redaction.[110] The manuscript was not used by Aneurin Owen, but it must have been known to him – it was in the Hengwrt collection, with other law manuscripts that he did use, and it was also included in the Hengwrt library catalogue drawn up by Owen's father, William Owen Pughe.[111] However, Owen did not assign a siglum to the manuscript – this was done in 2016 by Seminar Cyfraith Hywel – nor did he use the manuscript for any variant readings. It was listed by Thomas Charles-Edwards in his list of Welsh manuscripts, but without a siglum.[112] It is likely that it was Owen's omission of the manuscript that led to its being neglected for such a long time, which again highlights the importance of Owen's work in the general historiography of the Welsh laws and the impact it has had on studies even today.

If An is to be assigned to any redaction at all, then it belongs to Blegywryd, but it is to a great extent a forgotten representative of that redaction although the text does not follow the order of the Blegywryd texts particularly closely.[113] It would be safer to say that the manuscript belongs in the Blegywryd tradition, rather than in the Blegywryd redaction. In the same way that G belongs to the Iorwerth tradition and is listed with the Iorwerth redaction manuscripts, and F was once assigned to the Iorwerth redaction but is now better called a manuscript containing material from the Iorwerth tradition, An has enough sections that are recognisably from the Blegywryd tradition to warrant its inclusion with other Blegywryd manuscripts. However, the nature of the manuscript containing the text means that, like G, it has more in common with the other manuscripts included in this discussion. Elias points out that the manuscript is in three parts.[114] It does not have a prologue or Laws of Court – this is a common feature of most of the manuscripts discussed in this section – but it has several other sections taken from the Blegywryd tradition, showing a close affinity to manuscripts S, Tim and J; at times, it is closer to Tim and J, but at other points it is close to S.[115] It is not a copy of any of these, however, but may have been copied from their exemplar(s). The sections from Blegywryd are all practical and procedural – they are either sections found in *Arferion Cyfraith*, or they are parts of the text discussing justices and judgements; triads and *damweiniau* feature as genres of texts, and there is an interest in matters such as deposits, lending and borrowing.[116] The sections that

---

[109] Elias, 'Cam o'r Tywyllwch', 107–117.
[110] *Ibid.*, 107.
[111] *Ibid.*
[112] Charles-Edwards, *The Welsh Laws*, 102.
[113] Elias, 'Cam o'r Tywyllwch', 109.
[114] *Ibid.*, 108.
[115] *Ibid.*, 114.
[116] *Ibid.*, 109, 111–112, 114–115.

An has in common with S are likely to have been taken from a text known as *Rhol Dafydd Llwyd* ('Dafydd Llwyd's Roll').[117]

Most of the material found in An could be said to be useful for a practitioner of law, and at least one of the sources for the text – *Rhol Dafydd Llwyd* – had that practical purpose. There is also an interest in legal culture.[118] In addition, the manuscript itself is not a library text; it is in several different hands, is not particularly beautifully written, and there are markings throughout the text, including underlining, deleting and correcting.[119] This all suggests a manuscript created for a specific purpose, and even one that was used for that purpose, perhaps by someone who was working as a *brawdwr* ('justice'), in south Wales, or by someone who had a general interest in the practice of law. Elias notes that this is representative of the type of lawbook that was being made in south Wales at the time when Welsh law was coming to an end, and its links to S and J further support this.[120] However, as a sixteenth-century text, this would be in the last days of Cyfraith Hywel.

These manuscripts with their interest in the practical and useful aspects of Welsh law can highlight the way Welsh legal texts were developing: An represents a stage at which having a complete text of one of the redactions was no longer necessary or even relevant, but parts of the laws were still current. That is why the nature of the lawbooks changed, from comprising one of the traditional redactions, albeit expanded or reorganised, to texts such as An, which are a further step away from the more recognisable lawtexts. Rather than being 'anomalous' texts with 'additional material', these manuscripts show a different way of assembling the legal material that was available in any given area at a particular period in time.

Conclusion

The manuscripts examined in this chapter have much in common with each other. They were all neglected by scholarship in the twentieth century to some extent, largely because of the focus on the redaction texts and the more 'straightforward' manuscripts. That this division, and this emphasis on the value of the different texts, originates with Aneurin Owen and his *Ancient Laws* has been much of the subject of this present work. Two of the manuscripts discussed in this chapter – As and Mor – were classed as 'anomalous' by Owen. Others, Col, An and Lew, were omitted altogether from his study, despite the fact that they were kept in the Hengwrt library with other law manuscripts, and it is likely that this was a deliberate omission by Owen, perhaps because the texts were just too difficult to fit into his scheme. But if we move away from Owen's scheme and take a more open-minded approach to the texts of Welsh law, these manuscripts may cease to be 'difficult' and 'strange', and simply become 'different', and not different in any negative sense. Despite not being closely related in terms of content, they are linked by their background and purpose and, as such, can tell us a great deal about the social reality of Welsh law.

---

[117] *Ibid.*, 114. *Rhol Dafydd Llwyd* is discussed in Chapter 6. Dafydd Llwyd was a *dosbarthwr*, a man who worked with the law; his Roll would have contained legal material useful for him, including pleadings and material focusing on legal procedure.

[118] *Ibid.*, 108.

[119] *Ibid.*, 108.

[120] *Ibid.*, 108.

Each of these manuscripts, in its own way, is revealing about the development of the Welsh legal texts. As, Mor and H, and with Z added as a sister manuscript, are all north-east Wales texts, and they all contain material that was deemed to be useful, but useful to practitioners of law in a particular area where parts of Welsh law were still in use. Large parts of north-east Wales were in the March, and much has been said about the survival of Welsh law in the March of Wales.[121] But due to the neglect of these manuscripts, the written evidence of what was happening to Welsh law in the March has been hidden. The material in these manuscripts has an emphasis on procedural and administrative aspects – Z for example has details on fines and punishments, and reflects either a need for a text relating how to deal with particular situations, or alternatively an interest in income from the laws. The *cynghawsedd* text, some of which is included in all of these manuscripts, and a complete text of it in As, Mor and Z, may have been composed especially for a particular region, but it focuses on pleading, and this is the most practical element of court work: how legal cases were to be conducted and what would be said in court. This suggests that the material would be useful for a practitioner, and that in a region where Welsh and English law ran concurrently.[122] What these texts, As, Mor and H, along with Z, which also includes a 'standard' Cyfnerth text, tell us is that after the conquest the emphasis was less on the rules associated with Cyfraith Hywel, and more on the administration of law in a new situation where the legal rules may have changed, but the practicalities of legal cases continued to follow a recognisably Welsh pattern.

In contrast, while there is still an emphasis on the practical in F, G and Lew, these manuscripts all keep one foot in the classical Iorwerth tradition, while still reflecting post-conquest changes. There is less of an emphasis on particular tractates of the Welsh laws in these manuscripts, although some of them do include recognisable Iorwerth texts. The Iorwerth texts that are included are often more 'useful' texts on Land Law and suretyship; F also had sections of the Three Columns of Law, which were superseded by English law according to the Statute of Wales, but may have retained an interest in terms of the way things were done in the past. However, the main emphasis in these manuscripts is on pleading, *cynghawsedd*, *damweiniau*, and other texts that then travelled to south Wales and were incorporated in some of the Blegywryd practitioner texts. The same needs were arising in post-conquest Gwynedd as in the March: a system to allow the law to continue to operate, and was not the English system transplanted to a different place, but a Welsh version of the law, at one remove from Cyfraith Hywel perhaps, but still distinctly Welsh in both language and nature. It drew on the Welsh texts of the laws, but these manuscripts, with their emphasis on pleading and holding court cases, the administration of the law and the flexibility of the law, show the development of texts in north Wales, within the Iorwerth tradition but at one remove from the 'classical' texts of the 'golden age' of lawmaking in Gwynedd.

Finally, Col has great importance in that it is of a date with those very same 'classical' Iorwerth Gwynedd texts, but it is a different version of the same lawtexts. The emphasis in Col is on the flexibility of the legal texts in Gwynedd. It may have been produced in a flourishing Welsh legal centre, but the fact that the Iorwerth texts *could* be rewritten and revised in this way shows that the law was never a fixed or

---

[121] See for example the works of R. R. Davies, in particular: Davies, 'The Law of the March', Davies, 'The Twilight of Welsh Law'; and Davies, *Lordship and Society*. A more recent publication on the topic is Roberts, 'What's Yours is Mine'.

[122] Elias, 'Llawysgrif Peniarth 164', 44–46.

static entity but a living, changeable thing. Col shows that the law was flexible and adaptable even before the conquest made it urgently necessary for it to be so, and it is this inherent usefulness in the laws that paved the way for the later texts. Welsh legal texts, with a direct link to Cyfraith Hywel but a different purpose, continues to be created well into the fifteenth century, and this ensured the survival of Welsh law as a living intellectual system for centuries after the loss of Welsh independence.

CONCLUSION

There are several approaches to looking at the growth of law in medieval Wales. Often there is an emphasis on examining the texts for signs of antiquity, to attempt to recreate the earliest recoverable stage of the law. This tended to be the method used in early scholarly work on the laws, and is still an approach followed today. While Aneurin Owen focused on attempting to trace the laws back to the original book purported to have been created by Hywel ap Cadell, scholars today work on determining whether some parts of the law can be fitted into a concept of a 'Model Lawbook'. Seeking to recover pre-Norman Welsh law is a valid and important goal. It is pursued today without assuming a concrete link to Hywel Dda and without imposing particular frameworks on the lawtexts as we have them. However, examining sections of law to discover the earliest material does not mean that the earliest texts are more valid, more valuable, or more important than law that is not early. Later law has its importance too, and while it may not fit into a concept of a 'Model Lawbook', it may reveal a great deal about other things – the development of the law, the use of the texts, the practice of law in post-conquest Wales. That is what this volume has sought to do. Rather than looking backwards and focusing on Hywel Dda and the pre-Norman origins of the lawtexts, this volume asserts the importance of examining all of the lawtexts, and in their own contexts. It does not aim to dismiss the earlier law, or the three traditional redactions of Cyfraith Hywel, but instead looks at the neglected sections of law and considers how these fit in with the sections that have received more attention.

Approaching the lawtexts with fixed presuppositions presents many problems. This is not to dismiss Aneurin Owen's great work of examining Cyfraith Hywel in its entirety and published as *Ancient Laws and Institutes of Wales*. Owen's was an immense work of scholarship, with far-reaching consequences. Indeed, there is great value to be had in examining the historiography of the Welsh lawtexts. However, assumptions of early editors often have a serious effect on the development of academic fields and, in the case of the Welsh lawtexts, they have caused certain aspects of the laws to be treated in particular ways. Large swathes of legal material and large sections of the law manuscripts remain neglected, unedited, not easily available to scholars, to the detriment of the subject area. A full picture of medieval Welsh society, of the work of learned elites, of the creation of manuscripts, of the development of functional prose and, indeed, of law and administration can never be gained from neglecting a large part of the sources.

The work of the justices and the compilers of legal texts is central to this approach. The best place to start examining the law of medieval Wales remains the texts themselves, but free of constraints such as attempting to force certain manuscripts or sections of texts into a fixed form that may never have existed. The justices and compilers of the Welsh lawtexts drew their material from a variety of sources – early written law was certainly one, but they also incorporated custom, material discussing procedure, certain other genres of functional prose, and material with a more pedagogical purpose. The compilers themselves often did not distinguish between the many and varied sources that they had at their disposal. Alongside redaction texts of the laws that followed a fixed or semi-fixed form, and whose recognisable tractates are found in some or all of the Welsh redactions, the compilers also included other genres, material from different legal sources, and within the same manuscripts, which contained the redaction texts. The material from other sources was often not treated differently by the compilers; it was included along with the redactions. While we find references to certain material being viewed differently, perhaps due to the way it was composed or its assumed authority, on the whole there was no sense in medieval Wales that some legal material was more important than other material. Certainly there is no reflection of this kind of division in the manuscripts. Even when a book of law received a name – *Rhol Dafydd Llwyd, Llyfr Cynog, Llyfr Cynghawsedd* – the material that was not included in such named books was not seen as less important.

The law manuscripts themselves were very flexible, and were seen as such by the compilers who created them. The manuscripts of the Iorwerth redaction may be highly organised texts, but even so their form was not necessarily fixed. The compilers and the justices may have wanted, or needed, the law to appear authoritative, but the references throughout the Iorwerth texts to the 'debate pattern' show that the law itself was always changing in response to the changes in society, and that there were plenty of options. There was flexibility to adapt sections of law, to bring in material from different exemplars and material useful to the circumstances in which the book of law was being created. The law could even incorporate previously unwritten customs, and there were steps on how to do this. The Blegywryd texts show evidence for the practice of law and the work of the *dosbarthwyr*, who needed written texts to which they could refer. They often start with a recognisable text of the Blegywryd redaction, but some at least have a second part that seems more varied, and is often not found in the same form, or following the same order, in any other manuscript. Instead of dismissing this material as 'a tail', a new way of viewing these manuscripts is to see them as organised texts, with a tripartite division – as in the Iorwerth redaction – and the third part arranged according to purpose rather than according to subject. This would explain why the third part of the Blegywryd manuscripts appears disorganised and confusing, but that is not the case if they are viewed as incorporating material on the practice of law, administration, and procedure. In south Wales, the region of the Blegywryd redaction, there is evidence that many legal texts were in circulation, including but not confined to the recognisable Blegywryd texts, and the compilers could and did choose their material from these sources. It is this selection and exploiting of the legal material that affects the way some manuscripts appear, and this explains the complexity of the surviving texts, and is the reason they defy neat categorisation.

Examining the Welsh lawtexts without applying limits and terms such as 'additional' or 'anomalous', or indeed the concept of 'a tail', will give a clearer picture of this situation. Each lawbook should be viewed on its own terms. All of the material in any given lawbook should be examined, regardless of whether it fits neatly into a redaction, whether the material is unique to that manuscript, or whether it appears disorganised. If the material is legal, then it should be seen as law, and not excluded through imposing any criterion of validity on it. Sections ordered by subject have the same value as sections ordered by genre – and the way a section of text is organised is perhaps less important than what is in the section, and also what is absent. Older portions of text may appear alongside post-conquest ones, but rather than drawing

Conclusion

firm lines between the material, an alternative approach is to question why this is the case by considering the purpose of the material.

The law of medieval Wales may 'suffer from what must be one of the most complicated textual traditions known to any field of study',[1] but this complexity can be re-evaluated positively as a sign of the flexibility and open-mindedness of the men behind the texts. They were creating books of law for specific purposes and, as such, these lawbooks were not supposed to be tidy texts: they were the result of the lawyers' eclecticism, and the selection of sections of texts that they needed, regardless of their origin. The textual tradition of medieval Welsh law does not necessarily need to be complex, if we approach the manuscripts with an open mind, and with a consideration of the purpose of the books rather than attempting to shoehorn certain texts into a fixed format, one that may never have existed in reality. In doing so, all of the law of medieval Wales would be treated equally, regardless of its shape or organisation, or the early or late date of its composition. Looking at the growth of law in medieval Wales in its own context will give us a new picture of the texts of Cyfraith Hywel. This will see all of the law as a single entity, all with the same status, and this will have huge benefits for studying all aspects of medieval Wales, and indeed, medieval society in general.

---

[1] Stacey, *The Road to Judgment*, 17

ACKNOWLEDGEMENTS

This book has been a long time in the making, many years. I started working for my D.Phil. at Jesus College, Oxford, in 1998, and at that time my thesis had the unmemorable title 'The development of Welsh law after 1282, with special reference to NLW Wynnstay MS.36 and NLW Peniarth MS.164'. But informally, my supervisor, Prof. Thomas Charles-Edwards, and I would refer to this work as 'Ancient Laws II', since the aim was that I focused on the under-studied texts in the second volume of Aneurin Owen's great work. The two manuscripts selected as the basis for the study, however, contained large collections of triads, and the triads took over somewhat. Therefore, my thesis was renamed and became an edition and study of the triads, later published as *The Legal Triads of Medieval Wales*. The work I had started on other aspects of AL II was stored away, and it was there in the background of my other work on Cyfraith Hywel. It has taken around 20 years for this work to take the final shape, and it is pleasing that 2021 marked 180 years since the publication of Owen's *Ancient Laws and Institutes of Wales*; it seems fitting that I finished the work towards the end of 2021.

This book was also finished at a tumultuous time, during a global pandemic, and following periods of lockdown and limited access to published books and research material. However, in many ways, I faced greater challenges in the ten years or so before the pandemic. These have been years of either unemployment or precarious employment and, while I know I am not alone in finding it seemingly impossible to obtain a permanent university position in the present climate, this has had a huge effect on me and my family. Several friends passed away, and are sorely missed. Losing my wonderful friend Claire Jamset in 2019 has been particularly hard to come to terms with. She was in the room next door to mine when the earliest parts of this work was being created, and helped me with the Latin texts. It has been an unimaginably cruel and difficult time for me personally, but working on this book has been a comfort. In many ways I feel that publishing this book is closing a door on a certain part of my life and, while that is a good thing, I am also sad to say goodbye to it.

Given the length of time from the early genesis of parts of this work, and the gradual development of what was originally assumed would be a journal article to becoming a full-length monograph, the list of people who I wish to thank is immense, and would cover every person with whom I have had an academic conversation since starting my doctorate. Here, however, I wish to single out people who have assisted me in the preparation of this book. Very early drafts of chapters were read by Adam Chapman, Ceridwen Lloyd-Morgan and Emma Cavell. Their helpful comments gave me the confidence to submit a proposal to Boydell. Caroline Palmer at Boydell has been instrumental and beyond helpful in dealing with various aspects of bringing this work to press, and has dealt with every query efficiently and sensitively. Elizabeth McDonald and Christy Beale have also been instrumental in the publication process, and my experience with all at Boydell has been extremely positive. Robin Chapman Stacey very kindly read drafts of all of the chapters and suggested a new structure

Acknowledgements

for the work – this was after she had anonymously (!) peer reviewed two chapters for my anonymous (!) proposal for Boydell. It appears that anonymity is not really possible in the field of Cyfraith Hywel. I am extremely grateful to Robin for all of her helpful suggestions, and indeed for reading the work more than once, which goes above and beyond the call of duty. Thomas Charles-Edwards was my supervisor for my doctorate, and I still value his guidance and supervision; he also read a draft of the entire book, and made many comments and suggestions, and this work has benefited greatly from his help. Likewise, Barry Lewis read the entire work and again his assistance was invaluable. Naturally, any remaining errors are my own. Diolch i chi i gyd. Others who have assisted with comments and discussions on particular aspects of this work include, in no particular order, Emma Cavell, with whom I had lively discussions about customs, developed in Chapter 3, and Thomas Watkin, who discussed Roman law and Justinian with me. I had helpful and informative conversations with Rhiannon Comeau, Christine James, Ceridwen Lloyd-Morgan and Paul Russell among others, and all at Seminar Cyfraith Hywel have contributed with their excellent comments following presentations about parts of my research. Gruffudd Antur, Daniel Huws and Maredudd ap Huw have all given me important information on the manuscripts. During the last stages of preparing the draft, Elena Parina kindly stepped in and cast fresh eyes over a section of the work, shook it into shape, and helped me fit it in to the whole; Ben Guy kindly gave me permission to follow his (genius) format for my bibliography, and the Index of Manuscripts, and he was also very generous in sharing copies of his own work. Several people on social media answered my desperate eleventh-hour pleas for particular texts and works, and provided it quickly for me. Cath D'Alton created the map, and Owen McKnight at my Alma Mater, Jesus College, Oxford, was generous in allowing the use of the image of MS 57. Ken Rees and Dave Walsh Gibbon were superb in helping me secure an image from the Sun Clock at Gerddi Hywel Dda for the cover, and I am thrilled that that was able to happen. My husband, Tim Petts, created the index for this book; this is the third time he has indexed a book of mine and once again he has done an excellent job. Diolch o waelod calon i bawb.

My biggest gratitude however goes to my family, Tim, Iestyn and Goronwy, and also to my parents. Without their support and co-operation, and indeed their long suffering, this book would not have happened at all, but in the scheme of things the book does not matter; our lives together are more important, and I value each and every one of you for your love and support and for sticking with me through everything.

GLOSSARY

This glossary is a guide to words and terms found in the lawtexts, and discussed in this work. Several of these are technical terms for which there is no English equivalent and these are left untranslated in the work. This is intended as a guide only, and more information can be found in other studies of the Welsh lawtexts and reference works.

adnau Deposit.

amobr In marriage in medieval Welsh law, this is one of the payments that take place; it is a fee to the lord, and is seen as paid for the woman's virginity.

amod pl. *amodau*. Contract.

arfer pl. *arferoedd*. Practice or usage. This is found in the phrase *arfer cyfraith*, pl. *arferion cyfraith*, and is the name for a section of the Blegywryd texts. This is discussed in considerable detail in Chapter 5.

bonheddig Noble, a man whose ancestry is known.

braint Status, and also a special right or status.

brawd A judgement, also found in the office of *brawdwr*, a judge or justice; *brawdwr llys*, the court justice; *brawdwr o fraint swydd*, a justice by virtue of office; *brawdwr o fraint tir*, a justice by virtue of land. Also *brawdlyfr*, a judgement book, sometimes applied to the lawtexts themselves.

briduw In a contract, rather than having a surety, God is invoked as security.

camlwrw A fine, the smaller of the two penalties mentioned in Welsh law; contrasted with the larger *dirwy* fine. It was a fine of three cows or 15s, payable to the king or the lord.

canllaw An advocate who would help the litigant in legal cases. Little work has been done on this office, and that of the *cyngaws*, which seems to be similar. It is likely that these men had some form of legal qualifications or training, but they were distinct from the professional justices.

cantref The larger of the administrative units in medieval Wales, with the *cwmwd* ('commote') being a smaller division of the *cantref*.

cowyll A gift to a virgin bride from her husband, similar to the English 'morning gift'.

cwyn Plaint, the statement of events that would be declared to open legal proceedings.

Cyfar Co-tillage or joint-ploughing, a section in the Iorwerth lawbooks.

cyfarch cyffyll Stock-enquiry.

cyfran Division (of land).

Cynefodau Customs.

cyngaws Similar to the *canllaw*, the *cyngaws* shared a legal case with the litigant and provided expert guidance; a pleader.

Glossary

cynghawsedd   Also in the form *cyngheusaeth*, a genre of legal writing sometimes called 'model pleading', examples of which are found collected together as *Llyfr Cynghawsedd* ('The Book of Pleading'). The emphasis in *cynghawsedd* texts is on legal procedure.

cynghellor   The main officer in local administration. He worked with the *maer* but was superior to him.

dadannudd   pl. *dadannuddiau*. A ceremonial legal action for claiming land where the claimant would argue that his father had previously held the land.

damweiniau   Also as collections known as *Llyfr Damweiniau*, the form is a statement giving a possible legal situation and the legal solution. The sentences often open with the formula *O derfydd*, 'If it happens'.

Deddfgrawn   pl. *Deddfgronau*. A collection or corpus of laws, a legal compilation.

Diasbad uwch Annwfn   'A cry above *Annwfn* [the underworld]', also taking the form *diasbad uwch adfan*, 'a cry above emptiness'. It is a relatively obscure section in the laws, and refers to the cry of a man whose status changes from being a proprietor of family land to being a non-proprietor, a retrograde step in terms of status and land ownership.

dirwy   The major fine of 12 cows or £3 payable to the king or the lord, in contrast to the *camlwrw*.

dosbarthwr   An expert in *Cyfraith Hywel*, a justice or legal practitioner.

ebediw   Death duty for a man, calculated according to his status.

galanas   The act of homicide, or the payment for homicide, or a man's life-value payable for loss of life.

gorfodog   Bailsman.

gwarant   Guarantee, or more commonly guarantor.

gwybyddiaid   'Knowers', one of two witnesses in Welsh law. *Gwybyddiaid* would testify that something had happened and that they had personal knowledge of this.

Holiadon   'Interrogatories', this is Aneurin Owen's word for the collection of question-and-answer sections which occur in some law manuscripts, and are discussed in Chapter 4, and also in Chapter 5. The word is an unusual formation from the word *holi*, 'to ask, enquire'.

Llyfr   Book, and used throughout the laws to refer to different sections and collections of laws.

maer   The local administrative officer linked to the *cynghellor*, but lower in status.

mamwys   Claiming land through the mother's side.

naw affaith   The nine abetments, the opening part of the tractates on homicide, theft, and fire. The abetments list nine cases where a man can be punished for homicide, theft, or fire by association, for example in not preventing these things from taking place, or instigating the acts without carrying them out personally.

Naw Tafodiog   The Nine Tongued-Ones, a list of nine special witnesses whose testimony is to be believed in all cases.

profi ygneid   Also taking the form *profi ynadon*, 'proving/testing judges', the name in the manuscripts for a collection of question-and-answer statements, *holiadon* (see above).

Glossary

rhingyll The serjeant, responsible for maintaining order and enforcing commands issued from a higher authority (the royal court or a court of law).

sarhaed Literally 'insult', the payment for a deliberate injury or loss.

swyddog Officer, one holding an office

Tair Colofn Cyfraith The Three Columns of Law, a major tractate in the Welsh lawbooks discussing homicide, theft, and arson.

wynebwerth The oldest term for honour-price, interchangeable with *sarhaed*.

Wyth Pynfarch The Eight Packhorses (of the lord). Sources of casual income for the lord.

ymwrthyn Contention.

ynad pl. *ygneid* or in Modern Welsh *ynadon*. Justice or judges, discussed in full in Chapter 3.

BIBLIOGRAPHY

Antur, G., "'I Mewn Hen Ysgrifen Gron': Llawysgrifau Lewys Glyn Cothi', in S. E. Roberts, S. Rodway and A. Falileyev (eds.), *Cyfarwydd Mewn Cyfraith: Studies in Honour of Morfydd E. Owen* (Welsh Legal History Society Vol. XVII, Bangor, 2022), 1–15.
Baker, J. H., *An Introduction to English Legal History* (4th ed., London, 2002).
Beale, P., *A Dictionary of English Manuscript Terminology 1450–2000* (Oxford, 2008).
Bieler, L., 'The Irish Penitentials', *Scriptores Latini Hiberniae* 5 (1963).
—— 'Towards an Interpretation of the So-Called "Canones Wallici"', in J. A. Watt, J. B. Morrall and F. X. Martin (eds.), *Medieval Studies Presented to A. Gwynn* (Dublin, 1961), 387–392.
Binchy, D. A., *Celtic and Anglo-Saxon Kingship: The O'Donnell Lectures for 1967–8* (London, 1970).
Birks, P. and McLeod, P., *Justinian's Institutes* (London, 1987).
Bowen, I., *The Statutes of Wales* (London, 1908).
Brand, P., 'An English Legal Historian Looks at the Statute of Wales', in T. G. Watkin (ed.), *Y Cyfraniad Cymreig: Welsh Contributions to Legal Development* (Welsh Legal History Society Vol. III, Bangor, 2005), 20–56.
Bromwich, R. (ed. and transl.), *Trioedd Ynys Prydein: The Triads of the Island of Britain* (3rd ed., Cardiff, 2006).
Brundage, J. A., *The Medieval Origins of the Legal Profession: Canonists, Civilians, and Courts* (Chicago and London, 2008).
Brynmor-Jones, D., 'The Brehon Laws and their Relation to the Ancient Welsh Institutes', *Transactions of the Honourable Society of the Cymmrodorion* (1904), 7–36.
—— 'Foreign Elements in Welsh Law', *Transactions of the Honourable Society of the Cymmrodorion* (1916–1917), 1–51.
—— *The Study of the Welsh Laws* (Dolgellau, 1889).
Burdett-Jones, M. T., 'A Note on a Welsh Legal Manuscript, British Library, Cotton Caligula Aiii', *National Library of Wales Journal* 25 (1988), 249–251.
Carpenter, D., 'Confederation not Domination: Welsh Political Culture in the Age of Gwynedd Imperialism', in R. A. Griffiths and P. R. Schofield (eds.), *Wales and the Welsh in the Middle Ages: Essays Presented to J. Beverley Smith* (Cardiff, 2011), 70–88.
Carr, A. D., *Llywelyn ap Gruffudd, ?–1282* (Cardiff, 1982).
—— and D. Jenkins, *Trem Ar Gyfraith Hywel* (Hendy Gwyn ar Daf, 1985).
Carr, G., *William Owen Pughe* (Cardiff, 1983).
Cavell, E., 'Widows, native law and the long shadow of England in thirteenth-century Wales', *English Historical Review* 133, Issue 565 (December 2018), 1387–1419.
Charles-Edwards, G., 'The Scribes of the Red Book of Hergest', *National Library of Wales Journal* 21 (1979–1980), 246–256.
—— and T. M. Charles-Edwards, 'The continuation of 'Brut y Tywysogion' in Peniarth MS. 20', in T. Jones and E. B. Fryde (eds.), *Ysgrifau a Cherddi Cyflwynedig i Daniel Huws* (Aberystwyth, 1994), 293–305.
Charles-Edwards, T. M., '*Cynghawsedd*: Counting and Pleading in Medieval Welsh Law', *Bulletin of the Board of Celtic Studies* 33 (1986), 188–198.
—— 'Dynastic Succession in Early Medieval Wales', in R. A. Griffiths and P. R. Schofield (eds.), *Wales and the Welsh in the Middle Ages: Essays Presented to J. Beverley Smith* (Cardiff, 2011), 70–88.
—— *Early Irish and Welsh Kinship* (Oxford, 1993).

Bibliography

—— 'Early Medieval Kingships in the British Isles', in S. Bassett (ed.), *The Origins of Anglo-Saxon Kingdoms* (London, 1989), 28–39.

—— 'The *Galanas* Tractate in Iorwerth: Texts and the Legal Development', in T. M. Charles-Edwards and P. Russell (eds.), *Tair Colofn Cyfraith* (Welsh Legal History Society Vol. V, Bangor, 2007), 92–107.

—— '*Gorsedd, Dadl* and *Llys*: Assemblies and Courts in Medieval Wales', in A. Pantos and S. Semple (eds.), *Assembly Places and Practices in Medieval Europe* (Dublin, 2004).

—— 'The Heir-apparent in Irish and Welsh Law', *Celtica* 9 (1971), 180–190.

—— 'Honour and Status in Some Irish and Welsh Prose Tales', *Ériu* 29 (1978), 123–141.

—— 'Iorwerth Manuscript E (and B)', in T. M. Charles-Edwards and P. Russell (eds.), *Tair Colofn Cyfraith* (Welsh Legal History Society Vol. V, Bangor, 2007), 258–307.

—— 'The "Iorwerth" Text', in D. Jenkins and M. E. Owen (eds.), *The Welsh Law of Women* (Cardiff, 1980), 161–185.

—— 'The "Iorwerth" Text', in T. M. Charles-Edwards, M. E. Owen and D. B. Walters (eds.), *Lawyers and Laymen* (Cardiff, 1986), 137–178.

—— 'Kinship, Status and the Origins of the Hide', *Past and Present* 56 (1972), 3–33.

—— 'Law in the Western Kingdoms between the Fifth and the Seventh Century', in A. Cameron, B. Ward-Perkins and M. Whitby (eds.), *The Cambridge Ancient History, 14. Late Antiquity: Empire and Successors, A.D. 425–600* (Cambridge, 2000), 260–287.

—— 'Medieval Welsh law', in H. Birkhan (ed.), *Bausteine zum Studium der Keltologie* (Vienna, 2005), 409–413.

—— '*Nei, keifn,* and *kefynderw*', *Bulletin of the Board of Celtic Studies* 25 (1972–1974), 386–388.

—— 'The Seven Bishop-Houses of Dyfed', *Bulletin of the Board of Celtic Studies* 24 (1970–1972), 247–262.

—— 'Some Celtic Kinship Terms', *Bulletin of the Board of Celtic Studies* 24 (1970–1972), 105–122.

—— 'The Texts: i. Introduction', in T. M. Charles-Edwards, M. E. Owen and D. B. Walters (eds.), *Lawyers and Laymen* (Cardiff, 1986), 117–118.

—— 'The Textual Tradition of Llyfr Iorwerth Revisited, or why both J. Gwenogvryn Evans and Daniel Huws may be Right', in S. E. Roberts, S. Rodway and A. Falileyev (eds.), *Cyfarwydd Mewn Cyfraith: Studies in Honour of Morfydd E. Owen* (Welsh Legal History Society Vol. XVII, Bangor, 2022), 21–45.

—— 'The Textual Tradition of Medieval Welsh Prose Tales and the Problem of Dating', in B. Maier and S. Zimmer (eds.), *150 Jahre "Mabinogion" – Deutsch-Walisische Kulturbeziehungen, Buchreihe der Zeitschrift für Celtische Philologie* 19 (Tübingen, 2001), 23–39.

—— *Wales and the Britons, 350–1064* (Oxford, 2012).

—— *The Welsh Laws* (Writers of Wales, Cardiff, 1989).

—— and N. A. Jones, '*Breintiau Gwŷr Powys*: The Liberties of the Men of Powys', in T. M. Charles-Edwards, M. E. Owen and P. Russell (eds.), *The Welsh King and his Court* (Cardiff, 2000).

—— and F. Kelly (eds.) *Bechbretha* (1983).

—— M. E. Owen and P. Russell (eds.), *The Welsh King and his Court* (Cardiff, 2000).

—— M. E. Owen and D. B. Walters (eds.), *Lawyers and Laymen: Studies in the History of Law Presented to Professor Dafydd Jenkins on his Seventy-fifth Birthday, Gŵyl Ddewi 1986* (Cardiff, 1986).

—— and P. Russell (eds.), *Tair Colofn Cyfraith. The Three Columns of Law in Medieval Wales: Homicide, Theft and Fire* (Welsh Legal History Society Vol. V, Bangor, 2005).

Cichon, M., 'Insult and Redress in Cyfraith Hywel Dda and Welsh Arthurian Romance', *Arthuriana* 10 (2000), 27–43.

—— 'Mishandled Vessels: Heaving Drinks and Hurling Insults in Medieval Welsh Literature and Law', *Canadian Journal of History* 43 (2008), 227–240.

Clanchy, M. T., 'Remembering the Past and the Good Old Law', *History* 55, no.184 (1970), 165–176.

Bibliography

Cule, J., 'The Court Mediciner and Medicine in the Laws of Wales', *Journal of the History of Medicine and Allied Sciences* 21 (1966), 213–236.
Daube, D., 'Codes and Codas', in D. Daube, *Studies in Biblical Law* (Cambridge, 1947).
Davies, R. R., 'The Administration of Law in Medieval Wales: The Role of the *Ynad Cwmwd (Judex Patrie)*', in T. M. Charles-Edwards, M. E. Owen and D. B. Walters (eds.), *Lawyers and Laymen* (Cardiff, 1986), 258–273.
—— *The Age of Conquest: Wales 1063–1415* (Oxford, 1991).
—— 'Law and National Identity in Thirteenth-Century Wales', in R. R. Davies, R. A. Griffiths, I. G. Jones and K. O. Morgan (eds.), *Welsh Society and Nationhood: Historical Essays Presented to Glanmor Williams* (Cardiff, 1984), 51–69.
—— 'The Law of the March', *Welsh History Review* 5 (1970), 1–30.
—— *Lordship and Society in the March of Wales, 1282–1400* (Oxford, 1978).
—— 'The Status of Women and the Practice of Marriage in Late-Medieval Wales', in D. Jenkins and M. E. Owen (eds.), *The Welsh Law of Women* (Cardiff, 1980), 93–114.
—— 'The Survival of the Blood Feud in Medieval Wales', *History* 54 (1969), 338–357.
—— 'The Twilight of Welsh Law 1284–1536', *History* 51 (1966), 143–164.
Davies, W., 'Braint Teilo', *Bulletin of the Board of Celtic Studies* 26 (1974–1976), 123–137.
—— *The Llandaff Charters* (Aberystwyth, 1979).
—— 'Settling Disputes in Early Medieval Spain and Portugal: A Contrast with Wales and Brittany?', in R. A. Griffiths and P. R. Schofield (eds.), *Wales and the Welsh in the Middle Ages: Essays Presented to J. Beverley Smith* (Cardiff, 2011), 70–88.
—— *Wales in the Early Middle Ages* (Leicester, 1982).
Downer, L. J., *Leges Henrici Primi* (Oxford, 1972).
Dumville, D. N., 'The Ætheling: A Study in Anglo-Saxon Constitutional History', *Anglo-Saxon England* 8 (1979), 1–33.
—— 'On the Dating of the Early Breton Lawcodes', *Études Celtiques* 21 (1984), 207–221.
Edwards, J. G., 'The Historical Study of the Welsh Lawbooks', *Transactions of the Royal Historical Society* 12, no.5 (1962), 141–155.
—— *Hywel Dda and the Welsh Law-Books*, The Hywel Dda Millennary Lecture (Bangor, 1929); reprinted as 'Hywel Dda and the Welsh Law-books', in D. Jenkins (ed.), *Celtic Law Papers* (Brussels, 1973), 135–160.
—— 'The Language of the Law Courts in Wales: Some Historical Queries', *Cambridge Law Review* 6 (1975), 5–9.
—— 'The Royal Household and the Welsh Lawbooks', *Transactions of the Royal Historical Society* 5th ser, 13 (1963), 163–176.
—— 'Studies in the Welsh Laws since 1928', *Welsh History Review Special Number: The Welsh Laws* (1963), 1–17.
Elias, G. A., *Yr Ail Lyfr Du o'r Waun. Golygiad Beirniadol ac Eglurhaol o Lsgr. Peniarth 164 (H)*, (Texts and Studies in Medieval Welsh Law V, 2 vols., Cambridge, 2018).
—— 'Cam o'r Tywyllwch: Nodyn ar Lawysgrif Cyfraith LlGC Peniarth 166', *Studia Celtica* 50 (2016), 107–117.
—— 'Llawysgrif Peniarth 164 a Pharhad Cyfraith Hywel yn yr Oesoedd Canol Diweddar', *Llên Cymru* 33 (2010), 32–50.
—— '*Llyfr Cynog* of Cyfraith Hywel and St Cynog of Brycheiniog', *Welsh History Review* 23 (2006), 27–47.
—— *Llyfr Cynyr Ap Cadwgan* (Pamffledi Cyfraith Hywel/Welsh Law Pamphlets, Aberystwyth, 2006).
Ellis, T. P., 'The Catholic Church in the Welsh Laws', *Y Cymmrodor* 42 (1931), 1–68.
—— 'Hywel Dda: Codifier', *Transactions of the Honourable Society of Cymmrodorion* (1926–1927), 1–69.
—— 'The Land in Ancient Welsh Law', *Aberystwyth Studies X: The Hywel Dda Millenary Volume* (1928), 65–102.
—— 'Legal References, Terms and Conceptions in the "Mabinogion"', *Y Cymmrodor* 39 (1928), 85–148.
—— '"Mamwys": Textual references', *Y Cymmrodor* 40 (1929), 230–250.

Bibliography

—— *Welsh Tribal Law and Custom in the Middle Ages* (2 vols., Oxford, 1926).
Emanuel, H. D., 'Blegywryd and the Welsh Laws', *Bulletin of the Board of Celtic Studies* 20 (1962–1964), 256–260.
—— 'The Book of Blegywryd and MS. Rawlinson 821', in D. Jenkins (ed.), *Celtic Law Papers* (Brussels, 1973), 161–170.
—— 'The Latin Texts of the Welsh Laws', *Welsh History Review Special Number: The Welsh Laws* (1963), 25–32.
—— *The Latin Texts of the Welsh Laws* (Cardiff, 1967).
—— 'Llyfr Blegywryd a Llawysgrif Rawlinson 821', *Bulletin of the Board of Celtic Studies* 19 (1960–1962), 23–28.
—— 'The Seven Keys of Wisdom: A Study in Christian Humanism', *Studia Celtica* 5 (1970), 36–47.
Eska, C. and J. Wolf, 'The *Surexit* Memorandum Revisited: Legal Writing and Legal Process in Ninth-Century Wales', *Cambrian Medieval Celtic Studies* 79 (2020), 19–36.
Evans, J. G., *Facsimile of the Chirk Codex of the Welsh Laws* (Llanbedrog, 1909).
—— *Report on Manuscripts in the Welsh Language* (2 vols., London, 1898–1910).
Finnemore, J., *Social Life in Wales* (London, 1922).
Fletcher, I. F., *Latin Redaction A of the Law of Hywel* (Pamffledi Cyfraith Hywel/Welsh Law Pamphlets, Aberystwyth, 1986).
—— 'The Text of Latin Redaction A', in D. Jenkins and M. E. Owen (eds.), *The Welsh Law of Women* (Cardiff, 1980), 147–159.
Foster, I. Ll., 'Summary and Suggestions', *Welsh History Review Special Number: The Welsh Laws* (1963), 61–67.
Flechner, R., *The Hibernensis Book 1 – A Study and Edition / Book 2 – Translation, Commentary and Indexes* (Washington DC, 2019).
Gallagher, J. M., 'Grounds for Divorce? Applying *Nau Kynywedi Teithiauc* to Math uab Mathonwy', *Peritia* 28 (2017), 77–90.
Grant, A., 'Gwenogvryn Evans and Cyfraith Hywel', *National Library of Wales Journal* 36 (2004), 1–12.
Griffiths, R. A., 'Gruffydd ap Nicholas and the Fall of the House of Lancaster', *Welsh History Review* 2 (1965), 213–231.
—— 'Gruffydd ap Nicholas and the Rise of the House of Dinefwr', *National Library of Wales Journal* 13 (1964), 256–265.
—— *The Principality of Wales in the Later Middle Ages: The Structure and Personnel of Government. I. South Wales 1277–1536* (Cardiff, 1972).
—— 'William Rees and the Modern Study of Medieval Wales', in R. A. Griffiths and P. R. Schofield (eds.), *Wales and the Welsh in the Middle Ages: Essays Presented to J. Beverley Smith* (Cardiff, 2011), 70–88.
Goodman, R. T., '"In a Father's Place": Anglo-Saxon Kingship and Masculinity in the Long Tenth Century', Unpublished Ph.D. (Manchester University, 2018).
Griscom, A., 'The Book of Basingwerk and MS Cotton Cleopatra Bv', *Y Cymmrodor* 35 (1925), 49–110.
Gruffydd, R. G., 'A Glimpse of Medieval Court Procedure in a Poem by Dafydd ap Gwilym', in C. Richmond and I. Harvey (eds.), *Recognitions: Essays Presented to Edmund Fryde* (Aberystwyth, 1996) 165–176.
Guy, B., 'Historical Scholars and Dishonest Charlatans: Studying the Chronicles of Medieval Wales', in B. Guy, G. Henley, O. W. Jones and Rebecca Thomas (eds.), *The Chronicles of Medieval Wales and the March: New Contexts, Studies and Texts* (Turnhout, 2020), 69–106.
—— *Medieval Welsh Genealogy: An Introduction and Textual Study* (Woodbridge, 2020).
Hall, G. D. G., (ed. and transl.), *The Treatise on the Laws and Customs of the Realm of England Commonly Called Glanvill* (Oxford, 1965).
Hamp, E. P., 'gwaesaf', *Bulletin of the Board of Celtic Studies* 40 (1993), 119.
—— and P. K. Ford, 'Welsh *Asswynaw* and Celtic Legal Idiom', *Bulletin of the Board of Celtic Studies* 26 (1974–1976), 147–160.

Bibliography

Harris, M., 'Compensation for Injury: A Point of Contact between Early Welsh and Germanic Law?', in T. G. Watkin (ed.), *The Trial of Dic Penderyn and Other Essays* (Welsh Legal History Society Vol. II, Bangor, 2002), 39–76.

—— 'Dychwelyd at Gyfeiriadau, Termau a Chysyniadau Cyfreithiol yn y Mabinogi', *Y Traethodydd* 158 (2003), 17–39.

Haycock, M. E., 'Llyfr Taliesin', *National Library of Wales Journal* 25 (1987–1988), 357–386.

Hayden, D. and P. Russell, (eds.), *Grammatica, Gramadach and Gramadeg: Vernacular Grammar and Grammarians in Medieval Ireland and Wales* (Amsterdam and Philadelphia, 2016).

Heffer, S., *Like the Roman: The Life of Enoch Powell* (London, 1998).

Hellmann, S., *Pseudo-Cyprianus, de XII abusivis saeculi* (Texte und Untersuchungen zur Geschichte der altchristlichen Literatur 34, Leipzig, 1909).

Howells, D., 'The Four Exclusive Possessions of a Man', *Studia Celtica* 8–9 (1973–1974), 48–67.

Hudson, J., *The Formation of the English Common Law: Law and Society in England From the Norman Conquest to Magna Carta* (London and New York, 1996)

Huws, D., 'Descriptions of the Welsh Manuscripts', in T. M. Charles-Edwards, M. E. Owen and P. Russell (eds.), *The Welsh King and his Court* (Cardiff, 2000), 415–424.

—— *Five Ancient Books of Wales* (Chadwick Memorial Lectures 6, Cambridge, 1995).

—— 'Yr Hen Risiart Langfford', in M. E. Owen and B. F. Roberts (eds.), *Beirdd a Thywysogion* (Cardiff, 1996), 302–325.

—— 'Leges Howelda at Canterbury', *National Library of Wales Journal* 19 (1975), 340–343.

—— 'Leges Howelda at Canterbury: A Further Note', *National Library of Wales Journal* 20 (1977–1978), 95.

—— 'Llyfrau Cymraeg 1250–1400', *National Library of Wales Journal* 28 (1993–1994), 1–21.

—— 'The Manuscripts', in T. M. Charles-Edwards and P. Russell (eds.), *Tair Colofn Cyfraith* (Welsh Legal History Society Vol. V, Bangor, 2007), 196–212.

—— 'The Manuscripts: B.L. Cotton Caligula A. iii', in T. M. Charles-Edwards, M. E. Owen and D. B. Walters (eds.), *Lawyers and Laymen* (Cardiff, 1986), 119–132.

—— 'The Manuscripts: B.L. Cotton Cleopatra A. xiv', in T. M. Charles-Edwards, M. E. Owen and D. B. Walters (eds.), *Lawyers and Laymen* (Cardiff, 1986), 132–135.

—— *Medieval Welsh Manuscripts* (Cardiff, 2000).

—— *Peniarth 28: Darluniau o Lyfr Cyfraith Hywel Dda* (National Library of Wales, Aberystwyth, 1988).

Ifans, D., *William Salesbury and the Welsh Laws* (Pamffledi Cyfraith Hywel/Welsh Law Pamphlets, Aberystwyth, 1980).

Ireland, R., 'Law in Action, Law in Books: The Practicality of Medieval Theft Law', *Continuity and Change* 17, issue 3 (2002), 309–331.

Jackson, C., *The Diary of Abraham de la Pryme, the Yorkshire Antiquary*, Publications of the Surtees Society Vol. 54 (Durham, 1870).

James, C., 'Ban Wedy i Dynny: Medieval Welsh Law and Early Protestant Propaganda', *Cambrian Medieval Celtic Studies* 27 (1994), 61–86.

—— 'Dafydd (Llwyd): Dosbarthwr', in N. S. B. Cox and T. G. Watkin (eds.), *Canmlwyddiant, Cyfraith a Chymreictod: A Celebration of the Life and Work of Dafydd Jenkins 1911–2012* (Welsh Legal History Society Vol. XI, Bangor, 2011).

—— 'Llyfr Cyfraith o Ddyffryn Teifi: Disgrifiad o BL. Add. 22,356', *National Library of Wales Journal* 27 (1991), 383–404.

—— "Llwyr Wybodau, Llên a Llyfrau': Hopcyn ap Tomas a'r Traddodiad Llenyddol Cymraeg', in H. T. Edwards (ed.), *Cwm Tawe* (Llandysul, 1993), 4–44.

—— *Machlud Cyfraith Hywel: Golygiad Beirniadol ac Eglurhaol o Lsgr. BL Add. 22356 (S)* (Texts and Studies in Medieval Welsh Law, published online in 2013, <http://cyfraith-hywel.org.uk/cy/machlud-cyf-hyw.php>).

—— 'Parhad, Pragmatiaeth, Propaganda: Llawysgrifau Cyfraith Hywel yn yr Oesoedd Canol Diweddar', *Cof Cenedl* 22 (2007), 33–67.

Bibliography

—— 'Tradition and Innovation in some Later Medieval Welsh Lawbooks', *Bulletin of the Board of Celtic Studies* 40 (1993), 148–156.

—— 'Ysgrifydd Anhysbys: Proffil Personol', *Ysgrifau Beirniadol* 23 (1997), 44–72.

Jaski, B. 'King and Household in Early Medieval Ireland', in B. T. Hudson (ed.), *Familia and Household in the Medieval Atlantic Province* (Tempe, 2011), 89–122.

Jenkins, D., *Agricultural Co-Operation in Welsh Medieval Law* (Cardiff, 1982).

—— 'Ail Olwg ar Lawysgrif Colan', in T. Jones and E. B. Fryde (eds.), *Ysgrifau a Cherddi Cyflwynedig i Daniel Huws* (Aberystwyth, 1994), 63–78.

—— '*Arianfys, Efyddfys,* Goldfinger', *Bulletin of the Board of Celtic Studies* 21 (1964–1966), 308–309.

—— '*Bardd Teulu* and *Pencerdd*', in T. M. Charles-Edwards, M. E. Owen and P. Russell (eds.), *The Welsh King and his Court* (Cardiff, 2000), 142–166.

—— 'The Black Book of Chirk: A note', *National Library of Wales Journal* 15 (1967–1968), 104–107.

—— 'Borrowings in the Welsh Lawbooks', in P. Brand, K. Costello and W. N. Osborough (eds.), *Adventures of the Law: Proceedings of the Sixteenth British Legal History Conference* (Dublin, 2003), 19–39.

—— '"Camsyniadau F.W. Maitland': Y Genedl Alanas Yng Nghyfraith Hywel', *Bulletin of the Board of Celtic Studies* 22 (1966–1968), 228–236.

—— (ed.), *Celtic Law Papers: An Introductory to Welsh Medieval Law and Government* (Brussels, 1973).

—— *Conspectus of the Manuscripts of the Cyfnerth Redaction* (Texts and Studies in Medieval Welsh Law I, Cambridge, 2010).

—— 'Crime and Tort and the Three Columns of Law', in T. M. Charles-Edwards and P. Russell (eds.), *Tair Colofn Cyfraith* (Welsh Legal History Society Vol. V, Bangor, 2007), 1–25.

—— 'Custom in Welsh Medieval Law', in A. Gouron (ed.), *La Coutume, Deuxième Partie: Europe Occidentale Médiévale et Moderne* (Brussels, 1990), 421–433.

—— 'The "Cyfnerth" Text', in D. Jenkins and M. E. Owen (eds.), *The Welsh Law of Women* (Cardiff, 1980), 132–145.

—— *Cyfraith Hywel: Rhagarweiniad i Gyfraith Gynhenid Cymru'r Oesau Canol* (Llandysul, 1970).

—— '*Cynghellor* and Chancellor', *Bulletin of the Board of Celtic Studies* 27 (1976–1978), 115–118.

—— *Damweiniau Colan* (Aberystwyth, 1973).

—— 'The Date of the "Act of Union"', *Bulletin of the Board of Celtic Studies* 23 (1968–1970), 345–346.

—— 'Deddfgrawn William Maurice', *National Library of Wales Journal* 2 (1941), 33–36.

—— 'English Law and the Renaissance. Eighty Years On: In Defence of Maitland', *The Journal of Legal History* 2 (1981), 107–142.

—— 'Excursus: The Lawbooks and their Relation', in T. M. Charles-Edwards, M. E. Owen and P. Russell (eds.), *The Welsh King and his Court* (Cardiff, 2000), 10–14.

—— 'A Family of Medieval Welsh Lawyers', in D. Jenkins (ed.), *Celtic Law Papers* (Brussels, 1973), 121–133.

—— '*Gwalch*: Welsh', *Cambridge Medieval Celtic Studies* 19 (1990), 53–67.

—— 'Gwilym Was Da', *Cylchgrawn Llyfrgell Genedlaethol Cymru* 21 (1980), 429.

—— 'Hawk and Hound: Hunting in the Laws of Court', in T. M. Charles-Edwards, M. E. Owen and P. Russell (eds.), *The Welsh King and his Court* (Cardiff, 2000), 255–280.

—— 'The Horse in the Welsh Law Texts' in S. Davies and N. A. Jones (eds.), *The Horse in Celtic Culture: Medieval Welsh Perspectives* (Cardiff, 1997), 64–81.

—— 'A Hundred Years of Cyfraith Hywel', *Zeitschrift für Celtische Philologie* 49–50 (1997), 349–366.

—— *Hunting and Husbandry in Medieval Welsh Law* (Hallstatt Lecture 1993, Machynlleth, 1993).

—— *Hywel Dda a'r Gwŷr Cyfraith: Darlith Agoriadol* (Aberystwyth, 1977).

Bibliography

—— 'Iorwerth ap Madog: Gŵr Cyfraith o'r Drydedd Ganrif Ar Ddeg', *National Library of Wales Journal* 8 (1953), 164–170.
—— 'Iorwerth ap Madog a Hywel Dda': Review of *Llyfr Iorwerth: A Critical Text of the Venedotian Code of Medieval Welsh Law*, *Lleufer* 17 (1961), 17–33.
—— 'Kings, Lords, and Princes: The Nomenclature of Authority in Thirteenth-Century Wales', *Bulletin of the Board of Celtic Studies* 26 (1974–1976), 451–462.
—— 'Law and Government in Wales Before the Act of Union', in D. Jenkins (ed.), *Celtic Law Papers* (Brussels, 1973), 23–48.
—— 'The Lawbooks of Medieval Wales', in R. Eales and D. Sullivan (eds.), *The Political Context of Law* (Canterbury, 1985), 1–15.
—— *The Law of Hywel Dda: Law Texts from Medieval Wales* (Llandysul, 1986).
—— 'A Lawyer Looks at Welsh Land Law', *Transactions of the Honourable Society of the Cymmrodorion* (1967), 220–246.
—— 'Legal and Comparative Aspects of the Welsh Laws', *Welsh History Review Special Number: The Welsh Laws* (1963), 51–59.
—— 'Legal History at Aberystwyth', *Cambrian Law Review* 34 (2003), 27–56.
—— 'Llawysgrif Goll Llanforda o Gyfreithiau Hywel Dda', *Bulletin of the Board of Celtic Studies* 14 (1951–1952), 89–104.
—— (ed.), *Llyfr Colan* (Cardiff, 1963).
—— 'The Medieval Welsh Idea of Law', *Tijdschrift voor Rechtsgeschiednis* 49 (1981), 323–348.
—— 'Nodiadau amrywiol: (1) Gwad cyn dedfryd', *Bulletin of the Board of Celtic Studies* 25 (1972–1974), 112–118.
—— 'Nodiadau Cymysg: (1) distain; (2) cestyll: castra: lluestau; (3) nythod: nisi: llamysten', *Bulletin of the Board of Celtic Studies* 22 (1966–1968), 127–129.
—— 'Pencerdd a Bardd Teulu', *Ysgrifau Beirniadol* 14 (1988), 19–44.
—— 'Prolegomena to the Welsh Laws of Court', in T. M. Charles-Edwards, M. E. Owen and P. Russell (eds.), *The Welsh King and his Court* (Cardiff, 2000), 15–28.
—— 'Property Interests in the Classical Welsh Law of Women', in D. Jenkins and M. E. Owen (eds.), *The Welsh Law of Women* (Cardiff, 1980), 69–92.
—— Review of Melville Richards, *Cyfreithiau Hywel Dda, o Lawysgrif Coleg yr Iesu LVII*, *Welsh History Review* 1 (1960), 106.
—— 'Said: Gwrmsaid, Gwynsaid; Yslipanu', *Bulletin of the Board of Celtic Studies* 35 (1988), 55–61.
—— 'A Second Look at Welsh Land Law', *Transactions of the Honourable Society of the Cymmrodorion* (2001), 13–93.
—— 'The Significance of the Law of Hywel', *Transactions of the Honourable Society of the Cymmrodorion* (1977), 54–76.
—— 'Sylwadau ar y Surexit', *Bulletin of the Board of Celtic Studies* 28 (1978–1980), 607–612.
—— 'Towards the Jury in Medieval Wales' in J. W. Cairns and G. McLeod (eds.), *The Dearest Birth Right of the People of England: The Jury in the History of the Common Law* (Oxford, 2002), 17–46.
—— 'Welsh Law in Carmarthenshire', *The Carmarthenshire Antiquary* 18 (1982), 17–25.
—— 'The Welsh Marginalia in the Lichfield Gospels Part I', *Cambridge Medieval Celtic Studies* 5 (1983), 37–66.
—— 'The Welsh Marginalia in the Lichfield Gospels Part II: The 'Surexit' Memorandum', *Cambridge Medieval Celtic Studies* 7 (1984), 91–120.
—— 'Yr Ynad Coch', *Bulletin of the Board of Celtic Studies* 22 (1966–1968), 345–346.
—— 'Ysgar Mewn Cyfraith a Chrefydd', *Y Traethodydd* 125 (1970), 35–47.
—— and E. Anners, 'A Swedish Borrowing from Welsh Medieval Law?', *Welsh History Review* 1 (1960), 325–333.
—— and M. E. Owen (eds.), *The Welsh Law of Women* (Cardiff, 1980).
Jenkins, Geraint H. (ed.), *A Rattleskull Genius: The Many Faces of Iolo Morganwg* (Cardiff, 2009).

Bibliography

Johnson, L., '*Amobr* and *Amobrwyr*: The Collection of Marriage Fees and Sexual Fines in Late Medieval Wales', *Transactions of the Honourable Society of the Cymmrodorion* 18 (2012), 10–21.

—— 'Sex and the Single Welshwoman: Prostitution and Concubinage in Late Medieval Wales', *Welsh History Review* 27 (2014), 253–281.

Johnston, N., 'An Investigation into the Locations of the Royal Courts of Thirteenth-century Gwynedd', in N. Edwards (ed.), *Landscape and Settlement in Medieval Wales* (Oxford, 1997), 41–69.

Jones, G. R. J., 'Llys and Maerdref', in T. M. Charles-Edwards, M. E. Owen and P. Russell (eds.), *The Welsh King and his Court* (Cardiff, 2000), 296–318.

—— 'The Models for Organisation in Llyfr Iorwerth and Llyfr Cyfnerth', *Bulletin of the Board of Celtic Studies* 39 (1992), 95–118.

Jones, J. Ll., 'Gweilydd', *Bulletin of the Board of Celtic Studies* 11 (1941–1944), 37–38.

Jones, O., Williams E. and Pughe, W. O. (eds.), *The Myvyrian Archaiology of Wales: Collected out of Ancient Manuscripts* (2nd edn., Denbigh, 1870).

Jones, T., *Brut y Tywysogyon or the Chronicle of the Princes Peniarth MS. 20 Version, Translated with an Introduction and Notes* (Cardiff, 1952).

Jones, T. G., 'Social Life as Reflected in the Laws of Hywel Dda', *Aberystwyth Studies X: The Hywel Dda Millenary Volume* (1928), 103–128.

Jones Pierce, T., 'The Law of Wales – the Kindred and the Bloodfeud', in J. B. Smith (ed.), *Medieval Welsh Society: Selected Essays by T. Jones Pierce* (Cardiff, 1972), 289–308.

—— 'The Law of Wales – the Last Phase', in J. B. Smith (ed.), *Medieval Welsh Society: Selected Essays by T. Jones Pierce* (Cardiff, 1972), 369–389.

—— 'Social and Historical Aspects of the Welsh Laws' in J. B. Smith (ed.), *Medieval Welsh Society: Selected Essays by T. Jones Pierce* (Cardiff, 1972), 353–368.

Kelly, F., *A Guide to Early Irish Law* (Dublin, 1988).

—— 'An Old Irish Text on Court Procedure', *Peritia* 5 (1986), 74–106.

Keynes, S. and Lapidge, M., *Alfred the Great: Asser's Life of King Alfred and Other Contemporary Sources* (London, 1983).

Kirby, D. P., 'Hywel Dda: Anglophil?', *Welsh History Review* 8 (1976), 1–13.

Koch, J. T. (ed.), *Celtic Culture: A Historical Encyclopedia* (5 vols., Aberystwyth, 2006).

Lambert, T., *Law and Order in Anglo-Saxon England* (Oxford, 2017).

Larson, L. M., *The King's Household in England Before the Norman Conquest* (Madison, 1904).

Levi, T. A., 'The Laws of Hywel Dda in the Light of Roman and Early English Law', *Aberystwyth Studies X: The Hywel Dda Millenary Volume* (1928), 5–64.

Lewis, E. A., 'The Proceedings of the Small Hundred Court of the Commote of Ardudwy in the Court of Merioneth from 8 October 1325, to 18 September 1326', *Bulletin of the Board of Celtic Studies* 4 (1928–1929), 153–166.

Lewis, H., *The Ancient Laws of Wales* (London, 1889).

Lewis, S., *Braslun o Hanes Llenyddiaeth Gymraeg. Y Gyfrol Gyntaf: Hyd at 1535* (Cardiff, 1932).

Lewis, T., 'A Bibliography of the Laws of Hywel Dda', *Aberystwyth Studies X: The Hywel Dda Millenary Volume* (1928), 151–182.

—— 'Copy of the Black Book of Chirk Peniarth MS 29 National Library of Wales Aberystwyth', *Zeitschrift für Celtische Philologie* 20 (1936), 30–96.

—— *Glossary of Medieval Welsh Law* (Manchester, 1913).

—— *The Laws of Hywel Dda: A Facsimile Reprint of Llanstephan MS 116 in the National Library of Wales* (London, 1912).

Lieberman, M., *The March of Wales 1067–1300* (Cardiff, 2008).

—— *The Medieval March of Wales: The Creation and Perception of a Frontier, 1066–1283* (Cambridge, 2010).

Linnard, W., 'Beech and the Lawbooks', *Bulletin of the Board of Celtic Studies* 28 (1978–1980), 605–607.

—— 'The Nine Huntings: A Re-Examination of Y Naw Helwriaeth', *Bulletin of the Board of Celtic Studies* 31 (1984), 119–132.

Bibliography

—— *Trees in the Law of Hywel* (Pamffledi Cyfraith Hywel/Welsh Law Pamphlets, Aberystwyth, 1979).
Lloyd, J. E., 'The Date of the Act of Union of England and Wales', *Bulletin of the Board of Celtic Studies* 7 (1934), 192.
—— *A History of Wales from the Earliest Times to the Edwardian Conquest* (2 vols., London, 1911).
—— 'Hywel Dda: The Historical Setting', *Aberystwyth Studies X: The Hywel Dda Millenary Volume* (1928), 1–4.
Lloyd, N., 'Meredith Lloyd', *Journal of the Welsh Bibliographical Society* 11 (1975–1976), 133–192.
Lynch, P., 'Court Poetry, Power and Politics', in T. M. Charles-Edwards, M. E. Owen and P. Russell (eds.), *The Welsh King and his Court* (Cardiff, 2000), 167–190.
Mac Cana, P., 'Irish *Maccóem*, Welsh *Makwyf*', *Ériu* 42 (1991), 27–36.
MacNeill, E., 'Ireland and Wales in the History of Jurisprudence', in D. Jenkins (ed.), *Celtic Law Papers* (Brussels, 1973), 171–192.
Maitland, F., 'The Laws of Wales – the Kindred and the Blood Feud', in H. A. L. Fisher (ed.), *The Collected Papers of F. W. Maitland* (Cambridge, 1911), vol. I, 202–229.
—— 'The Tribal System in Wales', in H. A. L. Fisher (ed.), *The Collected Papers of F. W. Maitland* (Cambridge, 1911), vol. III, 1–10.
Maund, K., *The Welsh Kings: The Medieval Rulers of Wales* (Stroud, 2000).
McAll, C., 'The Normal Paradigms of a Woman's Life in the Irish and Welsh Texts', in D. Jenkins and M. E. Owen (eds.), *The Welsh Law of Women* (Cardiff, 1980), 7–22.
Means, R., 'Politics, Mirrors of Princes and the Bible: Sins, King and the Well-Being of the Realm', *Early Medieval Europe* 7 (1998), 345–357.
Milsom, S. F. C., *Historical Foundations of the Common Law* (Oxford, 1981).
Morris, J. E., *The Welsh Wars of Edward I* (Oxford, 1901).
Morris-Jones, J., 'Taliesin: Appendix II, The Surexit Memorandum', *Y Cymmrodor* 28 (1918), 268–279.
Mühlhausen, L., *The Chirk Codes of the Welsh Laws, nach dem Facsimile von J. Gwenogvryn Evans, Umschrift* (n.p., 1932).
Musson, A., *Medieval Law in Context: The Growth of Legal Consciousness from Magna Carta to the Peasants' Revolt* (Manchester, 2001).
Owen, A. (ed. and transl.), *Ancient Laws and Institutes of Wales* (2 vols, London, 1841).
Owen, M. E., 'The Animals of the Law of Hywel', *Carmarthenshire Antiquary* 45 (2009), 5–27.
—— 'Bwrlwm Llys Dinefwr: Brenin, Bardd a Meddyg', *Carmarthenshire Antiquary* 32 (1996), 5–15.
—— 'Cyfnerth Manuscript X', in T. M. Charles-Edwards and P. Russell (eds.), *Tair Colofn Cyfraith* (Welsh Legal History Society Vol. V, Bangor, 2007), 238–257.
—— 'The "Cyfnerth" Text', in T. M. Charles-Edwards, M. E. Owen and D. B. Walters (eds.), *Lawyers and Laymen* (Cardiff, 1986), 179–200.
—— 'Y Cyfreithiau (1) – Natur y Testunau', in G. Bowen (ed.), *Y Traddodiad Rhyddiaith yn yr Oesau Canol* (Llandysul, 1974), 196–218.
—— 'Y Cyfreithiau (2) – Ansawdd y Rhyddiaith', in G. Bowen (ed.), *Y Traddodiad Rhyddiaith yn yr Oesau Canol* (Llandysul, 1974), 220–244.
—— 'Cynllwyn a Dynyorn', *Bulletin of the Board of Celtic Studies* 22 (1966–1968), 346–350.
—— 'The Excerpta de Libris Romanorum et Francorum and Welsh Law', in T. M. Charles-Edwards and P. Russell (eds.), *Tair Colofn Cyfraith* (Welsh Legal History Society Vol. V, Bangor, 2007), 171–195.
—— 'A Fifteenth-Century Lawbook From Cefnllys', *Transactions of the Radnorshire Society* 81 (2011), 77–93.
—— 'Functional Prose: Religion, Science, Grammar, Law', in A. O. H. Jarman and G. R. Hughes (eds.), *A Guide to Welsh Literature Vol. 1* (Cardiff, 1992), 248–276.
—— 'Gwŷr Dysg Yr Oesoedd Canol', *Ysgrifau Beirniadol* 17 (1990), 42–62.

Bibliography

—— 'Llawysgrif Gyfreithiol Goll', *Bulletin of the Board of Celtic Studies* 22 (1966–1968), 338–343.
—— (ed. and transl.), 'The Laws of Court from Cyfnerth', in T. M. Charles-Edwards, M. E. Owen and P. Russell (eds.), *The Welsh King and his Court* (Cardiff, 2000), 425–477.
—— 'Medics and Medicine', in T. M. Charles-Edwards, M. E. Owen and P. Russell (eds.), *The Welsh King and his Court* (Cardiff, 2000), 116–141.
—— *Y Meddwl Obsesiynol: Traddodiad y Triawd Cyffredinol yn y Gymraeg a'r Myvyrian Archaiology of Wales* (Aberystwyth, 2007).
—— '*Meddygon Myddfai*: Who Were They and What Did They Know?', *Carmarthenshire Antiquary* 47 (2011), 30–43.
—— 'Royal Propaganda: Stories from the Law-Texts', in T. M. Charles-Edwards, M. E. Owen and P. Russell (eds.), *The Welsh King and his Court* (Cardiff, 2000), 224–254.
—— 'Shame and Reparation: Women's Place in the Kin', in D. Jenkins and M. E. Owen (eds.), *The Welsh Law of Women* (Cardiff, 1980), 40–68.
—— 'Tân: The Welsh Law of Arson and Negligent Burning', in T. M. Charles-Edwards and P. Russell (eds.), *Tair Colofn Cyfraith* (Welsh Legal History Society Vol. V, Bangor, 2007), 131–145.
—— 'Y Trioedd Arbennig', *Bulletin of the Board of Celtic Studies* 24 (1970–1972), 434–450.
—— 'Welsh Triads: An Overview', *Celtica* 25 (2007), 225–250.
Parry-Williams, T. H., 'The Language of the Laws of Hywel Dda', *Aberystwyth Studies X: The Hywel Dda Millenary Volume* (1928), 129–150.
Patterson, N. W., 'Honour and Shame in Medieval Welsh Society: A Study of the Role of Burlesque in the Welsh Laws', *Studia Celtica* 16/17 (1981), 73–103.
—— 'Patrilineal Kinship in Early Irish Society', *Bulletin of the Board of Celtic Studies* 37 (1990), 133–165.
Powell, J. E., 'Floating Sections in the Law of Hywel', *Bulletin of the Board of Celtic Studies* 9 (1937–1939), 27–34
—— 'The Trinity College manuscript of Hywel Dda', *Bulletin of the Board of Celtic Studies* 8 (1936), 120–124.
Pryce, H., 'Anglo-Welsh Agreements, 1201–77', in R. A. Griffiths and P. R. Schofield (eds.), *Wales and the Welsh in the Middle Ages: Essays Presented to J. Beverley Smith* (Cardiff, 2011), 70–88.
—— 'The Context and Purpose of the Earliest Welsh Lawbooks', *Cambrian Medieval Celtic Studies* 39 (2000), 39–63.
—— 'Duw yn Lle Mach: Briduw yng Nghyfraith Hywel', in T. M. Charles-Edwards, M. E. Owen and D. B. Walters (eds.), *Lawyers and Laymen* (Cardiff, 1986), 47–71.
—— 'Ecclesiastical Sanctuary in Thirteenth-century Welsh law', *The Journal of Legal History* 5.3 (1984), 1–13. Reprinted in A. Kiralfy et al. (eds.), *Custom, Courts and Counsel* (London, 1985), 1–13.
—— 'Early Irish Canons and Medieval Welsh Law', *Peritia* 5 (1986), 107–127.
—— 'Yr Eglwys a'r Gyfraith yng Nghymru'r Oesoedd Canol', in G. H. Jenkins (ed.), *Cof Cenedl* X (Llandysul, 1995), 1–30.
—— 'Harry Longueville Jones, FSA, Medieval Paris and the Heritage Measures of the July Monarchy', *Antiquaries Journal* 96 (2016), 391–414.
—— 'The Household Priest (*Offeiriad Teulu*)', in T. M. Charles-Edwards, M. E. Owen and P. Russell (eds.), *The Welsh King and his Court* (Cardiff, 2000), 82–93.
—— 'Lawbooks and Literacy in Medieval Wales', *Speculum* 75 (2000), 29–67.
—— (ed.) *Literacy in Medieval Celtic Societies* (Cambridge, 1998).
—— 'Mathrafal: The Evidence of Written Sources', *The Montgomeryshire Collections* 83 (1995), 61–65.
—— 'Medieval Welsh Law', *Newsletter of the School of Celtic Studies* (Dublin Institute of Advanced Studies) 4 (1990), 30–34.
—— *Native Law and the Church in Medieval Wales* (Oxford, 1993).
—— 'The Prologues to the Welsh Lawbooks', *Bulletin of the Board of Celtic Studies* 33 (1986), 151–182.

Bibliography

―― 'Welsh Custom and Canon Law, 1150–1300' in K. Pennington, S. Chodorow and K. H. Kendall (eds.), *Proceedings of the Tenth International Congress of Medieval Canon Law* (Vatican City, 2001), 781–797.
Rees E. and Walters, G., 'The Dispersion of the Manuscripts of Edward Lhuyd', *Welsh History Review* 7 (1974), 148–180.
Rees, W., *South Wales and the March 1284–1415: A Social and Agrarian Study* (Oxford, 1924).
Rhys, J. and D. Brynmor-Jones, *The Welsh People* (London, 1900).
Richards, M., *Cyfreithiau Hywel Dda yn ôl Llawysgrif Coleg yr Iesu LVII* (2nd ed., Cardiff, 1990).
―― *The Laws of Hywel Dda* (Liverpool, 1954).
Roberts, B. F., 'The Red Book of Hergest Version of *Brut y Brenhinedd*', *Studia Celtica* 12–13 (1977–1978), 147–186.
―― 'Rhai Swynion Cymraeg', *Bulletin of the Board of Celtic Studies* 21 (1964–1966), 197–213.
Roberts, S. E., 'Addysg Broffesiynol yng Nghymru yn yr Oesoedd Canol: Y Beirdd a'r Cyfreithwyr', *Llên Cymru* 26 (2003), 1–17.
―― '"By the Authority of the Devil": The Operation of Welsh and English Law in Medieval Wales', in S. Meecham-Jones and R. Kennedy (eds.), *Authority and Subjugation in the Writing of Medieval Wales* (New York, 2008), 85–97.
―― 'Creu Trefn o Anhrefn: Gwaith Copïydd Testun Cyfreithiol', *National Library of Wales Journal* 32 (2002), 397–420.
―― 'Cyfraith, Carchar a Chastell: Hynt a Hanes Llawysgrif Gyfreithiol', *Transactions of the Honourable Society of the Cymmrodorion* (2013), 24–40.
―― 'Dafydd Jenkins – Scholar of *Cyfraith Hywel*', in T. G. Watkin and N. S. B. Cox (eds.), *Canmlwyddiant, Cyfraith a Chymreictod* (Welsh Legal History Society Vol. XI, Bangor, 2013), 222–228.
―― 'Emerging from the Bushes: The Welsh Law of Women and the Legal Triads', in J. F. Eska (ed.), *Law, Literature and Society: CSANA Yearbook 7* (Dublin, 2008), 58–76.
―― '"Gwreic wyf fi": Transition to Womanhood in Medieval Wales', in S. Niebrzydowski (ed.), *Middle-Aged Women in the Middle Ages* (Cambridge, 2011), 25–36.
―― 'The Iorwerth Triads', in F. Edmonds and P. Russell (eds.), *Tome: Studies in Medieval Celtic History and Law in Honour of Thomas Charles-Edwards* (Woodbridge, 2011), 155–174.
―― 'Law Texts, Celtic [2] Welsh', in J. T. Koch et al. (eds.), *Celtic Culture: A Historical Encyclopedia* (Santa Barbara, 2006), 1112.
―― 'Law Texts and their Sources in Medieval Wales: The Case of H and Tails of Other Legal Manuscripts', *Welsh History Review* 24 (2008), 41–59.
―― 'Legal Practice in Fifteenth-Century Brycheiniog', *Studia Celtica* 35 (2001), 307–323.
―― (ed. and transl.), *The Legal Triads of Medieval Wales* (Cardiff, 2007).
―― (ed. and transl.), *Llawysgrif Pomffred: An Edition and Study of Peniarth MS 259B* (Leiden and Boston, 2011).
―― 'Living off the Land in Medieval Welsh Law', in Rh. Comeau and A. Seaman (eds.), *Living off the Land: Agriculture in Wales c. 400–1600 AD* (Oxford, 2019), 78–92.
―― 'More Plaints in Medieval Welsh law', *Studia Celtica* 48 (2014), 171–199.
―― 'Plaints in Welsh Mediaeval Law', *Journal of Celtic Studies* 4 (2004), 219–261.
―― 'A Rather Laborious and Harassing Occupation': The Creation of the *Ancient Laws and Institutes of Wales* (1841)', in T. Gobbitt (ed), *Law, Book, Culture in the Early and High Middle Ages* (Leiden and Boston, 2020), 376–397.
―― '*Tri Dygyngoll Cenedl*: The Development of a Triad', *Studia Celtica* 37 (2003), 163–182.
―― *The Welsh Legal Triads* (London, Selden Society, 2015). Also published as 'The Welsh Legal Triads' in T. G. Watkin (ed.), *The Welsh Legal Triads* (Welsh Legal History Society Vol. XII, Bangor, 2015), 1–22.
―― 'What's Yours is Mine: Cyfraith Hywel and the Law of the March' (Mortimer History Society Essay Prize Winner, 2018/2019). *Journal of the Mortimer History Society* 3 (2019), 1–15.
―― and James, C. (ed. and transl.), *Archwilio Cymru'r Oesoedd Canol: Testunau o Gyfraith Hywel* (Texts and Studies in Medieval Welsh Law IV, Cambridge, 2015).

Bibliography

Roderick, A. J., 'The Dispute Between Llywelyn ap Gruffydd and Gruffydd ap Gwenwynwyn (1278–1282)', *Bulletin of the Board of Celtic Studies* 8 (1936), 248–254.

Rowland, J., 'The Maiming of Horses in Branwen', *Cambrian Medieval Celtic Studies* 63 (2012), 51–69.

Russell, P., 'The Arrangement and Development of the Three Columns Tractate', in T. M. Charles-Edwards and P. Russell (eds.), *Tair Colofn Cyfraith* (Welsh Legal History Society Vol. V, Bangor, 2007), 60–91.

—— '*Canyt oes aruer*. Gwilym Wasta and the laws of court in Welsh law', *North American Journal of Celtic Studies* 1, no.2 (2017), 173–188.

—— 'The Etymology of *Affaith* "Abetment"', *Bulletin of the Board of Celtic Studies* 38 (1991), 104–110.

—— 'From Plates and Rods to Royal Drink-Stands in Branwen and Medieval Welsh Law', *North American Journal of Celtic Studies* 1, no.1 (2017), 1–26.

—— 'The Languages and Registers of Law in Medieval Ireland and Wales', in J. Benham, M. McHaffie and H. Vogt (eds.), *Law and Language in the Middle Ages* (Leiden and Boston, 2018), 83–103.

—— 'Latin D', in T. M. Charles-Edwards and P. Russell (eds.), *Tair Colofn Cyfraith* (Welsh Legal History Society Vol. V, Bangor, 2007), 213–237.

—— 'The Laws of Court from Latin B', in T. M. Charles-Edwards, M. E. Owen and P. Russell (eds.), *The Welsh King and his Court* (Cardiff, 2000), 478–526.

—— 'Llyfr Du o'r Waun', in J. T. Koch (ed.), *Celtic Culture: A Historical Encyclopedia* (Santa Barbara, 2006), 1175.

—— '*Priuilegium sancti Teliaui* and *Breint Teilo*', *Studia Celtica* 50 (2016), 41–68.

—— '*Y Naw Affaith*: Aiding and Abetting in Welsh Law', in T. M. Charles-Edwards and P. Russell (eds.), *Tair Colofn Cyfraith* (Welsh Legal History Society Vol. V, Bangor, 2007), 146–170.

—— 'Orthography as a Key to Codicology: Innovation in the Work of a Thirteenth-century Welsh Scribe', *Cambridge Medieval Celtic Studies* 25 (1993), 77–85.

—— 'Poetry by Numbers': The Poetic Triads in *Gramadegau Penceirddiaid*', in D. Hayden and P. Russell (eds.), *Grammatica, Gramadach and Gramadeg* (Amsterdam and Philadelphia, 2016), 161–180.

—— *The Prologues to the Medieval Welsh Lawbooks*, Basic Texts for Brittonic History 3 (Cambridge, 2004).

—— 'Scribal (In)Competence in Thirteenth-Century North Wales: The Orthography of the Black Book of Chirk (Peniarth MS. 29)', *National Library of Wales Journal* 29 (1995–1996), 129–176.

—— '*Swydd, Swyddog, Swyddwr*: Office, Officer and Official', in T. M. Charles-Edwards, M. E. Owen and P. Russell (eds.), *The Welsh King and his Court* (Cardiff, 2000), 281–295.

—— (ed. and transl.), *Vita Griffini Filii Conani: The Medieval Latin Life of Gruffudd ap Cynan* (Cardiff, 2006).

—— (ed. and transl.), *Welsh Law in Medieval Anglesey. British Library, Harleian MS 1796 (Latin C)* (Texts and Studies in Medieval Welsh Law II, Cambridge, 2011).

Samuel, W. I., 'The Ancient Laws of Dyfed', *The Pembrokeshire Historian: Journal of the Pembrokeshire Local History Society* 3 (1971), 42–52.

Schofield, P. R., 'English Law and Welsh Marcher Courts in the Late Thirteenth and Early Fourteenth Centuries', in R. A. Griffiths and P. R. Schofield (eds.), *Wales and the Welsh in the Middle Ages: Essays Presented to J. Beverley Smith* (Cardiff, 2011), 70–88.

Seebohm, F., *The Tribal System in Wales* (London, 1895).

Shaw, P. A., 'Telling a Hawk from an Herodio: On the Origins and Development of the Old English Word *Wealhhafoc* and its Relatives', *Medium Ævum* 82 (2013), 1–22.

Sheringham, J. G. T., 'Bullocks with Horns as Long as their Ears', *Bulletin of the Board of Celtic Studies* 29 (1981–1982), 691–708.

Smith, J. B., 'Dower in Thirteenth-Century Wales: a Grant of the Commote of Anhuniog, 1273', *Bulletin of the Board of Celtic Studies* 30 (1982–1983), 348–355.

Bibliography

—— 'Dynastic Succession in Medieval Wales', *Bulletin of the Board of Celtic Studies* 33 (1986), 199–232.
—— (ed.), 'Edward I and the Conflict of Laws', in M. Prestwich, R. H. Britnell and R. Frame (eds.), *Thirteenth Century England VII: Proceedings of the Durham Conference 1997* (Woodbridge, 1999), 189–205.
—— 'Judgment Under the Law of Wales', *Studia Celtica* 39 (2005), 63–103.
—— 'Land Endowments of the Period of Llywelyn ap Gruffudd', *Bulletin of the Board of Celtic Studies* 34 (1987), 150–164.
—— *Llywelyn ap Gruffudd: Prince of Wales* (Cardiff, 1998; 2nd ed. 2014).
—— *Llywelyn ap Gruffudd: Tywysog Cymru* (Cardiff, 1986).
—— (ed.), *Medieval Welsh Society: Selected Essays by T. Jones Pierce* (Cardiff, 1972).
—— 'Ynad Llys, Brawdwr Llys, Iudex Curie', in T. M. Charles-Edwards, M. E. Owen and P. Russell (eds.), *The Welsh King and his Court* (Cardiff, 2000), 94–115.
—— and Smith, Ll. B., 'Wales: Politics, Government and Law', in S. H. Rigby (ed.), *A Companion to Britain in the Later Middle Ages* (Malden, 2007), 309–334.
Smith, Ll. B., '"Cannwyll Dibwyll a Dosbarth": Gwŷr Cyfraith Ceredigion yn yr Oesoedd Canol Diweddar', *Ceredigion* 10 (1986), 229–253.
—— 'A Contribution to the History of "Galanas" in Late-Medieval Wales', *Studia Celtica* 43 (2009), 87–94.
—— 'Disputes and Settlements in Medieval Wales: The Role of Arbitration', *English Historical Review* 106 (1991), 835–860.
—— 'Family, Land and Inheritance in Late Medieval Wales: A Case Study of Llannerch in the Lordship of Dyffryn Clwyd', *Welsh History Review* 27 (2014), 417–458.
—— 'Fosterage and God-parenthood: Ritual and Fictive Kinship in Medieval Wales', *Welsh History Review* 16 (1992), 1–35.
—— 'The Gage and the Land Market in Late-Medieval Wales', *The Economic History Review* 29 (1976), 537–550.
—— 'The Gravamina of the Community of Gwynedd against Llywelyn ap Gruffudd', *Bulletin of the Board of Celtic Studies* 31 (1984), 158–176.
—— 'Proofs of Age in Medieval Wales', *Bulletin of the Board of Celtic Studies* 38 (1991), 134–144.
—— 'The Statute of Wales, 1284', *Welsh History Review* 10 (1980), 127–154.
—— 'Tir Prid: Deeds of Gage of Land in Late-Medieval Wales', *Bulletin of the Board of Celtic Studies* 27 (1976–1978), 263–277.
—— 'A View from an Ecclesiastical Court: Mobility and Marriage in a Border Society at the End of the Middle Ages', in R. R. Davies and G. H. Jenkins (eds.), *From Medieval to Modern Wales: Historical Essays in Honour of Kenneth O. Morgan and Ralph A. Griffiths* (Cardiff, 2004), 64–80.
Stacey, R. C., 'The Archaic Core of Llyfr Iorwerth', in T. M. Charles-Edwards, M. E. Owen and D. B. Walters (eds.), *Lawyers and Laymen* (Cardiff, 1986), 15–46.
—— 'Clothes Talk from Medieval Wales', in T. M. Charles-Edwards, M. E. Owen and P. Russell (eds.), *The Welsh King and his Court* (Cardiff, 2000), 338–346.
—— 'Divorce, Medieval Welsh Style', *Speculum* 77 (2002), 1107–1127.
—— 'Hywel in the World', *Haskins Society Journal* 20 (2008), 175–203.
—— 'Instructional Riddles in Welsh Law', in L. Jones and J. F. Nagy (eds.), *Heroic Poets and Poetic Heroes: A Festschrift for Patrick K. Ford* (Dublin, 2004), 336–343.
—— 'King, Queen and *Edling* in the Laws of Court', in T. M. Charles-Edwards, M. E. Owen and P. Russell (eds.), *The Welsh King and his Court* (Cardiff, 2000), 29–62.
—— *Law and the Imagination in Medieval Wales* (Philadelphia, 2018).
—— 'Law and Literature in Ireland and Wales' in H. Fulton (ed.), *Literature and Society in the Celtic Lands* (Dublin, 2005), 65–82.
—— 'Learning to Plead in Medieval Welsh Law', *Studia Celtica* 38 (2004), 107–124.
—— 'Legal Writing in Medieval Wales: Damweiniau I', in T. M. Charles-Edwards and R. J. W. Evans (eds.), *Wales and the Wider World: Welsh History in an International Context* (Oxford, 2011), 57–85.

Bibliography

—— *The Road to Judgment: From Custom to Court in Medieval Ireland and Wales* (Philadelphia, 1994).
—— 'Speaking in Riddles', in P. Ní Chatháin and M. Richter (eds.), *Ireland and Europe in the Early Middle Ages: Texts and Transmission/Irland und Europa im früheren Mittelalter: Texte und Überlieferung* (Dublin, 2002), 243–248.
—— 'Ties that Bind: Immunities in Irish and Welsh Law', *Cambridge Medieval Celtic Studies* 20 (1990), 39–57.
—— (transl.), '*Berrad Airechta*: An Old Irish Tract on Suretyship', in T. M. Charles-Edwards, M. E. Owen and D. B. Walters (eds.), *Lawyers and Laymen* (Cardiff, 1986), 210–233.
—— 'Welsh Law (Native and Canon)' in D. Loades (ed.), *Reader's Guide to British History* (2 vols, New York and London, 2003), 1348–1349.
Stephenson, D., *The Governance of Gwynedd* (Cardiff, 1984).
—— 'The Laws of Court: Past Reality or Present Ideal?', in T. M. Charles-Edwards, M. E. Owen and P. Russell (eds.), *The Welsh King and his Court* (Cardiff, 2000), 400–414.
—— *Medieval Powys: Kingdom, Principality and Lordships, 1132–1293* (Woodbridge, 2016).
—— *Medieval Wales c.1050–1332: Centuries of Ambiguity* (Cardiff, 2019).
—— 'The Middle Ages in the pages of the Montgomeryshire Collections: some re-considerations', *Montgomeryshire Collections* 100 (2012), 67–86.
—— *Thirteenth Century Welsh Law Courts: Some Notes on Procedure and Personnel* (Pamffledi Cyfraith Hywel/Welsh Law Pamphlets, Aberystwyth, 1980).
Stoker, D., 'William Wotton's Exile and Redemption: an Account of the Genesis and Publication of Leges Wallicae', *Welsh Book Studies* 7 (2006), 7–106.
Taylor, A., *The Shape of the State in Medieval Scotland 1124–1290* (Oxford, 2016).
Thornton, D. E., 'The Death of Hywel Dda: A Note', *Welsh History Review* 20 (2001), 743–749.
Thurneysen, R., 'Celtic Law', in D. Jenkins (ed.), *Celtic Law Papers* (Brussels, 1973), 49–70.
Vinogradoff, P., *The Growth of the Manor* (London, 1905).
—— and F. Morgan (eds.), *Survey of the Honour of Denbigh 1334* (London, 1914).
Wade-Evans, A. W. (ed. and transl.), 'Text of Pen. MS. 37 (fols. 61–76) with Translation', *Y Cymmrodor* 17 (1904), 129–163.
—— (ed. and transl.), *Welsh Medieval Law, Being a Text of the Laws of Howel the Good* (Oxford, 1909; repr. Darmstadt, 1979).
Walters, D. B., 'Comparative Aspects of the Tractates on the Laws of Court', in T. M. Charles-Edwards, M. E. Owen and P. Russell (eds.), *The Welsh King and his Court* (Cardiff, 2000), 382–399.
—— *The Comparative Legal Method: Marriage, Divorce and the Spouses' Property Rights in Early Medieval European Law and Cyfraith Hywel* (Pamffledi Cyfraith Hywel/Welsh Law Pamphlets, Aberystwyth, 1980).
—— 'The European Legal Context of the Welsh Law of Matrimonial Property', in D. Jenkins and M. E. Owen (eds.), *The Welsh Law of Women* (Cardiff, 1980), 115–131.
—— 'The General Features of Archaic European Suretyship', in T. M. Charles-Edwards, M. E. Owen and D. B. Walters (eds.), *Lawyers and Laymen* (Cardiff, 1986), 92–116.
—— '*Meddiant* and *Goresgyn*', *Bulletin of the Board of Celtic Studies* 31 (1984), 112–18.
—— 'Roman and Romano-Canonical Law and Procedure in Wales', *Recueil de mémoires et travaux publié par la Société d'histoire du droit et des institutions des anciens pays de droit écrit* 15 (1991), 67–102.
Waters, W. H., *The Edwardian Settlement of North Wales in its Administrative and Legal Aspects (1284–1343)* (Cardiff, 1935).
Watkin, M., 'The Black Book of Chirk and the Orthographia Gallica Anglicana', *National Library of Wales Journal* 14 (1965–1966), 351–360.
—— 'The French Linguistic Influence in Mediaeval Wales', *Transactions of the Honourable Society of Cymmrodorion* (1918–1919), 146–222.
Watkin, T. G., 'Ceremonies, Survivals and Syncretism: Ritual Search in Roman Law and in the Native Laws of Wales', in F.M. d'Ippolito (ed.), *Φιλία: Scritti per Gennaro Franciosi* (Naples, 2007), 2851–2864.
—— 'Cyfraith Cymru', in Tegid Roberts (ed.), *Yr Angen am Furiau* (Llanrwst, 2009), 64–80.

Bibliography

—— 'The Death and Later Life of Legal Symbols: Welsh Legal Symbols after the Union with England', in R. Schulze (ed.), *Symbolische Kommunikation vor Gericht in der frühen Neuzeit* (Berlin, 2006), 213–224.
—— 'Länderbericht: Legal History in England and Wales', *Zeitschrift für Neuere Rechtsgeschichte* 21 (1999), 436–450.
—— 'Legal Cultures in Mediaeval Wales', in T. G. Watkin (ed.), *Legal Wales: Its Past, Its Future* (Welsh Legal History Society Vol. I, Bangor, 2001), 21–39.
—— *The Legal History of Wales* (Cardiff, 2007; 2nd ed. 2012).
—— 'Oxwich Revisited: An Examination of the Background to Herbert's Case (1557–1558)', *Transactions of the Honourable Society of Cymmrodorion* 8 (2002), 94–118.
—— 'Saints, Seaways and Dispute Settlements', in W. M. Gordon and T. D. Fergus (eds.), *Legal History in the Making* (London and Ronceverte, 1991), 1–10.
—— (ed.), *The Welsh Legal Triads and Other Essays* (Welsh Legal History Society XII, Bangor, 2015).
—— and N. S. B. Cox (eds.), *Canmlwyddiant, Cyfraith a Chymreictod. A Celebration of the Life and Work of Dafydd Jenkins, 1911–2012* (Welsh Legal History Society XI, Bangor, 2013).
Wiliam, A. Rh., 'Y Deddfgronau Cymraeg', *National Library of Wales Journal* 8 (1953), 97–103.
—— 'Llyfr Cynghawsedd', *Bulletin of the Board of Celtic Studies* 35 (1988), 73–85.
—— *Llyfr Cynog* (Pamffledi Cyfraith Hywel/Welsh Law Pamphlets (Aberystwyth, 1990).
—— (ed.) *Llyfr Iorwerth: A Critical Text of the* Venedotian Code *of Medieval Welsh Law* (Cardiff, 1960).
—— 'Restoration of the Book of Cynog', *National Library of Wales Journal* 25 (1988), 245–256.
—— 'The Welsh Texts of the Laws', *Welsh History Review Special Number: The Welsh Laws* (1963), 19–23.
Williams, G., *Liability for Animals: Distress Damage Feasant and the Duty to Fence* (Cambridge, 1939).
Williams, I., 'costawg', *Bulletin of the Board of Celtic Studies* 11 (1941–1944), 81–82.
Williams, N. J. A. and T. M. Charles-Edwards, 'The Etymologies of *diffoddi* and *differaf/diffryt*', *Bulletin of the Board of Celtic Studies* 23 (1968–1970), 213–217.
Williams, S. J. (ed.), *Detholion o'r Hen Gyfreithiau Cymreig* (Cardiff, 1938).
Williams, S. J. and J. E. Powell (eds.), *Llyfr Blegywryd* (Cardiff, 1942).
Wormald, P., *The Making of English Law: King Alfred to the Twelfth Century. Vol I: Legislation and its Limits* (Oxford, 1999).
Wotton, W. and M. Williams (eds.), *Cyfreithjeu Hywel Dda ac Ereill seu Leges Wallicae Ecclesiasticae & Civiles Hoeli Boni et Aliorum Walliae Principium* (London, 1730).

Reference Works and Online Resources

13th Century Welsh Prose Manuscripts <https://pure.aber.ac.uk/portal/en/datasets/13thcentury-middle-welsh-prose-manuscripts(3abf4ef1-e364-4cce-859d-92bf4035b303).html>
Cyfraith Hywel Website <http://www.cyfraith-hywel.org.uk>
Dictionary of Welsh Biography (National Library of Wales) <https://biography.wales>
Digital Bodleian Online, Jesus LVII <https://digital.bodleian.ox.ac.uk/objects/91819125-25f1-4533-9fdd-99a4d1c84491/>
Geiriadur Prifysgol Cymru: A Dictionary of the Welsh Language (2nd edn., Cardiff, 2006) [GPC2]
National Library of Wales, Digital Mirror <*https://www.llyfrgell.cymru/darganfod/oriel-ddigidol/llawysgrifau/yr-oesoedd-canol*>
OED Online <www.oed.com/>
Oxford Dictionary of National Biography (Oxford University Press, 2004).
Rhyddiaith Gymraeg 1300–1425 <http://www.rhyddiaithganoloesol.caerdydd.ac.uk/>
Welsh Chronicles Research Group <http://croniclau.bangor.ac.uk/index.php.en>

INDEX

Abetments, Nine, *see Naw affaith*
Adnau 121, 129, 176
Additional material 10, 20, 39–48, 133–5, 147–8, 156–9, 161, 165–6, *and see also* Ch. 4, Ch. 7, *and* Conclusion, *passim; and Cynghawsedd, Damweiniau,* Triads
   Classification by Owen 34–6, 103–4, 134, 162, *and see also* Anomalous Laws
   Difficulty with classification 36–9, 43–7, 131–2, 133–5, 137, 155–9, 162–3, 184–6, 198, 188, 206, 210
   Reappraisal 131, 133, 148–9, 155–9, *and see also* Chs. 5–7 *passim*
Agriculture 69, 70, *and see also* Corn Damage, *Cyfar,* Value of Wild and Tame
Amod 74, 148, 150–1, 154
Ancient Laws and Institutes of Wales, see Ch. 2 *passim. See also* Additional material, Anomalous Laws
   Codes, division of manuscripts between 29, 30–1, 34–7, 38–9, 40, 13, 189, 198
   Codes, naming of 11
   Difficulty of navigating 34
   Idea for a study of Welsh laws 27
   Manuscripts consulted 30, 37
   Manuscripts not consulted 32, 205
   Publication 27–8
   Questions over true authorship 27–8
   Use of sigla 30, 37, 205
   Working method 26, 29, 33–4, 104, 122, 148, 187, 189–90
Animals 12, 18, 24, 69–71, 116, *and see also* Value of Wild and Tame
Anomalous Laws 34–40, *and see also* Additional material, *Ancient Laws and Institutes of Wales*
   Division in *Ancient Laws* 11, 33, 46, 48, 134, 140, 162, 188
   Manuscripts deemed 'anomalous' by Owen 187–91, 193, 202, 206
   Material deemed 'anomalous' by Owen 10, 42–4, 105, 110–12, 120, 127, 129

   Material later in date deemed 'anomalous', 103, 162–3, 184
   Material not deemed 'anomalous' by Owen 148–9
Arbitration 58
Arferion Cyfraith 72–3, 165, 169, 171, 178, 204–5, *and see also* Ch. 5 *passim*
   As third part of Blegywryd 133, 138–9, 145, 148, 158, 171
   Introduction to 128, 137, 143, 146–7, 149, 156, 169
   Incomplete 145–6
   Status as additional material questioned 139, 145, 148–9
Athelstan of Mercia 6

Black Book of Chirk, The, *see* Index of Manuscripts – Peniarth 29 (A)
Bleddyn ap Cynfyn 4, 5, 54, 70, 82–3, 95, 121
Blegywryd Athro 51–2, 54, *and see also* Blegywryd redaction
Blegywryd redaction 41–2, 75, *and see* Ch. 5, *passim, and see also Llyfr Blegywryd*
   Aneurin Owen's categorizations 11, 31, 32, 34, 127, 189–90
   Compared with Iorwerth 63, 76, 78, 85, 108, 141
   Custom 72–3, 75, 83
   Linked to Latin D 14–15, 18, 70, 75, 144, 148, 158, 175
   Manuscripts 14–15, 20–1, 47, 53, 59, 74, 106–7, 111–17, 125, 161, 163–81, 184–5, 189, 194, 203–4, 205, 210, *and see also* Ch. 5 *passim*
   Southern origins 81, 117, 186, 196, 207, *and see also* Ch. 5 *passim*
   Texts found in 55, 56, 57, 69–70, 79–80, 120, 111–15, 120, 125, 127, 130, 141, 204, 207, 210
   The justice 56, 57, 59–60, 62, 64, 66, 85
   Third part 126, 128, *and see also* Ch. 5, *passim*
   Treatment of Laws of Court 63, 64, 74, 115, 192–3
   Triads in 73, 74, 78, 105, 162, 189, 199–201
Book of Llandaf 7–8, 51

Index

Book of Trev Alun 122–3, 124, 153, 190
Book of the White House, Old, see *Llyfr y Ty Gwyn*, *Llyfr Hywel*
Bracton 41, 49, 72 n.135
Braint 59, *and see also Swydd a Braint Brawdwr*
Brawd 55, 57, 67, 116, 138, *and see also* Justices – *Brawdwr*
Brawdlyfr 65, 116, 170
Breint Teilo 8
Briduw 90–1
Brut y Tywysogion 28

Camlwrw 58
Canllaw 65 n.98, 111, 118, 123, 193
Cantref 56
Cefnllys 182, 184
Corn damage 12, 43, 68–72, 96, 98, 108–9, 142, 154, 180, 183, 193
  Contrast with English law 72
  Iorwerth version contrasted with others 70–1, 79
  Links to Iorwerth ap Madog 68, 69, 108
  Test Book 12, 68, 69, 77, 79, 80, 81, 108, 127
'Corpus Hoelianum', see *Deddfgrawn*
Cowyll 88, 98
Customs 23, 40, 50, 72–5, 77, 79–80, 81, 138, 146, 147, 204, 209, 210, *and see also Arferion Cyfraith*, Custom as a source of law *under* Cyfraith Hywel
  Importance 74–5
  In the March 9
  Triads 41, 73–4
  Upholding customs 73–4, 83, 85
Cwyn, Cwynion, see Plaints
Cyfar 68–72, 77, 80, 96, 97–8, 154, 183, 193, 195
  Links to Iorwerth ap Madog 68, 69, 79, 108
  Test Book 12, 17, 68, 69, 79, 108, 127
Cyfarch Cyffyll 80, 98
Cyfnerth ap Morgenau 51, 52, 53, 67, *and see also* Cyfnerth redaction
Cyfran 112, 114
Cyfnerth redaction 16–18, 32, 39, 51–3, 68, 82, 106, 108, 140–4, 161–2, 164, 184, 189, 194
  Gwentian Code renamed 11, 32, 51–3
  Laws of Court in Y 15, 17–18, 32, 115, 177–9, 181, 189
  Texts found in 59, 68–71, 76, 78–9, 105–6, 115, 120, 136, 162, 171, 176, 177–81

Cyfraith Hywel, *see also* Hywel ap Cadell, Law manuscripts, *and individual law topics*
  As lawyer–made law 50
  As *volksrecht* 5, 49, 74
  Comparison to a realm of phantasy and illusion 34
  Comparison to canon or English law 5, 71, 81
  Comparison to rocket science 3
  Custom as a source of law 72–5, 83, *and see also* Customs
  Dating 6, 7, 8, 9, 12
  Influence of Irish law 7
  Unifying factor for Wales 4, 40
Cyfraith Hywel website 10 n.46, 20
Cynefodau, see Customs
Cyngaws 65 n.98, 111–14, 119, 123, 193
Cynghawsedd 21, 39, 42, 44, 55, 58, 65, 78, 80, 105, 110–20, 123–5, 127, 130, 131, 133, 162–3, 169, 178, 207
  In As and Mor 19–20, 37, 110, 116, 164, 189–90, 202–4
  In B 13, 21, 42, 64, 81, 109, 110, 112
  In F 20, 110, 115, 194, 197–8
  In G 13, 110, 112, 115, 194
  In H 19, 110, 201
  In J 110, 154–5
  In Lew 13, 111, 195–6
  In S 117
  In Q 110, 168
  In Z 110, 116, 164
  Lack of modern edition 44, 130
  Linked to North Wales texts 111, 117, 119–20
  Linked to plaints 122, 123–5
  Llyfr Cynghawsedd 13, 43, 58, 81, 105, 110–11, 112–14, 116, 195, 197, 201, 210
  '*O derfydd*' opening 113
  Purpose 113–14
  Replacing *Llyfr Damweiniau* 80, 109
  Status as additional material questioned 111, 114, 131
Cynghellor 61, 143
Cynog, St 66, 105, 121, 122, *and see also Llyfr Cynog*
Cynyr ap Cadwgan 51–4, 66, 82, *and see also Llyfr Cynyr ap Cadwgan*

Dadannudd 112–13, 119
Dafydd Llwyd ap Gwilym 62, 67, 171, 206 n.117
Damweiniau 67, 76–8, 105–10, 111–12, 113, 120, 126, 131, 133, 162–3, 185, 207
  Absent in B and C 80–1, 108–9

236

Index

As 'the poor stepchild' of Welsh law 184
In A 106
In An 205
In Col 19, 106, 163, 191–2
In D and E 13, 106
In Ep 106
In F 20, 107, 112, 197–8
In G 13, 106, 112, 115, 194
In J 106, 154–5
In K 184
In Latin B 142
In Lew 13, 107, 111, 171, 195
In Llanforda (lost) 106
In Mor 203–4
In Q and K 13, 15, 106–8, 109, 166, 167–8, 182–3
In S and Tim 171, 182
In U 36–7, 106, 141–2, 162, 141 *and* 141 n.44, 142
Lack of modern edition 44, 106
Llyfr Damweiniau 13, 44, 64, 78–81, 98–100, 106 n.14, 106–8, 148, 166, 180, 185, 191–2, 195
'*O derfydd*' opening 78, 105, 113
Seen as separate to other texts 21, 43, 105, 162, 184
Status as additional material questioned 44, 108–9, 131
Treatment in *Ancient Laws* 38–9
Treated separately by editors 19, 43–4, 67, 104 n.5, 111, 130 n.126, 163, 184
'Debate Pattern', 76–81, 85, 210, *see also* Iorwerth redaction
Deddfgrawn 26, 47, 188–9, 193–4
De duodecim abusiuis saeculi, see Deuddeg Annoeth
Deheubarth 4, 67, 83
 Association with Blegywryd redaction 11, 63, 134
 Contrast with Gwynedd or Powys 45, 81–2
 Landowner justices 56, 59, 61, 170
Deuddeg Annoeth 173, 175
Diasbad uwch Annwfn 92
Dimetian Code, *see* Blegywryd redaction
Distress Damage Feasant 71–2
Dosbarthwr, see Dosbarthwyr under Justices

Edward I of England 4, 8, 9, 30
Einion ap Gwalchmai 51
Emyn Curig 150–1, 153–4

Family Law 77, 78–9, 83, 94, 127, 155
Fire 113 n.46, 197, 198–9, *and see also Naw Affaith*

Galanas 64, 84, 93–4, 117, 119, 124, 125–6, 127, 129–30, 142, 165–6, 177–8, 183, 194, 197
Glanville 49
Gorfodog 91
Goronwy ap Moriddig 52, 53–4, 67
Gruffudd ab yr Ynad Coch 50
Gruffudd ap Cynan 4
Gruffudd ap Nicolas 165, 182
Gwair ap Rhufon 52, 67
Gwarant 176
Gwentian Code, *see* Cyfnerth redaction
Gwilym Wasta 14, 15, 139, 145, 173, 175, 180
Gwrnerth Lwyd 52–3
Gwybyddiaid 138, 145
Gwynedd 4, 45, 56, 72, 79, 95, 109, 140, 168, 170, 192–3
 Contrast with Powys 81–4
 Earliest law manuscripts 8
 Evidence for lawyers in 50, 52, 54
 Golden era of Welsh law 8, 9, 12, 19, 207
 Lawbooks in 62–3, 64, 66, 67, 71, 77, 82
 Venedotian Code, *see* Iorwerth redaction

Hendy Gwyn ar Daf, *see* Whitland
Henry III of England 8
Holiadon 105, 107, 113–14, 117, 125–30, 144, 180, 182, 194, 203–4
 Status as additional material questioned 131
Honourable Society of the Cymmrodorion, The 27
Humphreys Parry, John 27–8
Hywel ap Cadell (Hywel Dda) 4, 5–7, 11, 24, 30, 36, 40, 52, 63, 122, 209
 Uncertainty of contribution to law 5–6, 7, 44, 49 n.4, 209
 See also Llyfr Hywel
Hywel ap Gruffudd Lloyd 196
Hywel Dda, *see* Hywel ap Cadell
Hywel Fychan (fab Hywel Goch) 14–15, 114, 133, 168

Iddig Ynad 52–3
Ieuan ab Phylip 182
Ieuan ap Dafydd ap Howel 124
Interrogatories, *see Holiadon*
Iolo Morganwg 30 *and* 30 n.42, 39, 190
Iorwerth ap Madog ap Rhahawd 12, 25, 52, 53, 54, 66, 67–8, 69, 71, 77, 79–81, 96, 98, 108, 109, 131, 140, 144, 193, 197, *and also* Iorwerth redaction *and* Test Book

Connection to Iorwerth redaction   12, 51, 54, 63, 64
References to him removed from B   13, 64
Iorwerth redaction   11–13, 21, 39–40, 42–3, 62–4, 67–8, 131, 133–7, 207, *and also* Iorwerth ap Madog ap Rhahawd *and* Test Book
  Authors   52–4
  Dating   12, 15, 32, 54, 63, 114, 140, 185, 193
  Debate Pattern   76–81, 87–100
  In Q and S   166–72
  Manuscripts   11–13, 17, 19–20, 31–2, 54, 59, 62, 64, 68, 125, 128, 143, 156, 163, 171, 181–4, 185, 189–99
  Naming   11–12, 32
  Southern version   151, 153–5, 157, 167–9, 182–4
  Texts in   15–17, 43–4, 55–6, 58, 59, 66, 68–75, 76–81, 83, 87–98, 105–16, 123–4, 126–7, 162–3, 166–7, 177–81, 203–4
  Tripartite arrangement   133–7, 140–5, 210
Irish law   7, 24, 69 n.120, 143, 173
Is Aled   203 n.105

Jones, John (of Gellilyvdy)   200
Justices
  As creators of the law   50, 53, 54, 85
  Brawdwr   55–61, 64–5, 206, *and see also Brawdlyfr*
  Challenging decisions of   64, 66
  Comparison to the king's role in legal cases   56
  Dosbarthwyr   61–3, 67, 75, 85, 171, 185, 196, 206 n.117, 210
  Duties   60, *and see also Swydd a Braint Brawdwr, Brawd, Brawdlyfr*
  Education of   56, 57
  Flexible definition of   52
  In genealogies   50
  Landowners acting as   8, 56, 59–61, 62 n.81, 64, 65
  Named in some lawbooks   51
  Officer of the royal court   55–7, 60
  Role   50, 58, 65, 85, 116, 119
  Role in arbitration   58
  Role in court sessions   58
  Role in society   55
  Terminology in the lawtexts   55, 59
  Training   57, 60, 74, 114, 119, 126–7, 130, 142, 144–5, *and see also Cynghawsedd, Damweiniau,* Test Book
  Twelve selected to make the law at Whitland   52
  Value of the court justice's tongue   57, 65, 73
  Variations between north and south Wales   8, 9, 56, 59, 62, 206
  Ynad, ygneid   50, 52–3, 55, 60, 113, 118, 174
    Profi yneid   56, 126–7, 144, 148–52, 154–5, *and see also Holiadon*
Justices' Test Book, *see* Test Book

Land Law   77–9, 84, 91–4, 127, 152–3, 154–5, 166, 176–7, 178, 194, 201, 203–4, 207, *and see also* Laws of Country
  Cynghawsedd   111–14, 117, 119, 123, 201
  Holiadon   127
  Legal case for land in Iorwerth   55, 56, 58, 111, 162
  Plaints   124
Law manuscripts   9–20, *and see also* the Index of Manuscripts
  Composite   15, 32, 46–7, 154, 162–4, 177, 179, 184–5, 187, 190–1, 193–6
  Dating   3, 6–7, 10–20, 23, 36, 45, *and see also* the Index of Manuscripts
  Editors' personal problems   26–7
  'Floating Sections', *see* Powell, J. Enoch
  Latin versions   3 n.1, 8, 14, 17, 18–19, 26, 30, 36, 39 n.84, 44, 51, 53, 59, 66, 68, 70–1, 74–5, 79, 84, 114, 120, 137, 142–5, 192
  Presuppositions by earlier editors   23–4, 134, 161
  Prologues   6, 24, 52, 63, 166, 194, 197, 200, 205, *and see also* Test Book
  Purpose   23, 50, 62–3, 65–6, 73, 113, 164, 166, 171, 177, 181, 185, 204, 206–7, 210–11
  Size   62, 120, 196
  Source for wider studies   3, 21, 23
  Structure and organisation   24–5, 66, 161, and Ch. 5 *passim*
Law of Women   13, 18, 53, 76, 87–8, 203, *and see also* Laws of Country
  In Iorwerth texts   183
  Missing from K   180–1
  Similarity of tractate in different redactions   78
Laws of Country   24, 76, 137–8, 140, 141, 143, 144, 149, 192
  In Blegywryd texts   170–1, 177, 178
  In Cyfnerth texts   141, 179
  In Iorwerth texts   12, 108, 136, 144, 183–4
  In Y   179–81

238

Index

Outdated section 184
Removal of portions by Iorwerth ap
    Madog 67, 68, 79
Laws of Court 12, 203–4
    Court Justice 55–7, 60, 64, 74
    In Blegywryd texts 16, 20, 42, 60, 63,
        64, 74, 137, 140, 143, 166, 170, 172
    In Cyfnerth texts 140, 141, 142
    In Iorwerth texts 12, 70, 76–7, 87, 108,
        138, 140, 144, 167, 168, 181, 183, 185,
        194
    In Y 15, 17–18, 32, 115, 177–81, 189
    Omitted from manuscripts 15, 20–1, 25,
        42, 60, 63 *and* 63 n.91, 64, 138, 159,
        167 n.28, 168, 170, 172, 179, 181–2,
        183, 185, 192–3, 194, 205
    Opening tractate in lawbooks 24, 63
    Outdated 15, 63, 77, 131, 170, 181–2, 192
    Royal background to law 63–4, 171, 181
Lawyers, *see* Justices
Leges Wallicae 26–7, 28–9, 32
Lewys Glyn Cothi 13, 109, 123, 153, 168,
    181, 182
Lewys Ysgolhaig 13, 171, 195, 196
Lichfield Gospels, *see* Surexit Memorandum
Llanforda lost manuscript 106–7
Llyfr Blegywryd 15, 20, 39, 41, 75, 134,
    145–6, 165, 169, 172–3, 175–6, 177, 185
    Attempt to recreate original 21, 42, 46
    Division of material deemed
        additional 41, 46, 135, 156, 163
Llyfr Cynghawsedd, *see* Cynghawsedd
Llyfr Cynog 66, 130 n.126, 175, 188, 210
    Collection of various legal materials 43,
        105, 122, 128, 129, 193–4
    Links to Powys 82–3, 121
    Relationship to G 112, 115, 120–2, 173,
        175, 193–4
    Relationship to Mor 203–4
    Relationship to Q 175
Llyfr Cynyr ap Cadwgan 51, 52, 82, 173,
    see also Cynyr ap Cadwgan
Llyfr Coch Hergest, *see* Red Book of
    Hergest
Llyfr Damweiniau, *see* Damweiniau
Llyfr Gwyn Hergest, *see* White Book of
    Hergest
Llyfr Gwyn Rhydderch, *see* White Book of
    Rhydderch
Llyfr Hywel 25, 113, 114, 131
'Llyfr Iestyn', 67
Llyfr Prawf Ynaid, *see* Test Book
Llyfr Taliesin 17
Llyfr y Ty Gwyn 25, 39, 40, 67, 197
Llywelyn ab Iorwerth 8, 12, 19

Llywelyn ap Gruffudd 4, 8, 50
Longford, Richard 164
Lord Rhys, *see* Rhys ap Gruffudd

Madog ap Maredudd 82
Maelienydd 52, 82, 184
Maer 143, 169–70
Magna Carta 5 n.9, 8
Mamwys 112
March, The
    Law in 9, 117 n.55, 119, 120, 124, 127,
        182, 183–4, 201–2, 207
    Status of 4, 9, 207
Maredudd ap Bleddyn 82
Maurice, William 10
    Naming of manuscripts 19, 181, 191
    Work on Welsh laws 10–11, 26, 27, 29,
        47, 188, 195, 196, 203
    Work used by Aneurin Owen 11, 26, 30,
        195
Mechniaeth, *see* Suretyship
Merthyr Cynog 121
Model lawbook, concept of 39–47, 48, 103,
    114, 209
Monumenta Historica Britannica 28
Morgenau (Ynad) 52
Myvyrian Archaiology of Wales, The 30

Naw Affaith 84, 130, 142, 165, 183, 189, 197,
    216
Naw Tafodiog 117, 119, 183–4, 192

Owen, Aneurin 27, Ch. 2 *passim*, *and see
    also Ancient Laws and Institutes of
    Wales*

Petrie, Henry 27–8, 29, 34
Plaints 39, 105, 107, 131, 151–2, 153–4, 162,
    166, 168, 185, 189–90, 194
    Linked to *cynghawsedd* 122, 123–5
    Status as additional material
        questioned 131
Ploughing 69, 96–8, 201, *and see also
    Cyfar*
Powell, J. Enoch 41, 46, 135, 167
    'Floating Sections', 41–3
    views on triads 42–3
Powys 4, 31 n.49, 56, 67, 81–4, 121, 122,
    142, 168, 170
Procedure 57, 79–80, 115, 117, 122, 135, 141,
    142, 144, 147–9, 166, 168, 169, 180–2,
    184, 195, 199, 200–2, 204–5, 207, 209,
    210, *and see also Arferion Cyfraith*
    Action for land 78, 113 n.44
    Adapting theft procedure for different
        topics 118–19

Development of law to reflect
procedure 85
Explanation of court procedure 58, 61–2, 71
For accepting or denying a son 83
For appointing an inexperienced court
justice 74
For questioning judgements 72
Use of lawbooks in court procedure 65, 67, 73
Pughe, William Owen 27–8, 205
Punishment for shaving a man's head while
he is asleep 128

Red Book of Hergest 15, 133, 168, 182
Redactions 11–21, 45, 48, 104–5, *and see
also* Blegywryd redaction, Cyfnerth
redaction, Iorwerth redaction
As grouping of manuscripts 10, 25, 31–2
Editions, single redaction 39–42, 104
Manuscripts not fitting the
pattern 19–20, 25, 31–2, 37, 46–7, 187–208
Naming 11, 40, 51–2, 67
Rhingyll 141
Rhol Dafydd Llwyd 15, 62, 67, 156, 170–2, 185, 206, 210
Rhys ap Gruffudd (Lord Rhys) 5, 11, 54, 81, 83

Saith Esgopty Dyfed 7, 121, 204
Sarhaed 53, 57, 59, 81, 84, 94, 115, 124, 126–30, 178, 204
Scribes 3, *and see also* Gwilym Wasta,
Hywel Fychan, Lewys Glyn Cothi,
Lewys Ysgolhaig
Errors by 129, 152–3
Lack of scribes recording all
judgements 72
Of A 13
Of Bost 151–3
Of C 137
Of Col 192
Of F and L 15, 198
Of G and U 13, 115, 116, 128, 194
Of J 15, 114, 133, 167–8, 182, 198
Of K 109, 182
Of L 149, 157
Of Lew 196
Of N, O and Tr 15, 145, 175, 177
Of Q 109–10, 114, 165, 180, 182, 198
Of S and Tim 108, 156, 164, 168, 170, 172, 182, 185
Of V and W 17, 141
Of Y 178

Working methods 116, 128, 129, 152 n.73, 157, 165, 172, 177, 178, 180, 185, 198
Seminar Cyfraith Hywel 16, 19
Assigning of sigla 20, 37 n.77, 190 n.23, 202 *and* 202 n.100, 205
Comparison to secret society 3
Senchas Már 24
Seven Bishop-Houses of Dyfed, *see Saith Esgopty Dyfed*
Statute of Rhuddlan (Statute of Wales) 8, 30, 36, 154, 207
Suretyship 58, 71, 7-9, 88–91, 99, 115, 118
Surexit Memorandum 7
Swydd a Braint Brawdwr 60, *and see also* Justices
Swyddog 59, 136, *and see also Swydd a Braint Brawdwr*

Tails 10, 46–8, 134–5, 145–8, 155, 157–9, 161–71, 184–5, 210, *and see also* Additional material
Tair Colofn Cyfraith, see Three Columns of Law
Teilo, St. 8
Test Book
'Appendix' 12 *and* 12 n.57, 68, 193 n.39
As training for justices 56, 73, 126–7, 144–5, 196
Contents of 68–9, 77, 79, 80–1, 96, 108, 127, 130, 140, 145, 183, 192
Drawing on other books 17, 25, 52–4, 66–7, 69–71, 143
Expectation for justices to know 63, 73, 79, 126, 130, 140, 144, 156
In Iorwerth texts 12, 108, 133, 136, 140–3, 181–3, 193
In non-Iorwerth manuscripts 17, 120–1, 136, 141, 180, 195, 197–8
Practical material 21, 64, 127, 144, 158, 181, 196
Prologue 52, 54, 67, 108, 145, 197
Title 55–6, 137 n.24, 144–5
Work of Iorwerth ap Madog 25, 52, 54, 63–4, 66–8, 71, 79–80, 108, 140
Theft 5 n.13, 117–19, 154, 156, 178, 180, 197, 201, *and see also* Three Columns of Law
Three Columns of Law 12, 24, 45, 77–9, 84, 94–6, 127, 130, 145, 165–6, 177–8, 197, 204
Tractates 46–8, 79, 111, 130–1, 135, 139, 148–9, 162, 169, 184, 189, 194, 197, 210, *and see also index entries for specific legal topics*

Index

As divisions of law manuscripts   10, 23, 104–5
In Blegywryd manuscripts   63, 105, 142, 167
In Cyfnerth manuscripts   16–17, 105, 142, 181
In Iorwerth manuscripts   63, 76–8, 180, 183, 207
In Latin manuscripts   19
Missing in some manuscripts   25
Order of tractates in manuscripts   47, 63–4
Variety in nature and form   24–5, 163, 164, 185

Triads
Arferion Cyfraith triad   135–9, 141, 143
As tractate   16, 17, 23–4, 138, 167, 176, 199
Collection   19, 20–1, 38, 141, 142, 164, 165, 166, 173, 176, 175–6, 180, 199
Collection in Q and K   13, 105, 107–8, 109, 110 n.30, 167, 168, 182, 189 n.2
Cyfnerth   17, 137 n.25, 140, 141, 180
Feature of Blegywryd   105, 135, 138, 141, 166, 167, 176, 180, 189, 199
'Floating Sections', *see* Powell, J. Enoch
Individual triads   52, 57, 59, 61, 74, 78, 126, 129, 130, 139, 149, 176, 195, 199

Not 'additional material', 41–2, 104 n.4

Value of equipment   68, 77, 79, 80, 96
Value of Wild and Tame   12, 77, 79, 96, 116, 145, 166, 183
Vaughan, Robert, Hengwrt 200
Venedotian Code, *see* Iorwerth redaction

Wade-Evans, Arthur   40
  renaming of Codes   11, 17
  warning about Welsh law   34
Wake, William   26
Welsh Medieval Law (Wade-Evans)   39, 40
White Book of Hergest   122, 123, 124, 153, *see Llyfr Gwyn Hergest*
White Book of Rhydderch   149, *see Llyfr Gwyn Rhydderch*
Whitland   36, 44, 46, 52, *see also Llyfr y Ty Gwyn*
Williams, Moses   10, 26–7, 29
Wotton, William   10, 26–7, 28–9
Wynebwerth   94
Wynnstay Hall   30
Wyth Pynfarch   117

Ymwrthyn   112, 113
Ynad, see Justices

INDEX OF MANUSCRIPTS

Aberystwyth, National Library of Wales
Llanstephan 29 (Llan)   14, 16, 32, 74, 145–6, 148, 172
Llanstephan 116 (Tim)   14–16, 32, 46, 62, 67, 74–5, 108, 145–9, 151, 155–6, 158, 163–4, 167–8, 168–72, 182–3, 185, 196, 205
Llanstephan 121 (copy of H)   200
NLW 20143A (Y)   14–18, 32, 115, 125–6, 145–6, 148, 155–6, 177–81, 185, 189
NLW 24029A (Bost)   13–15, 32, 74, 122–8, 135, 145–58, 165, 169–72, 180, 194
Peniarth 28 (Latin A)   18–19, 70, 142–4, 192
Peniarth 29 (A, The Black Book of Chirk)   11–13, 31–2, 44, 76, 79, 80, 87–98, 106–8, 137, 185, 189, 200
Peniarth 30 (Col)   19, 40, 43–4, 64, 66, 69–70, 79, 106–7, 163, 189, 190–3, 206–8
Peniarth 31 (R)   14–15, 32, 69, 137, 145–6, 172
Peniarth 32 (D)   11–13, 31, 64, 76, 99–100, 106–8, 180, 182, 185, 189
Peniarth 33 (M)   14–15, 31, 137, 145–6, 172, 203
Peniarth 34 (As)   19–20, 37, 39, 110, 116–20, 125–6, 129, 148, 156, 164, 189, 191, 201–4, 206–7
Peniarth 34 (F)   15, 19–20, 31–2, 37, 107, 110–12, 115, 121, 188, 189–90, 194, 196–9, 205, 207
Peniarth 35 (G)   11–13, 31, 66–7, 106–7, 110–16, 120–4, 125–9, 148, 155–6, 173–5, 188, 189, 190, 193–4, 196, 205, 207
Peniarth 36A (O)   14–16, 20–1, 32, 42, 69, 74, 137, 145–6, 163, 172–3, 175–7, 203
Peniarth 36B (N)   14–15, 32, 69, 137, 145–6, 172, 175
Peniarth 36C (Mor)   19–20, 37, 39, 110, 116–21, 125–6, 129, 145, 148, 155, 164, 189, 191, 201–4, 206–7
Peniarth 37 (U)   13, 16–17, 32, 36–7, 69–70, 106–7, 115, 128, 141–2, 148, 156, 162, 179, 193
Peniarth 38 (I)   14–15, 31, 145–8, 178–9
Peniarth 39 (Lew)   11–13, 32, 107, 111–12, 171, 190, 194–6, 206–7

Peniarth 40 (K)   11–13, 31–2, 107–10, 122–5, 148, 151, 153, 155, 167–8, 180–5, 189, 192, 194
Peniarth 164 (H)   19, 31–2, 37–9, 110, 116–20, 163–4, 189, 191, 197, 199–202, 207
Peniarth 166 (An)   19–20, 37, 190–1, 205–6
Peniarth 258 (Ep)   14–16, 32, 37, 106, 122, 145–9, 156, 164–5, 189, 190
Peniarth 259A (P)   14–16, 32, 69, 145–6, 148, 164, 172
Peniarth 259B (Z)   16–18, 19–20, 32–3, 51, 68–9, 110, 116–21, 125, 129, 134, 156, 163–4, 169, 172, 177, 181–5, 197, 199–204, 207
Peniarth 278 (Copy of H)   200
Wynnstay 36 (Q)   13–16, 30, 32, 37–9, 51, 105, 106–10, 112–15, 121, 122–9, 134, 145–9, 151, 153, 155–8, 163–4, 165–71, 173–5, 176, 178–84, 185, 189, 194–6, 198, 199
Wynnstay 37 and 38 ('Deddfgrawn William Maurice')   10, 15, 26, 29–30, 47, 188

Cambridge, Corpus Christi College
454 (Latin E)   18–19, 70–1, 142–3

Cambridge, Trinity College
O.7.1 (Tr)   14–16, 20–1, 32, 42, 75, 145–6, 148, 163, 172–5

Cardiff, Central Library
2.7 (Crd)   14, 15

London, British Library
Add. 14,931 (E)   11–14, 31, 64, 76, 79, 87–100, 106, 108, 125, 128, 137, 185, 189
Add. 22,356 (S)   14–16, 20, 32, 39, 46–8, 51, 62, 75, 108, 117, 122, 125–9, 134, 145–51, 155, 163–4, 166–7, 168–72, 177–9, 182–3, 185, 187, 195–6, 199, 205–6
Add. 31,055 (Dd, copy of the lost White Book of Hergest)   37, 122–4, 190, 194
Cotton Caligula A. iii (C)   11–13, 31, 64, 68, 76, 87–98, 108–9, 137, 145, 182–3, 185, 189

Index of Manuscripts

Cotton Cleopatra A. xiv (W)   16–18, 69, 141, 176, 179
Cotton Cleopatra B. v (X)   16–18, 32, 69, 164, 179
Cotton Titus D. ii (B)   11–14, 21, 31, 42–3, 64, 68, 76, 80–1, 108–10, 112–14, 144, 163, 183–4, 185, 189
Cotton Titus D. ix (L)   14–16, 20–1, 31, 38, 42, 75, 125–6, 127–9, 133–5, 145–58, 163, 165–6, 169–72, 180, 197
Cotton Vespasian E. xi (Latin B)   18–19, 66–7, 70, 84, 120, 142, 143–4, 192
Harleian 1796 (Latin C)   18–19, 70, 142–3, 192
Harleian 4353 (V)   16–18, 32, 51, 69, 141
Harleian 958 (T)   14–15, 32, 74, 137, 145–6, 148, 172

London, The National Archives
PRO 36/44   29, 34

Oxford, Bodleian Library
Rawlinson C. 821 (Latin D)   14–15, 18–19, 51, 53, 59, 70, 71, 74–5, 120, 137, 145–6, 148, 158, 192

Oxford, Jesus College
57 (J)   14–16, 31, 75, 106, 110, 112–14, 125–9, 133–5, 138, 143, 146–58, 163, 165, 167–72, 180, 182–4, 185, 198, 204–6
111 (The Red Book of Hergest)   15, 133, 168, 182

Oxford, Merton College
323 (Latin E)   18–19, 70–1, 142–3

Private Ownership
Bodorgan Hall, Anglesey, Copy in Bangor 21108 (Mk)   16–18, 32, 51, 69, 141, 145, 148, 176

STUDIES IN CELTIC HISTORY

Already published

Details of earlier titles are available from the publisher

XXV · SAINTS' CULTS IN THE CELTIC WORLD
Steve Boardman, John Reuben Davies and Eila Williamson (ed.)

XXVI · GILDAS'S *DE EXCIDIO BRITONUM* AND THE EARLY BRITISH CHURCH
Karen George

XXVII · THE PRESENT AND THE PAST IN MEDIEVAL IRISH CHRONICLES
Nicholas Evans

XXVIII · THE CULT OF SAINTS AND THE VIRGIN MARY IN MEDIEVAL SCOTLAND
Steve Boardman and Eila Williamson (ed.)

XXIX · THE TRANSFORMATION OF THE IRISH CHURCH IN THE TWELFTH CENTURY
Marie Therese Flanagan

XXX · HEROIC SAGA AND CLASSICAL EPIC IN MEDIEVAL IRELAND
Brent Miles

XXXI · TOME: STUDIES IN MEDIEVAL CELTIC HISTORY AND LAW IN HONOUR OF THOMAS CHARLES-EDWARDS
Fiona Edmonds and Paul Russell (ed.)

XXXII · NEW PERSPECTIVES ON MEDIEVAL SCOTLAND, 1093–1286
Matthew Hammond (ed.)

XXXIII · LITERACY AND IDENTITY IN EARLY MEDIEVAL IRELAND
Elva Johnston

XXXIV · CLASSICAL LITERATURE AND LEARNING IN MEDIEVAL IRISH NARRATIVE
Ralph O'Connor (ed.)

XXXV · MEDIEVAL POWYS: KINGDOM, PRINCIPALITY AND LORDSHIPS, 1132–1293
David Stephenson

XXXVI · PERCEPTIONS OF FEMININITY IN EARLY IRISH SOCIETY
Helen Oxenham

XXXVII · ST SAMSON OF DOL AND THE EARLIEST HISTORY OF
BRITTANY, CORNWALL AND WALES
Lynette Olson (ed.)

XXXVIII · THE BOOK OF LLANDAF AS A HISTORICAL SOURCE
Patrick Sims-Williams

XXXIX · PERSONAL NAMES AND NAMING PRACTICES IN
MEDIEVAL SCOTLAND
Matthew Hammond (ed.)

XL · GAELIC INFLUENCE IN THE NORTHUMBRIAN KINGDOM:
THE GOLDEN AGE AND THE VIKING AGE
Fiona Edmonds

XLI · READING AND SHAPING MEDIEVAL CARTULARIES:
MULTI-SCRIBE MANUSCRIPTS AND THEIR PATTERNS
OF GROWTH. A STUDY OF THE EARLIEST CARTULARIES
OF GLASGOW CATHEDRAL AND LINDORES ABBEY
Joanna Tucker

XLII · MEDIEVAL WELSH GENEALOGY
Ben Guy

XLIII · THE LEGACY OF GILDAS: CONSTRUCTIONS OF AUTHORITY
IN THE EARLY MEDIEVAL WEST
Stephen T. Joyce

XLIV · HISTORY AND IDENTITY IN EARLY MEDIEVAL WALES
Rebecca Thomas

XLV · THE GROWTH OF LAW IN MEDIEVAL WALES, c.1100–c.1500
Sara Elin Roberts

XLVI · THE MEDIEVAL WELSH 'ENGLYNION Y BEDDAU':
THE 'STANZAS OF THE GRAVES', OR 'GRAVES OF THE WARRIORS
OF THE ISLAND OF BRITAIN', ATTRIBUTED TO TALIESIN
Patrick Sims-Williams (ed.)

XLVII · STORYTELLING IN GAELIC FROM AD 700 TO THE PRESENT:
TRUTH, TRADITION AND TRANSLATION
Alice R. Taylor-Gri iths and Seosamh Mac Cárthaigh (ed.)

XLVIII · VIKINGS IN EARLY MEDIEVAL IRELAND:
CHURCH-RAIDING, POLITICS AND KINGSHIP
Colmán Etchingham

XLIX · CLASSICAL MYTH IN MEDIEVAL IRELAND
Brigid Ehrmantraut

www.ingramcontent.com/pod-product-compliance
Lightning Source LLC
Chambersburg PA
CBHW071613240426
R18188700001B/R181887PG43668CBX00002B/1